ORGANIZATIONAL SURVIVAL IN THE NEW WORLD

The Intelligent Complex Adaptive System

KM
Ci PRESS

KNOWLEDGE
MANAGEMENT
CONSORTIUM
INTERNATIONAL

About KMCI Press

POWERFUL KNOWLEDGE FOR KNOWLEDGE PROFESSIONALS

KMCI Press is an exciting publishing partnership that unites the Knowledge Management Consortium International (KMCI), the leading organization for knowledge management professionals, and Butterworth-Heinemann's Business group and Digital Press imprints, one of the premier publishers of knowledge management books.

KMCI Press publishes authoritative and innovative books that educate all knowledge management communities, from students and beginning professionals to chief knowledge officers. KMCI Press books present definitive and leading-edge ideas of the KMCI itself, and bring clarity and authoritative information to a dynamic and emerging profession.

KMCI Press books explore the opportunities, demands, and benefits knowledge management brings to organizations and defines important and emerging knowledge management disciplines and topics, including:

- Professional roles and functions
- Vertical industry best practices and applications
- Technologies, including knowledge portals and data and document management
- Strategies, methodologies, and decision-making frameworks

The Knowledge Management Consortium International (KMCI) is the only major not for profit member organization specifically for knowledge management professionals, with thousands of worldwide members including individuals in the professional and academic fields as well as leading companies, institutions, and other organizations concerned with knowledge management, organizational change, and intellectual capital.

For information about submitting book proposals, please see our website at http://www.kmci.org

Titles from KMCI Press

The Springboard: How Storytelling Ignites Action in Knowledge-Era Organizations Stephen Denning

Knowledge Management Foundations Steve Fuller

World Congress on Intellectual Capital Readings Nick Bontis

Enterprise Information Portals and Knowledge Management Joseph M. Firestone, Ph.D.

The New Knowledge Management: Sustainable Innovation Through Second-Generation Knowledge Management Mark W. McElroy

Key Issues in the New Knowledge Management Joseph M. Firestone, Ph.D. & Mark W. McElroy

ORGANIZATIONAL SURVIVAL IN THE NEW WORLD

THE INTELLIGENT COMPLEX ADAPTIVE SYSTEM

Alex Bennet
&
David Bennet

A New Theory of the Firm

KNOWLEDGE
MANAGEMENT
CONSORTIUM
INTERNATIONAL

ELSEVIER
BUTTERWORTH
HEINEMANN

AMSTERDAM • BOSTON • HEIDELBERG • LONDON
NEW YORK • OXFORD • PARIS • SAN DIEGO
SAN FRANCISCO • SINGAPORE • SYDNEY • TOKYO

Butterworth–Heinemann is an imprint of Elsevier

 Recognizing the importance of preserving what has been written, Elsevier prints its books on acid-free paper whenever possible.

Library of Congress Cataloging-in-Publication Data – application submitted

ISBN-13: 978-0-7506-7712-7
ISBN-10: 0-7506-7712-0

British Library Cataloguing-in-Publication Data
A Catalogue record for this book is available from the British Library.

The publisher offers special discounts on bulk orders of this book.
For information, please contact:

Manager of Special Sales
Elsevier
200 Wheeler Road, 6th Floor
Burlington, MA 01803
Tel : 781-313-4700
Fax: 781-313-4882

For information on all Butterworth-Heinemann publications available, contact our World Wide Web home page at http://www.bh.com

10 9 8 7 6 5 4 3

Printed in the United States of America

CONTENTS

PART I   THE GROUNDWORK

Chapter 1   MOVING BEYOND THE BUREAUCRATIC MODEL, 3

The Metamorphosis: Breaking Free of the Cocoon, 4;   Challenges to Becoming World Class, 8

Chapter 2   THE PRESENT AND FUTURE DANGER,
OR WHY WE NEED TO CHANGE, 13

The Five Major Drivers, 13;   Change, Uncertainty, and Complexity, 17;   Why We Need a New Theory of the Firm, 21

PART II   THE THEORY

Chapter 3   THE INTELLIGENT COMPLEX
ADAPTIVE SYSTEM (ICAS), 25

Definitions and Assumptions, 26;   The ICAS Model, 28;   Emergent Characteristics, 29; An Introduction to the Eight Emergent Characteristics of the ICAS, 30;   An Introduction to the Four Major Processes, 33

Chapter 4   EXPLORING THE EMERGENT PROPERTIES OF THE ICAS, 37

Organizational Intelligence, 37;   Unity and Shared Purpose, 41;   Optimum Complexity, 43;   Selectivity, 46;   Knowledge Centricity, 47;   Flow, 50;   Permeable Boundaries, 53;   Multidimensionality, 55

LIST OF FIGURES AND TABLES

FOREWORD

During the last decade it has become obvious to many managers that to succeed they need more effective models of the firm and to implement better organizational principles and practices. Traditional methods and perspectives are not good enough to ensure enduring success in today's emerging business environments. Globalization and emergence of the "knowledge economy" have made effective application and competitive quality of knowledge—intellectual capital assets—decisive competitive factors. It is clear that the new world is more complex and more difficult to manage than that to which we have been accustomed.

Work itself is becoming more complex as enterprises automate routine tasks and ask employees to handle more difficult work requirements. At all levels of the organization we are asked to deliver customized products and services that will provide the greatest value to our external and internal customers. We are asked to respond faster with better work products and fewer errors. We are asked to develop relationships and improve customer loyalty and supplier teaming while looking out for the objectives of multiple stakeholders. We are asked not only to learn faster than our competitors but also to innovate faster. We are asked to participate knowingly in implementing our enterprise's strategy and deliver its intents. And we are asked to do all of this with minimal resources, effort, and problems.

To respond to these demands we increasingly need to rely on intellectual capital assets utilized by individuals who are positioned to deal with the demanding situations. We need new organizational and management paradigms, since conventional ones are limited in their capabilities to build and marshal the intellectual capital assets that make it possible to excel in the new environment. Part of the answer to these demands is to delegate decisions to knowledgeable people who are close to the points of action where detailed information is good and understanding of contexts and situations is clear. Additional answers lie in implementing better organizational structures and management philosophies and practices that reflect and support new directions and strategies which facilitate new approaches.

However, for managers, it has been far from clear how to determine which principles to adopt and how to implement them. It is in this void that Alex and David Bennet present the intelligent complex adaptive systems (ICAS) model for a powerful and comprehensive organizational and operational enterprise. The Bennets, initially separately and now jointly, have pursued the quest for better organizational principles and operations to achieve enterprise objectives more effectively. As a result of this quest, the authors, with their deep respect for building upon proven experiences and solid scientific findings, have been able to integrate multidisciplinary theory and practice to conceptualize and describe the ICAS. They provide a clear and comprehensive roadmap—a model for managers who wish to pursue more powerful approaches to operate their enterprises more effectively—to match the needs of the new environment. They provide a comprehensive exposé of the principles and practices—an application model—supported by underlying rationales that make it possible for readers to obtain understanding, objectives, expectations, and knowledge of how to approach implementation of practices within their organizations.

Managers who wish to pursue new directions need help. In particular, they need understanding of what is possible and how to achieve it. Cognitive science tells us that when at all possible, people make decisions and undertake actions by imitating role models or replicating prior experiences and that it is difficult to decide what to do and how to do it without a roadmap. By learning and internalizing descriptions and methodologies—particularly the ICAS model as presented by the Bennets—people are able to build personal understandings and mental models for "what it is possible to achieve," "what to do," "why do it," and "how to do it" that can motivate and guide them in implementing new approaches.

The path to better enterprise principles and practices is not simple. In this book, the Bennets have addressed requirements that need to be satisfied to create suitable paradigms and implement workable solutions that will improve enterprise performance. Whereas the ICAS may not have been implemented in full by any enterprise, it does not represent "a figment of the imagination" in the minds of the authors. Alex Bennet, in her position at the U.S. Department of the Navy, had extensive experience in implementing aspects of the ICAS. In his own organization, David Bennet gained in-depth practical experience with ICAS concepts. Other organizations have implemented aspects of the ICAS and report it to be of significant importance. On June 17, 2003, the Financial Times reported that several Chief Executive Officers, among them Lord John Browne of BP and Rich Fairbank of Capital One, consider their enterprises complex adaptive systems that are heavily reliant on intellectual capital assets to provide exceptional performance. Given such convictions, they attempt to manage their organizations accordingly. This is similarly the case with the U.S. Marines.

One might ask: "Why is the ICAS so important? What makes it so different that we should expend effort to pursue it?" One answer is that the ICAS ties together and integrates wide-ranging capabilities to address the new challenges in a comprehensive manner. The ICAS, as explained by the Bennets, focuses on the need for the enterprise to act intelligently. It is designed to make the people within the enterprise—and hence the enterprise itself—deal effectively with complex environments consisting of tightly interconnected and frequently changing systems where considerable adaptiveness is required to generate the evolution needed to survive as the world changes and new insights are gained.

Many enterprises have started to consider their organizations to be complex evolving systems—far from the Newtonian mechanisms or machines assumed by Tayloristic scientific management theory. The increasing realization is that the past models of predictable, controllable, and routine operations constitute wishful thinking rather than what actually happens. The reality is that most work operations are variable and require adaptation to be delivered competently.

The ICAS builds upon the realization that overall enterprise performance results from the myriad of individual decisions and actions of personnel, groups, and operational units at every level of the organization. The behavior of each party is shaped by individual attitudes, objectives, perspectives, and resources—including intellectual capital assets. These vary and can never be fully known. As a result, the individual behaviors are partly unpredictable and the resulting overall behavior becomes complex. To address these complexities, the design focus of the ICAS has been to provide a management system that will foster, support, and generate durable enterprise performance and success in spite of the challenges.

Successful management leads to a search for constant progress, progress that results from finding the best and most effective fit to satisfy current and future customers and survive in competitive environments (compete successfully). Adaptation by the proactive enterprise to current and perceived future contexts leads to improved and more effective actions and operations—to progress. From this perspective, the gradual and at times stepwise or revolutionary improvements become evolution. As the authors point out, this evolution results from practical implementation of Argyris and Schön's double-loop learning.

The Bennets acknowledge that the principal actors in any enterprise are people and that the main resources that make people effective are the intellectual capital assets that they possess or otherwise have available to conduct work. These intellectual capital assets must constantly be renewed through collaboration, learning, and innovation to sustain the advantages that the enterprise wishes to maintain to remain competitive. Hence, the ICAS relies extensively on deliberate and systematic knowledge management (KM).

KM, although at times equated with advanced information management, is central to the people-focused perspectives of the ICAS model. Clearly, in today's technological environment the ICAS must rely extensively on technological capabilities for facilitation and support provided by communication and information processing infrastructures of information technology and intelligent automatic processing and actions of cognitively simple tasks, and for functions such as discovery of historic patterns by knowledge discovery in databases (KDD).

In the new context of the global knowledge economy, many have suggested that we need new perspectives for how to manage complex organizations. In this book, the authors provide a systematized and integrated paradigm for a new model of the firm that will be of great value for those who wish to conduct business differently and successfully in the years to come.

This is a bold book that pulls together principles and considerations that for many would be separate entities that are difficult to unite. Unfortunately, the world is integrated and unless we treat it as such it is difficult to steer our enterprises to perform well. As a result of Alex and David Bennet's willingness to tackle the difficulties head on, the book is unique in providing a truly interdisciplinary model that integrates practical management practices into a cohesive and congruent whole. This book should be a valuable guide for all managers who aim to compete successfully in the global knowledge economy.

Karl M. Wiig
Arlington, Texas
June 2003

PREFACE

This work is an accumulation of two lifetimes of study and experience, yet it continues to change, and new ideas continue to emerge, even as we write, and so we can only imagine the potential offered to organizations through the intelligent complex adaptive system (ICAS) approach. This book is intended as an idea-generator and resource for organizations, and their leaders and workers, who choose to survive—and thrive—in the new world of complexity.

We have not attempted to duplicate the significant work that has been published on complexity, emergence, learning and knowledge management, themes running throughout this text. Where appropriate, we have provided references to these works. What we have worked hard at doing is developing a cohesive, consistent new theory of the firm built around the concept of intelligent complex adaptive systems. To this end, we have included foundational information on systems and complexity, learning and knowledge management, and have offered new approaches to thinking and knowing in support of the ICAS.

At the pragmatic level, we have included both strategic and tactical information aimed at developing a design for the new ICAS organization. Areas of specific focus include structure, culture, and leadership, together with major emergent characteristics. The new knowledge worker is discussed in terms of the new skills and competencies needed for organizational survival.

In a very real sense, this book wrote itself. Just as optimum complexity is a critical part of the ICAS, this book is written with a bent toward achieving optimum length and depths of subject matter. For example, this means that the way we address complexity, a relatively new field, is very different than the way we address relationship network management, which builds on a long history of social relationships. As another example, the length of discussion about the eight emergent characteristics of the ICAS is very different than the length of the discussion about emergent characteristics of the environment, which are observable by every leader.

This book begins with a brief overview of the history of organizations, with additional detail provided in the Appendix. The intent of this material is to demonstrate the historic relationship of organizations and their environments before presenting a model for organizational survival in the complex, uncertain, and rapidly changing environment of today and tomorrow. To be effective, this new organization must be integrated, cohesive, and meld theory and practice. With this in mind, Part II discusses the theory of the organization and Part III focuses on application and implementation. These two parts present a number of new concepts, some of which may be unfamiliar to readers and challenge the status quo. For these reasons, Part IV provides introductory material on those significant new concepts essential for organizational success such as complexity thinking, knowing, and relationship network management.

While the book is necessarily organized in a linear fashion, a linear approach to reading the text may not be the best for some learners. Rather, base the reading approach on your personal and professional preferences, interests and requirements. For example, if complexity is a fairly new concept to you, go immediately to Chapter 19 and become familiar with the terminology before tackling the theory behind the ICAS. Understanding complexity will also provide a tremendous benefit to the implementation approach in Part III, as will the understanding of systems (Chapter 18). You will note in the following graphic that Part IV (on knowledge worker skills and competencies) supports Part III (on structure, culture, and leadership), and Part III, in turn, supports Part II (the theory).

If you are already familiar with the history of organizations, and the rise of knowledge organizations, you might want to skip the first chapter, give a cursory review to Chapter 2, since it discusses the current and future environment, and then dive directly into the theory of the ICAS. In like fashion, you may use Part IV, The Knowledge Solution, as a resource as you move through Part II, The Theory, and Part III, The ICAS in Practice. For those who are more interested in application than theory, after reviewing complexity thinking, you may choose to read the overview of the ICAS model provided in Chapter 3 and immediately move into Part III.

Because of the interconnection of thinking and acting throughout the book, and the potential for spot reading and future referencing, we have included enough repetitiveness throughout to provide context and clarity where the material resides. We also provide references to other chapters that have additional depth on specific or related topics.

We do not propose the ICAS organizational model as a panacea for all ailing organizations. Nor do we believe it is necessarily worthwhile for organizations and individuals who operate in a relatively stable environment to adopt this approach. Our concern, however, is that as the environment and our society becomes more complicated and complex, because complexity builds upon itself, more and more organizations, particularly those who operate at the edge of the state-of-the-art, will be faced with the huge challenge of operating effectively in

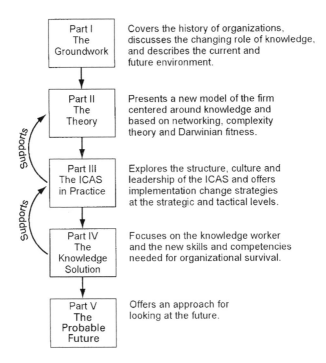

a turbulent environment. Toward this end, we provide a number of ideas, considerations, relationships, and competencies that, when put together in the right way for a given situation and environment, will provide considerable help in responding to that environment.

ACKNOWLEDGMENTS

Our utmost respect to those thought leaders and the many professionals referenced throughout this book and our colleagues and friends who have informed our thinking and spurred us onward to this new theory of the firm.

Our deep thanks to Joe Firestone who encouraged us to write the early work on the ICAS, and then published that work in *Knowledge and Innovation: Journal of the KMCI*. How appropriate that this book is coming into existence through the KMCI Press.

Our appreciation to the employees of the former Dynamic Systems, Inc. and the Department of the Navy who have served as a testing ground for so many of these ideas. Our particular thanks to Dan Porter and Jack Hawxhurst, with whom continuous dialogues helped surface many early ideas, and to Rachael Sedeen, who helped to graphically represent many of these early ideas. Also, our thanks to Bob Turner for his insights on communities of practice. Our appreciation to Charlie Seashore, our friend and mentor who had the good fortune to be the first to read the material that makes up Part I. We are also appreciative of Argosy Publishing for their professional design and editing of the final graphics used in this book. Our editors included: Antonella Elisabetta Collaro, Jef Boys and Jane Shaw.

Our heartfelt thanks to our editor, Karen Maloney, Academic Press/ Butterworth-Heinemann/Elsevier, who was ever willing to listen to—and support—our needs, and to our publisher, Butterworth-Heinemann, who we hope will continue publishing in this important area of study.

Our deep appreciation to our ten children and eight grandchildren who keep us mentally acute and physically moving. A special thanks to our youngest son, Andrew, who moved in and took over our day-to-day research and retreat center and farm responsibilities, enabling us to focus on and complete the writing of this book.

Finally, our thanks to you, our colleagues and readers. We hope you are as interested in, and concerned about, the future performance of our organizations and our knowledge workers as we are. We take this opportunity to invite you to visit us at Mountain Quest Institute nestled in the Monongahela Forest of the West Virginia Allegheny Mountains* and look forward to your thoughts, suggestions, and dialogue. We have a great deal to learn together!

*See www.mountainquestinstitute.com

INTRODUCTION

How well will your organization perform over the next two decades, and how do you know? The optimal performance of an organization is that performance which allows the organization to achieve its goals and objectives over time. In the highly competitive environment of business, success can be described as sustainable competitive advantage. For government and not-for-profit organizations, success may be considered as sustainable high performance. Sustainability means over the long term; competitive advantage means ahead of the competition, that is, the most desired producer or supplier as seen by the marketplace. Sustainable competitive advantage also means that the organization is a respected organization with a high reputation and an admirable image to other stakeholders such as employees, stockholders, the community, and the environment.

While many firms have momentary success, only to die out or to become gobbled up, the problem of sustainability challenges leaders everywhere. Along with vision and purpose, a significant factor driving organizations is their external environment, particularly its predictability or compatibility. Over the past decade or so the general environment can best be described as one of accelerating rate of change, nonlinearity, increasing uncertainty, and growing complexity. To our knowledge, no environment in history can match the intensity of changes and the complexity of the present landscape. If you believe as we do that technology, change, and complexity each feed on themselves and on each other, then the future holds an even greater challenge than the present.

Even the past has not been so kind to many organizations, as can be seen by the fact that blue-chip firms have difficulty staying in the Fortune 100 for very many years. As time passes, the environment has always taken on new characteristics. What worked yesterday may not work today and most likely will not work tomorrow. De Geus (1997), after describing a Shell study on long-lived companies, noted that "Every company we found that had been in existence for 100 years or more had gone through a period of adaptation so profound that it had had to thoroughly alter its core business portfolio" (p. 144). Our concern at the present is that the future environment is taking on significantly new and different parameters that will have a significant, most-likely negative, impact on organizations who continue to operate in their historical mode.

Collins and Porras (1997), in seeking the fundamental factors creating high performance, found core ideology, a strong drive for progress, alignment, and a well-designed organizational structure to be universal requirements that are independent of time. While we agree with these factors up to a point, in the future progress and organizational structures may take on a different meaning. If our forecast of the future is correct, the rate of change and the growth of knowledge and technology will be so rapid that unless we change the basic nature of our organizations, long-term linear progress may be rare and even medium-term progress may be a challenge. The impact of these trends on people is to create personal anxiety and professional concern as leaders and knowledge workers struggle to interpret and outmaneuver these environmental effects. The old rules and principles of management no longer seem to be working very well, particularly for organizations at the forefront of change and complexity. How effective will these rules and principles be in ten or more years?

If the current rules of management and organizational forms are becoming outdated, what then will work? What changes do we need to consider in order to gain sustainable performance in our organizations? Where is the real value in our organization, in our customer's firms, in our society? How should we restructure our organizations, and why? How can we better match the marketplace to deal with its paradoxical behavior? Questions and concerns such as these drove our own interest in and concern about future organizational performance.

This book presents a large number of ideas—some new, some old, and some extremely unusual—that, when taken together, compose a new theory of the firm. However, this theory does not represent a specific organizational design. That would be futile because every organization exists in its own unique environment in time and space and with its own organizational structure, culture, leadership, and health parameters that need to be matched to the local and anticipated environment. Instead, what we have done is to propose a nominal description of the firm, what we call the intelligent complex adaptive system (ICAS), in itself a result of the interconnections (possibly entanglements) and mutual interactions of a number of ideas, concepts, and structures. We use the ICAS as a vehicle for describing and communicating these ideas, and also to demonstrate their contribution to the integrity and effectiveness of the organization as a whole. We have also tried to explain why the different considerations of the ICAS will improve sustainable organizational performance when taken as a whole. There are perhaps a number of new ideas that the reader may not be familiar with, such as emergence, knowing, dynamic balancing, etc. We believe that new problems and challenges require new modes of thinking, new concepts, new actions, and—the most difficult of all—new ways of behaving!

At the highest level, the ICAS is an organization designed to continuously adapt to and co-evolve with its environment. In doing so, the organization must exhibit flexibility and agility coupled with the ability to create and apply new ideas and actions to determine what will and will not work. One of our assumptions is that in such a highly complex and dynamic environment it will be difficult at best, and probably impossible, to anticipate the future of that environment or the environment's response to a given ICAS action. This leads us to the importance of the knowledge worker, who is the individual at the point of contact and at the point of action between the organization and its customers. These workers must have the competency and the freedom to take effective actions wherever possible and to utilize the full resources of their ICAS organization. The ICAS has been designed to create and provide the knowledge needed by its workforce. Examples are the extensive use of teams, communities, and relationship networks to leverage knowledge and broaden the experience of knowledge workers. In addition, creation of a knowledge-centric organization, supported by knowledge management and other characteristics such as flow and optimum complexity, will greatly assist knowledge workers in learning and decision-making. If the knowledge worker is at the point of action, then the knowledge they need to take effective actions becomes a critical factor in the ICAS. What an organization can do to help create, store, leverage, and apply knowledge in support of the knowledge worker is described in some detail in several chapters of the book.

A third major consideration after the knowledge worker and knowledge is the ability of the organization as a whole to support and create an environment in which the knowledge worker can operate with maximum effectiveness. This organizational environment includes the structure, culture, leadership, support of learning, and integrative competencies needed by knowledge workers, and an overall strategy that includes dynamic balancing and the correlation of forces.

The major characteristics of the model proposed in this book arise from the multiple lower-level interactions and relationships found within and external to the ICAS. Because these major characteristics cannot be traced directly to individual actions or relationships, the approach to designing, building, and maintaining the ICAS must be one of a gardener or orchestra conductor who creates and orchestrates an environment within which the right things are encouraged to happen.

One of our main ideas for the ICAS comes out of the work done by Nobel Laureate Gerald Edelman and his associates who seek to understand consciousness through research in neuroscience (Edelman and Tononi, 2000). We also have learned from, and made use of, Karl Wiig's seminal studies on knowledge management (Wiig, 1993). Csikszentmihalyi's extensive work on flow theory provides insight from psychology into the desirable internal movement of relationships and data, information, and knowledge (Csikszentmihalyi, 1990).

Ralph Stacey provides many ideas from his studies on complex adaptive systems and organizations (Stacey, 1996).

In summary, this book offers a description of a next-generation organization designed to meet the challenge of accelerating change, nonlinearity, increasing uncertainty, and growing complexity. While the characteristics, structures, and ideas proposed are designed to work cohesively, individually they may be of help to any organization. However, caution must be used in selecting isolated ideas and applying them within a different context than intended. As always, "context is king."

REFERENCES

Collins, J. C. and J. I. Porras. *Built to Last.* New York: Harper Business, 1997.

Csikszentmihalyi, M. *Flow: The Psychology of Optimal Experience.* New York: Harper Perennial, 1990.

de Geus, A. *The Living Company: Habits for Survival in a Turbulent Business Environment.* Boston, MA: Harvard Business School Press, 1997.

Edelman, G. M. and G. Tononi. *A Universe of Consciousness: How Matter Becomes Imagination.* New York: Basic Books, 2000.

Stacey, R. D. *Complexity and Creativity in Organizations.* San Francisco, CA: Berrett-Koehler Publishers, 1996.

Wiig, K. *Knowledge Management Foundations—Thinking about Thinking—How People and Organizations Create, Represent, and Use Knowledge.* Arlington, TX: Schema Press, 1993.

This book is dedicated to
Those who have urged us onward and
Those who wish to join us on this Quest.

The significant problems we face cannot be solved
at the same level of thinking we were at
when we created them.

Albert Einstein

PART I

THE GROUNDWORK*

Chapters 1 and 2, supported by the Appendix, set the context for a new theory of the firm.

Chapter 1 moves through the bureaucratic model to foundational concepts of the early and mid twentieth century, skimming such questions as: How do organizations evolve? What did organizations look like at the beginning of the twentieth century? What is the relationship of organizations to their environment? How is information technology changing that environment? What does it mean to be world-class? What are the challenges to becoming a world-class organization?

Chapter 2 explores the fundamental forces that will challenge future organizational survival in an environment filled with accelerating change, rising uncertainty, and increasing complexity. These forces are presented from both a systems-level perspective and in terms of connectivity; data, information, and knowledge; access; speed and digitization. These fundamental forces of the environment—along with the growing anxiety of individuals in organizations—are the four major descriptors relative to the future environment.

---

*Many of these concepts were originally published as "Rise of the Knowledge Organization" in Barquin, R. C., A. Bennet, and S. G. Remez (eds), *Knowledge Management: the Catalyst for Electronic Government*, Vienna, VA: Management Concepts, Inc., 2001, and reprinted with that title in Holsapple, C. W. (ed), *Handbook on Knowledge Management 1: Knowledge Matters*, New York: Springer-Verlag, 2003.

Chapter 1

MOVING BEYOND THE BUREAUCRATIC MODEL

With the rise of large corporations in the early twentieth century came a strong interest in research in fields such as leadership, management, organizational theory, and capitalism. Frederick Taylor, Henri Fayol, Mary Parker Follet, Chester Bernard, Adam Smith, Herbert Simon, Abraham Maslow, etc. (the list goes on and on), all contributed to the foundational research and set of organizational concepts of the early and mid twentieth century. This era created the formal foundation of management and organizational theory. Although the origins lay in Weber's bureaucracy, church and state autocracy, and military leadership, these were all modified by the social, political, and capitalistic drives in the free world after World War II. The new theories and concepts such as Theory X, Theory Y, Theory Z, Charismatic and Transformational Leadership, General Systems Theory, and Organizational Linking Pins became popular and a noticeable shift occurred from bureaucracy toward a more benign and malleable organizational structure. Tools such as Management by Exception, Span of Control, Kurt Lewin's Force Field Analysis, and Taichi Ohno's Toyota Production Line techniques helped both managers and workers to implement change throughout their organizations. While some changes occurred, most organizations continued to be hierarchical and as Whyte (1956) noted in his widely read *Organization Man*, large organizations were still forcing people into molds and stereotypes. Knowledge and information were held close by supervisors and managers and protected as they represented power and authority. Economic progress was relatively steady and, until the 1970s, fairly predictable. During this post-bureaucratic era the key factors were a combination of Tayloristic time and motion management and participative management, slowly bringing some of the workforce into the arena of worker responsibility and empowerment.

Organizations strove for clear rules and policies that all employees were expected to follow with few exceptions and little initiative. Of course, many of the tools encouraged innovation, but unfortunately few organizations saw the need to risk doing anything drastically different. In colloquial language, during the 1950–1970 period, most large organizations were fat, dumb, and happy. Although pressured by a better-educated workforce and the growing ranks of knowledge professionals to provide a more participative environment, most large organizations held steadfastly to their belief in the fundamental hierarchical structure.

As the affluence, mobility, and expectations of the workforce in developed countries continued to rise, coupled with the explosive growth of information and communication technologies and the subsequent increase in the creation of knowledge, organizations found themselves in situations of restructure or collapse. The old mechanical metaphor could no longer function in the nonlinear, dynamic, complex global web of the mid 1990s. Many organizations failed, many were acquired, and the best set about seeking the popular vision of the "world-class" corporation. The stage was now set for the rise of the information and knowledge organizations, with the information organizations taking the lead via computers and communications technology in the early 1980s and 1990s and the knowledge organizations, currently in their early form, focusing on networking and knowledge creation, sharing, and application. We now consider the fundamental characteristics of these modern leading-edge knowledge organizations.

THE METAMORPHOSIS: BREAKING FREE OF THE COCOON

Peter Drucker (1993) broadly describes the current shift from industry to information to knowledge, which started around 1960 and is expected to continue until 2010 or 2020, as follows: "We are entering the knowledge society in which the basic resource is no longer capital, or natural resources, or labor, but is and will be knowledge, and where knowledge workers will play a central role" (quoted in Skyrme, 1999, p. 11). Since these concepts are used extensively in describing the current and future organization, it is important to clarify our interpretation of the terms data, information, and knowledge. We are acutely aware of the many definitions and interpretations of the words data, information, and knowledge and we do not propose that "our" use is "the" correct one. Rather, we take a pragmatic stance and offer the following meanings to these terms. Following Wiig (1993), we consider data to be sequences of numbers and letters; spoken words; pictures; even physical objects when presented without context. We take information as data with some level of context and meaning, noting that both context and meaning require human interpretation and understanding. It is usually presented to describe a situation or condition and therefore has added value over data. Knowledge is built on data and information, often heavily dependent on context, and created within the individual. Knowledge represents understanding of situations and their context, insights into the relationships within a system, and the ability to identify leverage points and weaknesses and to understand future implications of actions taken to resolve problems. It represents a richer and more meaningful awareness and understanding that resonates with how the "knower" views the world. Knowledge is frequently considered actionable. In brief, knowledge is the human capacity to take effective action in varied and uncertain situations. By capacity we mean both potential and actual ability. We now address the characteristics of the best of the best organizations in the year 2000.

Time accelerates. Distance shrinks. Networks expand. Information overwhelms. Interdependencies grow geometrically. Uncertainty dominates. Complexity boggles the mind. Such is the environment and the context within which current organizations must compete, survive, and thrive (see Chapter 2).

This situation is a result of many years of evolution driven by a number of major factors. Of significance is the increasing economic affluence of the worker in the developed countries coupled with increased education level. This has resulted in a strong demand by workers to be recognized, respected, and allowed to participate and have determination in their work. Economic growth and technology provide both the means and pressures for mobility, thereby giving individuals the freedom to leave their jobs for other, more challenging positions. While the last 50 years has seen many ups and downs in terms of employment, productivity, interest rates, investments, etc., overall the recent decades have provided increasing wealth and economic success.

Consistent with this history, every organization lives at the pleasure of its environment—economic, sociological, political, and technological. For example, state charters legitimize corporations, the Occupational Safety and Health Administration (OSHA) and Department of Labor mandate tight restrictions on both safety and personnel regulations, the Environmental Protection Agency (EPA) regulates organizational behavior relative to environmental impact, and the business media heavily influences corporate stock values depending upon local and temporal events. Technology plays a dominant role in determining both the landscape of competition and the cultural and educational needs of the workforce. It is arguably true that technology has played the strongest role in creating the present environment within which organizations must adapt and learn to excel compared to their competitors. For example, tremendous increases in processing speed, communication bandwidth, miniaturization of computers, and the development of complex algorithms and application programs have created the rapidly changing pace of society and the increasing need and capability for communication, collaboration, and networking, both virtual and real. The phenomenal rise of the Internet, coupled with the spin-offs of intranets, extranets, etc., have created a networking potential which drives all of society and corporations in terms of speed, interdependencies, global markets, and the creation and spread of memes (see p. 213) instantaneously throughout the world. Those organizations which have found ways to compete successfully within this nonlinear, complex, and dynamic environment may dominate their competitors by as much as 25 percent in growth rate and profitability relative to the average organization in their industry.

There are specific characteristics of these "world-class" organizations that are major determinants of their success. While most of today's organizations are far from world class, many of the better ones are working hard to improve their performance, that is, efficiency, effectiveness, and sustained competitive advantage, in order to stay competitive and in some cases prevent being acquired or going into bankruptcy.

Many of the tools, methods, structures, and principles that the best companies have found to drive high performance are neither new nor, in many cases, unique. For example, the ideas that Toyota created in the late 1940s and early 1950s relative to lean manufacturing in the automobile industry, although refined and improved, are still considered world class and, in fact, Toyota has been considered to be a leader throughout the world in automobile manufacturing (Womack et al., 1990). Taichi Ohno created the Toyota production system just after World War II as a response to changing customer demands and potential bankruptcy (Shingo, 1989). The system eventually included just-in-time supply parts delivery, workers on the factory floor taking responsibility for the production line quality and having authority to stop the production line, and teams of workers solving problems on the factory floor and learning cross-functional jobs to ensure continuous production line flows. Shingo notes that it took Toyota over 20 years to perfect the system (Shingo, 1989). Approximately 50 years later many of these ideas are still considered best practices and used by corporations throughout the world. Note that they represent a breaking away of the bureaucratic hierarchical chain of command and minimum freedom of the worker.

In *Built to Last*, Collins and Porras did a six-year study of 18 companies who had outstanding performance over time periods between 50 and 200 years (Collins and Porras, 1994). They sought the fundamental factors creating such performance. Considering their results with other research on long-lived world-class firms, we suggest the following factors as being representative of long-term, highly successful companies:

- Continuous striving to improve themselves and doing better tomorrow than what they did today, always remaining *sensitive* to their customers and their environment.

- Not focusing on profitability alone, but *balancing* their efforts to include employee quality of life, community relations, environmental concerns, customer satisfaction, and stakeholder return.
- A willingness to take risks with an insistence that they be prudent and an overall balanced *risk* portfolio. In general, they were financially conservative.
- A strong feeling about their core ideology, changing it seldom if ever. Their core values form a solid foundation and while each company's individual *values* were unique, once created they were not allowed to drift with the fashions of the day. These core values molded their culture, and created a strong sense of *identity*.
- Relative to their employees, these companies demanded a strong "fit" with their culture and their standards. Thus, employees either felt the organization was a great place to work and flourished, or they were likely short-term. At the same time these companies were tolerant of individuals on the margins who *experimented* and tested for possibilities.

Many current top organizations have made significant changes in the way they do business in the past decade and have been able to create performance through change management and deliberately develop the fundamental characteristics that support success. These characteristics must provide those responses needed to excel in the present environment. For example, time to market or the ability to develop new products rapidly is a key factor in many industries because of customer demands and the decreased production time made available by technology, concurrent engineering, and agile production techniques. The use of simulation, integrated product teams, and world-wide subject-matter experts operating virtually has created the capacity to quickly bring new knowledge and ideas together to rapidly produce products desired by a fickle and impatient market. Examples of this capability are mass customization, where economic order quantities of one are being pursued, and agility, the ability of an organization to move rapidly in response to changing and unique customer needs. Creativity and innovation have come to the forefront as key success factors with many organizations striving to develop and unleash these capacities throughout their workforce, using a combination of management, the workforce, and their customers.

Employee involvement has now been accepted and understood by world-class organizations and many "hope-to-bes." Examples are Wal-Mart, Hewlett-Packard, IBM, Texas Instruments, Motorola, and the Chaparral Steel Company. These world-class organizational structures have moved significantly away from bureaucratic decision-making, and have modified their hierarchies to include team-based organizations and horizontal structures with minimum "white space." These firms encourage cross-communication by all employees, supported by technology such as e-mails and groupware, and reward employees who play a strong role in influencing organizational direction and decision-making.

These organizations, working predominantly in the fast-moving world of information and knowledge application, also recognize the value of decisions made at the lowest qualified level and the payoff from smart workers who know their jobs. However, for employees at all levels to make effective decisions, they must understand the context within which those decisions are to be made. This context is provided through shared vision, clear values, and strong corporate direction and purpose, combined with open communication. As described by Peter Senge in *The Fifth Discipline*, smart companies put significant effort into transferring their vision, purpose, and goals to all employees. Good employee decision-making stems from understanding their work in terms of its impact on adjacent areas of the corporation and its direct impact on the customer. The first of these requires effective empowerment and systems thinking and the second results from customer orientation and focus (Senge, 1990). Note how far the leading companies have departed from Weber's description of bureaucracy (see Appendix) and how impotent his bureaucracy would be in the current world context. One could think of today's best organizations as flexible and sensitive hierarchies.

Nurtured by total quality management, the transfer of best business practices has recently become a hallmark of high-performing organizations. A number of tools have been developed in the recent past that have helped companies create environments that make maximum use of employee capabilities. These best business practices include total quality management (TQM), benchmarking, business process reengineering (BPR), lean production, value chain analysis, agility, integrated product teams, and the balanced score card. Common themes that result from the above practices offer insights into the difference between bureaucratic organizations and the current world-class organizations. Table 1-1 explicates some of the differences between the historic bureaucratic mode and the world-class mode.

CHALLENGES TO BECOMING WORLD CLASS

As valuable as these world-class practices are, their implementation continues to be a challenge to most organizations. Although many of these tools were originally touted as silver bullets, after they become popular, and companies try them without fully understanding the intricacies of their implementation, they frequently achieve less than anticipated results. Michael Hammer, one of the co-creators of BPR, has defined BPR as "the fundamental rethinking and radical redesign of business processes to achieve dramatic improvements in critical contemporary measures of performance" (Hammer and Champy, 1993, p. 32). We find that, ten years later, BPR is just now being understood well enough to provide a good chance of success, if applied to the right situation by experienced professionals. The unproven norm is that typically 70 percent of BPR implementations fail to meet

Table 1-1

Differences Between Bureaucratic and World-Class Organizations

Bureaucratic Mode	World-Class Mode
Focuses on organizational stability and the accuracy and repetitiveness of internal processes	Focuses on flexibility and customer response
Utilizes autocratic decision-making by senior leadership with unquestioned execution by the workforce	Utilizes practices that emphasize using the ideas and capabilities of employees to improve decision-making and organizational effectiveness
Uses technology to improve efficiency and expects employees to adapt	Brings technology into the organization to support and liberate employee involvement and effectiveness
Seeks to establish fixed processes to ensure precision and stability with little concern for value	Takes actions to eliminate waste and unnecessary processes while maximizing value added
Minimizes the use of teams to maintain strong control and ensures knowledge is kept at the managerial and senior levels. Axiom: "Knowledge is Power."(used as a metaphor)	Emphasizes the use of teams to achieve better and more balanced decision-making and to share knowledge and learning. Axiom: "Knowledge Shared is Power Squared." (used as a metaphor)

expectations. Many feel TQM has suffered the same phenomenon. As time progresses and more organizations learn how to successfully implement these tools, they will become more and more useful and significantly contribute to organizational improvement. From the authors' personal experience, major reasons for the difficulty in applying these tools comes more from the lack of infrastructure support and the inability to change culture than it does from the workforce and leadership. Research has indicated that the resistance from cultural inertia causes great difficulty in transferring knowledge to effectively implement better business practices (Brown, 1999).

For a practice to really provide long-term value, "The practice itself must be better understood and continuously improved through a process of ongoing learning. Second, as the business environment changes, it must be adapted and even reinvented into something better that fulfils an important need" (Skyrme, 1999, p. 5). Thus we see that in today's environment, *no solutions can be independent of either time or context*. This also applies to organizational structures. To the extent that this is true, there is not—and likely may never be—any single form of organizational structure that provides maximum overall effectiveness. However, all structures will need to facilitate agility, learning and knowledgeable decisions, and effective follow through.

A significant challenge still facing modern organizations is how to harness the benefits of information technology. While the rapid growth and widespread influence of this technology has resulted in huge investments by many corporations, there has been some disillusionment with its hoped-for increase in productivity. However, those companies that have recognized the close relationship between information technology and culture, using the technology to support people in achieving corporate objectives, have found information technology highly effective in creating a competitive advantage (Coleman, 1997). To achieve this not only requires selecting and adapting the technology to the organization's needs, but also a carefully designed process that brings the technology into the culture in a way that the workforce finds acceptable and is motivated to make the necessary workflow adaptations through cultural changes (Coleman, 1997).

In addition to the aforementioned difficulties in applying information technology and the requisite culture change, there are a number of fundamental barriers that many organizations face today as they attempt to become world class to develop and maintain continuous competitive advantage. It is widely known that change management is a broad and challenging field that offers many theories and processes to consider, but no guaranteed solutions. Fundamentally, the process of change is highly situational, complex, and dependent not only on the environment and the goals and objectives of the organization, but also on its specific history, culture, and leadership. Each year finds a number of new books and journal articles offering the latest and greatest solutions to implementing change. To the authors' knowledge, there is no "solution" to implementing change since each situation offers its own unique set of challenges, pitfalls, and potentially successful tactics.

Major opposition to new practices frequently comes from middle management's unwillingness to give up its prerogatives of decision-making and authority. Since most of the workforce gets their direct information from, and usually develops trust in, their immediate supervisors, they are heavily influenced by the attitudes and actions of these middle managers. This barrier has occasionally been overcome by senior management bypassing the mid-level and working directly with the workforce (Carlzon, 1987).

Although communication is always a problem, even in stable times, the difficulty in communication becomes acute under times of change and uncertainty. Rumors, informal networks, official organizational policies and rules, as well as personalities and fear of job loss or power shifts all heavily influence the accuracy, noise level, and effectiveness of people trying to share understanding. The classic solution seems to be to communicate as much as possible, as accurately as possible, and as often as possible, keeping everyone informed on events and changes in the organization. Although theoretically appealing, this practice may be impossible under conditions of anticipated mergers, serious reductions in market share, or new competitive threats. Also, in the extremes, too much communication can lead to trivia, time-wasting, gossip, and misunderstanding.

Before an organization can adopt new practices to significantly change the way it does business, it must be willing to admit that its current practices are inadequate. This requires a willingness to adapt new assumptions in terms of how the business works and what must be done, often referred to as a paradigm shift. Resistance to this paradigm shift is usually high and may go unrecognized by senior management. The historic paradigm that produced past success is so ingrained in the belief systems of most middle and upper managers, and the risk of adapting totally new assumptions about the business is so large, that the "double loop" learning required, as presented and explained so eloquently by Argyris and Schön (1978), becomes a major challenge.

Still another challenge to leadership is their willingness to give up authority and decision-making and to empower their workforce and teams to make decisions based upon local circumstances. This shift in authority from upper and middle management to the workforce essentially means giving up authority while keeping responsibility—something few people are willing to do. Yet, to successfully release the worker's knowledge and experience for organizational improvement, the context, direction, and authority to make local decisions must be made available to all personnel.

The leading organizations strive hard to become learning organizations so the entire workforce will learn while working and have the ability to adapt quickly to market changes and other environmental perturbations. Except for professional services and knowledge-based organizations, most of the workforce is not used to continuous learning as part of their job. In addition, many supervisors and managers believe that learning on the job is not appropriate. Thus, individuals who have worked for years without learning or even the expectation of having to learn on the job find it disconcerting and difficult to "learn how to learn" and to continuously keep updated in their area of expertise. Creating the emergent characteristic represented by a learning organization takes considerable more effort than simply offering courses and training people.

A final barrier particularly relevant to those organizations seeking to become knowledge organizations is that of creating a culture in which knowledge and knowledge sharing are valued and encouraged. Many in the workforce today consider knowledge as power and job security and are unwilling to share ideas and experience with their colleagues. The solution to this challenge is an area of current research and ideas are being offered and tested. As usual, they are situation dependent and represent another step toward complexity.

The evolution of organizations has passed from cooperative hunting bands to farming groups to cities/towns to bureaucracies. These changes took almost 35,000 years, or about 1400 generations. Yet over the past 50 years (two generations) organizations have moved from enlightened bureaucracies to employee-centered, team-based, networked, and information- and knowledge-intense structures struggling to keep pace with change. In one sense we are back to small bands of people working together to solve their common and immediate problems. In another, everyone lives, works, and relates in a totally new and strangely connected world.

In summary, at the forefront of organizational performance are the world-class organizations that have successfully adopted many of the practices known as best business practices. Through one means or another, they have been able to overcome the barriers and achieve organizations which represent the highest efficiency, effectiveness, sustained competitive advantage and, above all, an effective balance in satisfying stakeholders, customers, the workforce, the environment, and local community needs. The character of these organizations is unique to their history, their culture, their mission, and their environment. While there is still much experimentation with organizational design, and trial-and-error is on the daily menu, general patterns of success may be emerging. These patterns are creating new metaphors for organizations such as: agile production systems, living organisms, complex adaptive systems, self-organizing systems, virtual organizations, and the spiritual workplace. Which of these metaphors, or new ones to be generated in the future, will shadow the successes of the day 15–20 years ahead cannot be predicted, but reflection and speculation can be useful in describing potential/probable visions of what the best of the best organizations will look like in the future world. The metamorphosis of the butterfly is almost complete (see Appendix), and as organizations respond to the current (and future) environment to ensure survival and success, they are moving beyond the bureaucratic model and toward a new organizational theory. The concept of the intelligent complex adaptive system provides one model for those organizations.

REFERENCES

Argyris, C. and D. A. Schön. *Organizational Learning: A Theory of Action Perspective*. Philippines: Addison-Wesley Publishing Co., 1978.

Brown, J. S. "Conversation," *Knowledge Directions: The Journal of the Institute for Knowledge Management*, 1, Spring, 1999.

Carlzon, J. *Moments of Truth*. Cambridge: Ballinger Publishing Co., 1987.

Coleman, D. *Groupware: Collaborative Strategies for Corporate LANs and Intranets*. New Jersey: Prentice Hall, 1997.

Collins, J. C. and J. I. Porras. *Built to Last*. New York: Harper Business, 1994.

Drucker, P. F. *Post Capitalist Society*. Butterworth-Heinemann, 1993.

Hammer, M. and J. Champy. *Reengineering the Corporation*. New York: HarperCollins Publishers, 1993.

Senge, P. M. *The Fifth Discipline: The Art and Practice of the Learning Organization*. New York: Doubleday, 1990.

Shingo, S. *A Study of the Toyota Production System*. Cambridge: Productivity Press, 1989.

Skyrme, D. J. *Knowledge Networking: Creating the Collaborative Enterprise*. Boston: Butterworth-Heinemann,1999.

Whyte, W. H., Jr. *The Organization Man*. New York: Simon and Schuster, 1956.

Wiig, K. M. *Knowledge Management Foundations—Thinking About Thinking—How People and Organizations Create, Represent, and Use Knowledge*. Arlington, TX: Schema Press, 1993.

Womack, J. P., D.T. Jones, and D. Roos. *Machine That Changed The World*. New York: McMillan Publishing Co., 1990.

Chapter 2

THE PRESENT AND FUTURE DANGER, OR WHY WE NEED TO CHANGE

While it is impossible to predict the future, there are major trends driven by fundamental underlying forces that may give one some ability to at least comprehend its possibilities.

For example, while progress in science and technology is nonlinear, long-term advances in these fields have consistently led to an increase in knowledge, and advances in their application through businesses and other organizations have created the present world economy and standard of living. The technology to access data, information, and knowledge is growing rapidly over time and may well overwhelm our limited human ability to find, identify, and retrieve the data and information, and develop the knowledge we need in time to interpret and apply it to fast-changing crises and opportunities.

THE FIVE MAJOR DRIVERS

Recognizing that a great many factors and forces impact our organizations, and that their number will increase in the future, we suggest some drivers behind the change, complexity, and uncertainty that currently cast a shadow over many institutions. We believe these five drivers represent fundamental forces that will challenge future organizational survival. They are: connectivity; data, information, and knowledge (DINK); speed; access; and digitization (see Figure 2-1). In addition to impacting how firms must structure themselves and what strategies and form they take on, these drivers will also impact employees, customers, legislative policies, and international relationships, all of which carry over to influence every organization's ability to meet its objectives.

The first major force of the future environment is *connectivity*: the number and ease of connecting computers, different individuals, and different parts of the world. Technology has provided totally new ways of moving and transferring data, information, and knowledge among individuals, organizations, and governments. Anyone in the world can talk at any time to almost anyone else in the world in real time through the Internet, satellite, or fiber-optic cables. Virtual conferences and video cameras are commonplace and will soon be ubiquitous.

The result will be many more conversations at lower costs, the speeding up of the flow of ideas, and the need for faster decision-making and more sharing of understanding. Collaboration will involve experts from all over the world, brought together rapidly and efficiently to solve problems or brainstorm ideas.

The ability to enter into a formal dialogue with strangers is rapidly becoming a factor in success as the need for synergistic thinking and quick action approaches a survival necessity. The resulting pressures on organizations will mandate their ability to scan, select, and quickly respond to the consequences of this complex network and web of exchanges and actions. As the number of nodes in a network increases, the number of links rises at an explosive rate. As the links and their consequent relationships increase, so does the complexity. Thus we find that not only is the external environment becoming increasingly more complex, but, to survive, more and more organizations are being forced into a heretofore unthinkable level of internal complexity. Organisms (organizations), to survive in a competitive, evolutionary type environment, are often forced to become more complex. They need more options (possible actions) to

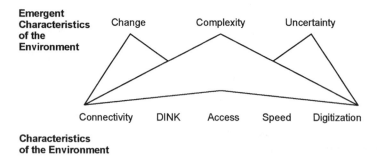

Figure 2-1
Emergent Characteristics of the Environment

give customers than their competitors offer. This creates a march toward internal complexity. How they handle this internal complexity will not only be a significant factor in their survival, but in their long-term success.

The second driver impacting organizations is *data, information, and knowledge*. In addition to possible overload from saturation, organizations will have technology and human systems that search and seek the data, information, and knowledge needed to meet their objectives. These systems must validate the information, categorize it, identify the context and develop the best interpretation, thereby laying the groundwork for knowledge creation and application. Each of these activities is difficult enough by itself, but when existing in an environment where information is a bombardment, changing quickly, and is noisy and possibly random, or with little meaning, the organization will be forced to develop new systemic and human capabilities that can respond to such terrain. This driver also challenges individuals to learn how to learn, create, leverage, and apply knowledge faster than the environment can change.

Speed is the next force behind the accelerating world: speed in the movement of goods and services, in the creation of new ideas through virtual collaboration, in the spread of information through increased bandwidth, in smart search engines and learning software, and in the sharing and diffusing of knowledge. Speed shortens time and creates a demand for faster decision-making. It also increases uncertainty by limiting the time available to comprehend what is going on. As discussed below, it exacerbates the problems of validation and assurance of information and knowledge. In general, the pace of every thing will continue to accelerate while simultaneously demanding that the human mind keep up. One challenge for the new organization is the resolution of the apparent conflict between the limitations of human processing speed and the increasing speed of change and growth of data, information, and knowledge.

Access is a recent problem emerging from the confluence of the three previous phenomena. It has several aspects. The first is how to identify the context of the information so that understanding can be extracted and relevant knowledge created by the user. The combination of large amounts of information coming from multiple networks using high-speed transfer systems and workers who need rapid, quality decisions makes this "context" extraction a difficult problem. When one considers the global sources of information and the language and cultural differences that come with international participants in communication networks the challenges become staggering. A second element of access is competition.

In the organization of the future, competitors will have the ability to quickly and reliably find information on each other, thereby improving their own competitive status and driving other competitors to match or exceed their own. The world of competitive intelligence is already turning in this direction for those with the human capital necessary to understand the whats and hows of

Internet superiority. In addition, every organization's customers will have access to more information and their standards and expectations of products and services will be high. A third effect of increasing access to information is the changed perspective and expectations of employees relative to their place of employment.

For example, employees with a broader understanding of their world can easily assess their own situation relative to their current employer versus other opportunities. To prevent possible job-hopping, employers will have to carefully monitor their internal structure, culture, and leadership styles to maximize employee loyalty.

A final impact of increased access to information is the opportunity of the organization to make use of information as a major internal process and competency. Data and information are necessary for knowledge and knowledge is the solution to external complexity. Any of the above characteristics of the environment may have one or all of these impacts on the organization.

Connectivity, speed, access and large amounts of information from everywhere on earth will seed the culture of the future. How the above characteristics can be turned into shared understanding and knowledge application for the good of the organization is unanswered at this time. A vital question is: "Can organizations adapt and learn and act fast enough to keep up with the environmental changes driven by these forces?"

The fifth driving force, perhaps underlying the other forces, is *digitization.* The digital economy, as it is popularly known, describes the overall movement to make maximum use of digital technology to create new technology products and increase efficiency. The scope of impact is almost unbelievable, covering computers, telephones, publishing, banking, education, medicine, and cyberspace.

Donald Tapscott (1998) considers the digital economy's driver to be an alliance of converging technologies. In his book, *Blueprint to the Digital Economy*, Tapscott offers the following forecast: "Clearly the first 40 years of the computing revolution have been a preamble. Much greater changes lie just ahead. The marriage of computers and communication networks is transforming most aspects of business and consumer activities. Organizations face enormous changes, many occurring simultaneously"(p. 1).

It seems clear to most students of the economy that the current and future world will be driven by technology as the number of networks and relationships increase and encourage consumers, businesses, the media, and government to expand their range of activities and options through communication and collaboration. As nanotechnology, biotechnology, the Internet highway, and smart machines embed themselves into the world of *Homo sapiens*, their very invisibility will quietly create an entirely different milieu. This new world will be as different and challenging as the shift from horse transportation to space travel. The changes are more than simply increasing speed, complexity, and connectivity.

The digital world brings its own set of rules, limitations, and constraints that demand a reorientation, restructuring, and, in many areas, a redesign from the bottom up for those organizations at the leading edge of the economy. This book offers a glimpse of what those firms in the knowledge industry may look like.

Each of the five major environmental forces discussed above influences the other four. For example, connectivity has made data, information, and knowledge more widespread, easier to generate, and available, while digitization has provided the technology for wide bandwidth connectivity as well as reduced cost and improved quality. These five characteristics of the environment represent major drivers that create an overall landscape upon which the organization of the future must live and adapt. In adapting, the organization itself will have to accept and master these five characteristics. Environmental complexity begets organizational complexity, which further increases environmental complexity. Here we can see the ever-increasing spiral from the early simplicity of bureaucracy to our current entry into the age of complexity.

CHANGE, UNCERTAINTY, AND COMPLEXITY

This new landscape can be described at the highest level by three characteristics that emerge from the interaction of these five forces. They are familiar to all readers as *change, uncertainty, and complexity.* To be more precise, we would describe the trend in the environment as accelerating change, rising uncertainty, and increasing complexity. These, in combination with the human response of anxiety, will be a central concern in much of this book.

Accelerating Change

It is convenient to consider several types of change. The first is the increasing speed with which transactions can occur throughout the world. As an example, those with which money can be wired anywhere in the world, the ability to have a credit card validated at a gas pump with no attendant needed, and the speed at which an experienced Internet operator can find and locate information world-wide. This speed-up of transactions means that things happen much more rapidly than they used to, even only ten years ago. It also means that when errors do happen to occur in the systems, then those errors are moved on and are very hard to trace back, since they represent history by the time they are detected.

The second type of change represents a change in the *types* of events or patterns that occur, created by the increasing number of interactions and advances in technology, enabling an increase in creative and innovative ideas. Examples would be computer-related phenomena such as viruses and hacking, such

Internet businesses as eBay and eLearning, cell phones, and even global positioning systems (GPS). All these things created in the recent past are significantly changing the way we do our jobs, the way we live our lives and the way businesses operate. There are several consequences of this that result directly from the increasing rate of change such as the increased rate at which learning needs to occur by knowledge workers and businesses in order to keep up with these advances. These learning needs not only necessitate more rapid learning, but also learning in new areas such as computer operations, software programs, working successfully with the Internet, and individuals learning to deal with more and new information. So another result of the increasing rate of change is the value and importance of knowledge in terms of recognizing the impact of these changes and being able to deal with them.

Undoubtedly, most readers at one time or another have been highly frustrated with the increasing rate of change and its impact on our personal and professional work. A common example is the large number of e-mails typically received by a given knowledge worker that must be processed or at least scanned prior to taking action. A second-order impact of the acceleration of change is to create situations where transactions and events and patterns are happening so fast that they tend to overwhelm the individual or the organization, resulting in feelings of confusion, bewilderment, and even anxiety.

Rising Uncertainty

Uncertainty can be considered the inability to predict what will happen next in a given situation or environment. When the environment is relatively stable and change is slow, it is easy to fall into patterns and routines that enable us to be aware of what is going to happen next. This leads to efficiency, self-confidence, and a comfort feeling, based on our past experiences, that we can handle whatever comes up in the future. When the future becomes uncertain to where we frequently cannot predict the results of what will happen based on our actions or forecast even what may happen, from our own personal and organizational perspectives the world seems to change. When uncertainty increases in the environment and in our jobs, it becomes harder and harder to decide or predict customer needs, what regulations are going to come down, what the value of money will be, what new products will be popular and which ones will not, or how long we should continue doing the same job.

From an organizational view it becomes harder and harder to plan for the future because, basically, the time horizon shrinks. When we don't know what will happen, then we have to decide what are the possibilities that A or B or C will happen and, if they do happen, what are the second-order effects going to be? Managers, leaders, and knowledge workers all find themselves in a position of speculating, using their experience, intuition, and best judgment to anticipate what they think will happen in the future. This uncertainty makes it harder and harder to make decisions with confidence and, in some cases, impossible to make decisions without hedging your bets, creating redundancy operations, doing detailed risk analysis, or using a trial-and-error approach. All of these are, of course, a result of increasing uncertainty and the increased level of risk it carries with it.

Uncertainty is driven by the inability to understand the current situation well enough to anticipate its reaction to any event that could occur. As uncertainty increases it becomes harder and harder to make rational decisions and, even in the short term, it may be a gambling approach. The consequences of this again result in dismay, frustration, and anxiety on the part of the individual or the organization. It may be possible to increase one's knowledge of the situation sufficiently to improve the probability of predicting what could happen, thereby reducing the level of uncertainty through increased knowledge. Approaches that offer the possibility of understanding the future and overcoming uncertainty would be scenario development, decision trees, computer modeling, linear extrapolation, and Delphi groups. The classical futurist approach is to take the future and divide it into what could possibly happen, what is likely and most probable to happen, and finally, what would be preferable to happen. Examples of the result of increasing uncertainty are the dotcom successes and failures of recent years, the airline industries significant problems as spin-offs of 9/11, and other numerous changes in the economy.

Increasing Complexity

The third major category is that of increasing complexity. Complexity is discussed in some detail in Chapter 19, but for now let's consider it as a large number of elements and their relationships such that there's an inability to predict or understand causal relationships among them due primarily to the number of relationships and their nonlinearity. Thus a complex system can take on a large number of states and possess characteristics that we call emergent in that these global characteristics cannot be directly derived from the individual elements and their relationships. The existence of complexity in the environment essentially makes it very difficult, if not impossible, to predict what will happen even in the near-term future in some cases. It also makes it very difficult to understand the system itself. An example that comes to mind is that a number of years ago when the U.S. economy was in bad shape with interest rates very high and the other economic parameters varying "out of bounds" a major news magazine asked seven Nobel Laureates for their interpretation, understanding, and opinion on what caused the economy to be the way it was. The interesting result was that every one of these seven experts had a different opinion and understanding of the causes. This is not at all to belittle Nobel Laureate economists, quite the contrary. What it does is indicate the complexity of the national economy—and that occurred 30 years ago!

In a complex situation, things can sometimes happen that appear contradictory and totally beyond comprehension. Because we are historically trained in rational thought and causal analysis, we tend to try to understand phenomena in the same way. In complex systems this simply cannot be done because the system cannot be analyzed from the bottom up, so to speak. Complexity, then, also leads to confusion, concern, an inability to make rational decisions with some confidence, and a feeling of total loss of control relative to what is going on. From a personal viewpoint, it also leads to frustration, perhaps fear, and certainly anxiety.

When we consider these three major environmental characteristics together—accelerating change, rising uncertainty, and increasing complexity—we get a potential picture of the direction in which the environment is going and perhaps some of the challenges it presents. It also suggests that to live in such a world requires a very robust and flexible organization with the ability to react quickly while adapting to changing external conditions. It also means that its workers must be able to live with such change and be constantly learning, fully using their skills, experience, and knowledge to understand, interpret, and act upon that environment. These requirements represent the genesis of the need for a new theory of the firm, one that we call the intelligent complex adaptive system, or ICAS.

In discussing change, uncertainty, and complexity above we have several times noted that the impact of each of these three on the individual, as well as their sum, is to potentially create a certain level of anxiety in terms of the perception of loss of control, not knowing what to do, and not knowing how to learn what to do. We would propose anxiety as a major human factor affecting the near-term and future environment. This means that we consider accelerating change, rising uncertainty, increasing complexity, and growing anxiety as the four major descriptors relative to the future environment.

Anxiety

Increasing anxiety within the workforce or organizations that must survive in the turbulent world may well cause loss of security, lack of trust, and a sense of undermining one's personal identity. Such stress can result, in a negative sense, in physical or psychological disorders or, in a positive sense, transformational change. Under these potential conditions, it is very important that individuals and the organization work hard to maintain an identity, a feeling of belonging and an "all for one and one for all" attitude. Thus one consequence of increased anxiety is that the successful organization must work hard to create a strong environment and culture within which people can effectively feel freedom, stability, and loyalty in the face of a dynamic, uncertain, and complex external environment. This necessitates the organization maintain a stability of values, integrity, and ethical behavior with a clear direction, vision, and purpose.

The environment of the new organization must be able to adapt to external environmental necessities both for its organizational success and survival and, as Merry (1995) notes, "adaptation is not a basic transformative change, but it is having a new range of possibilities. When people face growing uncertainty and stress, their resilience allows them to find novel forms of adaptation to the changing conditions" (p. 129). In other words, with a stressful external environment, people will naturally tend to find ways of reacting and adapting to that environment. The internal organizational environment needs to not only encourage and support those ways, but have the structure and culture to leverage this behavior.

WHY WE NEED A NEW THEORY OF THE FIRM

Historically, man has always sought a stable and predictable environment. It is usually during stable times that civilizations and societies have advanced. Organizations often act as barriers against uncertainty through their added resources, and by virtue of their size they can often offer stability to individuals. While organizational structures change, they rarely change daily, weekly, or monthly. And while cultures can move and shift, they are also relatively stable as far as the individuals within the organizations are concerned. This perception and feeling of stability of the organization helps alleviate concerns, fears, and anxieties over external uncertainties and complexities.

As Merry (1995) has noted, "To ensure regularity, predictability, and routine, men also impose order around them. People are not only passive seekers after certitude, reliability and predictability, they also actively impose these on the world around them. Where people cannot find order and regularity, they attempt to create them" (p. 20). While we agree with Merry that men have attempted to create stability, we also believe that as society becomes more and more complex and uncertain it will be harder and harder for individuals and organizations to control their external environment. What is happening now, and will continue to happen in the future, is that the successful organizations will be those who have developed the capacity to co-evolve in an ecological sense with their external environments through mutual interaction, internal adaptability, and rapid response. These organizations will develop a strategy, structure, culture, and overall health level that permits them to act intelligently, creating, leveraging, and applying knowledge in a manner that leads them to overcome environmental threats and take advantage of opportunities. This essentially means that these organizations can create and nurture sustainable competitive advantage over their competitors or, in the case of not-for-profit and government, create and nurture sustainable high performance. To do this is the challenge of all organizations hoping to survive—and grow—in the future.

REFERENCES

Merry, U. *Coping with Uncertainty: Insights from the New Sciences of Chaos, Self-Organization, and Complexity.* Westport, CT: Praeger Publishers, 1995.

Tapscott, D. *Blueprint to the Digital Economy: Creating Wealth in the Era of e-Business.* San Francisco, CA: McGraw-Hill, 1998.

PART II

THE THEORY*

Chapters 3, 4, and 5 provide different perspectives of the intelligent complex adaptive system organizational model. Chapter 3 provides an overview of the model, presents definitions and assumptions, explores the concept of emergence, and introduces the eight emergent characteristics and four major processes of the ICAS.

Chapter 4 builds on the emergent characteristic concepts presented in Chapter 3, repeating core statements, expanding those statements, and offering references in support of those statements. This increased depth of discussion is intended to build a deeper understanding of the ICAS approach in terms of model development.

Since ICAS performance relies heavily on the interaction and synergy among emergent characteristics, Chapter 5 explores the relationships among those eight emergent characteristics presented in the model. Figure 5-1 connects the characteristics of the environment, the emergent characteristics of the ICAS, and optimal performance.

*The initial concept of the ICAS was first distributed across the Federal government in toolkits published by the Department of the Navy. External to government, it first appeared in print as "Characterizing the Next Generation Knowledge Organization" and "Exploring Key Relationships in the Next Generation Knowledge Organization" published in Volume 1, Issues 1 and 2, respectively, of *Knowledge and Innovation: Journal of the KMCI.* A brief overview version of the ICAS titled "Designing the Knowledge Organization of the Future: The Intelligent Complex Adaptive System" was contributed to Holsapple, C. W. (ed), *Handbook on Knowledge Management 1: Knowledge Matters*, New York: Springer-Verlag, 2003.

Chapter 3

THE INTELLIGENT COMPLEX ADAPTIVE SYSTEM

As we begin to understand and hopefully anticipate the behavior of the current and future environment, it becomes clear that neither the classic bureaucratic nor the current popular matrix and flat organizations will provide the unity, complexity, and selectivity necessary for survival. A different approach is needed to create an organizational system that can enter into a symbiotic relationship with other organizations within its enterprise and with the external environment while retaining its own unity of purpose and selectivity of incoming threats and opportunities, i.e., turning the *living system* metaphor into a reality. This organization builds on the currently anticipated knowledge organization to become a living system composed of living subsystems that combine, interact, and co-evolve to provide the capabilities of an advanced, intelligent techno-sociological adaptive enterprise. The system we propose can best be described as an intelligent complex adaptive system (ICAS).

The ICAS is a conceptual model developed to bring out the most important capabilities necessary to live and contribute in an unpredictable, dynamic, and complex society. As an idealization, it is described in somewhat pure forms and perfect structures, neither of which is found in practice. The variation in human experience and behavior, together with the practical demands of the workforce and natural difficulties in communication create a reality that is often far from ideal. Nevertheless, new concepts, perceptions, relationships, and communications are essential if our organizations are to keep up with the pace, direction, and demands of society in the age of complexity.

DEFINITIONS AND ASSUMPTIONS

The term complex system means a system that consists of many interrelated elements with nonlinear relationships that make them very difficult to understand and predict. See Chapter 19 for a more detailed discussion of complex systems. The ICAS, as a complex organization, is composed of a large number of individuals, groups, and human subsystems that have nonlinear interaction and the capability to make many local decisions and strive for specific end states or goals. These components build many relationships both within the organization and external to the organization's boundaries that may become highly complex and dynamic. Together, these relationships and their constituents form the organization and its enterprise. The word *adaptive* implies that the organization and its subcomponents are capable of studying and analyzing the environment and taking actions that internally adjust the organization and externally influence the environment in a manner that allows the organization to fulfill local and higher-level goals.

Complex adaptive systems (organizations), then, are composed of a large number of self-organizing components that seek to maximize their own goals but operate according to rules and in the context of relationships with other components and the external world. In an intelligent complex adaptive system the actors are people. The organization may be composed of semi-hierarchical levels of workers, which can take the form of teams within teams, divisions or other structures that have common bonds. While workers are empowered to self-organize, they are not independent from the corporate hierarchy. Along with the increased freedom to organize and act at the lower levels of the organization comes a responsibility for awareness of local situations, organizational goals and values and the ongoing activities and available knowledge throughout the rest of the organization. By providing workers the encouragement to think and act on their own, the ICAS will manifest itself through eight characteristics essential for survival and growth in the previously described external landscape. *Organizational intelligence* is needed to provide the advantages of innovation, learning, adaptation, and quick response to new and trying situations. In further discussions, we use the terms "ICAS," "system," and "organization" interchangeably.

Though complex adaptive systems have been formally studied for several decades, current understanding of them can best be described as "work in process." Nevertheless, numerous examples of them include ant colonies, cities, the brain, the immune system, ecosystems, computer models, and, of course, organizations. There are some basic properties common to many complex adaptive systems. Examples are some level of self-organization, nonlinearity, aggregation, diversity, and flow. See Holland (1995), Battram (1996), and/or

Stacey (1996) for particularly lucid explanations. For more in-depth analyses of complex systems see Kauffman (1993), Axelrod (1997), Morowitz and Singer (1995), and Axelrod and Cohen (1999). There are a number of biological systems that possess capabilities needed by organizations to survive and compete. Neo-Darwinistic survival has produced organisms with modes of behavior that most organizations would consider unattainable. For example, cells and organs in the human body do their job and cooperate closely and continuously with other cells and organs. Because of their level of development, humans are not easily kept doing their job day-by-day and working without complaint or rebellion. However, they are individually and collectively far more innovative than cells and organisms. Thus, there exists a challenge to take advantage of the strengths of people while getting them to cooperate and collaborate to leverage knowledge and maintain unity of purpose. This balance will be the topic of further discussion (see Chapter 12). Nonetheless, we find it useful to use living systems as a source of metaphor and insight in developing our organization for the future.

One finding in the research on complex adaptive systems is that they have the ability to exist and operate in a state that is between pure stability and complete instability in a region that contains both stability and instability. In this mode, the organization is able to be innovative and creative, while concomitantly keeping its identity and cohesion (Stacey et al., 1996). According to Stacey, this state is achieved only when each of five parameters: information flow, connectivity, degree of diversity among workers, level of anxiety and degree of power differentials. What these levels should be is a matter for research and trial-and-error to determine. Certainly they are all sensitive to culture, situational context and external forces. Note that if any (or all) of these parameters become too high, the organization may be pushed into saturation, confusion, or chaos—leading to an inability to respond and adapt to the environment. If all of the parameters are low, for example if the information flow among workers is low, people work in isolation and as in a classical bureaucracy everyone follows the boss's orders without question, there will be little change, and no new ideas. The result would be an organization optimized for productivity in a stable, deterministic environment. Such an organization may not survive long in the age of complexity.

Certain assumptions were made in developing the ICAS model proposed in this book. One assumption is that nature, with her millions of years of experience through evolution, provides us with insights to understand the behavior of people working in complex organizations. Another source of ideas is consciousness and how the brain/mind works. Some characteristics of the human mind are helpful for understanding knowledge organizations in more than superficial ways. For example, a key to success in living organisms is how efficiently and effectively they handle information within their boundaries and in their interaction with the environment. Similar capabilities are needed by modern complex organizations.

THE ICAS MODEL

Organizations take inputs from their environment, transform those inputs into higher-value outputs and provide them to customers and stakeholders. Organizations solve problems (or take on opportunities) by creating options using internal and external resources in efficient and effective ways that create added value above and beyond the value of the inputs. Briefly, the organization solves problems (or takes on opportunities) that create options for action that then produce some internal or external value. Although they do this through available resources—people, ideas, technology, funds, facilities, etc.—as we move from the manufacturing to the information to the complexity age the most valuable resource becomes knowledge. Recall that in Chapter 1 we defined knowledge as the capacity (both potential and actual) to take effective action in varied and uncertain situations. This continuous ability to take effective action may require judgment, experience, context, insight, the right information, and the application of analysis and logic. Both understanding and meaning become requisite objectives before taking effective action. This ability to create value through effective action, i.e., knowledge, whether for employees, investors, customers, or other stakeholders, will be *the driving force* behind survival and growth. When the challenge is not routine the organization must be creative and generate innovative ways of solving problems and developing new opportunities. When facing non-routine situations, the organization, through its people working together or independently, must make decisions and take actions that produce their intended results. Making good decisions and taking effective actions each require knowledge; information alone is not up to the challenge when uncertainty, ambiguity, and nonlinearity dominate the landscape.

While this paradigm is easy to describe, it becomes very complicated and challenging in the real world, particularly when things are moving quickly, problems are not well understood, there are many opinions and options, and a successful outcome is dependent on uncertain events. Understanding and successfully applying the four processes of (1) creating new ideas, (2) solving problems, (3) making decisions, and (4) taking action to achieve a desired result is the major challenge to all organizations, including the ICAS. The processes themselves become core competencies that every intelligent organization must master.

The ICAS may need to be highly diversified or superbly coherent, depending on its mission, purpose, and environment. It will need to exhibit a unity of purpose and a coherence of action while being highly selective and sensitive to external threats and opportunities. An ICAS may have to rapidly bring together diverse knowledge located anywhere in (or beyond) the organization to solve problems and take advantage of opportunities.

Since only people can make decisions and take actions in a highly uncertain environment, there will be increasing emphasis on individual worker competency and freedom in terms of learning, decision-making, and taking actions. These will be leveraged through multiple and effective networks that provide sources of knowledge, experience, and insights from others. Dynamic networks will represent the critical infrastructure of the next-generation knowledge-based organization. Made available by increased bandwidth and processing power of both silicon and biotechnology, they will offer the opportunity for virtual information and knowledge support systems that connect data, information, and people through virtual communities, knowledge repositories, and knowledge portals. The foundation and grounding of future firms will be strengthened through a common set of strong, stable values held by all employees. Such values not only provide a framework that enhances empowerment but also motivate and strengthen the self-confidence of the workforce, thereby magnifying the effectiveness of the self-organized teams within the ICAS. To survive and successfully compete in the future world, these organizations will need to possess a number of emergent characteristics that taken together result in resilience, agility, adaptivity, and learning, all well-known traits of survival.

EMERGENT CHARACTERISTICS

As organizations change and take on new forms, they often do so through the creation and development of what complex systems theorists call emergent characteristics. Mills suggests three criteria for emergence: "First, an emergent character of a whole is not the sum of the characters of its parts; second, an emergent character is of a type totally different from the character types of the constituents; third, emergent characters are not deducible or predictable from the behaviors of the constituents investigated separately" (Auyang, 1998, p. 174).

The sources of emergent properties are both structural and relational. Auyang notes "Emergent characters mostly belong to the structural aspect of systems and stem mainly from the organization of their constituents" (Auyang, 1998, p. 176), whereas Holland (1998) writes "Emergence is above all a product of coupled, context-dependent interaction. Technically these interactions, and the resulting system, are *nonlinear*. The behavior of the overall system *cannot* be obtained by *summing* the behaviors of its constituent parts. [...]; However, we can reduce the behavior of the whole to the lawful behavior of its parts, *if* we take the nonlinear interactions into account" (pp. 121–122). Ingber (2000), in investigating biological design principles that guide self-organization and emergence, extends the normal complexity-based approaches that focus on nodes, connections, and resultant pattern formation to include the importance of architecture, mechanics, and structure in the evolution of biological forms. Human organizations abound with all of these phenomena. When emotions run high, the smallest event can create an explosion of feelings and action. Even routine human behavior is too complex to reduce to single causes. Relations create interdependencies that may result in completely new and unique ideas or actions, results that can rarely be traced back to any point of origin in the interaction that produced them.

Some examples of emergent phenomena suggested by Coveney and Highfield (1995) are: life is an emergent property arising from physicochemical systems organizing and interacting in certain ways; a human being is an emergent property of huge numbers of cells; a city is an emergent property of thousands or millions of humans; and a company is more than the sum of its technology, real estate, and people.

AN INTRODUCTION TO THE EIGHT EMERGENT CHARACTERISTICS OF THE ICAS

The ICAS, as an organization, must act like a biological system in many ways if it is to survive in a rapidly changing, nonlinear, complex, dynamic, and uncertain world. The eight emergent characteristics of the ICAS are shown in Figure 3-1 to highlight their relationships. These eight characteristics help provide the internal capability to deal with the future environment. We will briefly introduce each of them in this overview chapter. These are: organizational intelligence, shared purpose, selectivity, optimum complexity, permeable boundaries, knowledge centricity, flow, and multidimensionality. For a more in-depth treatment of these emergent characteristics, building on these overview descriptions, see Chapter 4.

Intelligence, according to *Webster's Dictionary* (1996), is the capacity for reasoning and understanding or an aptitude for grasping truths. When applied to organizations, Wiig (1993) broadens this view of intelligence and considers it the ability of a person to think, reason, understand, and act. He further considers intelligence as applying to organizations and includes the capabilities to innovate, acquire knowledge, and apply that knowledge to relevant situations. (From an organizational viewpoint, both employees and their organization can exhibit intelligent behavior.)

As a working concept for the ICAS model, *organizational intelligence* is taken to be the ability of an organization to perceive, interpret, and respond to its environment in a manner that simultaneously meets its organizational goals while satisfying its stakeholders, that is, its employees, customers, investors,

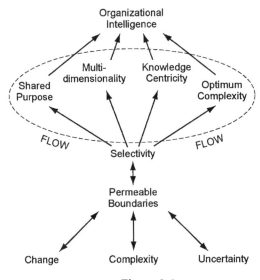

Figure 3-1
Emergent Characteristics of ICAS

community, and environment. Organizational intelligence is a descriptive term that indicates the measure of the organization's (and its workforce's) capacity to exhibit intelligent behavior.

Unity and shared purpose represents the ability of the ICAS organization to integrate and mobilize resources to (1) provide a continuous line of focus and attention and (2) pull together the relevant parts of the organization when and where they are needed. For an organization to work intelligently, it must be able to coordinate and unify its relevant resources to gain maximum situational understanding, knowledge, and concentration of energy to act and to respond. Faced with a large number of threats and opportunities and the potential need for quick reaction, the ICAS will have systems that constantly reach into, and maintain, continuous two-way communication with a large number of relatively independent subsystems (see Chapter 6 on structure and Chapter 7 on culture). According to complexity research (Stacey, 1996), these subsystems of agents should organize themselves to maximize their learning, innovation, and knowledge, that is, their ability to take effective action at the local point of the stakeholder interface.

Optimum complexity is a new concept in organizational theory. First consider the concept of complexity as it applies to organizations. Complexity is most simply interpreted as being a measure of the number of states (elements and/ or their relationships) in a system. While useful in many applications, there are difficulties with this interpretation when considering organizations. It is not the number of possible states—either in the organization or in its external environment—that need concern an organization. It is the *number of possible states that make a difference to the organization* that are important.

Consider now the two limits of internal complexity. If every component (worker, team, or group) were to act independently without coordination, a large number of independent states would be generated. But this would not be useful to the organization because there would be no alignment, synergy, or direction; in other words, no coherence, only isolated independent behavior. At the other extreme, if every component were constrained to behave in a predetermined way so that the organization became a rigid structure whose relationships were tightly controlled, the organization would become a classic bureaucracy and would be unable to deal with today's rapidly changing markets. It would be unable to adapt and respond fast enough to keep up with either its competitor's actions or its customer's needs. Neither the strong independent nor the tightly controlled forms of internal complexity will work. Somewhere in the middle region lies the organizational state of *optimum complexity*, the right level of internal complexity to deal with the external environment while maintaining overall order and unity of purpose.

Selectivity, as the filtering of incoming information from the outside world, will always occur. Individual attention is usually limited to one thing at a time. Because of the sheer volume and lack of control of outside information impinging on the system, natural selectivity at the boundaries of the organization may become erratic and create more random than purposeful action. This is exactly what system components (such as teams or self-organizing groups) are supposed to prevent. By analyzing incoming information through internal communication and "group digestion" of unusual events, the organization improves its filtering ability. Good filtering requires broad knowledge of the environment, specific knowledge of the customer, and a strong sense of the organization's strategic intent. Many opportunities can be lost if the organization cannot recognize and interpret the meaning and consequences of seemingly benign signals.

Knowledge centricity is the aggregation of relevant information derived from the knowledge of the organization's components that enables self-synchronization and increases collaborative opportunities while promoting strategic alignment. Knowledge centricity closely supports organizational intelligence, since to behave intelligently a complex adaptive system must achieve continuous, interdependent collaboration and interplay. Since information flows are dynamic in nature, powerful aids (such as search algorithms, intelligent agents, and semantic interpreters) are needed to allow people to rapidly retrieve information to formulate viable problem solutions but also give them the confidence that the information is current, accurate, and complete enough to make sound decisions. Knowledge, the actual and potential ability to take effective action, is at the heart of the ICAS.

Flow enables knowledge centricity and facilitates the connections and continuity that maintain unity and give coherence to organizational intelligence. The ICAS organization flourishes from the flow of data, information, and knowledge; the flow of people across and in and out of the organization; and flow in terms of the optimal human experience. The flow of data and information is both horizontal and vertical, including the continuous, rapid two-way communication between key components of the organization and top-level decision-makers that is essential to unity and shared purpose.

Permeable boundaries are an essential characteristic of the ICAS. The high degree of permeability required for a successful ICAS organization differentiates it from a classic bureaucracy. The virtual world of the ICAS breaks down the historic understanding of relationships and boundaries in terms of time and space. Over time as people come in and out of the organization driven by increasing and decreasing demands, the "boundaries" of the organization become more difficult to define. As ideas are exchanged and built upon, the lineage of these ideas becomes impossible to follow. Add all of this to a fluctuating, complex environment that is constantly changing and one can understand just how important permeability and porosity are to survival of the next-generation knowledge organization.

Multidimensionality represents organizational flexibility and can be discussed in terms of competencies that ensure ICAS knowledge workers have the ability to view the environment from many different perspectives and to apply a variety of thinking styles and core competencies to issues and problems (see Chapter 14). These capabilities give the organization an ability to continuously learn and apply this new knowledge; to identify and deal with risk; and to think in terms of systems, that is, to perceive and analyze situations in terms of wide scope of possibilities and long timeframes, all the while maintaining its organizational identity and unity. In other words, the organization must develop instincts and automatic competencies that are natural and become second nature at all times, what we call multidimensionality.

People are not machines and their variability and self-determination are essential for their efficacy. Thus, while a desirable emergent characteristic can be nudged and guided, it cannot be decreed. Every one of the eight characteristics of what we call the ICAS must emerge in one form or another from the nature of the organization, and cannot be predesigned and implemented by managerial fiat. We discuss this issue in more detail in Chapter 10.

AN INTRODUCTION TO THE FOUR MAJOR PROCESSES

These global characteristics, when they exist, support the conditions for the four major processes that deal effectively with the external environment and with stakeholders. These processes represent the primary ways that organizations prepare for and take actions (see Figure 3-2) that affect themselves and their environment and thereby ensure survival. The processes, which are introduced here and explicated in Chapter 8, are: (1) creativity, (2) problem-solving, (3) decision-making, and (4) implementation.

Creativity is the human act of generating new ideas, perspectives, understanding, concepts, or methods that help in solving problems or building new products. The organization has significant influence on the development and effectiveness of *creativity* through its strong influence over the working environment within which employees interact. A creative environment requires open communication, collaboration, a playful attitude, and critical thinking, coupled with a clear vision and objective. Such an environment encourages new ideas and different ways of seeing things, resulting in employee out-of-the-box suggestions for solving problems.

Problem-solving is one of the most important processes in the organization. Problems can be solved by individuals, teams, networks, or communities of people. Taking inputs from the creative process as needed, the problem-solving process provides the link between problems and decisions. The output of the problem-solving process is a set of alternatives that provide ways to achieve a desired situation or problem solution.

Decision-making refers to the selection of one or more alternatives generated by the problem-solving process. There is no single way to make decisions: it is both an art and a science. Decision-making cannot be avoided where responsibility is concerned. In a complex adaptive system all workers may be purposeful goal-seeking decision-makers. In the ideal ICAS decisions are made at all levels, with each level having a domain of decision authority commensurate with their experience and scope of responsibilities. Although team decision-making is more complex and often more time-consuming than individual decision-making, most

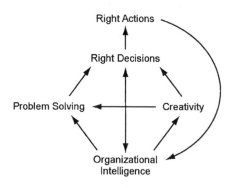

Figure 3-2
Optimal Performance

of the difficult and complex decisions are likely to be made by teams because of the potential improvement in decision quality.

Finally, results make the difference. Making high-quality decisions is essential to getting good results, but it is not enough. Taking good decisions and turning them into actions and changes that create improved products is a major challenge for all organizations. When individuals who have responsibility for *implementation* are aligned with the decision, implementation becomes much more effective. Big decisions that set the fundamental tone and nature of the ICAS require greater understanding and support throughout the organization. Ultimately, implementation is built on relationships and knowledge. Efficiency and clarity of communication, coupled with openness and a sincere concern to share understanding and get active participation, assure effective implementation of ICAS decisions.

In this chapter we have suggested certain organizational characteristics that will contribute to long-term success in the future storms and opportunities that lie ahead. The following chapters in this part explore these characteristics in greater depth, investigate the relationships among these emergent characteristics, and discuss the interdependency among these characteristics and the four major organizational processes.

REFERENCES AND RELATED READING

Auyang, S. Y. *Foundations of Complex-System Theories in Economics, Evolutionary Biology, and Statistical Physics.* Cambridge, England: Cambridge University Press, 1998.

Axelrod, R. *The Complexity of Cooperation: Agent-Based Models of Competition and Collaboration.* Princeton, NJ: Princeton University Press, 1997.

Axelrod, R. and M. D. Cohen. *Harnessing Complexity: Organizational Implications of a Scientific Frontier.* New York: The Free Press, 1999.

Battram, A. *Navigating Complexity: The Essential Guide to Complexity Theory in Business and Management.* Sterling, VA: Stylus Publishing, 1996.

Bennet, A. and D. Bennet. "Characterizing the Next Generation Knowledge Organization," *Knowledge and Innovation: Journal of the KMCI,* 1, No. 1, 2000, 8–42.

Coveney, P. and R. Highfield. *Frontiers of Complexity: The Search for Order in a Chaotic World.* New York: Fawcett Columbine, 1995.

Csikszentmihalyi, M. *Flow: The Psychology of Optimal Experience.* New York: Harper Perennial, 1990.

Edelman, G. M. *The Remembered Present: A Biological Theory of Consciousness.* New York: Basic Books, 1989.

Holland, J. H. *Hidden Order: How Adaptation Builds Complexity.* Reading, MA: Helix Books, 1995.

Holland, J. H. *Emergence from Chaos to Order.* Reading, MA: Helix Books, 1998.

Ingber, D. E. "Biological Design Principles that Guide Self-Organization, Emergence, and Hierarchical Assembly: From Complexity to Tensegrity," in Y. Bar-Yam (ed.), *Unifying Themes in Complex Systems.* Cambridge, England: Perseus Books, 2000.

Kauffman, S. A. *The Origins of Order: Self-Organization and Selection in Evolution.* New York, NY: Oxford, 1993.

Morowitz, H. J. and J. L. Singer (eds). *The Mind, the Brain, and Complex Adaptive Systems.* Reading, MA: Addison-Wesley Publishing Company, 1995.

Pinchot, G. and E. Pinchot. *The End of Bureaucracy and the Rise of the Intelligent Organization.* San Francisco, CA: Berrett-Koehler Publishers, 1993.

Stacey, R. D. *Complexity and Creativity in Organizations.* San Francisco, CA: Berrett-Koehler Publishers, 1996.

Stacey, R. D., D. Griffin, and P. Shaw. *Complexity and Management: Fad or Radical Challenge to Systems Thinking?* New York: Routledge, 2000.

Webster's *Encyclopedic Unabridged Dictionary of the English Language.* New York: Portland House, 1996.

Wiig, K. *Knowledge Management Foundations—Thinking about Thinking—How People and Organizations Create, Represent, and Use Knowledge.* Arlington, TX: Schema Press, 1993.

Chapter 4

EXPLORING THE EMERGENT PROPERTIES OF THE ICAS

This chapter builds on the introductions to the emergent characteristics of the ICAS provided in Chapter 3, reinforcing significant concepts, digging deeper into those concepts, and citing major works in the literature that have contributed to those concepts. Chapter 5 is then focused on exploring the relationships among these eight emergent characteristics. We begin with:

ORGANIZATIONAL INTELLIGENCE

As introduced in Chapter 3, intelligence is the capacity for reasoning and understanding or an aptitude for grasping truths. Wiig (1993) broadens this to include the individual's ability to think, reason, understand, and act and the organization's capabilities to innovate and acquire knowledge and apply it to relevant situations. Pinchot and Pinchot (1993) describe the intelligent organization as one that can face many competitors simultaneously and deal effectively with all of them and attend to all the details and supporting competencies that add up to cost-effective, superior performance. They further note that "the quality of relationships between members of the organization is a strategic issue that determines the very fabric of the organization" (Pinchot and Pinchot, 1993, p. 70).

McMaster (1996) refers to organizational intelligence as "the capacity of a corporation as a whole to gather information, to innovate, to generate knowledge, and to act effectively based on the knowledge it has generated. This capacity is the basis of success in a rapidly changing or highly competitive environment. Organizational intelligence refers to a capacity which is inherent in a system of organization. It is greater than the sum of the intelligence, information, and knowledge of each individual in that organization" (p. 3).

Building on the work cited above, we have defined organizational intelligence as the ability of an organization to perceive, interpret, and respond to its environment in a manner that simultaneously meets its organizational goals while satisfying its stakeholders, that is, its employees, customers, investors, community, and environment. We also use organizational intelligence as a descriptive term indicating the measure of the organization's (and its workforce's) capability to exhibit intelligent behavior.

Intelligent behavior of individuals, groups, and organizations (Wiig, 1993) can be understood in terms of (1) demonstrating behavior traits that are effective and acceptable; (2) being well prepared; (3) choosing the right posture in each situation; (4) being able to solve problems well; and (5) being able to make high-quality decisions and take effective actions for their implementation. Each of these can be studied to find the specific competencies needed for success in each area.

For example, intelligent behavior traits range from listening to others, remaining objective and flexible to learning, and thinking before acting. Independent thought, the ability to collaborate well in pressure situations, and having strong principles all help create credibility and trust, and support good long-term relationships. Such relationships greatly enhance the speed and quality of decision-making and situational assessment. Intelligent behavior from an organizational perspective means that external firms, customers, and partners will look with favor on the idea of interacting with the organization. Intelligent behavior leads to good working relationships at every level. According to McMaster (1996) relationships are the foundation of human intelligence. While good relationships have always been important, in the future they will be critical because of the advance of technology and the increasing role of knowledge in handling time compression and complexity.

Being well prepared means maintaining continuous context knowledge of surroundings, thinking ahead (anticipating possible events and evaluating worst-case scenarios), and rapidly developing opportunities that will be advantageous at all levels of the organization. Tomorrow's world will require a good knowledge of systems thinking and the ability to integrate large numbers of divergent data and information into a cohesive unity of understanding. We discuss this challenge in the section on "Unity and Shared Purpose."

For an organization to behave intelligently as a complex adaptive system, it must achieve continuous, interdependent collaboration and interplay among all levels of its system. This means balancing the knowledge and actions of its people to achieve both the lowest-level tasks and highest-level vision of the organization, creating a distributed intelligence throughout the organization. This can be done by using teams and communities to amplify local intelligence levels, accelerate quality decision-making, and foster innovation and creativity.

Being well prepared enables the firm to choose the right tactics. This is not easy in a world supersaturated with information, access problems, and complex nonlinear changes and threats impacting the organization. Quick reaction capabilities must be assembled using the knowledge and expertise needed to act effectively. Locating the right knowledge, experience, and tools to effect right action and tactics is a major strength of an ICAS. While problem-solving and decision-making are well-known competencies, their implementation is made more difficult in the future world of change, complexity, and uncertainty. To perform these processes will require more data, information, and knowledge than any single person, and perhaps any one group, can possess. Just as no one part of the brain is responsible for a given thought or process (Greenfield, 1995), no one part of the ICAS will necessarily be sufficient to develop tactics, solve problems, or make decisions. Undoubtedly, this approach will be widely resisted by many managers and leaders. It has disturbing consequences for the historical balance among authority, responsibility, and accountability. These problems are already being faced with the extended use of teams (Bennet, 1997).

In discussing intelligent behavior, Wiig (1993) notes that knowledge plays a central role and suggests the following six knowledge areas that need to be developed:

- Knowledge of knowledge
- Thinking about thinking
- "World knowledge" of society, sciences, people, etc.
- Knowledge of primary work-related domains
- Knowledge of private life, hobbies, etc.
- Basic knowledge of "walking," "talking," 3 Rs, social skills, etc.

A study of knowledge workers in Bell Labs by Kelly and Caplan (1993) identified nine capabilities that lead to high performance. Their capabilities are laid out in some detail and, in general, agree with Wiig's (1993) description. What has not been done as far as we know is an investigation of each capability to see how it can be expanded to teams and larger components of an organization to create the desired level of organizational intelligence.

Although data and information are necessary for acting intelligently, it is the knowledge that is created and acted upon that is the critical factor for the ICAS. As previously noted, there is currently much discussion and many interpretations of the terms data, information, and knowledge. Since we are concerned with making organizations work better, we take a somewhat pragmatic stance. Recall that we introduced the concept of data as sequences of numbers and letters; spoken words; pictures; even physical objects when presented without context, and information as data with some level of context and meaning, noting that both context and meaning require human interpretation and understanding. Knowledge, while made up of data and information, can be thought of as much greater understanding of a situation, relationships, causal phenomena, and the theories and rules (both explicit and implicit) that underlie a given domain or problem.

According to Wiig (1993), "Knowledge can be thought of as the body of understandings, generalizations, and abstractions that we carry with us on a permanent or semi-permanent basis and apply to interpret and manage the world around us. [...]; we will consider knowledge to be the collection of mental units of all kinds that provides us with understanding and insights" (p. 82). Thus knowledge is what each of us uses to determine *what something means*. In addition, it should not to be separated from action or from pragmatic concerns. McMaster (1996) says "Knowledge is information that is integrated with the entire system in such a way that it is available for action at potentially appropriate times" (p. 83). Data, information, and knowledge support organizational intelligence through the competency and demonstrated actions of both individuals and groups within the organization.

Knowledge includes facts, laws, theories, rules-of-thumb, insights, intuition, gut feel, judgment, causal relationships, leverage points, expectations, concepts, etc., and is usually about or of something, some area or domain of the world. Taking another perspective, data provides the where and when answers, information provides the what and who, and knowledge answers the why and how questions. As stated in Chapter 1, we take knowledge to be the capacity (potential and actual) to take effective action in uncertain and varied situations. For purposes of understanding this text, it is important to note that knowledge only exists in human minds.

In summary, an organization needs to exhibit intelligent behavior to provide the best response to its environment and to influence that environment in an effective way. Such intelligence must be coordinated throughout the organization at every level so there is a unity of purpose and a consistency of history as the firm evolves and grows through a co-evolution process with its environment. At the ICAS level, the characteristic of intelligence results from a large number of individual agents and their relationships, supported by technology and other artifacts.

Since organizational intelligence has no specific location within the ICAS organization, it must come from lower-level actions, processes, and characteristics. That is, organizational intelligence is an emergent property of the ICAS. It results from the structure, culture, and leadership of the organization through the interactions and behavior of ICAS knowledge workers. We now turn to the other characteristics that, taken together, support intelligent behavior.

UNITY AND SHARED PURPOSE

As introduced in Chapter 3, unity and shared purpose represent the ability of the ICAS organization to integrate and mobilize its resources to (1) provide a continuous line of focus and attention and (2) pull together the relevant parts of the organization when and where they are needed. Senge (1990) addresses a partial solution to this problem in his management book, *The Fifth Discipline*. He emphasizes the importance of a shared vision where employees participate in the development of a corporate vision, and can then make decisions and take actions consistent with the direction set by senior leadership. One can hardly disagree with this so long as the environment is reasonably stable and the vision does not change frequently. In the future world, however, one can expect more changes within every organization that operates close to the field where knowledge and information are the prime movers. Under these conditions, structures and relationships must be established that support and ensure continuous, rapid two-way feedback between key components throughout the organization *and* the central nexus where top-level decisions are made or orchestrated.

In the fifth of a series of books describing his research on consciousness, Edelman and his coauthor, Tononi (2000), propose the mechanism that provides unity to consciousness, thereby creating a continuous history of thought and a consistency of identity and action:

Our analysis leads to several conclusions. First, conscious experience appears to be associated with neural activity that is distributed simultaneously across neuronal groups in many different regions of the brain. Consciousness is therefore not the prerogative of any one brain area; instead, its neural substrates are widely dispersed throughout the so-called thalamocortical system and associated regions. Second, to support conscious experience, a large number of groups of neurons must interact rapidly and reciprocally through the process called reentry. If these reentrant interactions are blocked, entire sectors of consciousness disappear, and consciousness itself may shrink or split. Finally, we show that the activity patterns of the groups of neurons that support conscious experience must be constantly changing and sufficiently differentiated from one other. If a large number of neurons in the brain start firing in the same way, reducing the diversity of the brain's neuronal repertoires, as is the case in deep sleep and epilepsy, consciousness disappears (p. 36).

Recognize that the brain has roughly 100 billion neurons, each with an average of 1000 connections to other neurons. Information is stored in the connections between neurons and in patterns of connecting neurons, which change continuously, dependent on external sensory inputs and other internal pattern inputs. It is also known that different regions of the brain process different parts of a visual image and that all of the outputs of these processes are combined to make the image a unitary whole so that the perceiver "sees" a self-consistent, integrated picture (Edelman and Tononi, 2000). This ability to maintain different parts of the brain in harmony and to pull them together is exactly the challenge of the future organization, where the external environmental complexity continually impinges on many parts of the firm and may not in itself have coherence or consistency. Evolution's solution to the brain's so-called "binding problem" is to create certain neuron paths that provide continuous two-way communication between key operating networks (Edelman and Tononi, 2000).

Finally, if we consider neural dynamics (the way patterns of activity in the brain change with time), the most striking special feature of the brains of higher vertebrates is the occurrence of a process we have called reentry. Reentry [...]; depends on the possibility of cycles of signaling in the thalamocortical meshwork and other networks mentioned earlier. It is the ongoing, recursive interchange of parallel signals between reciprocally connected areas of the brain, an interchange that continually coordinates the activities of these areas' maps to each other in space and time. This interchange, unlike feedback, involves many parallel paths and has no specific instructive error function associated with it. Instead, it alters selective events and correlations of signals among areas and is essential for the synchronization and coordination of the areas' mutual functions (Edelman and Tononi, 2000, p. 48).

What are we to make of these findings? Clearly an individual is not a neuron and consciousness is not a good description of our future organization. But, if we think about the patterns of interaction and the way information is shared and unified there are some telling lessons here.

As stated earlier, for our new organization to work intelligently, it must be able to simultaneously unify its relevant parts to gain maximum situational understanding, knowledge, and concentration of power to act and to react. Because of the large number of threats and opportunities and the urgent need for fast response, the ICAS will put in place systems to reach into, and maintain, continuous two-way communication with a large number of relatively independent subsystems.

According to complexity research (Stacey, 1996), these subsystems of agents should be self-organizing to maximize their learning and innovation. In addition, self-organizing groups are capable of creating emergent properties and are better at dealing with surprises and unknowable futures than the normal organizational structure. Stacey (1996) addresses this topic head on when he says:

[...]; The immediate conclusion drawn is that ignorance can be overcome by greater investment in gathering information, funneling it to some central point where it can be analyzed, and then feeding it back to the actors. The dominant schema therefore leads people to believe that ignorance can be overcome by research into organizational excellence, incompetence can be overcome by training and developing managers, and systems can be used to prevent bad behavior [...]; From the complexity perspective, however, we reach the opposite conclusion, namely, that the future is truly unknowable. Creative futures emerge unpredictably from selforganizing interactions between members; therefore, they clearly cannot use some forecast of long-term outcomes to decide between one action and another (pp. 268–269).

The need for unity and shared purpose and also for local freedom, empowerment, and self-organization presents an apparent paradox. The solution lies in accepting both as necessary for intelligent behavior and in structuring relations among subsystems and organizational levels such that there is enough flexibility and coordination for both to coexist, each rising to meet local and organizational needs as appropriate.

Note that self-organization need not imply the lack of rules. A shared vision, common values, and widespread communication of context information all support empowerment and self-organization. In any case, both rules and the freedom to self-organize are needed. The specific balance between rules for alignment and coherence of operations and empowerment for local work flow optimization and innovation is both situationally dependent and dynamic. There is no pat formula for a desired balance (see Chapter 12).

When achieved, unity and shared purpose create an integration of internal activities that makes the whole organization greater than the sum of its parts. The synergy, differentiation, and variety of its subsystems provide the internal complexity needed to deal with the complexity of the outside world. To be effective, this complexity must be able to provide not only a large variety of responses but any particular response must be coherent (or at least not inconsistent) with the rest of the ICAS organization. The unity of the organization's actions is closely associated with its perception of external events. This is where the flow of information, knowledge, and experience becomes so important. Although an organization can be aware of several mutually incoherent events at the same time, if these are not integrated at some level, the responses may be inconsistent and deleterious. This emphasizes the need for continuous and widespread common context sharing at the appropriate levels throughout the organization.

A final word of caution: too strong a unity and shared purpose can become stifling if it prohibits divergent thinking or remains focused on one goal for too long. The unity needed is the unity of direction and the coherence of action, together with its context knowledge. Specific goals and tactics will change frequently due to the nonlinearity and dynamics of the external world.

OPTIMUM COMPLEXITY

Complexity is a popular research area ranging from artificial life to complex adaptive systems to social systems. Its use in management has been to carry over ideas that were developed in the hard sciences to the soft sciences. In a recent book, Axelrod and Cohen (1999) note that: "Social systems exhibit dynamic patterns analogous to physical, biological, and computational systems. This is perhaps the fundamental reason we pursue complexity research" (p. 12). In a discussion of the relationship between complexity and information they offer the following:

If complexity is often rooted in patterns of interaction among agents, then we might expect systems to exhibit increasingly complex dynamics when changes occur that intensify interaction among their elements. This is of course exactly what the Information Revolution is doing: reducing the barriers to interaction among processes that were previously isolated from each other in time or space. Information can be understood as a mediator of interaction. Decreasing the costs of its propagation and storage inherently increases possibilities for interaction effects. An Information Revolution is therefore likely to beget a complexity revolution (p. 12).

From our perspective, we see the Knowledge Revolution on the close-in radar screen and the Complexity Revolution soon to follow. The two phenomena are somewhat interdependent with a challenge and response type of relationship where each drives the other. Increasing complexity drives the need for more knowledge and more knowledge creates more complexity. As a result, neither revolution is likely to ever end. More likely, after initial surges, they will co-evolve, with continuous shifting of stresses and strains between them. Nevertheless, as early preparation for an anticipated complexity avalanche, we are suggesting possibilities for organizational characteristics that will more effectively respond to complexity.

As introduced in Chapter 3, complexity is commonly interpreted as being a measure of the number of elements and/or their relationships in a system. While useful in many applications, there are difficulties with this interpretation when considering organizations. It is not the number of possible states, either in the organization or in its external environment that need concern an organization. It is the number of possible states *that make a difference* to the organization that counts. Of the almost infinite number of states of information, material, or energy that impinge upon the organization, only a few of them are meaningful and make a difference. The ability to recognize this difference can become a useful way for the ICAS to reduce its own internal complexity as well as the impact of the external complexity in its environment. When done well, selectivity reduces confusion, simplifies decisions, and makes attention easier, more focused, and more powerful.

As discussed earlier, considering the internal design of the ICAS, we can see that if every worker and every subsystem (team, group, or organizational element) were to act independently and randomly, the largest number of states would be generated. But this would not be useful to the organization, because there would be no coherence, only random behavior. At the other extreme, if every worker and every subsystem were constrained to behave in a predetermined way such that the organization became a rigid structure with a large number of elements with tightly controlled relationships, such as a "perfect" bureaucracy, then this rigidity would kill the organization in our future world. An example from physics would be a perfect gas versus a rigid solid structure. Both could be said to have high complexity due to their large number of elements and relationships.

From an organizational perspective, neither extreme is acceptable. The right balance between unity and diversity has not been found and may not exist. Both unity and diversity may coexist, or the balance may vary with the specific external environment and the ICAS form. Most likely there is a range of operation and a range of external conditions over which the organization can function and sustain itself. However, to the extent that Edelman's research on the brain offers insights into organizations (Edelman and Tononi, 2000), the ICAS will not be able to function at either extreme—strong control or full freedom. When operating in this middle range, complex adaptive system theory, in consonance with Darwin's concept of fitness, suggests that the three key factors are variation, interaction, and selection. Clearly this combination enhances the ability of organizations to survive in an environment of rapid change, complexity, and competition. Variation provides new ideas and options, interaction with the environment provides feedback, and selection reduces complexity and amplifies what works and discards what does not. It is evolution's survival strategy in an unknown future and ICAS strategy in an unknowable environment.

Variation comes from new employees, virtual teams, learning, and a willingness to explore new strategies and tactics. A dynamic balance between highly variable processes and tightly controlled ones can allow both variability and consistency. Interactions are the fundamental phenomenon of the ICAS. They must be "managed" so as to achieve balance between interactions that make the difference to the organizations—those that amplify knowledge and direct resource capabilities—and so as to minimize interactions that waste time. Selection of incoming information represents the filter that prevents internal information saturation and determines what the organization will pay attention to.

Although the internal complexity of the organization can be influenced by structure, relationships, process design, and culture, a major determinant is the individual. Each individual is an attenuator and amplifier of complexity within their local environment. Their behavior, knowledge, intentions, purposes, and expectations can either increase or reduce the complexity within their subsystem.

Team leaders, managers, and influential workers throughout the ICAS may play a large role. Internal complexity must be carefully understood. A large variety of options and actions to meet goals is desirable, yet random actions, wrong approaches, and shadow governance can do significant harm to the organization.

We have returned to the issue of balance. Internal complexity is neither good nor bad, rather it is the role that complexity plays in supporting ICAS objectives that counts. A major conclusion is that complexity will play a strong role in the ICAS and therefore it must be identified, monitored, and nurtured, keeping in mind that it arises from processes and relationships within the organization, and from the transmission of data, information, and knowledge through the organization's permeable boundaries. A second conclusion is that too much internal complexity can lead to chaos, while too little complexity limits the organization's ability to respond and deal with the complexity of the external world. Applying Ross Ashby's law of requisite variety to organizations, we suggest that to successfully manage external complexity one has to have more options, i.e., more complexity, than the thing managed (Ashby, 1964). There are no easy solutions to the problem of using internal complexity to *live* with external complexity, though the next section will address one approach to the problem—selectivity.

SELECTIVITY

At any given moment, every individual and every organization has a huge number of signals impinging on its boundaries: data, information, sounds, images, ideas, etc. We are not even aware of many of these signals; for example, sounds above 20,000 hertz, or infrared radiation. How the organization prevents itself from being overwhelmed with these signals and is able to select, receive, process, and maintain a balance of unity, variety, and flexibility is an amazing feat. Yet both organizations and people do this every waking moment of every day. As the external environment becomes more influential through its change, complexity, and uncertainty parameters, the ability to select and control which signals make a difference may be the first line of defense (and opportunity) for the ICAS organization.

As noted in Chapter 3, selectivity, or the filtering of incoming information from the outside world, will always occur. Individual attention is limited by physiology to one thing at a time (groups may have difficulty staying on a single topic). If left to itself, natural selectivity may become random and create more noise than purposeful action within the organization. This is exactly what subsystems such as teams or self-organizing groups are supposed to prevent. Although opportunities may be lost due to the non-recognition of the meaning and consequences of seemingly benign signals, by analyzing incoming information through internal communication and "group digestion" of unusual events, the organization can improve its filtering ability.

One approach to signal-to-noise filtering of incoming information is to establish value systems that are consistent across the organization, coupled with the unity and shared purpose discussed above. These provide ICAS members with guidelines and context knowledge—the basis for effective interpretation and filtering of signals. Values provide a means of rejecting signals that the organization chooses not to respond to. They are preconditions for intelligent behavior.

Shared purpose and current organizational tactics make visible what signals the organization is interested in. If people are clear about the priorities that really matter to the organization, and keep these firmly in their awareness, they will be able to quickly evaluate incoming signals and make the appropriate decisions.

This ability to discriminate among incoming signals (discernment and discretion) can become an art, to be continuously refined and perfected. The shared knowledge of what makes a difference to the organization will become more important as the rate of change increases. Such knowledge will usually be grounded in the tacit knowledge of individuals. It cannot become wholly explicit, however, because such knowledge may not be shared fast enough to keep up with change. Knowledge repositories (explicit knowledge, i.e., data and information stored such that it can be easily transferred, easily understood and used by others) and flow (discussed below) play a big role in knowledge sharing and in the ICAS of the future.

Sometimes the incoming signals may appear unrelated to the organization's purpose, yet are significant. Edelman and Tononi (2000) address this as follows: "All selectional systems share a remarkable property that is as unique as it is essential to their functioning: In such systems, there are typically many different ways, *not necessarily structurally identical,* by which a particular output occurs" (p. 86). This degeneracy means that for a given input, different parts of the organization can produce the same output or interpretations. This capability reflects organizational insurance. If an important signal comes in it can be dealt with properly, even if structural changes have occurred within the ICAS.

As different subsystems evolve and change, the selection ability of the organization as a whole must remain strong. When the selection function loses its coherence the organization deteriorates, potentially into confusion, infighting, and misdirected energy, resulting in a loss of competitive advantage and eventually death or merger.

KNOWLEDGE CENTRICITY

In the new knowledge world where ideas are central, knowledge shared is power squared. Knowledge is one of those rare things you can give away and still have. Hoarders of knowledge have limited value to the organization and become the primary cultural barriers to learning. As knowledge is shared, and through reciprocal sharing, innovation springs into being. This sharing relationship must be built on a foundation of trust.

A *knowledge-centric organization* (KCO) is one in which knowledge is recognized as a key success factor and is systematically managed through knowledge management (KM) best practices. When maximum synergy exists between individuals in the workforce and KM, the organization amplifies its resource effectiveness, thereby providing sustainable competitive advantage and performance excellence. For this to occur, the organization must be able to sustain a dynamic balance wherein the individual and the KM system continuously adapt to each other through cultural expectations, flexibility, and empathy.

A KCO is, quite simply, an organization that organizes virtually around the knowledge needs of its decision-makers at every level. In a continuous cycle, it is first a builder (creating websites and database structures to house and transfer content); then an operator (orchestrating interactions among individuals, teams, and communities and serving as a media agent between organizations); then a knowledge broker (overseeing and operating the exchange of goods, services, and knowledge transactions).

One might ask if knowledge exists only in human minds, how can an organization store, transfer, and share knowledge? The answer has several aspects. First, IT venders have been quick to label their hardware and software as intelligent or knowledge-based. This is a loose interpretation of the terms, since their technology creates, stores, and moves binary or analog patterns that only have meaning if translated by humans with the appropriate experience and ability to understand and develop meaning. That said, data and information can be structured in such a way that makes it more or less easier for other people to re-create understanding in their own minds that is close to the understanding of the originator. Thus some stored digital patterns are more easily converted into user knowledge than others. Such systems (and others of lesser capability) are often called knowledge systems or knowledge repositories. However, just as when two people are sharing knowledge in a one-on-one conversation, the only things that are physically transferred are sound pressure waves and photons or light rays. Listeners must transform these wave patterns into understanding by combining them with their personal experience, learning, feelings, and goals in order to create knowledge.

As members of a KCO, ICAS workers will integrate knowledge sharing into their everyday lives. New employees reporting to work may spend days acclimating to their new surroundings and learning new processes and procedures. Using the principles of a KCO, the ICAS can drastically reduce the learning cycle time, providing access to the breadth of command knowledge and the ability to quickly and accurately draw upon critical lessons learned to make work time more efficient.

In the KCO, knowledge repositories, automated libraries, computer services, databases, etc. offer the capability for not only storing huge amounts of data and information but also efficient and intelligent retrieval and assemblage capability. Powerful search algorithms, intelligent agents, and semantic interpreters allow employees to rapidly retrieve information needed for problem-solving and decision-making. To become knowledge centric, the ICAS will pass through the following steps: building awareness; preparing the organization for knowledge sharing and learning; defining strategic goals, performing a knowledge audit, and identifying the knowledge needed; developing and monitoring knowledge systems and processes; promoting environments for knowledge creation; building and supporting communities; and reviewing, assessing, and sharing stories.

Knowledge management will be embedded throughout the ICAS as a process for optimizing the effective application of intellectual capital to achieve organizational objectives. Intellectual capital includes human capital, social capital, and organizational capital, all three being essential contributors of the organization's enterprise knowledge, and all valued at the bottom line of the ICAS, with each employee taking responsibility for ensuring intellectual-capital growth. Knowledge centricity is closely related to organizational intelligence.

As noted in Chapter 3, in order for any complex adaptive system to behave intelligently it must achieve continuous, interdependent collaboration and interplay among all levels of the system. This capability highlights the importance of both internal and external networks as they heavily influence the relationships and amplify knowledge diffusion among agents, components, and external systems. As these networks increase, the organization becomes more complex, harder to manage by those seeking direct control, but potentially capable of handling more complexity in its environment. Teams and communities accelerate quality decision-making and foster innovation and creativity. (See the following discussions of flow and processes.)

A knowledge-centric ICAS will recognize the value of information and knowledge in decision-making. It will connect people to people, people to systems, and systems to people to ensure availability and delivery of the right information at the right time for decision and action. The creation, storage, transfer, and application of knowledge (and perhaps wisdom) will have been refined and developed such that it becomes a major resource of the ICAS as it satisfies customers and adapts to environmental competitive forces and opportunities. The bottom line for a knowledge-centric ICAS is optimal performance. It achieves this by (Bennet, 1999):

1. *Aligning strategic direction.* The more information is shared, the better people collaborate, the more aligned the organization is in moving toward its vision of the future. This shared vision harnesses the collective energy of people and accelerates improvement.
2. *Enhancing mission performance.* Operational and business performance improves as best practices are shared and new ideas build on ideas shared.

Knowledge management drives development of a knowledge base relating to the organization's core competencies.

3. *Increasing collaboration opportunities.* The collaborative and sharing aspects of knowledge centricity will enrich the exchange between people and ideas at all levels of the ICAS.

4. *Driving process improvement.* As the sharing of information becomes embedded in day-to-day activities, the flow and exchange of best practices increases, providing the fluid for true process improvement. In addition, the high visibility of content areas across the organization facilitates the exchange of new ideas regarding process change.

5. *Facilitating learning.* Knowledge centricity provides the opportunity for individuals to put new knowledge into practice while exposing them to new challenges. Since the value of individual knowledge becomes a major asset to the ICAS, an individual's contribution to this knowledge bank becomes recognized and rewarded.

6. *Facilitating availability of expertise.* Knowledge centricity utilizes "tacit" knowledge, defining content areas and identifying sources, thus providing intermediation between knowledge needs and knowledge sources. This "brokering" translates into availability of expertise which can be brought to bear on emerging issues.

7. *Increasing innovation and creativity.* As information begets information, ideas beget ideas. Knowledge centricity provides access to a rich pool of ideas, providing a foundation for others to build upon, sowing the seeds for innovation and creativity.

8. *Enhancing job performance.* Knowledge centricity provides the opportunity for adaptability in rapidly changing situations. Knowledge workers can quickly access, integrate and act on new knowledge, and efficiently find out what they don't know from a vast pool of organizational knowledge.

The knowledge-centric characteristics will ensure that learning will be continuous and widespread, utilizing mentoring, and classroom and distance learning, and will likely be self-managed with strong infrastructure support.

FLOW

As introduced in Chapter 3, flow enables knowledge centricity and facilitates the connections and continuity that maintain unity and give coherence to organizational intelligence. The emergent characteristic of flow in the ICAS can be discussed in terms of the flow of data, information, and knowledge; the movement of people in and out of organizational settings; and the optimal human experience. Flow, moving across networks of systems and people, is the catalyst for creativity and innovation. Social capital is the medium of exchange in this human framework.

The Flow of Data, Information, and Knowledge

The flow of data, information, and knowledge is facilitated through teams and communities, and can be accelerated through event intermediation. Teams, small groups, task forces, etc., accomplish specific objectives while concomitantly sharing data, information, and knowledge with other people who may come from diverse parts of the ICAS. Communities of practice or interest, knowledge portals, and knowledge repositories also facilitate the sharing of information and knowledge. Managers are often unaware that the greatest benefit from a team's effort is the long-term payoff in future collaboration among team members. An ICAS that deliberately nurtures flows will factor this payoff into team formation and team member selection.

Event intermediation is not a new idea. All too often employees work and strive to create change with only slightly visible results. Then, when some event occurs which connects all this prior activity, the understanding of change value jumps to a new strata of recognition, and the entire plane of behavior shifts upward to a new starting point. This pattern recurs again and again throughout history. The ICAS of the future will orchestrate such events, formally and informally, as both change and knowledge sharing become a way of life.

Note that the flow of "knowledge" is in reality the flow of data and information with enough context and understanding built around the data and information—and the sensemaking capability built into the user—such that the user can effectively re-create the desired knowledge.

The Flow of People In and Out of the Organizational Setting

The fluid flow of people in and out of the ICAS must support the organization's need for flexibility in responding to demands of the global marketplace. The workforce grows and shrinks, engaging free agents, and buying intellectual capital as needed. Employees will have to be systems thinkers so they can quickly grasp the context and implications of rapidly changing events in response to orchestrated mobility throughout the ICAS. A benefit of moving people will be the increase in variety of talent mixes throughout the organization. These flows will also prevent long-term rigidity and maintain organizational plasticity. In addition, continual change within the ICAS will maintain a population of new ideas that can make a difference in organizational performance. A continual flow of employees into and out of the organization will be needed to stay in touch with the environment and to maintain high internal standards of performance.

The Optimal Human Experience

The concept of autotelic work is tied to the optimal experience of flow, a state where people are so involved that nothing else seems to matter. An individual, or a team, is said to be in a state of flow when the activity at hand becomes so intense that the normal sense of time and space disappears, and all energy is invested in the task. In a team setting, individuals lose the sense of identity or separateness during the experience, then afterward emerge from the experience with a stronger sense of self. Individuals involved in this flow state feel a sense of exhilaration and joy. As these optimal experiences are repeated, they develop a sense of experiencing their real reason for being, coupled with a strong feeling of being in control.

Each of us has experienced flow at times in our lives: playing a good tennis match, meeting a short deadline, or enjoying team camaraderie during an intense task. Autotelic workers create their own experience of flow. They are often creative, curious, and lead vigorous lives, taking everything that comes along in their stride. They are "life-long learners" who enjoy everything they do, and, along the way, spread a bit of joy to those around them.

Although flow cannot be turned on and off, individuals and teams can develop the ability to experience flow and create environmental conditions that facilitate its onset. The experience of flow has been developed and studied by Csikszentmihalyi (1990) over the past 30 years and is best described in his book entitled *Flow: The Psychology of Optimal Experience*. According to him, the conditions required for a team flow experience are:

1. Tasks must have a good chance of being completed, yet not be too easy.
2. The team must be able to concentrate on what it is doing. Interruptions, distractions, or poor facilities prevent concentration.
3. The task should have clear goals, so that the team knows when it has succeeded.
4. Immediate feedback should be provided to the team so that it can react and adjust its actions (Csikszentmihalyi, 1990).

The phenomenon of flow results in individuals and teams giving their best capabilities to tasks at hand. Team members come away with feelings of accomplishment, joy, and well-being that influences their willingness to trust and openly communicate with other team members, enhancing collaboration and team performance. The bottom line for the ICAS is a high level of performance. The bottom line for the employee is personal growth and self-satisfaction.

PERMEABLE BOUNDARIES

The bureaucratic model defined clear boundaries between jobs, between levels of management, and between organizations. But those who are succeeding in today's world have already recognized the blurring of those boundaries as man and machine create virtual networks around the globe.

Boundaries between the individual, other individuals, the social organization, and the organizational culture are the places where ideas are formed and change occurs. Social psychology (Gold and Douvan, 1997) is the study of how influence is exerted across those boundaries, or "zones of interpenetration." The permeable and porous boundaries in the ICAS are those among individuals, the social organization, and the organizational culture, as well as those across organizations and, indeed, across countries. Using terms from social psychology: (1) the individual is an entity having motives and resources; (2) relations between individuals (interpersonal relations) are composed of identities; (3) the social organization is composed of interdependent sets of roles; and (4) the organizational culture is a system of shared beliefs. Individual motives and resources, and, within the system (at whatever system level you focus upon) identities, roles, and shared beliefs provide the elements that will determine the permeability of boundaries.

As introduced in Chapter 3, the virtual world of the ICAS tears down our historic understanding of relationships and boundaries in terms of time and space. As people come in and out of the organization driven by increasing and decreasing demands, over time the "boundaries" of organizations become more difficult to define. As ideas are exchanged and built upon, the lineage of these ideas becomes impossible to follow. Add all of this to a fluctuating, complex environment and we begin to understand just how important permeable and porous boundaries are to the survival of the next-generation knowledge organization.

The boundaries of *Phylum porifera*, what we call a sponge, provide a metaphor for the changing boundary conditions of the ICAS. Sponges are simple, multicellular animals that have minimal interdependence among their cells. In 1907 an embryologist, H. V. Wilson (Arms and Camp, 1987), discovered that a living sponge could be pushed through fine silk so that it was broken up into individual cells and cell debris. Over the next three weeks, the cells started crawling around and aggregating into larger masses until a functional sponge was re-formed. Although we would not suggest pushing a living organization through fine silk, nevertheless, the splitting and reaggregating around goals (in the sponge's case survival) is a metaphor appropriate for the ICAS. With the living body, atoms and molecules constantly die and are replaced. The structure of the cell retains its identity even while the matter that composes it is continually altered. The cell rebuilds itself in line with its own pattern of identity, yet is always a part of emerging action, alive and responding even in the midst of its own multitudinous deaths.

The permeable boundary of an ICAS will allow the organization to optimize its results through teaming, partnering, alliances, and close relationships with customers and all stakeholders. Teaming, partnering, and alliances are terms we give to more formal relationships between organizations. They imply the intent of one or more organizations to work together to improve the efficiency and effectiveness of a common goal, and to reduce the costs of disagreements.

These formal relationships driven by economic need and potential are much like a marriage. For success, they must be built on trust, open communications, and a thorough understanding of themselves and each other. The social psychology boundary model can also be applied to teaming, partnering, and alliances, i.e., the elements that will determine the permeability of organizational boundaries are motives and resources, identities, goals, interdependent sets of roles, and shared beliefs.

Let's use the value of one, the individual, to understand relationships and boundaries in terms of space. We usually think of the boundary of the individual as framed by the outside of the physical body. This is not the case. Each of us sets up special boundaries that reflect our relationships with those around us. There are many models for this personal space, and many more variables affecting the validity of those models. For discussion purposes, we will use the widely accepted categories proposed by Burgoon (1988):

- Intimate distance—reserved for intimate encounters and physical contact.
- Personal distance—used in close interpersonal relationships or for private discussions.
- Social distance—used for relatively impersonal encounters such as informal social interaction and business meetings.
- Public distance—reserved for formal interactions and presentations.

There is sensory involvement (involving cutaneous, visual, olfactory, auditory, and thermal receptors) ranging from high to low in both intimate and personal relationships. Social relationships are outside the range of touch, but do include some involvement of the other senses. Public distance minimizes kinesthetic involvement. Although Burgoon (1988) attempted to assign distances to each of these categories, later social science research has shown that the variance of the norm was highly dependent on gender, age, degree of acquaintance, social status, personality, etc. Still, the construct itself has considerable value for addressing the changes in special relationships—the variance of—boundaries among individuals and organizations.

In the ICAS, distances are closing. Proximity to others is as far away as the nearest computer, but built on a human network. Indeed, the social capital of an organization determines success or failure. The architectural firm of Thompson & Rose proposed nomadic, rounded work shells that can be minimized and connected in groups of varying sizes or disconnected, and distances to provide personal space (*Business Week*, 2000). This architectural concept provides an excellent seating model for the ICAS, providing ease of movement from personal space to collective space. It also opens personal distance through the elimination of walls and closes social distance through connected collective space.

What is missing from this model is technology. As wires become a constraint of the past, technology will be more portable, floating at an intimate distance from employees, that distance reserved in the past for intimate encounters and physical contact. This hands-on-keyboard relationship will bring private discussions, business meetings, and presentations over remote distances into closer proximity, but still build on human networks and relationships. In private discussions, faces will project across distances; in business meetings visible body movements and the rise and fall of expressions will provide context; during presentations, dialogue will occur throughout and exchange of ideas will build intimacy from a distance.

MULTIDIMENSIONALITY

From the perspective of evolution, man, because of his intelligence, adaptability, and robustness, has become the dominant species in a world where only the fittest survive. If the ICAS is to survive in the future environment, it must have the instinctual ability to sense, learn, and respond with a wide repertoire of actions. To become the fittest of the fit in the anticipated intensely competitive organizational arena of the future, the ICAS must be able to demonstrate agility and robustness at all levels of its structure.

As introduced in Chapter 3, this requires the organization to continuously forget and learn; to identify and deal with risk; to think in terms of systems; to perceive and analyze in terms of wide scope and long timeframes; and, finally, to keep its identity and unity. The organization must develop instincts and automatic competencies that are natural and become second nature at all levels. We label this group of basic competencies multidimensionality. While no one of these is more important than the others—it depends upon local circumstances—we will address systems thinking first because of its scope and potential payoff. See Chapter 18 for a more in-depth treatment of systems.

Systems thinking became widely known in the late 1960s with von Bertalanffy's book on general systems theory (von Bertalanffy, 1968). Since then, systems research has moved away from general systems theory to Forrester's system dynamics and Senge's Systems Thinking to the research on complexity and complex adaptive systems coming out of the Santa Fe Institute and other researchers. From an organizational viewpoint, the importance of being able to understand and analyze systems lies in the perspective afforded by systems thinking and the ability to look for fundamental systemic characteristics. This ability includes both holistic and reductionist considerations, and can greatly aid in recognizing leverage points both within the organization and in the environment.

Systems thinkers naturally become aware of the surrounding context of their work and can recognize the impact of actions in one part of the organization on other parts. With people and teams scattered throughout the ICAS with this capability, the organization can adapt flexibly and respond within the proper context. System thinking also encourages a broader perspective in both space and time. Carried to the extreme, everything is connected to everything else. System thinkers look for these connections, and interpret and generate actions correspondingly (see Auyang, 1998; Morowitz and Singer, 1995; Bar-Yam, 2000; Checkland and Holwell, 1998).

Another dimension of import to survival is that of forgetting and learning. Team learning in particular (Senge, 1990) has been recognized as essential for adaptive enterprises. Unfortunately, the concomitant need to forget is usually forgotten. To learn means to change, and to change means to give up something. But giving up is difficult and is usually resisted because of the discomfort it causes. To continuously change and adapt, the organization must continuously let go of past beliefs.

Argyris and Schön (1978) have extensively researched the difficulties of learning and changing and have identified the fundamental reasons why organizations find it so hard to adapt. Their major finding is that organizations build in special systems and defenses that prevent them from learning and questioning their basic beliefs and assumptions. Their solution is called double-loop learning—a technique for getting individuals to review and question their basic assumptions.

Another dimension is that of risk. In an uncertain world risk becomes part of life. A robust organization must be willing and able to take on and manage risks in a manner that maximizes the probability of success while at the same time protecting against disasters. This requires the ability to estimate future events and assess the immediate and future result of contemporary changes. The discussion of knowledge earlier in this chapter would indicate the importance of workers and subsystems having knowledge of their areas of work and being able to accurately judge cause and effects. The effective management of risk should be an invisible characteristic of the culture—built into the way the work gets done. The areas of probability assessments, scenario development, and simulations are supportive of risk management. Studies on management risk analysis may also be helpful (see Morecroft and Sterman, 1994; van der Heijden, 1996; Bennet, 2000).

To be able to shift its frequency of operations, the ICAS must be built around processes and core competencies that are flexible and robust. This means that both the supporting technology and the workforce are capable of multiple tasks and are open to rearrangements through virtual connections or rapid reprogramming.

Workload and resource problems must be amenable to quick resolution, with all parts of the ICAS working together in support of a response to outside perturbations or opportunities. A rapid shift in operating tempo is where the unity and shared purpose are tested for truth.

In summary, the range and depth of outside forces that the ICAS can effectively respond and adapt to is a fundamental measure of its survival capability. At the same time, its sustainable competitive advantage will be measured by its robust ability to take advantage of a wide range and depth of opportunities, originating both within and external to the firm. Other integrative competencies related to multidimensionality include: complexity thinking, relationship network management, knowing, and learning. These are discussed in Chapters 16 through 21. Multidimensionality as applied to knowledge workers is addressed in Chapters 14 and 15.

REFERENCES

Argyris, C. and D. A. Schön. *Organizational Learning: A Theory of Action Perspective*. Philippines: Addison-Wesley Publishing Co., 1978.

Arms, K. and P. Camp. *Biology*, 3rd ed. New York: Saunders College Publishing, 1987.

Ashby, W. R. *An Introduction to Cybernetics*. London: Methuen, 1964.

Auyang, S. Y. *Foundations of Complex-System Theories in Economics, Evolutionary Biology, and Statistical Physics*. Cambridge, England: Cambridge University Press, 1998.

Axelrod, R. and M. D. Cohen. *Harnessing Complexity: Organizational Implications of a Scientific Frontier*. New York: The Free Press, 1999.

Bar-Yam, Y. *Unifying Themes in Complex Systems*. Cambridge, England: Perseus Books, 2000.

Bennet, A. "The Virtual Town Hall: Vehicle for Change," *CHIPS Magazine*, Fall, 1999, 6–7.

Bennet, D. *IPT Learning Campus: Gaining Acquisition Results Through IPTs*. Alexandria, VA: Bellwether Learning Center, 1997.

Bennet, D. "AAV RAM/REBUILD: Management Review Integrated Product Team Report." Marine Corps Report, 2000.

Burgoon, J. K. "Spatial Relationships in Small Groups," in R. Cathcart and L. Samovar (eds), *Small Group Communication*. Dubuque, Iowa: Wm. C. Brown Publishers, 1988.

Business Week. "21st Century Corporation." August 2000, 153.

Checkland, P. and S. Holwell. *Information, Systems and Information Systems: Making Sense of the Field*. New York: John Wiley & Sons, 1998.

Csikszentmihalyi, M. *Flow: The Psychology of Optimal Experience*. New York: Harper Perennial, 1990.

Edelman G. and G. Tononi. *A Universe of Consciousness: How Matter Becomes Imagination*. New York: Basic Books, 2000.

Gold, M. and E. Douvan. *A New Outline of Social Psychology*. Washington, D.C.: American Psychological Association, 1997.

Greenfield, S. *Journey to the Centers of the Mind: Toward a Science of Consciousness*. New York: W. H. Freeman and Company, 1995.

Kelly, R. and J. Caplan. "How Bell Labs Creates Star Performers." In Harvard Business Review, 71, July–August 1993, 128–139.

McMaster, M. D. *The Intelligence Advantage: Organizing for Complexity*. Boston: Butterworth-Heinemann, 1996.

Morecroft, J. D. W. and J. D. Sterman (eds). *Modeling for Learning Organizations*. Portland, Oregon: Productivity Press, 1994.

Morowitz, H. J. and J. L. Singer (eds). *The Mind, The Brain, and Complex Adaptive Systems*. Reading, MA: Addison-Wesley Publishing Company, 1995.

Pinchot, G. and E. Pinchot. *The End of Bureaucracy and the Rise of the Intelligent Organization*. San Francisco, CA: Berrett-Koehler Publishers, 1993.

Senge, P. M. *The Fifth Discipline: The Art and Practice of the Learning Organization*. New York: Doubleday, 1990.

Stacey, R. D. *Complexity and Creativity in Organizations*. San Francisco, CA: Berrett-Koehler Publishers, 1996.

van der Heijden, K. *Scenarios: The Art of Strategic Conversation*. New York: John Wiley & Sons, 1996.

von Bertalanffy, L. *General Systems Theory: Foundations, Development, Applications*. New York: George Braziller, 1968.

Wiig, K. *Knowledge Management Foundations—Thinking about Thinking—How People and Organizations Create, Represent, and Use Knowledge*. Arlington, TX: Schema Press, 1993.

Chapter 5

RELATIONSHIPS AMONG EMERGENT PROPERTIES

It is the interweaving of the eight emergent characteristics that creates the rich tapestry of the ICAS. While each of the emergent characteristics individually contributes to ICAS performance, the overall organizational design is intended to create a performance that relies heavily on the interaction and synergy among these characteristics. For example, flow greatly assists and improves on the effectiveness of knowledge centricity and team decision-making. In this chapter we will investigate some of the interactions and relationships among these characteristics that provide the overall capacity of the organization to achieve sustainable competitive advantage.

MAJOR RELATIONSHIPS IN THE ICAS

Figure 5-1 shows the major characteristics in the ICAS model and the top-level conceptual relationships among them. The rectangle at the top identifies the four major processes and their broad relationships to each other. It also shows that organizational intelligence has a major role in the quality of those processes. The middle rectangle identifies the eight emergent characteristics of the ICAS organization, together with their major relationships. The bottom two rectangles represent the major characteristics in the external environment.

As the rate of change of problems, demands, and opportunities speeds up, and with it the increased variability and unpredictability of the environment, the ICAS must react faster and with pinpoint accuracy. Underlying such a

59

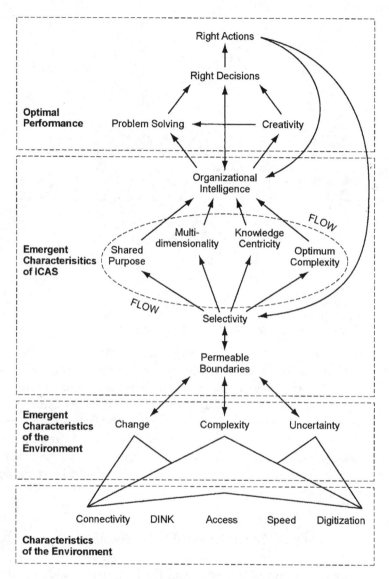

Figure 5-1
Relationships of the Eight Emergent Characteristics

capability is the generic concept of relationships. Relationships among individuals, across internal boundaries, between people and technology, and with external customers and other stakeholders are the mainstay of trust, collaboration, rapid action, and intelligent behavior. How well these relationships are created and maintained is the key to adaptation and optimum performance. In this chapter we are concerned with how the emergent characteristics of the ICAS (Figure 5-1) relate to each other and how, as a group, they support the four major processes of (1) creativity, (2) problem-solving, (3) decision-making, and (4) implementation.

Organizations take inputs from their environment, transform those inputs into higher-value outputs and provide these to the environment. They do this by using internal and external resources in efficient and effective ways that create added value above and beyond the value of the incoming resources. Briefly, the organization solves problems (or takes on opportunities) that create options for action that then produce some product or services. It does this through its available resources–people, technology, relationships, experience, partnering, etc. When the challenge is not routine the organization needs to be creative and generate new ways of solving problems and developing new products. At this point it must make a decision as to what action will best produce the desired solution, then carry out the action in a manner that best ensures the anticipated outcome.

While this sequence is easy to describe, it becomes very complex and challenging in the real world, particularly when things are moving quickly, the problem is not well understood, there are many opinions, and a successful outcome is dependent on external events. Successfully implementing such processes is a real challenge to ICAS organizational intelligence. The processes themselves become the production tools that every intelligent organization must master. For a more in-depth discussion of these processes see Chapter 8.

THE DRIVERS OF ORGANIZATIONAL INTELLIGENCE

Since organizational intelligence is the generic *competency behind the processes* we will focus on its relationship to the other emergent characteristics. In Chapter 3 we interpreted organizational intelligence as the ability of an organization to perceive, interpret, and respond to its environment so as to meet its goals while satisfying stakeholders. In the future environment that we have characterized as rapidly changing, highly complex, and unpredictable, the acts of perceiving, interpreting, and responding effectively become complicated and challenging in and of themselves. Perception, the adaptive discrimination of an object or event from background or other objects or events (Edelman, 1989) becomes difficult because nothing stays the same for very long and the variety and disconnectedness of things make discrimination and/or coherence difficult. Interpretation, or sense-making, becomes hard because of the complexity of events and their seeming independence. Context is frequently hidden in the noise of crises. To determine meaning requires an understanding of both context and continuity of phenomena. Both kinds of understanding are made difficult by complexity and randomness. Nevertheless, this is the challenge faced by the ICAS and all other organizations that would thrive in the future.

An intelligent complex adaptive system must be able to generate, manage, and apply knowledge in a rapid, coherent manner. Knowledge, while including data and information, is the potential and actual ability to take effective action–requiring one to create understanding and find meaning in a situation by recognizing the relationships, causal phenomena and theories and rules underlying them. To generate shared unity and consistency of understanding, the organization must coordinate relevant information and knowledge across regions and among teams and other autonomous units. Finally, intelligence depends upon Wiig's suggested competencies of good behavior, being well prepared, adopting the right posture, good problem-solving, and effective actions (Wiig, 1993). Thus we consider some of the key variables underlying organizational intelligence to be knowledge, coordination, and individual and team competency. Beginning with unity and shared purpose, we now consider how organizational intelligence is supported by the other emergent characteristics of the ICAS.

Shared Purpose and Organizational Intelligence

The ICAS characteristic we have called unity and shared purpose plays a significant role in support of organizational intelligence. Perhaps its most important contribution is to help integrate and unify the various parts of the organization.

An ICAS is made up of a number of self-organized, autonomous units providing innovation and rapid response to its stakeholders. At the same time, the entire organization must be able to marshal resources that maximize its response capability as needed. For this to occur, every part of an ICAS should have a clear understanding of the direction and purpose of the overall organization. This shared vision serves as the standard for behavior, as the goal for actions, and as the metric for measuring competency and success. On a broader scale, unity and shared purpose brings the organization into focus, creating a common culture and a sense of belonging and ownership compatible with the autonomy of each team or unit. All self-organizing units must operate within certain rules or boundary conditions whose nature depends upon the units, the organization, and its immediate environment. These rules may vary from unit to unit but they should be self-consistent throughout the ICAS. For example, many departments create their own shared assumptions and expected behavior patterns that work for them in their particular environment. These assumptions and behaviors, seen across the whole organization, must be compatible with each other and with the organization's basic purpose and value set. The organization's values may both restrict behavior and action and encourage creativity and proactivity. Knowing what is and is not acceptable, where the organization is going and how it will get there provides self-organizing units the needed freedom in decision-making and implementation. At the same time it constrains them to stay within the boundaries of the ICAS purpose and objectives.

Unity and shared purpose also serves to integrate ICAS activities and enables the ICAS to mobilize resources to gain the synergy of complementary talents and to coalesce personnel resources to meet surge requirements. By synergy we mean the working together of two or more people when the results are greater (and usually different) than the sum of their individual talents. If all parts of the ICAS can be kept informed and up to date on the overall direction of the organization, the autonomous units can then respond rapidly, collectively, and collaboratively, without the often-seen confusion over what is wanted or needed, or why. When an ICAS is behaving intelligently it is similar to the conscious mind working intentionally, using its unconscious experience, its incoming information, and its full capability to focus on the task at hand. The unconscious experience of ICAS is composed of both individual tacit knowledge and the unconscious patterns of relationships that exist throughout the organization. Such an organizational capability as this requires a number of special collaborative communication channels to facilitate continuous dialogue and unity of purpose. These channels need to be open, meaningful, and easy to use. They also serve as knowledge sharing, problem identification, and performance self-awareness vehicles. They should not be management- or performance-monitoring vehicles as this may dampen their usage. To be effective, a culture of trust, openness, and collaborative relationships should be created and nurtured by all organizational personnel.

Another way that unity and shared purpose supports organizational intelligence is through its contribution to situational understanding. When people agree and understand the organization's vision and purpose, they tend to see the present *and* potential world. This allows them to apply their experience and professionalism to problems and opportunities in ways that can best contribute to ICAS objectives. Some departures from this uniform outlook are essential to prevent organizational paradigm lock that can prevent alternative views from being seriously considered.

Unity and shared purpose encourages self-organized autonomous units to contribute to overall organizational objectives while concomitantly maintaining their individuality and creativity. These latter characteristics are badly needed to respond intelligently to the dynamic complexity of the external environment. Creativity provides new ideas, solutions, and ways of perceiving and acting upon the environment. Individuality provides a range of options available to the organization. These options increase the organization's own internal complexity, and paradoxically if they are structured properly through the culture and communication channels discussed above, they can be used to counter the challenges presented by very high complexity in the external environment.

Finally, it must be recognized that unity and shared purpose represents an ICAS characteristic that communicates and enables in such a way as to provide a balance between focus and diversity. It is not meant to be a funneling of activity that prevents variety or inhibits new adventures. Neither must it become a permanent direction or fixed purpose. Times change, forces shift, and responses must be agile and precise. It is the ability of the ICAS to effectively change its focus as an entire organization that signifies the sought-after intelligent behavior. We can look at unity and shared purpose as necessary but not sufficient for organizational intelligence. Another ICAS characteristic that contributes to organizational intelligence is multidimensionality.

Multidimensionality and Organizational Intelligence

Multidimensionality represents a number of capabilities that provide an ICAS with the ability to view the environment from many different perspectives and to apply a variety of thinking styles to issues and problems. There is no one part of an ICAS, or one individual in the organization, that possesses these capabilities; they must be spread throughout the system.

Thinking skills such as systems and complexity thinking, logic, creative approaches, analysis, judgment, and intuition are all needed at some time during an organization's operations. The time and space dimensions of thinking become important when organizations try to recognize and anticipate patterns in their environment. For example, when markets shift or political changes are bubbling around, it is important to be able to estimate the right time scale of anticipated changes, be it three months or ten years. A similar need occurs over space as external forces vary over spatial scales, i.e., local, regional, or global. Historically, lower-level personnel in organizations thought and acted in the short-term and senior managers thought and prepared for long-term trends. In the future, external forces are likely to require all ICAS units to scale both their thinking and their actions to match environmental patterns. As they learn to do so, organizational intelligence will increase because of the improved interpretations and responses that result. Risk has always been part of organizational life. As complexity, change, and uncertainty increase so will the risk of making poor decisions, developing non-marketable technology, or losing a competitive edge. The ability to recognize, understand, manage, and influence risk will then have to become a competency throughout the ICAS. This will require technical competencies such as probability theory, modeling, trend analysis, and forecasting techniques. As the world accelerates into ultracomplexity, successful thinking about risk will demand instinct, intuition, and broad social and cultural knowledge, coupled with a deep understanding of the flow of events and the second-order impact of actions. This need will tax the organizational intelligence of all firms.

As can be seen, a broad range of thinking and implementation skills are categorized under the heading of multidimensionality, all of which relate directly to the ability of the ICAS to perceive, interpret, and respond to its environment. Each ICAS will determine its own specific set of skills and competencies needed for its particular objectives and environment. The set of skills and competencies addressed in this book represents fundamental capabilities that most organizations are likely to need.

We next consider knowledge centricity and its relationship to organizational intelligence.

Knowledge Centricity and Organizational Intelligence

Knowledge and its application are at the heart of the ICAS organization. Its knowledge-centric characteristic ensures the creation, sharing, and availability of the right knowledge to the right people at the right time. Recall that knowledge centricity is closely related to organizational intelligence in that to behave intelligently, any complex adaptive system must achieve continuous, interdependent collaboration and interplay among all levels of the system to facilitate knowledge diffusion among agents, components, and external systems. Knowledge, the deep understanding and sense of context and meaning in situations, is a critical part of intelligent behavior and thinking.

The concept of knowledge centricity places knowledge as central to the ICAS, the nerve center of the organization. Since knowledge is created within the individual, knowledge centric also means people centric. Since it is people, or teams, that exhibit intelligence, the application of their intellectual capital is the mechanism for achieving the mission and vision of the organization. Because the creation of new knowledge is as important as the sharing and use of current knowledge, continuous learning becomes an essential requirement for perceiving, interpreting, and responding to the external environment of the ICAS. Knowledge centricity therefore promotes organizational learning, directly impacting organizational intelligence, multidimensionality, and selectivity. Knowledge centricity, through its three mechanisms of human, social, and organizational capital, provides the data, information, and knowledge needed for ICAS units to perform their functions and responsibilities. It provides the socio-technical subsystems and processes that tie the organization together to ensure unity of purpose though coherent operations and quality decision-making. Like flow (discussed below), it supports all parts of the ICAS, giving it a quick reaction capability and a higher level of organizational intelligence.

Optimum Complexity and Organizational Intelligence

As stated earlier, we see the Knowledge Revolution on the close-in radar screen and the Complexity Revolution soon to follow. It is to operate effectively within this incoming explosion of complexity that we anticipate the ICAS, or some similar organizational construct, will become essential for survival and growth. Although complexity is often taken to be a measure of the number of states that a system can take on, for our use we consider complexity to be a measure of the number of *meaningful* states that a system can have. Meaningful refers to those states that make a difference to the ICAS, that is, those states that influence the organization's ability to meet its goals and objectives. This discrimination will significantly lower the number of states and hence the complexity of a system. It also injects the subjective interpretation of meaningfulness into the description. However, an ICAS must look at the world from its own perspective, which means from its own objectives, vision, history, and culture. While evolving in a hypercomplex environment it must optimize its own internal complexity and minimize external complexity by whatever means possible. Using its own criteria of meaningfulness, the ICAS will ignore, or filter, external states that are unimportant to its purpose and internally generate new ways of taking advantage of opportunities or rebutting threats.

One approach is to clearly determine an ICAS's purpose and shared vision and ensure that all members of the ICAS are able to apply their knowledge of the shared vision and purpose to discern meaning from both internal and external events, problems, and opportunities. Doing this enables the organization to filter many unwanted and oftentimes confusing states. To do this will require individuals to develop a knowledge base of the entire ICAS within the framework of its reason for being. When this is achieved, the internal organization, with its multidimensionality and knowledge centricity, can have the maximum number of possible states that can make a difference in terms of its ability to perceive, interpret, and respond to the external environment. It will also have the minimum acceptable complexity by eliminating all states that are not relevant to the vision and purpose of the ICAS.

Stated in another way, the organization strives to achieve its own maximum useful complexity and its own minimum unnecessary complexity. This level of optimum complexity provides support to organizational intelligence by offering the largest useful variety of possible perceptions and actions to respond to the increasingly complex external environment. In return, the ability to develop knowledge, to learn and forget, and to coordinate actions and share information, all enable self-organizing units and individual agents to determine relevance of activities and events and to use their local optimum complexity to effectuate responses. Achieving an organizational state of optimum complexity also guides the scope and depth of data, information, and knowledge needed by the ICAS. In other words, it can create boundaries for the knowledge-centric characteristics that support the rest of the organization, and particularly its organizational intelligence.

THE INTERWEAVING OF FLOW

Flow provides the connections, the continuity, and the coalescing patterns of behavior that ensure the unity of behavior and the exercise of organizational intelligence. Flow moves throughout the emergent characteristics of unity and shared purpose, multidimensionality, knowledge centricity, and optimum complexity. Recall that we discussed flow in terms of the free flow of data, information, and knowledge; the flow of people in and out of the organizational setting; and the optimal human experience.

The Flow of Data, Information, and Knowledge

The flow of data, information, and knowledge moves across networks of systems and people, is shared through teams, communities and events, and is facilitated through knowledge repositories and portals. It enables knowledge centricity. This free flow of data, information, and knowledge in the ICAS is built on push/pull strategies. While the organization is responsible for building structures and vehicles to facilitate this free flow, and for embedding the awards and incentives to maximize this flow, it is ultimately each individual's responsibility to assure they have what they need when they need it to make the best decisions (in alignment with the mission and vision of the organization). This flow is both horizontal and vertical, including the continuous, rapid two-way communication between key components of the organization and top-level decision-makers that is essential to unity and shared purpose. With the influx of new data and information comes the need to develop discernment and discretion, the ability of individuals, teams, and organizations to recognize the data and information that is of benefit or importance to work, business, or growth, and discard or ignore that which is of no benefit or importance. In the world of today, with access to exponentially increasing amounts of data and information, the capability of discernment and discretion will strongly contribute to achieving the optimum complexity for organizational success.

Earlier we discussed the interdependent relationship of the Knowledge Revolution and the Complexity Revolution, a challenge-and-response type of relationship where each drives the other. Selectivity (discernment and discretion at the highest level of decision-making) determines the data and information that are meaningful and make a difference within the organization, or in the external world of concern to the organization, building the optimum complexity for responding to the external environment and internal demands (see Figure 5-1).

This free flow of data and information is as much about people as for people; the context of the data and information must be part of the flow, including information about people's capabilities, interests, and potential. As the richness of context builds in the ICAS, the realization of the multidimensionality or potential multidimensionality of the organization also builds. Specific skills and capabilities of individuals and teams become common knowledge, a part of organizational capital.

The Flow of People In and Out of the ICAS

A continual flow of employees into and out of the organization allows the organization to stay in close touch with the environment, increasing the innovative ideas available. While effective acclimatization of new employees ensures continuous improvement, unity and shared purpose may be negatively impacted by the flow of people in and out of the organizational setting, primarily due to the time delay involved in creating alignment of new people via the vision and culture of the organization. The effect on multidimensional capabilities can be framed in both negative and positive contexts. The positive context would focus on bringing new capabilities in-house; the negative context would focus on the potential loss of capabilities. However, the true ICAS recognizes that it is not necessary to have resources in-house, only to be able to access them when needed. Thus, if relationships are maintained, employees who leave the organization remain part of the organizational capability bank, becoming potential resources to meet future needs.

Since the ICAS is knowledge centric, knowledge central to the business of the organization is captured and shared. The more groups and teams are used in the organization, the more this core knowledge is used, shared, and built upon in terms of innovation and the creation of new knowledge. While each individual is important to this process, it is the continuous flow of data and information among people provided with context that generates organizational learning.

Flow in Terms of the Optimal Human Experience

Flow in terms of the optimal human experience in the organizational setting occurs when there is close alignment of people and organizational goals. Autotelic workers are those workers whose work and family lives are challenging yet harmoniously integrated, where their personal goals are closely aligned with organizational goals (Csikszentmihalyi, 1990). Thus, unity and shared purpose are essential ingredients to achieving flow in the organizational setting. Multidimensionality, knowledge centricity, and optimum complexity are characteristics that support individuals achieving the optimal human experience, providing the depth and breadth of potential and experience that help achieve the optimum state for flow. In his treatment of flow, Csikszentmihalyi says that people are able to achieve harmony of mind, and grow in complexity, even when some of the worst things imaginable happen to them (Csikszentmihalyi, 1990). The inference here is twofold: that people work toward harmony of mind and that the growth of complexity is a natural complement of life.

PERMEABLE BOUNDARIES AND SELECTIVITY

Permeable boundaries and selectivity work hand-in-hand to ensure the organization's ability to meet needs and take advantage of opportunities, while retaining the ability to select and control what makes a difference. Selectivity, the filtering of incoming information from outside the organization includes the use of discernment and discretion applied at every level of decision-making within it. Any permeable boundary is by definition a selection system, since permeability by its nature is specifically designed to be porous, i.e., to provide for the movement in and out of people and information, but with safeguards to prevent the entry of information that does not make a difference to the ICAS. Permeable boundaries also may blur the historic understanding of relationships in terms of time and space, often placing people and information simultaneously both inside and outside of the perceived organizational construct.

Permeable boundaries and selectivity directly impact all of the other six emergent characteristics as they represent the gateway to the external world. The balance between what and how much information and what kind of relationships span the boundaries and what selection rules are followed to focus effort and reduce external complexity is a critical part of the success of ICAS. On the one hand, partners, virtual networks, image management, and close customer relations are vital to a sustained competitive advantage. On the other hand, the organization may be overwhelmed (and confused) by the almost infinite number and variety of external demands, threats, and random events. Thus, the rules that the ICAS develops to selectively manage its external complexity are major challenges. Since the ICAS is composed of a large number of self-organizing autonomous agents, these rules must be both firm corporate policy and robust enough to permit local flexibility. These rules and their balance will come from unity and shared purpose for uniformity and consistency, from knowledge centricity for understanding, and from organizational intelligence for learning and application.

There is another side of selectivity that becomes important. Looking at the ICAS from the outside, some organizational responses will be reinforced by the environment and others will be rejected. This environmental selection phenomenon serves to select the best ICAS responses, and in doing so reinforces their internal generation. This is the Darwinian mechanism that promotes the ICAS's learning and adaptation. These successes and failures that occur through the porous boundary and the selectivity process may be the single most important events that determine the survival or failure of the organization. As the pace of external change rises, the speed and fidelity with which the autonomous agents can react, learn, and relay their perceptions and interpretations across the entire ICAS organization will determine its ability to adapt, learn, and forget. Both flow and knowledge centricity drive this communication and collaboration process. Multidimensionality and organizational intelligence determine the rate of learning, forgetting, and how well the organization can implement effective responses.

The relationships and interfaces among all of the emergent characteristics may well be the single strongest leverage point within the ICAS organization. Because these characteristics are emergent, rather than designed, the challenge is to identify the underlying rules and general principles among the self-organizing autonomous units that will create the desired set of relationships.

From this short discussion of the relationship between permeable boundaries and selectivity, it is also clear that the character of these two emergent character-istics is very different from the six previously discussed, and that those other six are dependent on permeable boundaries and selectivity. However, ICAS activities and processes may be independent of selectivity and permeable boundaries for a short time. For example, projects underway in an organization have defined directions and boundaries; at least for some period of time, regardless of the activity of the environment, i.e., excepting some life-threatening event, they take on a life of their own. Yet eventually to ensure success they must respond to the ever-changing external environment.

CONCLUDING THOUGHTS

We find that for an ICAS to be effective, the organizational relationships among all eight of the emergent characteristics (organizational intelligence, unity and shared purpose, optimum complexity, selectivity, knowledge centricity, flow, permeable boundaries, and multidimensionality) become a critical parameter and provide the high leverage point of the system. The characteristics are closely intertwined and therefore highly dependent upon each other. This interdependency, while partially due to the overlap of functions and roles of the characteristics, derives primarily from their relationships with each other. To perform their roles, they must be closely coupled and mutually supportive. This interdependency is what potentially can give the ICAS its rapid response, variety of activities, and resilience against threats. While each of these eight emergent characteristics contributes to the over-all ICAS, their correlation is what leads to superior performance. As time passes and the environment changes, the relative importance of each characteristic will undoubtedly change–challenging all parts of the organization to recognize and act upon the new balance needed within the organization. Continuous adaptation means constant internal change, which leads to internal uncertainty with its attendant risk.

As with current organizations, the real gemstone is the individuals who perform the day-to-day work that creates value. How they perceive their working world is significantly influenced by the organization's self-image, its culture, and its reason for being. While this internal environment is nurtured by superior leadership and good management, the essence of performance comes from the interplay between individuals and their organization's *umwelt*. This system— people, technology, knowledge, policies, processes, actions, and challenges—is created through the generation and evolution of the eight emergent characteristics described earlier. These, when coupled with the four major processes, strong values, and an enlightened leadership, will produce an organization fit for the future.

REFERENCES

Csikszentmihalyi, M. *Flow: The Psychology of Optimal Experience.* New York: Harper Perennial, 1990.

Edelman, G. M. *The Remembered Present: A Biological Theory of Consciousness.* New York: Basic Books, 1989.

Wiig, K. *Knowledge Management Foundations—Thinking about Thinking—How People and Organizations Create, Represent, and Use Knowledge.* Arlington, TX: Schema Press, 1993.

PART III

THE ICAS IN PRACTICE*

What structure is needed to create an organizational system that can enter into a symbiotic relationship with its environment while simultaneously retaining unity of purpose and selectivity of incoming threats and opportunities? Chapter 6 begins the ICAS implementation journey, setting the stage for a new way of thinking about organizations by laying out a learning structure which supports the eight emergent characteristics of the ICAS. Chapter 7 continues this journey by exploring the type of culture that will energize and help each knowledge worker make the right decisions and take the best actions. Chapter 8 focuses on the four major processes—creativity, problem-solving, decision-making, and implementation—that enable the ICAS to apply its capabilities to produce products, support customers, and deal with external influences. Chapter 9 discusses new rules and roles for leaders and managers, a leadership built on collaboration and empowerment existing throughout the organization.

---

*The four major processes of organizations were initially addressed in the *IPT Learning Campus: Gaining Acquisition Results Through Integrated Product Teams* produced by the Bellwether Learning Center for the Department of the Navy in 1997. A focused version of the change agent strategy, which was de facto implemented in the Department of the Navy (DON), was published as "Managing Change" in Porter, D., A. Bennet, R. Turner, and D. Wennergren (eds), *The Power of Team: The Making of a CIO*, 2002. With permission from DON, this strategy appeared as "The Force of Knowledge: A Case Study of KM Implementation in the Department of Navy" in Holsapple, C. W. (ed.), *Handbook on Knowledge Management 2: Knowledge Directions*, Heidelberg, Germany: Springer-Verlag, 2003.

In Chapter 10 the important property of emergence is readdressed in terms of its potential impact on the structure, culture, leadership, and strategy of the ICAS organization, specifically developing the example of culture. This leads into Chapter 11, which presents a change strategy at the level of the change agent, complete with real-world actions. With the pieces beginning to fall into place, Chapter 12 soars back to the systems level of the organization to take a close look at strategy, balance, and what we call the correlation of forces.

The final chapter in this part uses story to exemplify and amplify the fundamental differences between historically successful organizations that rely on formal structure and a mechanical model and those who rely on adaptation and a more organic approach, preparing themselves to succeed in the uncertain and complex future ...; a future that will challenge every organization.

Chapter 6

THE LEARNING STRUCTURE OF THE NEW ORGANIZATION

In our research it quickly became clear that neither the classic bureaucratic nor the currently popular flat organization could provide both the unity and selectivity necessary for the ICAS. A different structure is needed to create an organizational system that can enter into a symbiotic relationship with its cooperative enterprise, virtual alliances, and external environment while simultaneously retaining unity of purpose and selectivity of incoming threats and opportunities. This organization is a living system composed of other living—systems teams within teams, interacting communities, self-organization within organization—that combine and interact to provide the capabilities of an advanced, intelligent techno-sociological adaptive enterprise.

The objective of structure is to provide a framework and foundation for the workforce to meet its mission/vision while maintaining sustainable competitive advantage in a turbulent environment. The structure must align with the vision and strategy over the long term while at the same time supporting the immediate needs of the workers and managers. In a turbulent world, strategy is more a direction than an end goal and vision is a characterization of the future firm rather than a detailed description. In an unknowable future, strategy and vision must be malleable, but not too malleable.

Senge (1990) and others have pointed out that it is the structure of every organization that predominantly drives its behavior. Complexity theory (Axelrod and Cohen, 1999) recognizes the fundamental role that relationships and individuals play in creating the emergent or global characteristics of human complex adaptive systems. While to some degree structure can be established by senior management, culture—also influential in determining organizational performance—is more difficult to establish. Culture is addressed in Chapter 7. Here we look at what structure will best support the organization as an intelligent complex adaptive system in the age of complexity.

Using our hypothesis that an organization's value added comes from the totality of actions of all employees every day, it follows that the objective and responsibility of the ICAS is to ensure that every employee takes the most effective actions necessary to achieve sustainable competitive advantage. For this to occur, each employee must have a clear understanding of the corporate vision and objectives, and the knowledge, resources, and freedom to make decisions and act in concert with others as needed. Structure commonly means the display of formal responsibilities via an organization chart. It also includes the roles and relationships among leaders, managers, teams, and other subcomponents in the organization (Handy, 1993). Establishing the roles, relationships, authorities, and freedom of employees provides the framework and context within which their work is performed. This framework significantly influences how the work gets done if, and only if, it is in consonance with employee needs and activities, as they perceive it, relative to getting the work done.

GUIDING PRINCIPLES FOR STRUCTURING THE ICAS ORGANIZATION

Based on complexity theory and organizational experience, we propose a number of guiding principles for structuring the ICAS organization. These are:

1. *The structure needs to be compatible with the culture and both should be ecologically matched to the environment and the organization's purpose, strategy, and vision.* Cultures are heavily influenced by the interplay of structure, vision, and external environment. For example, a learning culture would not be compatible with a bureaucracy and a military-like structure would not work well in an academic culture.
2. *The structure design supports the workforce in their daily decision-making and actions.* In other words, the structure contains the informal network as much as possible and it supports the knowledge needs of workers, managers, and leaders.
3. *The structure supports the long-term needs of the workforce, including learning, professional development, and career management.* The technology, roles and responsibilities, facilities, and policies all need to function effectively to satisfy both short-term and long-term ICAS needs. Short-term organizational needs such as flexibility, adaptability, surge requirements, cycling, mesh networks, technology opportunities, coherence of activities, operational tactics, and stakeholder demands often place different

demands on the structure than long-term activities such as learning, adaptability, strategy, knowledge management, core competencies, career management, stakeholder satisfaction, and public image.

4. *The structure supports leader and manager needs for loose–tight control of resources.* For example, the ICAS needs only loose control over self-organization, empowerment, and internal communication, but may need tight control over financial transactions, career assignments, near-fatal decision-making, and strategic direction.

5. *The structure supports and encourages the emergence of the eight characteristics of the ICAS.* That is, the structure, in alignment with the culture and leadership approach, helps facilitate the emergence of the eight characteristics of organizational intelligence, shared purpose, selectivity, optimum complexity, permeable boundaries, knowledge centricity, flow, and multidimensionality.

DEVELOPING THE ICAS STRUCTURE

The history of organizations is rich in its variety of formal organizational structures, from the earliest bureaucracies with their formal, rigid, and hierarchical forms to some of the modern seamless, boundaryless, team-based structures (Sadler, 2001; Ashkenas et al., 2002; Pasternack and Viscio, 1998; Mohrman et al., 1995). Historically, organizational structures have been based on geography, functionality, product, industry, and size. Each structure evolves through experience and trial-and-error until an acceptable form provides an ecological balance with its culture, its market, and its environment. That this stability is hard to maintain is easily seen by watching managers periodically reorganize as they attempt to improve communication, reduce costs, realign processes, or achieve some other stated goal. This restructuring is often justified as necessary to keep up with the competition, or respond to changes in the markets. Just as often it occurs from internal unhappiness with productivity or organizational cohesion. This restructuring is usually accompanied by new policies, rules, systems, and procedures designed to improve the organization.

Managers, assuming that they are in control of their organization, face surprise and disappointment when their system does not work the way they intended. As this occurs, they are continually getting together and "fixing" their organizations—over and over again. As Stacey et al. (2000) describe, the problem is that the way the work gets done is not the way managers think it gets done. The informal networks, the practical decisions and actions, and the common sense in doing a job end up driving the day-to-day operations in most organizations. This disjuncture between official policy and how the work actually gets done has been a long-term problem for many organizations. It is created by a mismatch between the official structure and the needs of the workers. When these two clash, the needs of the workers will often take precedence. That is why informal or shadow networks exist in organizations.

Structure is a global characteristic of the ICAS, and as such impacts all lower-level systems from departments to teams to individuals. In a fast-moving environment that daily requires flexible responses and local context awareness, there may be no time to restructure, set new policies, or send problems up the chain for higher resolution. The structure must permit, encourage, and support local, daily self-governance, empowerment, and decisions over a broad range of action space. At the same time, the structure needs to allow rapid access to knowledge sources and senior decision-makers when the situation calls for it. In other words, the structure must allow variety and local empowerment most of the time, yet ensure cohesion and unity of purpose and direction over the entire ICAS. Ideally the formal and informal networks and chains of commands would be the same, but this is unlikely if not impossible, even in the best of organizations. Formal networks, policies, and relationships are created to establish broad, global operating conditions. They cover many smaller subsystems. In a dynamic world, each lower-level group will face some unique, unpredictable situations and decisions that are not covered in the global policies, etc. This local optimization, necessarily done by front-line knowledge workers, requires them to be somewhat self-sufficient, using their information networks as a support system.

The specific structure for an ICAS organization is highly dependent upon the vision, direction, and products of the firm. Every ICAS organization will have a slightly different structure due to the nature of the product mix, markets, its own history, workforce, leadership, and the environment in which it works. As a minimum, we assume that for an organization to *need* an ICAS structure it is operating in a turbulent environment, and is primarily a knowledge-based organization. This latter assumption is a weak one, because even production lines are likely to have significant computerized capability in their products and smart products are becoming the norm. More and more organizations are moving toward knowledge as their main source of value to customers.

Another consideration is the need for a stable part of the ICAS structure to ensure that those routine functions are done with maximum quality and efficiency. Examples might include legal, contracts, personnel, finance, and operations departments. If the ICAS produces assembly line products, the structure should support six-sigma quality and high efficiency. Here, there is the need for clear procedures and rigorous discipline coupled with local assembly line empowerment, team problem-solving, and innovation. In the research and development phase of product development, the organization needs a structure that encourages multidisciplined teams such as integrated product teams, innovation and market attractiveness coupled with firm budgets, and development deadlines. If the ICAS contains a services department or a professional services group, the overall structure must be both formal and informal, tight and loose, rigid and lax, narrowly focused and highly flexible, resistant to rapid changes and continuously learning, and quickly adapting to changing customers or missions. This all sounds paradoxical, and it is. Living with paradox is a mandate from the future. Fortunately, paradoxes are in the eyes of the beholders. Nature doesn't create paradox, man does.

It seems clear that there is no single homogenous structure that will provide the ICAS with all of its needs. Living in a turbulent environment and dependent on the specific nature of the business, the ICAS will have to function in several arenas, each arena calling for a different structural form. For example, professional services firms have contracts, legal, and human resource departments that operate with a reasonable degree of stability, therefore flourishing in a hierarchical, well-defined structure. Yet the professional/customer side of the firm requires a much more flexible structure to maximize its long-term effectiveness. Recognizing that there are many variations in between, we address the two extremes: the segment of the firm that works in a stable, predictable environment, and that part of the firm that operates in the turbulent world of rapid change, uncertainty, nonlinearity, and complexity. This latter world is, of course, the reason for the ICAS.

The standard hierarchical structure is used for those areas of the firm that operate in a relatively stable, predictable environment. Clear lines of authority, responsibility, and accountability are delineated along with individual, although perhaps broad, position descriptions for each job. Advancement and salary increases are based on performance and capacity for higher-level responsibilities. Position, quality, and efficiency are the name of the game. As mentioned previously, possible functional areas that would operate within this structure would include: human resources, contracts, finance, legal, and operations. Responsibilities of these departments are usually to keep their functions operating smoothly, watching for opportunities to help the firm move toward its vision, acting as a watchdog for internal day-to-day decisions and processes, and external commitment to ensure that corporate policies and rules are followed.

Since we are primarily concerned with that part of an organization that lives in the turbulent environment, the question becomes: What organizational structure will best support the ICAS? We have previously noted that the successful organization must be creative, flexible, adaptable, and capable of rapidly responding to surprise, yet maintain cohesion of direction and an internal learning capability. Figure 6-1 provides a high-level visual representation of one potential structure.

To provide this balance between a local freedom to act and an organizational unity of purpose and vision requires some unique structural characteristics. First, as discussed above, there will always be a hierarchy of some sort to maintain authority and accountability for the firm's funds and objectives. That said, there must also be the widespread use of teams, communities, networks, and technology to ensure that the worker has the knowledge, empowerment, trust

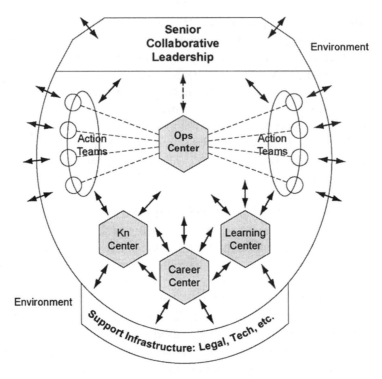

Figure 6-1
A Potential ICAS Structure

and support to act effectively. A third element is the ability to coordinate or align the efforts of local knowledge workers to prevent organizational chaos.

THE USE OF TEAMS

One approach that has worked well in the development and production of complex products is to structure the organization as teams within teams within teams (Bennet, 1998). At the level where the work gets done, teams may be permanently created and assigned responsibility for a given product or area of service, or they are created ad hoc to address a specific opportunity or issue. Using the teams-within-teams concept, the team leader of a lower-level team becomes a team member of the next higher-level team, or a team may be formed that reports directly to a manager at whatever level is appropriate for the task. This team-within-team relationship is embedded within the organization as shown in Figure 6-1.

Teams have a number of characteristics that match well with ICAS needs: they can leverage information and knowledge; they can be created and dissolved as needed; they broaden team-member competency and increase their understanding of the organization; and they bring a diversity of thinking, knowledge, and behaviors to bear on threats or opportunities.

Teams usually need a higher-level champion and, most importantly, the freedom to self-organize and decide how to do their work. Clear, one-page, written charters that provide resources, authority, timelines, and objectives are critical to team success. Successful team leaders (and team members) know how to collaborate, facilitate, and implement the four major processes discussed in Chapter 8. Good team leaders are not autocratic, rather they encourage the team to collaborate and make decisions. Team leadership may or may not be rotated among all team members, with the team leader being first among equals rather than the boss. Ideally, all of the workforce would be trained in facilitation, communication, teamwork, systems thinking, and the other integrative competencies.

While teams add a significant capability to the ICAS, they are not without some cost. Managers give up authority while keeping responsibility, something few people like to do. Nonlinear elements in the market can quickly lead to explosive threats that require immediate assessment, understanding, and action. When this occurs there may not be time for a team to handle the issue. The ICAS cannot afford to get bogged down in approval chains or in getting a team together in a short-fused emergency. When these occur, and they are very rare, the hierarchy can be used, or bypassed, as the local team leader finds necessary.

Teams also need space and technology to make them efficient. All of these cost time and money. The bottom line is that teams offer a significant benefit to the firm in a turbulent environment, but that benefit is not free. Three major costs are training and development of the workforce, structural support via space and technology, and senior management backing and nurturing. Team success depends as much on senior management support and structural systems as it does on the workers.

The ICAS utilizes several forms of teams and communities. There are ongoing operational teams that have a continuous flow of people in and out of the teams; action teams that have a limited life cycle as needed; communities of practice and interest (CoPs and CoIs) that evolve and dissipate as the interests and needs of the organization and its knowledge workers focus and refocus; and, finally, there are meshes, special teams created to handle surprise complex threats and opportunities that require both teams and an extremely rapid response.

OPERATIONAL TEAMS

There are specialized, permanent operational teams that enable the ICAS to adapt, react, and sustain coherence. These include: the Operations Center, the Knowledge Center, the Learning Center, and the Career Management Center. These centers are represented in relation to action teams in Figure 6-1.

The Operations Center

The Operations Center is a single team chartered to keep current on all unusual events and patterns occurring in the firm's external environment. It also serves as the nerve center for the ICAS by receiving brief status reports from line managers and team leaders relative to their external environment. The Ops Center then analyzes, interprets, and makes sense of the events, patterns, and structures in the environment. In doing so, it interacts closely with team leaders and knowledge workers and does not become just a strategic forecasting study group. As an integration center, it feeds back what it learns and thinks to the workforce to provide them with the context and higher-level understanding of what is going on in the environment and how the ICAS could be affected. By having a continuous, two-way communication with all teams throughout the ICAS, the Center helps provide a real-time interpretation of events, patterns, and deep knowledge. The Ops Center basically provides the context and framework for dealing with uncertainty, surprises, and complexity in the external world. It may draw upon all expertise within and external to the ICAS as needed.

It is convenient to consider two levels of analysis of the outside world. The first is classical strategic and future-oriented studies of high-level changes related to economic, social, technological, and political dimensions, plus others of special interest. Such analysis proposes answers to many what-if questions, builds various scenarios to identify possible futures and tries to develop most probable future worlds. These are useful, somewhat academic, usually wrong, but very good learning exercises. If this higher-level, long-term strategic analysis is needed, it is done by a separate group in close concert with the tactically oriented Ops Center. The second level of analysis is at the knowledge worker level, where day-to-day events, and conversations with customers and market representatives provide a wealth of ideas, trends, possibilities, and perspectives that are often forerunners of near-term events and trends. These local inputs represent the pulse of the turbulent and fast-changing boundary of the firm. It is here that the emergent characteristics of permeability and selectivity work to intelligently gather these inputs. The integrative competencies of learning, knowing, systems and complexity thinking, and relationship network management position the knowledge worker to perceive, interpret, and assess this turbulence (see Chapters 14–21). We then add the support of the knowledge worker's team and community activities (CoPs and CoIs), and the Ops Center's broader perspective and integrative capacity via its two-way continuous communications throughout the enterprise. This combination significantly improves the ICAS's capacity to deal with its environment.

The Ops Center, in providing high level integration and interpretation of the outside world, plays a role similar to human consciousness. Recall our reference in Chapter 4 to Edelman and Tononi's (2000) work on consciousness and their explanation of how the brain maintains its unity of consciousness. In this role, the Ops Center serves as the focal point for contemplating and, where possible, integrating incoming signals from the environment. For this team to be most effective, it cannot be in a position of control. Its primary function is as integrator and facilitator of environmental context knowledge up, down and across the organization. As such it requires excellent technological support, a small number of people, and immediate two-way access to everyone in the firm. Its members will develop a good understanding of the firm, its direction, and vision, while concomitantly understanding systems, complexity, and collaboration, and acquire deep knowledge of the environment.

A number of advantages come from rotating people through the Center for six-month or one-year assignments. First, the flow of information and knowledge across the organization is increased as individuals return to their new assignments. Second, during their time at the Ops Center, individuals build cross-organizational relationship networks and have the opportunity to gain senior-level visibility and a better understanding of corporate-level perspectives. All of these elements build more effective employees while enhancing their individual career potential. After leaving the Center, returning workers merge their new networks with their long-time networks, spreading the word about how the organization works. Finally, rotations prevent the Center from becoming a typical bureaucratic barrier, since no one is there long enough to take control. Senior Ops Center leadership may well need to stay several years to provide continuity, but rarely more than three years. The head of the Ops Center, the Chief Operations Officer, would be a vice president and report directly to the president of the ICAS. The Chief Operations Officer would also be the team leader of the Support Center Team composed of the Chief Knowledge Officer, Chief Learning Officer and the Career Development Officer, each of whom leads their respective center.

The Knowledge Center

The Knowledge Center works under the Chief Knowledge Officer of the firm and has the responsibility for implementing knowledge management throughout the ICAS (see Chapter 15). The Knowledge Center is the focal point for locating the information, knowledge, and experience of the ICAS. This includes data banks, yellow pages, knowledge audits, subject matter experts, communities, knowledge portals, relevant technology, lessons learned, good practices, resumes, and resource libraries. Like the Ops Center, the Knowledge Center is small, with some full-time staff and a larger number of line knowledge workers cycling through to learn about the corporation and become well-versed in the sources and areas of knowledge. With the Learning Center, the Knowledge Center co-sponsors and/or supports communities of interest and practice that emerge and evolve throughout the organization. They also lead and support an extended Knowledge Center Virtual Community that touches every element of the organization. Members of the Knowledge Center Virtual Community are responsible for ensuring that organizational elements and teams continuously update and connect data and information needed by other elements and teams throughout the organization, i.e., each organizational element and team within the organization has responsibility for connecting and providing the context for the data and information in their areas of expertise.

The Knowledge Center represents a critical integration resource for the ICAS by helping all employees find information and individuals with the needed knowledge. While this intermediation function is important in terms of connecting people and knowledge, it is not the only source of the firm's knowledge, since each knowledge worker will have their own relationship networks, coworker sources, and communities of practice and interest (see Chapter 21).

The Learning Center

The Learning Center is the focal point for both individual and organizational learning. In addition to the normal skills and information learning, the Center is responsible for ensuring that ICAS core competencies are kept at the forefront of the state-of-the-art and the synergistic capabilities that stem from group experience and past collaboration are maintained as people flow in and out of the organization.

The Learning Center reaches out primarily into the organization and to external sources to find needed expertise to keep up with changes in disciplines needed by ICAS knowledge workers, though it may have its own expertise in the integrative and core competencies. The Center is responsible for identifying next-generation knowledge that the ICAS will need in the near future to maintain competitive advantage. It will also identify next-generation problems, that is, gaps between the ICAS's current knowledge and what it needs to know. While the Learning Center co-supports communities as needed, it does not control them.

The Learning Center supports mentoring virtual learning networks designed to provide employees with learning opportunities within the ICAS that relate to specific needs of the organization. These networks are both structured, distance learning lessons and informal, local community networks operating as local communities of practice. Subject areas such as the integrative competencies, team-building, leadership, managing change, etc. are included (see Chapters 14–21). A primary value of virtual learning networks is their availability 24 hours a day, 7 days a week, which puts the responsibility for accessing and learning on the knowledge worker. They are also an excellent source of just-in-time learning for all knowledge workers. The Chief Learning Officer is a member of the ICAS Support Center Team, responsible for coordinating all Learning Center efforts with the Ops Center, the Knowledge Center, and the Career Management Center.

The Career Management Center

The Career Management Center has responsibility for supporting the career development of all knowledge workers, including team leaders, managers, and senior executives. It advises workers on career needs, and works with mentors and their mentees to provide guidance and support as requested. The Center also sponsors external professional development programs and works with leaders and senior executives in deciding new assignments for knowledge workers. To maintain a culture of learning and adapting, knowledge workers must change their work assignments at least every three or four years; exceptions should be rare. New work assignments bring new challenges and keep the mind flexible, active, and learning. The Career Management Center negotiates ICAS current and future needs and individual knowledge worker desires.

This Center works closely with the Learning Center to ensure connectivity of short-term and long-term learning goals of employees. The Center works closely with human resources as well and, in small organizations, it may also support or provide many of the human resource functions for the organization.

ACTION TEAMS

Action teams are the line teams responsible for getting the day-to-day work done through the ICAS. They are led by a collaborative team leader (see Chapter 9) and have a specific area of responsibility assigned by senior leadership. They operate with a great deal of freedom within their charter, and can self-organize and change their structure as needed, with the team leader being first among equals.

Depending upon the nature of their work, the team is usually made up of a diversity of disciplines with a variety of experience and thinking styles. They will be collegial in culture, interdependent through performance assessment, and have a flow-through of team members to ensure new ideas and prevent team stagnation. Effective teams need to operate at the edge of chaos, meaning that they need some level of instability to ensure creative approaches to problems. Typical team size is from 8 to 12 members, depending on the work responsibilities. If the work assigned requires more people, then subteams are formed by separating the work into smaller parts, always creating mechanisms that ensure close coordination and collaboration where necessary (Katzenbach and Smith, 1993; McDermott et al., 1998).

COMMUNITIES OF PRACTICE AND INTEREST

The ICAS has many ways of connecting people and knowledge. Communities represent another source of information and knowledge flow for the firm. Supported by the Knowledge and Learning Centers, communities of practice and communities of interest focused on specific knowledge areas flourish throughout the organization. The concept of embedded teams, communities, and relationship networks is represented in Figure 6-2. All of these operate in an interconnected and overlapping fashion providing the flow of ideas and leveraging of knowledge.

Communities of practice and interest are built on the tradition of professionals joining together to share skills and resources, and are vibrant learning centers and rich marketplaces for knowledge sharing. They are groups of knowledge workers who have a common practice or interest in a given area and use these networks to exchange ideas, solve problems, and keep up to date on the state of their art. Communities of practice (CoPs) have a shared domain of practice, i.e., members are actively engaged in applying the knowledge they are creating, sharing, and

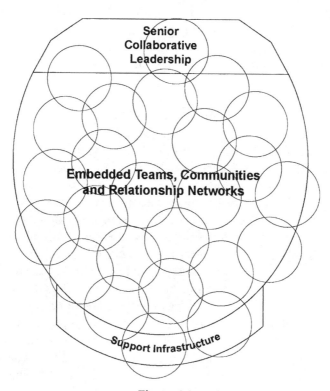

Figure 6-2
Teams, Communities, and Networks Embedded in the Structure

reusing. Communities of interest (CoIs) can bring together an eclectic group of thinkers and learners who are anxious to explore and share new ideas in an area outside their individual practice and beyond the current practice of the organization. Such communities provide a powerful opportunity for the ICAS to develop new applications and develop new employees. CoPs may have CoIs with the same focus areas, providing a learning opportunity for peripheral members, or for knowledge workers who are working to expand their areas of focus. CoIs may be short-lived and are always voluntary (Lesser, 2000; Lesser et al., 2000).

Communities of practice and interest may be either formal or informal in nature, though the true bonds in communities are their common focus on an area of practice or interest, and their willingness to learn and share their expertise. The knowledge focus of communities is aligned with the interests of the organization and its knowledge workers. While focused on knowledge, the goal of communities is to share and explore common problems and opportunities, and learn and develop better practices while doing real work. They are managed and supported by facilitating connections and networking, and have an evolving agenda.

Concentrating on value added, mutual exchange, and continuous learning, communities essentially build, sustain, and improve a professional practice for the sake of the individuals within the community and to the benefit of the organization. Their contribution to the organization is through higher-quality decision-making, more creative ideas, and faster problem-solving. Membership is not limited, but active participation is expected and listening is essential. Critical factors for success include a sense of importance, trust, personal passion, respect, key thought leader involvement, and open communications (Wenger, 1998).

Communities require management time and attention to get them started and fully integrated into the organization. In addition, whether formal or informal communities, the organization provides a corporate champion, the technology infrastructure through the Knowledge and Learning Centers, rewards and recognition programs, and pays for participants' time. Sustainance of communities requires a leader as well as the necessary technology systems and information repositories. Communities are primarily virtual communities whose network may—depending on the area of focus—extend beyond the boundaries of the ICAS to include partner firms, retired employees, or world-class experts. The mode of interchange is ubiquitous, available from any location 24 hours a day, 7 days a week.

The number, size, and scope of communities depend upon the firm's size, needs, and areas of interest. Communities may have as few as ten or as many as several hundred active members. They work best when they are voluntary and self-organizing. Individual communities may start, flourish, and die out as the ICAS evolves through time, and its environment and professional needs vary. To survive, each community must add value to the firm and to those workers interested in the specific area of focus.

The benefits of communities accrue at the organizational, team, workgroup, and individual level. At the organization level, they have the ability to complement more formal team structures, facilitating collaboration across the organization, accelerating the rate of innovation, and improving the quality and speed of decision-making. Communities leverage the organization's investment in human capital, the management of knowledge, and organizational learning. They increase the organization's capacity for managing complexity, and the organization's ability to envision the future as employee potential becomes clearer.

At the team and workgroup level, communities can support any unit where assigned work is managed to meet an organization's commitments for products and services. They accelerate the use of best practices, provide a platform for knowledge sharing and access to just-in-time expertise, and increase the flexibility of teams and workgroups. At the individual level, communities extend the knowledge worker's reach, building new relationships and access to other knowledge workers across the organization. This increase in collaboration and the transfer of know-how makes creative problem-solving available to all, while facilitating just-in-time learning (Smith and McKeen, 2003; Bennet and Bennet, 2003). Communities of practice and interest also serve as the fodder for the mesh network.

THE MESH NETWORK

Meshes are special networks of individuals that have a deep knowledge of focus areas and are available on short notice. These people come to the mesh with a high level of organizational context and an understanding of ICAS's vision and purpose. Meshes are created for rapid response situations, thus the relation ships among mesh members should have already been developed in terms of knowledge and trust.

As illustrated in Figure 6-3, members of meshes are drawn primarily out of ongoing communities composed of internal and external knowledge workers who have experience and expertise in specific areas of immediate interest to the ICAS. When expertise is needed beyond internal resources, meshes may need to draw from extended silent networks that could include retired employees under an "as needed" consulting contract with the organization, knowledgeable individuals from partnering organizations, or experts who have had some previous relationship with the organization or individuals within the organization. While these individuals are usually aware of the potential need, these extended mesh networks are most often invisible until called upon to handle a significant situation requiring knowledge and experience relating to a specific problem or opportunity.

When an event occurs that may significantly impact the ICAS, a combination virtual and face-to-face mesh meeting is called within 24 hours. Relevant material is sent to all mesh members within six hours of such event. After a fast

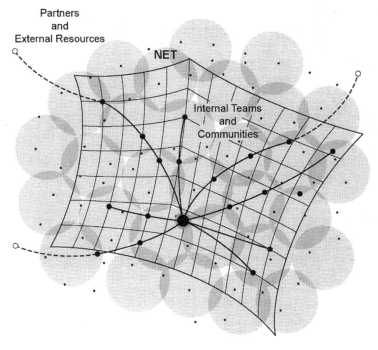

Figure 6-3
The Mesh

exploration and development of context, and building an understanding of the problem or opportunity, the mesh self-organizes, selects a leader and drafts a short charter before commencing work—all of this accomplished in a timeline of approximately four hours. Administrative procedures, resources, internal working agreements, etc. are automatically implemented, providing full support to the process. This identification of expertise, pre-organization and pre-commitment is somewhat similar to the concept used by the Federal Emergency Management Agency (FEMA) to respond to national emergencies. FEMA develops formal relationships and operating responsibilities and procedures prior to the need for response. After completing its task and transitioning any further work to others—which is accomplished in as short a period as possible— the mesh prepares an after-action report for the Operations Center and then is dissolved. Members of the mesh continue to provide advice and guidance on any follow-on work as requested. Members of the mesh are also charged with continuing interaction in their community and team settings to disseminate information and champion implementation of measures as required.

In summary, meshes are intended to be transient teams that specialize in a specific area of expertise and a quick response capability. Their members know the organization, and have the trust and respect of its leaders and knowledge workers. Most of them are full-time employees, scattered throughout the ICAS, and up to speed on corporate direction, vision, tactics, and culture. Because they are active participants in organization communities, they have built-in relationship networks. They are the emergency crews that, working with the local knowledge workers, come in, generate the quick-response actions, and then go back to their normal responsibilities. Their experience and special knowledge is known to the organization through the Knowledge Center. Some may be ex-employees, outside specialists, or specialists from partnering firms.

SIGNIFICANT STRUCTURAL FACTORS

There are a number of factors that play a significant role in the structure of the ICAS. These include: authority, responsibility, and accountability; roles and responsibilities, technology, time and space, and policies and rules. Each of these factors is discussed below in terms of the ICAS structure.

Authority, Responsibility, and Accountability

Since the ICAS will have a mix of hierarchical structure, action teams within teams, communities, and specialized organizations such as the Knowledge Center, authority, responsibility, and accountability relationships will vary with each part of the structure. As knowledge workers and teams are given the responsibility of self-organizing within defined limits, they will also have the authority to implement the four major processes of creating ideas, problem-solving, decision-making, and implementation, all within preset limits. See Chapter 8 for a discussion on the processes and limits.

All team members carry equal responsibility for results, although the team leader has more responsibility for the team's performance than the team members. Decisions are made by the team, not by the team leader acting alone. As for leaders who oversee several teams, they carry the responsibility to meet corporate goals and objectives and to nurture, move, and remove workers. Senior leadership recognizes that while long-term profitability and competitive advantage are necessary, both of these results are global attributes of the firm and result from the sum of the daily actions of all workers. At the local level there will be some mistakes, trial-and-error activities, and errors in judgment. In a turbulent environment where no one can predict the future, the goal is to take the most effective actions possible. Leaders and their teams will be held accountable for long-term results, and for creating a local culture and atmosphere in which the workforce can be, and is, empowered, collaborative, and self-organizing. With these characteristics, knowledge workers can create new ways of dealing with their problems and opportunities arising in the environment, and have ownership in the results of their efforts with the full backing of the enterprise.

Having the freedom to make decisions and decide how to achieve their goals, knowledge workers are accountable over the long-term for their actions. Their accountability is primarily for effectiveness (getting the desired results), and secondarily for efficiency (doing things at the least cost), although, as always, funds are limited and efficiency is important. When working in a complex environment, doing the right things often means losing some efficiency. For example, learning, networking, keeping the knowledge center up to date with what is learned, sharing knowledge with others, trying new ways of supporting customers, and spending time thinking about complex situations could all be considered inefficient in a bureaucratic organization. Yet without these activities, the ICAS will not be able to function, let alone excel, in its volatile world. The focus is on making and implementing *effective* decisions (see Chapter 8 for guidelines).

Efficiency and effectiveness are independent only in a stable environment, where the products and services and customer desires do not change significantly. Under these conditions, effectiveness is essential for long-term customer loyalty, while efficiency maximizes profit or sustainable competitive advantage.

In a changing environment, organizations must make tradeoffs between efficiency and effectiveness. A highly efficient company may make products at the lowest cost but it may not spend funds to learn and anticipate future changes in customer demands. It will be profitable over the short term but unable to keep customers over the long term. In order to maintain the learning rate, flexibility, and agility to effectively survive in an uncertain, complex environment, the company must expend time, funds, and personnel resources; that is, become a learning, knowledge-centered, complex adaptive system to enhance its long-term effectiveness at the expense of efficiency. Thus, as the markets become more volatile, prices will rise. The solution is for the complex adaptive corporation to add more value to its products and services through knowledge management, new products, and customer loyalty. The newly achieved knowledge, organizational learning, and complexity are put to advantage from the customer's viewpoint, otherwise the organization will sacrifice both customers and profits at the same time, a disaster in the making for any organization. (See Chapter 19 for additional discussion of balance.)

Not all knowledge workers are able to function in the above manner. Managers and team leaders have to take action when the challenge exceeds the capability of individuals. There may be a mismatch between the individual and the assignment, the individual may need more experience, or perhaps the individual is just not interested in working in a complex world. In any of these situations, and others, fair and quick action must be taken for the good of both the ICAS and the individual. Empowerment and self-organization cannot tolerate people who will not learn, take responsibility, work with others, and give their commitment to the firm.

Roles and Responsibilities

To achieve the ICAS vision, leaders take on new roles and responsibilities. It is their role as gardener (not decision-maker) to give up authority while retaining responsibility, admitting that they may not know more than their knowledge workers about any given problem, and trusting in their people to think and do the right things. Leaders are available for advice; for integrating the efforts of their knowledge workers when needed; for nurturing an atmosphere of trust, collaboration, confidence, and integrity; for listening and being a sounding board; and for overriding their knowledge workers *only when they believe that a fatal mistake is about to be made*. Mistakes will happen, losses will occur. These are a necessary part of living in a turbulent environment, and having freedom to make mistakes is the price for creativity, agility, learning, and optimum complexity. What is critical is that knowledge workers learn from all mistakes. Leaders are accountable for getting results *and* supporting their knowledge workers.

Knowledge workers do not have jobs with specific position descriptions. Jobs restrict people, allow them to hide behind words on a sheet of paper, and encourage stagnation and comfort. In the ICAS world, knowledge workers have a simple position description: *Do whatever is necessary to get the assignment done within the ethics, values, moral standards and policies of the organization*. Bureaucratic managers would cringe at such an approach because it makes justifying performance evaluations difficult. Nevertheless, for knowledge workers to have the freedom to accomplish their assignments they must have the freedom to act, as well as the personal accountability for those actions. In fact, knowledge workers take on more responsibility and accountability when they do not have "jobs."

The ICAS approach places more strain on leaders who must continually reassign workers as the workload, situation, and requirements change. It also presses the organization to manage knowledge workers' careers by assignment sequences. As mentioned earlier, to prevent employees from becoming stale, no one should be in the same job for more than about three years. This rotation creates a culture of change, learning, and continuous growth. It does reduce efficiency in the short term due to learning curve costs, but it increases effectiveness over the long term through broader employee competency and growth.

Technology

Technology is a keystone of ICAS performance. Yet it should be invisible, ubiquitous, and a natural part of the work processes. As a foundation of the infrastructure, technology is essential in supporting the multiple networks, teams, knowledge repositories, virtual organizational structures, and information needs throughout the ICAS. There is considerable technology to support virtual communication via real-time video and graphics. There are several good voice-actuated computer software programs that allow an individual to talk directly to a computer and, for many knowledge workers, speed up the process of entering information into a computer. Artificial intelligence research is also making some headway relative to decision support systems such as neural networks, genetic algorithms, fuzzy systems, and case-based reasoning, and the marriage between the human mind and artificial intelligence provides tremendous processing and thinking advantages.

As technology moves into the nanotechnology and organic world, its capability will surely expand to provide even better support to the ICAS. Note, however, that as good as technology is at processing speeds and memory size, it does not operate like the human brain. To date, and probably for the foreseeable future, no computer can come close to a person in terms of context recognition and intuition, judgment, and feeling. As good as technology is at storing and transmitting information, it cannot store or transmit knowledge.

Time and Space

Time can be an ally or an enemy, depending on the organization's understanding of it and the resources available to respond to emergent opportunities and threats. The ICAS organization is structured for knowledge availability and quick response, providing the potential for achieving high performance and competitive advantage. There are also problems that either diminish or disappear entirely over time. Knowledge workers at the point of action are in a good position to make—or not make—time-sensitive decisions, since only they can sense the pace of change in the local environment. However, they may not be aware of longer-term patterns of change in the global environment. Here is a case where the Ops Center, team leaders, and knowledge workers need to collaborate and share context and perspectives to make the most knowledgeable decisions.

Another aspect of time is as a boundary condition for focused sharing and interactions. For example, in relationship network management (Chapter 21), knowledge workers manage their interactions to ensure future access and sustain trust and respect in their relationships with other workers, a necessity for quick response. This sharing is a significant factor in managing time—a scarcity in every organization—since linear cause-and-effect relationships between events and ideas may be hidden by complexity. In addition, with ideas flowing across the organization in a nonlinear fashion, multiple knowledge workers (decision-makers) can combine information and identify patterns that might never be accessed in a linear ask-and-respond sequence. The use of repositories that capture thoughts with context, including sources of thoughts together with an enterprise taxonomy built on natural languages and workflows, provides knowledge workers the ability to slow the flow of ideas, or even hold them in abeyance until needed. Much has been written about time management in terms of numbers. A challenge to the new knowledge worker is to think about time in terms of the flow of ideas.

Space represents part of the context within which knowledge workers communicate, cooperate, coordinate, and collaborate. As such, spatial surroundings play a large role in the efficiency and effectiveness of teams as they meet to create ideas or solve problems. A popular slogan describing the impact of communication and information technology on organizations is known as "the death of distance." In fact, space has been shrunk as knowledge workers use the Internet and networks to communicate and collaborate with others around the organization and the world.

That said, technology has not replaced face-to-face conversations where trust, personal feelings, and individual character play a role in sharing understanding, reaching agreement, or making a decision. Group creativity is best when the group is in the same room. *Ad hoc* coffee pot conversations can be very productive. The more conference rooms that are strategically located throughout the ICAS, the more people will share what they know and jump into work sessions to help solve problems. While knowledge workers need quiet time in their offices, they also need conversation time and team time.

From an organizational view, spaces should be designed to provide teams, groups, and individual workers with the best technology and surroundings for all of these. In knowledge firms, the intellectual value of the firm may be five to ten times as much as the book value. The cost of space is far less than the cost of salaries. Thus, providing effective space for knowledge workers has a high leveraging effect on their performance, provided the structure, culture, and leadership back it up. As von Krogh et al. (2000) have pointed out, "[...]; effective knowledge creation depends on an enabling context. What we mean by an enabling context is a shared space that fosters emerging relationships. Based on the Japanese idea of ba (or "place"), such an organizational context can be physical, virtual, mental, or—more likely—all three" (p. 7).

For example, the location of workspaces can be significant. People who are spatially close to each other have a much higher frequency of interactions than those far apart. People who need to have frequent meetings should be in the same area if possible. Conference rooms for video teleconferencing need to be readily accessible, as well as the technology for retrieving information stored in knowledge banks, the Internet, etc. Advanced graphic creation, display, and merging should also be available, and a large number of software programs to support knowledge workers and teams in such areas as creative thinking, analysis, graph construction, system design, decision-making, etc.

A relaxed, informal, comfortable, and well-laid-out conference room or coffee mess helps a team's productivity and reduces distractions. Technology such as electronic whiteboards, projectors, flipcharts, good and adjustable lighting, swivel chairs, and plenty of room can significantly affect the outcome of brainstorming, dialogue, and other synergistic processes. All conference and meeting rooms need to be equipped with interface technology so that access to networks throughout the ICAS is quickly available. Many conference rooms are really lecture halls in disguise, implying lectures, inequality of participants, formality, etc., and leaving little room for learning, open communication, and widespread participation during meetings. Whereever possible think in circles, ovals, and small groups when designing conference rooms.

Policies and Rules

While some rules may be required, most directives in the ICAS are issued in the form of guidance, providing room for the connectedness of choices so important to success. Different elements of the organization have different focus areas, and operate in somewhat different structures according to work requirements. Also, the fact that elements are composed of different people with different capabilities who may have varied cultures causes the "how" part of achieving a common vision to vary from element to element. The ICAS structure provides room for empowerment and decision-making at the lowest possible level, while simultaneously ensuring a clear understanding of the organization's direction and values.

Although specific policies and rules depend upon the individual firm, there are some generic ideas that foster the nature and spirit of the desired environment. Some examples of important ICAS heuristics are:

- All knowledge workers have some stake in the firm.
- All prioritized e-mails and phone calls are answered within 24 hours.
- No one can say "no" to a new idea except a senior leader.
- Everyone has access to anyone in the firm.
- If time is short and no one is available, make the decision and explain later.
- Use your team and personal network for all difficult decisions.
- Everyone knows the size of their action space; everyone tries to earn a larger space.
- At staff meetings, leaders take the time to ensure knowledge workers understand the line-of-sight question, the direction and the values of the ICAS.
- Context and potential consequences are always addressed before any significant action is taken.
- Real-time lessons learned and after-action reports are prepared and disseminated and sent to the Knowledge Center.
- Knowledge workers have assignments and careers, not jobs, and are reassigned about every three years. Thus, they work for the company, not a given individual.
- All knowledge workers have a responsibility to monitor the external environment for threats and opportunities and to report them ASAP to the appropriate, *accessible* person.

- Career development is the joint responsibility of the ICAS and every knowledge worker.
- A team's responsibility transfers directly to every team member.
- Trust and integrity are not useful characteristics, they are conditions of employment.

STRUCTURE IN SUPPORT OF THE EMERGENT CHARACTERISTICS

The ICAS structure supports the major characteristics of intelligent behavior, unity and shared vision, knowledge centricity, flow, optimum complexity, integrative competencies, selectivity, and porous boundaries. Let's briefly consider each of these in terms of how they can be supported by the structure.

Intelligent behavior means being prepared, being able to solve problems, thinking things through, positioning oneself for success, and having sound judgment. By using self-organizing teams supported by technology, the Knowledge Center, and the Ops Center, the ICAS is able to sense, interpret, and respond to external situations with a high degree of intelligence and experience. Virtually the entire organization will/can be available if the need warrants. With a structure that encourages team decision-making, and at the same time allows rapid access to the entire organization, including the chain of command, both day-to-day actions and emergency situations can be optimized. As accountability and responsibility are pushed downward through the company, bringing them closer to the situations where action is needed, the quality of decisions and their ability to implement increases. The Operations Center provides the integration and alignment of decision-making throughout the firm, ensuring consistency of direction at all levels of the ICAS.

Unity and shared vision ensures cohesion of activities and identity and sense of purpose for the ICAS and for every employee. Continuous and widespread communication throughout the ICAS, the mobility of managers and knowledge workers, team charters and staff meeting agendas, and the integration efforts of the Operations Center and the Knowledge Center all serve to create organizational unity and widely understood vision.

Flow is facilitated by effective communication, trust, knowledge sharing, technology, people moving around in the organization, a clear direction, team structure, communities, the integrative competencies, good spaces for conversations and learning, and an open door policy for all employees. Where workers have careers instead of jobs, they are not directly competing with each other. Career advancement is based on their contribution to the entire firm as well as their local accomplishments.

Selectivity is the ability to filter incoming signals from the environment to identify those important to the ICAS. Selection cannot be performed by a single group within the firm. Signals come from everywhere, and all knowledge workers are attuned to their possible impact on the ICAS. Whether an environmental event is important or not depends upon its local context, the organization's direction, the local team's immediate objectives and goals, and recognition of what constitutes a threat to the organization and what constitutes an opportunity. The ability for knowledge workers to filter external events and patterns is aided by their mastery of the integrative competencies, the context awareness maintained by each team, and knowledge sharing through the Learning Center, the Operations Center, meshes and lessons learned reports, communities and personal relationship networks.

Optimum complexity is achieved when the options available to a team to deal with their external situation are sufficiently greater than the complexity of that situation. By using teams, networking and all available knowledge resources of the ICAS, the local variety of options available to teams can be made sufficient to at least successfully counter, if not influence, that external situation. Since systems and complexity thinking are familiar to all knowledge workers, ICAS is able to better perceive, interpret, and respond to uncertainty, rapid change, and variety in its environment.

Knowledge centricity is supported by the Knowledge Center, learning, ubiquitous networking, and the integrative competencies, as well as teams, communities, relationship networks, information systems, and technology. As an organization becomes aware of the important role that knowledge plays in understanding and responding to complex situations, it tends to create and use more knowledge. Knowledge grows on knowledge. In current high-tech companies and professional service firms, intangible assets can be eight to ten times the value of tangible assets. As the world moves toward services, information, and knowledge, the value of knowledge will increase relative to other organizational assets (Sveiby, 1997).

Porous boundaries are created first by corporate policies of listening and responding to all customers and being open to partnerships, joint ventures, alliances, and virtual teaming. The real day-to-day interactions that go on between the ICAS knowledge workers and their customers will significantly influence how open the firm is to data, information, events, etc. that occur in the external environment. All workers must be sensitive to the importance of what happens daily in their world of relationships. Even if senior leadership wants to work with other organizations and workers watch for things that happen outside the ICAS, there is still the internal problem of unquestioned beliefs, and unknown internal biases and prejudices that act to preclude seeing what is really happening. The integrative competencies of learning, knowing, and systems and complexity thinking help objectify incoming information.

The integrative competencies are supported by a knowledge and learning culture and by the Knowledge Center and team structure. Knowledge worker mobility and career management help make clear the need for the various integrative competencies, while self-organization and team empowerment pressure workers to know how to work together, learn, and understand their tasks. Emphasis on context, knowledge, collaboration, trust, and responsibility with the entire organization in mind brings home the need for mastering the competencies. The Learning Center, extensive network technologies, and a collaborative culture make it easy for knowledge workers to learn the integrative competencies they need and use them to make the best decisions and take the best actions.

REFERENCES

Ashkenas, R., D. Ulrich, T. Jick, and S. Kerr. *The Boundaryless Organization: Breaking the Chains of Organizational Structure*. San Francisco: Jossey-Bass, 2002.

Axelrod, R. and M. D. Cohen. *Harnessing Complexity: Organizational Implications of a Scientific Frontier*. New York: The Free Press, 1999.

Bennet, A. and D. Bennet. "The Partnership between Organizational Learning and Knowledge Management," in C. W. Holsapple (ed.), *Handbook on Knowledge Management 1: Knowledge Matters*. New York: Springer-Verlag, 2003.

Bennet, D. *IPT Learning Campus: Gaining Acquisition Results Through IPTs*. Alexandria, VA: Bellwether Learning Center, 1997.

Edelman G. and G. Tononi. *A Universe of Consciousness: How Matter Becomes Imagination*. New York: Basic Books, 2000.

Handy, C. *Understanding Organizations: How Understanding the Ways Organizations Actually Work Can Be Used to Manage Them Better*. New York: Oxford University Press, 1993.

Katzenbach, J. R. and D. K. Smith. *The Wisdom of Teams: Creating the High-Performance Organization*. New York: HarperCollins Publishers, 1993.

Lesser, E. L. *Knowledge and Social Capital: Foundations and Applications*. Boston: Butterworth-Heinemann, 2000.

Lesser, E. L., M. A. Fontaine, and J. A. Slusher. *Knowledge and Communities*. Boston: Butterworth-Heinemann, 2000.

McDermott, L. C., N. Brawley, and W. W. Waite. *World Class Teams: Working Across Borders*. New York: John Wiley & Sons, 1998.

Mohrman, S. A., J. A. Galbraith, E. E. Lawler, III, and Associates. *Tomorrow's Organization: Crafting Winning Capabilities in a Dynamic World*. San Francisco: Jossey-Bass Publishers, 1997.

Pasternack, B. and A. Viscio. *The Centerless Corporation: A New Model for Transforming Your Organization for Growth and Prosperity*. New York: Simon & Schuster, 1998.

Sadler, P. *The Seamless Organization: Building the Company of Tomorrow*, 4th ed. Dover, NH: Kogan Page US, 2001.

Senge, P. M. *The Fifth Discipline: The Art and Practice of the Learning Organization*. New York: Doubleday, 1990.

Smith, H. A. and J. D. McKeen. "Creating and Facilitating Communities of Practice," in Holsapple, C. W. (ed.) *Handbook on Knowledge Management 1: Knowledge Matters*. New York: Springer-Verlag, 2003.

Stacey, R., D. Griffin, and P. Shaw, *Complexity and Management: Fad or Radical Challenge To Systems Thinking*. New York: Routledge, 2000.

Sveiby, K. *The New Organizational Wealth: Managing & Measuring Knowledge-Based Assets*. San Francisco: Berrett-Koehler Publishers, 1997.

von Krogh, G., K. Ichijo, and I. Nonaka. *Enabling Knowledge Creation: How to Unlock the Mystery of Tacit Knowledge and Release the Power of Innovation*. New York: Oxford University Press, 2000.

Wenger, E. *Communities of Practice: Learning, Meaning, and Identity*. Cambridge: Cambridge University Press, 1998.

Chapter 7

THE ACTION CULTURE FOR SUCCESS

Although culture has been studied by scholars for many years and is a common concept among organizations, there is still no single definition of culture; it is something observed, felt, and lived, but cannot be defined in any precise set of words. Culture has been described as how the work gets done, as expected behavior, the amount of freedom given workers, the accepted or expected formal and informal relationships among workers, and even as a way of life or as a set of norms in the workplace. Culture often includes unstated assumptions about people, relationships, and knowledge. It develops over time from all of the interactions among the workforce modulated by a myriad of events and situations, both internal and external to the firm. Since culture is a characteristic that emerges from the members of the organizations and their interaction, it is unlikely that one could ever trace all of the influences and specific forces within a group of people that would create a given culture.

Culture is the source of organizational energy, or apathy, and a major determinant of organizational performance. As the varied descriptions of culture testify, it is a term that contains many factors that impact the effectiveness of the organization. The unstated rules of behavior inherent in culture and the acceptability of certain communication patterns over others are widely known but rarely discussed among workers. How the workforce perceives the organization, their feelings and expectations concerning management, and their image of the firm are all tied into culture. Every individual has an image of themselves and their role in the workplace. This self-image and how they feel about their own work and the organization is both in response to and directly affects culture, as well as playing a large role in determining both professional performance and personal satisfaction. In short, even though culture is a somewhat vague term, it is vital to the success of any organization.

From the perspective that the sum of all employee actions determines how well the firm performs, culture has to be understood as a vital factor in driving overall organizational performance. It is the *invisible medium* within which every knowledge worker moves, thinks, and acts every workday. It influences their feelings, frustrations, hopes, and motivations. Without being aware of it, workers adjust their behavior to conform more or less to the unstated expectations and beliefs of those around them. Like fish in water, we are all unaware of the influence of culture until we go to another organization. A culture can stifle independent thinking, reinforce power sources, or enhance collaboration and innovation. Thus this invisible medium we call culture plays a tremendous role in how the work gets done and how much knowledge workers contribute to the organization's goals.

In organizations that constrain the workforce, culture usually has a shadow or informal side, often called the informal network, which exists to get the work done in spite of official rules, policies, and formal procedures. Because culture has such an impact on the workforce, where all actions take form and determine organizational performance, the factors that drive culture become of critical importance to every organization. Culture emerges from a multidimensional set of influences that include the external environment, the workforce, managers and leaders, the structure, technology, the organization's history, and perception of the future. It results from the continuous interactions of all of these factors, takes time to develop and is very hard to change once it stabilizes. While culture is not static, it is slow to change.

Whatever description is chosen for the concept of culture, it emerges from the day-to-day work of the organization and cannot be predetermined, although there are many things that leaders and managers can do to influence it. See Chapter 10 for some approaches to influencing and creating a desired culture.

TYPES OF CULTURE

Handy suggests that the success of an organization depends heavily on the match between its structure and culture and that there is a large variety among organizations with respect to their cultures and structures (Handy, 1993). A number of authors have found it useful to divide cultures into categories for analysis and explanation. Goffee and Jones have identified networked, fragmented, mercenary and communal cultures (Chowdhury, 2003). Deal and Kennedy (1990), in demonstrating that culture depends upon the characteristics of the environment, found four types of cultures, or "corporate tribes," that matched their environments: macho, work-hard/play-hard, bet-your-company, and the process cultures. Handy (1993) suggests another set of four types of cultures: the power, role, person, and task cultures. Recognizing that for clarity we will look at extreme and somewhat simplistic descriptions, let's consider each of Handy's culture types as potential ICAS candidates.

The Power Culture

The power culture is based on a single, centralized source of power and decision-making. These organizations are frequently small, entrepreneurial, and dictatorial. They operate as a centralized web, can react quickly, and depend for their success on the judgment and capability of a few or only one person. In sub-organizations the finance department is often a power culture, with the Chief Financial Officer having a tight reign over all financial areas. In extreme cases of a power culture, workers have little freedom to act on their own and may become robots.

Clearly, such a culture does not leverage knowledge or make the best use of resources. All incoming information would have to come into the power source, an impossible situation in today's information-saturated environment. Organizational change would depend completely upon the central power source, with the entire organization's future riding on one individual's capacity to interpret that future and act wisely. In a large sense, the power culture is the antithesis of the ICAS, since the ICAS leverages knowledge through the technology support and networking capacity of all knowledge workers and localizes sense-making and action at the point where it is most prolific. In addition, localized actors are supported by centralized guidance, specific structures such as the Knowledge Center and the Operations Center, and a connectedness of choices through a widespread, cohesive understanding and acceptance of organizational purpose and interdependencies.

The Role Culture

The role culture or bureaucracy operates through its functional components and experts. Job descriptions are the foundation of work, with strong reliance on their accuracy and implementation. Each worker has a specific role to play in the system, with managers ensuring that workers carry out their preassigned duties. Power comes with position and the entire organization becomes rule-bound and conservative, with most individuals protecting their jobs and power. Knowledge *is* power and tends to be hoarded and protected by managers and functional experts. Learning is only for new employees and those seeking promotions. Memos, procedures, policies, and audit trails become part of the expectations of all workers. Creativity is not encouraged because it breaks the status quo and threatens positional relationships. Processes and procedures are the dominant ways that work gets done. Efficiency is the hallmark of the role-based culture. Security and reliability are strengths of the organization, and long-term employment is the norm. If the environment and market of the role culture organization are stable, the organization can survive and be successful.

Change is difficult for the role culture and the typical reaction is to work harder and keep doing what was done in the past. Rapid response is very hard because it requires bypassing rules and procedures. Since decisions are hierarchical, there is a built-in bias against new ideas. Everyone in a decision chain has to say yes for an idea to be implemented, but any one person in the chain can kill the idea. From an ICAS selectivity viewpoint, role-based organizations are extremely selective because they only recognize those things that fall within their process and procedure spaces. For this reason, they miss many outside events and opportunities. Since the ICAS is intended to survive and excel in a turbulent, complex world, the role-based culture would stifle and paralyze it. Although the support functions may be process oriented, continuous learning will still need to occur as market changes necessitate new processes. As with the power culture, the role culture would have difficulty surviving in an ICAS-like environment. This culture would be unable to respond to external demands and competition would pass the organization by.

The Person Culture

The person culture puts the individual first, with everything else providing support. There is little or no overall cohesion throughout the organization. The person culture is more of a collection of individuals who band together to make it easier for each of them to do their own thing. There is no organizational objective, and little gain in knowledge or leveraging of resources. Other than a few agreed-upon rules, there is no mechanism for controlling individuals within the person culture, nor is there a mechanism for collaboration. This culture embeds more a group orientation than a team-based organization. Its capability would at best be the sum of the capabilities of all of its members. There is little synergy, no emergent properties, no organizational learning, and no gain in performance; it is more chaotic than complex adaptive (see Chapter 19). All of these limitations make it clear that such a culture is not capable of providing the performance needed by the ICAS in a turbulent environment.

The Task Culture

The task culture focuses on each task or project. Its goal is to get the job done. As Handy (1993) notes:

> To this end the culture seeks to bring together the appropriate resources, the right people at the right level of the organization, and to let them get on with it. Influence is based more on expert power than on position or personal power, although these sources have their effect. Influence is more widely dispersed than in other cultures, and each individual tends to think he has more of it. It is a team culture, where team's work tends to be the common enemy obliterating individual objectives and most status and style differences (p. 188).

The task culture works well where flexibility and quick response are important. This culture cannot be controlled in the sense of the "control" in a power culture. People are given some level of freedom and responsibility for accomplishing their assigned tasks, usually through a team. By creating teams as needed, there is a good capability for adapting to changing markets and environmental pressures. From a knowledge perspective, the task culture gets a gain from its effective use of teams and their ability to leverage team-member expertise into improved problem-solving and decision-making. However, it is very difficult for a task culture to develop knowledge workers with deep knowledge in specialized areas.

The task approach works well when funds are available and the organization is growing, and in low- and medium-risk environments. It is often used in product development, acquisition programs, and professional services. The common matrix organization, a compromise between project management and functional specialization, is a modern implementation of the task culture. However, during tough times, senior managers in task cultures feel that they must tighten control and ration resources, creating real internal problems with ongoing projects and the workforce. As management takes back control, rations resources, and moves people around, the organization may be pressed toward a role culture, emphasizing procedures and processes to ensure results.

The task culture would seem to be a good candidate for the ICAS, and in some ways it is. Many professionals prefer the task culture because of the freedom it provides them as well as the learning gained through team assignments. The culture is somewhat adaptive so long as the environment does not change too quickly. However, when rapid change occurs, local teams may have little or no additional support from the organization and can become overwhelmed. Even adding more resources does not solve the problem because of the learning curve time delay. By the time others get up to speed, the change has created something new. Flexibility is also a problem for task cultures because moving people around is difficult; people usually have jobs with specific position descriptions. Another problem is the lack of structures and social attributes needed to sustain cohesion throughout the organization. In task cultures, hierarchies are used above the teams and information must pass through these hierarchies, a fairly slow process for any medium or large organization. Thus the firm's reaction time may be too slow to keep up with the environment.

ASSUMPTIONS FOR THE ICAS CULTURE

Considering the types of cultures presented above, each has some attributes that could have a role in the ICAS. When fast, corporate-level decisions must be made, senior leadership must step up to the plate and make the hard choices. In support functions where operating stability is the norm, the efficiency of the role culture is well suited. When the ICAS needs experts on specialized topics, it may call upon individuals with deep knowledge who tend to do their own thing; and the task culture, with its teams and bent toward workforce freedom, provides a framework for ICAS self-organizing teams. However, none of these alone gives us enough of the culture needed to succeed in the future environment.

The ICAS culture is predicated on the following assumptions:

- Organizations will increasingly be faced with rapid change, uncertainty, nonlinearity, complexity, and anxiety.
- The future is unknowable (to regard as true beyond doubt) but not unfathomable (to penetrate to the meaning or nature of; to comprehend) (*American Heritage Dictionary*, 1992).
- Individual actions make *the* difference.
- All individuals are creative, and can learn and develop knowledge.
- Knowledge workers want to perform and contribute to an organization they respect.
- No one individual possesses the information or knowledge to understand complex situations.
- Knowledge can be leveraged through strategy, structure, and collaboration.
- Trust, mutual respect, fairness, and collaboration are critical for leveraging knowledge.
- To survive, the organization must support all of its knowledge workers. Learning, making mistakes, and changing behavior are survival and success necessities.
- Strong control is a myth, influence is possible, and dialogue is essential.

THE ACTION CULTURE

The ICAS culture is an action culture because of the importance of every individual knowledge worker taking the right action at the right place and time. The core of the action culture is built on the foundation of creating, leveraging, and applying knowledge anywhere, anytime it is needed. Recall our definition of knowledge as the potential and actual ability to take effective action, recognizing that effective action becomes harder and harder as the environment gets more dynamic, nonlinear, complex, and unknowable. If knowledge is the primary source for understanding the landscape and taking right actions, then knowledge must be the central consideration of the ICAS and its culture. A good structure will provide the framework for learning and getting the work done. A good culture will enhance worker attitudes and motivations for doing the work and taking effective actions.

From a culture viewpoint the question becomes: What kind of culture best supports the knowledge worker's motivation and ability to have, or get, the knowledge needed to take the most appropriate actions in an uncertain, unpredictable, and possibly unknowable situation? There is no one *right* culture for our turbulent world landscape; the scope of the culture throughout any given organization is dependent upon how much of the firm has to deal with this world landscape. The action culture seeks to combine the best of all worlds.

While creativity takes many forms, it typically needs the freedom to think, play, and share ideas with others. Trust, integrity, mutual respect, and a non-judgmental atmosphere play a significant role in real communication, that is, *the sharing of understanding*. They are also essential for the creation of new knowledge and for the leveraging of what several individuals know. Practices such as brainstorming, dialogue, inquiry, communities of practice, and group discussions all help knowledge workers share and create knowledge (Couger, 1995; Robinson and Stern, 1997).

To implement such practices the action culture exhibits an atmosphere of trust, open communication, collaboration, and freedom from fear and reproach. While there are managers and leaders, they are not autocratic or controlling but more like mentors, colleagues, and supporters. It will take unusual professionals to be able to take on responsibility for projects and at the same time give colleagues the freedom to think creatively and have a strong voice in their own activities. Leadership in the action culture is very different than the classical models offered in the past. Leadership is a distributed phenomenon, where individuals at all levels and in all specialties work with others to ensure multi-directional collaboration, line-of-sight activity consistent with organizational level objectives, and the rapid and effective leveraging of resources, especially knowledge. See Chapter 9 for a detailed discussion of collaborative leadership.

Power

Power in the action culture is rarely used and mostly invisible, with senior people guiding, setting the corporate direction, and making minimal decisions on local direction and implementation. There are limits set by leaders—limits designed to expand possibilities, focus attention, and create intentions. Limits can facilitate positive growth. When referring to ideas, each of us lives in a field of possibilities. The limits imposed by defining ideas within a framework encourages deeper understanding and spurs the emergence of new ideas, with the potential for those ideas to go far beyond the defining framework of their birth. In other words, setting limits provides focus that can lead to new thought. Although this may sound paradoxical, where limits overlap among workers new interpretations may arise, increasing options (optimum complexity) and simultaneously focusing attention and enhancing intentions. Much of the power in the ICAS lies with teams, with individual knowledge workers running a close second. Knowledge workers have significant influence over what actions they take, and the related responsibility. In any organization, some workers will perform better than others and those that do become the quiet leaders who easily and naturally guide others.

Flexibility

Individuals have considerable flexibility to move around in the organization. In fact, they are encouraged to do so to foster continuous learning and maintain the diversity and instability needed for creativity and adaptability. Knowledge workers are able to work alone, in teams, on multiple and different tasks, at varying paces, with other companies, and with senior leaders. Since all social relationships assume mutual respect and trust, there is no need for inhibition and reserve during vertical communication. Workers are assigned a senior or mid-level leader for career development and mentoring. These mentors have the responsibility of keeping the organization's fundamental values and assumptions alive and stable while transferring their tacit knowledge to others through shared experiences, mental models, and technical skills (Nonaka and Takeuchi, 1995; Nonaka, 1999).

Knowledge workers are expected to work with anyone and everyone in the ICAS, and to do so in a manner consistent with the company's values and purpose. They can learn this only through practice, by frequently sharing assignments with other workers. Each worker's relationships may extend throughout the ICAS and beyond if partnerships and other connections are considered. Networking, both personal and technological, is the norm and expected of all knowledge workers. Social relationships are a foundation of leveraging knowledge and all workers contribute and utilize them. Where an individual does not, or will not, collaborate and work with others, coworkers quickly recognize such behavior and must either accept, isolate or remove the worker, depending on circumstances. The action culture cannot afford very many loners who refuse to work together. *Knowledge shared is power squared* (Davenport and Prusak, 1998; Havens and Haas, 2000).

Careful selection and indoctrination procedures maximize the hiring of knowledge workers who can fit into the action culture. An individual's character, basic values, learning ability, capacity for professional growth, and social maturity may count more over the long term than special expertise or years of experience. Their tolerance for mistakes—and ability to learn from those mistakes—may count more than their desire for perfection. The action culture accepts mistakes as necessary for learning and changing. It encourages individual reflection and questioning of all significant decisions and builds upon diversity of thinking and the internal challenge of assumptions and hidden beliefs that mold conclusions. Intelligent behavior is rewarded and expected. Just as the ICAS exhibits intelligent behavior at the organizational level, its culture expects individuals to think things through, plan ahead, be good at solving problems, seek knowledge from others, and learn from everyone's mistakes.

Individuals working in an action culture have an unusual self-image. They see themselves as supporters, contributors, leaders, and teachers all at the same time. This requires strong egos but not large egos. The difference is that big egos live on flattery while strong egos have confidence in themselves and their thinking without the need to always be right. They take pride in their work, but much of it includes others' work as well. Their allegiance is to the company, not to an individual in the organizational chain. Their work will often be at the front lines where customers, partners, and regulators are offering opportunities or threats that they must continually balance with internal goals and limits.

The Environment

The environment places multiple and unusual demands on the ICAS workforce, that in turn impacts the resultant culture. These demands require rapid response, continuous learning, knowledge-leveraging through teams, risk-taking from trial-and-error actions, and creativity to develop optimum complexity. To survive, the ICAS culture must be adaptable to counter uncertainty, provide damage control to dampen nonlinear phenomena, and constantly ensure a connectedness of choices to maintain the ICAS purpose cohesion.

Cultural forms arise from adapting to local and environmental circumstances. The resulting culture then reacts back on the environment. This give-and-take, co-evolutionary relationship is a signature of organisms living in an ecology. Each participant, in this case the ICAS and its marketplace, molds and influences the other, thereby creating itself and its identity (Capra, 2002; Maturana and

Varela, 1987). The action culture is adaptive to the demands of the environment: stakeholders, technology advancements, government regulations, competitive practices, economic swings, and the overall business landscape.

How the Work Gets Done

In the ICAS the work gets done through interaction with the external world, self-organization at the local level, multiple collaboration through teams, networks and formal chains, knowledge creation, sharing and leveraging to respond to external requirements, flexible processes and procedures, invisible technology, and structural support centers that respond to workforce needs. A good structure provides the mechanisms for effectively *getting the work done*. A good culture can enhance worker attitudes and motivations for *doing the work*. While knowledge workers try to find ways of getting their work done with or without help from the structure or culture, their efficiency and morale can be significantly affected by the organization's structure and culture.

Technology plays a strong role in supporting ICAS knowledge workers and influences culture by providing information resources, network and communication technologies; knowledge, virtual learning, and community collaboration systems; and team collaboration artifacts such as electronic whiteboards, displays, and software packages. Video conferencing and the Internet greatly affect how information and knowledge are created and shared. Overall, technology helps create and support the ICAS emergent characteristics of flow, knowledge centricity, optimum complexity, and selectivity. As technology changes the way that work gets done, it influences the culture. Although ideally in the future technology would be invisible, currently it is the interrelationship between workers, software, and hardware that changes work processes and thereby knowledge worker behavior (Coleman, 1997; Kaku, 1997).

To further explore the role of culture in the ICAS organization, let's use a metaphor from Freudian psychology.

THE ORGANIZATIONAL EGO AND ID

From psychology (Freudian theory), we get the concept of the ego, that aspect of personality that encompasses the sense of "self" in contact with the real world. To represent the instinctive aspects of personality, Freud uses the concept of the id (Gerow, 1992). Viewing an organization as having a culture, an emergent characteristic similar to personality in an individual, we can extrapolate that culture is made up of both an ego and an id. The ego provides that portion of the inner identity of the organization that faces the world with rational thinking, and the id represents past experiences and beliefs converted to automated behavior and emotions through time.

The culture (ego and id) of the organization is a powerful energy force. While the organizational ego serves as the watchtower and processor for incoming information, the id provides the energy and spirit for action and resolve. Ego represents the rational, objective part of culture and id represents the emotional, subjective part. Whether viewed in the individual or organizational setting, the ego and id can be strong advocates or barriers to change, and both must be recognized and dealt with effectively.

All too often, senior managers believe that since their workforce is empowered and flexible, they need deal only with the ego side of culture, providing a set of reasons why change must occur and some plan to accomplish that change. They may consider the id side as touchy-feely and therefore unnecessary. Freudian theory reminds us that people act consistent with their personal knowledge, beliefs, instincts, and feelings—especially in times of possible danger and all significant organizational change will be perceived as threatening to some workers. Change can be addressed in terms of both the ego and id, with the super ego considered the moral standards that restrain the ego.

Sensory inputs provide the stimuli for the organizational culture's attention, or inattention. The external senses provide what Thomas Reid, a Scottish philosopher who lived, thought, and wrote over 200 years ago, called a conception and an invincible belief of the existence of external objects. Reid (1813) credited a "double Province" to the senses: to make us perceive and to make us feel. Reid uses the smelling of a rose as an example. When we smell a rose two separate and parallel things happen: a sweet, subjective smell enters through our olfactory system and we perceive the external and objective presence of a rose. What Reid is getting at is that the sense of smell is something that directly affects us as individuals, a subjective experience, a feeling. But the perception of an external presence provides us with objective facts to make judgments about the external objective world. We will see this same duality showing up later in the difference between having knowledge of x and knowing x, or having a deep knowledge that brings x into our being, our experience (see Chapter 20).

The culture of the organization, then, carries the residue (memory) of feelings about the organization and the external world, while at the same time it is constantly under the influence of its own belief set which is itself being continuously examined as new external and internal information flows within the organization (see Figure 7-1).

Thus, in the regular course of events, the organizational ego will modify itself and change or flow into a somewhat different ego. Such is the usual process with cultures. They change slowly, never losing all of their history nor accepting all of the new ways, with the id portion taking longer to adjust to the new changes than the ego. When an organization's culture undergoes traumatic shock such

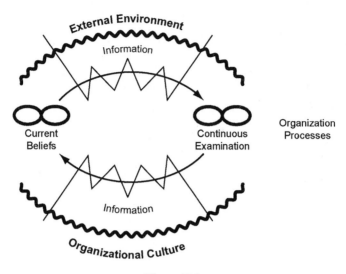

Figure 7-1
The Continuous Examination Process

as massive layoffs, mergers, or impending dissolution, there is a frantic attempt to create alternate stories or self-images to handle the situation. But egos have their id partners that carry the memory of the images and experiences of traumatic shock. If all humans behaved rationally, there would be very few overweight people, no smokers, and wars would be history. If organizational cultures followed their ego, most would be high performance, knowledge centric, and adaptive. However, such organizations are rarely found.

The ICAS culture learns to live with change and builds a strong ego to one that is in consonance with a strong id. As the ICAS experiences setbacks and successes, its id will become more robust and not react and respond with fear and skepticism as so often happens during times of stress. The id is also strengthened through the trust, networking, and mobility of the ICAS knowledge workers. There is nothing like experience and success, especially through bad times, to strengthen the will.

In the more highly competitive world of work, culture has long taken the brunt of blame when an organization is unable to change and successfully adapt to its environment; and, of course, this is often true. When a bureaucratic organization is floundering—or perceived to be floundering—management teams spend weeks developing new rules of work and behavior, then directing subordinates to follow them. While visible efforts are made to respond to these new rules, over time behaviors usually fall back into old habits that work. In short, most organizations get the job done around these new rules, not because of them. Every stable organization is stable for a reason. The reason is because there exists a balance of forces throughout the organization that are usually unseen but come into play when the organization becomes unbalanced. When this happens the counterforce serves to regain the original balance, another perspective on resistance to change (see Chapter 19).

In summary, the action culture is the invisible medium through which the ICAS knowledge worker seeks information, interprets and analyzes it, creates and shares knowledge, makes decisions, and takes action on issues and market opportunities. This culture plays a significant role in energizing and helping each worker make the right decisions and take the best actions. To do this, the culture has the characteristics of widespread trust, continuous learning, high integrity, and fair treatment of all workers. In addition it encourages creativity, allows a high degree of self-determination, and supports knowledge sharing and collaboration, all within an equalitarian base. The action culture is action oriented, flexible, and responsive to surprises. Since all cultures emerge from their organizations and cannot be predetermined, the action culture is nurtured, guided, and supported in a manner that will push it in the right direction. Chapter 10 addresses the challenge of creating and sustaining an action culture.

REFERENCES

American Heritage Dictionary of the English Language. Boston: Houghton Mifflin Company, 1992.

Capra, F. *The Hidden Connections: Integrating the Biological, Cognitive, and Social Dimensions of Life into a Science of Sustainability*. New York: Doubleday, 2002.

Chowdhury, S. (ed.). *Organization 21C: Someday All Organizations Will Lead This Way*. New York: FT Prentice-Hall, 2003.

Coleman, D. *Groupware: Collaborative Strategies for Corporate LANs and Intranets*. Upper Saddle River, NJ: Prentice-Hall, 1997.

Couger, J. *Creative Problem-solving and Opportunity Finding*. Danvers, MA: Boyd and Fraser Publishing Company, 1995.

Davenport, T. H. and L. Prusak. *Working Knowledge: How Organizations Manage What They Know*. Boston, MA: Harvard Business School Press, 1998.

Deal, T. and A. Kennedy. *Corporate Cultures: The Rites and Rituals of Corporate Life*. New York: Addison-Wesley Publishing Company, 1990.

Gerow, J. *Psychology: an Introduction*. New York: HarperCollins, 1992.

Handy, C. *Understanding Organizations: How Understanding the Ways Organizations Actually Work Can Be Used to Manage Them Better*. New York: Oxford University Press, 1993.

Havens, C. and D. Haas. "How Collaboration Fuels Knowledge," in J. W. Cortada and J. A. Woods, (eds), *The Knowledge Management Yearbook 2000–2001*. Boston, MA: Butterworth-Heinemann, 2000.

Kaku, M. *Visions: How Science Will Revolutionize the 21st Century*. New York: Anchor Books/Doubleday, 1997.

Maturana, H. R. and F. J. Varela. *The Tree of Knowledge: The Biological Roots of Human Understanding*. Boston: Shambhala, 1987.

Nonaka, I. "The Dynamics of Knowledge Creation," in R. Ruggles and D. Holtshouse (eds), *The Knowledge Advantage*. Oxford, England: Ernst & Young, 1999.

Nonaka, I. and H. Takeuchi. *The Knowledge-Creating Company: How Japanese Companies Create the Dynamics of Innovation*. New York: Oxford University Press, 1995.

Reid, T. *Essays on the Intellectual Powers of Man* (ed. D. Stewart). Charlestown: Samuel Etheridge, 1785, 1813.

Robinson, A. and J. Stern. *Corporate Creativity: How Innovation and Improvement Actually Happen*. San Francisco: Berrett-Kochler Publishers, 1997.

Chapter 8

THE FOUR MAJOR ORGANIZATIONAL PROCESSES

In their book entitled *Harnessing Complexity* Axelrod and Cohen (1999) used evolutionary biology, computer science, and social design to build a framework for improving how people work together. Using the concept of a complex adaptive system, they conclude that three qualities that organizations should cultivate are variation, interaction, and selection. Variety provides the range of ideas and options needed to counter external complexity. Interaction among knowledge workers provides variety and establishes the right balance between variety and uniformity—what we call *local freedom and organizational coherence*. Selectivity, in this framework, means deciding which ideas and actions are to be retained for their successes and which are to be shelved or discarded.

From an ICAS view, to successfully influence and adapt to a complex world, it has to continuously create a wide range of options (ideas, strategies, and actions), then select from that range those options that appear to solve the specific complex problems at hand. The ICAS must then take action on the selected options, observe the results and amplify the successful approaches while filtering out failures. Undoubtedly, this is a somewhat trial-and-error approach driven by the dynamic complexity of the environment but ameliorated by an understanding of complexity and the knowledge and knowing competency of ICAS knowledge workers and their teams. A key question then becomes, how can the ICAS implement this approach?

We suggest that in every organization there are four processes that are used continuously, although often they are unconscious, invisible, or merged together, depending on the problem and experience of the actor(s). Many actions are taken without realizing that a decision was made before taking the action. Often decisions are so natural that there is no problem-solving needed; no options are generated because it is assumed that the decision is clear. Creative ideas may not be needed if the problem is standard and easily understood. In a stable environment this is a natural way of doing work; in an unstable, unpredictable world it is smart to rethink the obvious solutions and take the time to go through all necessary processes before jumping into action. The processes can be performed by an individual acting alone or via teams or groups, and each process may be performed by different individuals or teams.

These four major processes—creativity, problem-solving, decision-making, and implementation—together constitute a procedure for ensuring all aspects of a situation are taken into account. There is no one right way to use the processes; their relevance and specific methodology depend on the problem, the knowledge workers, and their knowledge and goals. Through these processes, the ICAS applies its capabilities to produce products, support customers, and deal with external influences. Each of the four major processes is discussed below in some detail.

CREATIVITY

Plato viewed creativity as both mysterious and divine: "For the poet is an airy thing, a winged and a holy thing; and he cannot make poetry until he becomes inspired and goes out of his senses and no mind is left in him [...]; not by art, then, they make their poetry [...]; but by divine dispensation [...];" (Warmington and Rouse, 1984, p. 18). The romantic could substitute the word "exceptional" for "divine," glorifying creative people as gifted with talent (insight or intuition) that others lack. Arthur Koestler (1975) went beyond the inspirational and romantic and tried to understand how creativity happened. He felt that, "The moment of truth, the sudden emergence of a new insight, is an act of intuition. Such intuitions give the appearance of miraculous flashes, or short circuits of reasoning. In fact they may be likened to an immersed chain, of which only the beginning and the end are visible above the surface of consciousness. The diver vanishes at one end of the chain and comes up at the other end, guided by invisible links" (p. 211). Koestler's words insinuate more, but they do not explain the more.

Henri Poincaré (2001) suggests that creativity tugs on the unconscious. He describes four phases of creativity, later named by the mathematician Jacques Hadamard as preparation, incubation, illumination, and verification. The initial phase, *preparation*, is the conscious probing of a problem or an idea. The second phase, *incubation*, is while the conscious mind is focused elsewhere and may last for minutes, months, or years. During this time the unconscious mind may well be contemplating the challenge and trying to make sense of the situation. Poincaré credited this phase with the novelties denied through waking, rational thought. The flash of insight, or tug, comes in the third phase, *illumination*, when creative thoughts burst through the unconscious stirring of incubation into the conscious where it can be explored and tested in the fourth phase, *verification or validation*.

Poincaré (1982) visualized the creative thought mechanism of the unconscious as similar to the workings of the atom. "Figure the future elements of our combinations as something like the hooked atoms of Epicurus. During the complete repose of the mind, these atoms are motionless, they are, so to speak hooked to the wall [...]; On the other hand, during a period of apparent rest and unconscious work, certain of them are detached from the wall and put in motion. They flash in every direction [...]; [like] a swarm of gnats, or, if you prefer a more learned comparison, like the molecules of gas in the kinematic theory of gases. Then their mutual impacts may produce new combinations" (p. 389). The role of this preliminary conscious work is to mobilize certain of these atoms, "to unhook them from the wall and put them in swing [...];. After this shaking up imposed upon them by our will, these atoms do not return to their primitive rest. They freely continue their dance. Now, our will did not choose them at random; it pursued a perfectly determined aim. The mobilized atoms are therefore not any atoms whatsoever; they are those from which we might reasonably expect the desired solution" (Poincaré, 1982, p. 389).

Teams and communities can facilitate these phases of creativity. Ideas are probed through the dialogue of teams and the virtual interactions of communities, placed in incubation as knowledge workers intermingle these exchanges with actions. Illumination occurs in many forms, possibly by several members of the team or community, and as it is shared offers the potential for quick verification and validation, as well as the opportunity for additional probing leading to additional new ideas. These ideas are the mental implements used to gain competitive advantage. Since ideas build upon ideas, the more these implements are used, the more ideas available for use, and the more opportunity for the organization to develop and fulfill its own unique competitive advantage.

Boden (1991) breaks creative thought (or creative people) into two types: *P-creative* (psychological or personal) and *H-creative* (historical). P-creative ideas are fundamentally novel with respect to the individual mind, the person who has them, and H-creative ideas are historically grounded, fundamentally novel with respect to the whole of recorded human history. Her point is that the H-creative ideas, which by definition are also P-creative, are the ones that are socially recognized as creative, but P-creative ideas are possible in every human being. Boden purports that creativity as a personal quality is judged (during most of the person's lifetime, if not in obituaries) primarily in terms of P-creativity.

Global connectivity, access to an exponentially increasing amount of data and information, and expanding virtual relationship networks provide the opportunity for knowledge workers to build on others' ideas and to contribute their own insights to the network. It follows that this common virtual availability of ideas combined with P-creativity supports the continual emergence of new ideas, with the potential for similar ideas simultaneously emerging throughout the world. In this environment it is not just the creation of new ideas, but how quickly the organization can comprehend, select, and act on these new ideas that will provide sustainable competitive advantage.

The team leaders and senior leadership of the ICAS have significant influence on the development and effectiveness of creativity throughout the organization. The team leader has strong influence over the operating environment within which team members interact. A creative environment requires open communication, collaboration, a playful attitude, and critical thinking, coupled with a clear vision and objective. Such an environment encourages new ideas and different ways of seeing things, resulting in team member out-of-the-box suggestions for solving problems.

Creative ideas, like everything new, have uncertainty that inherently carries risk with it. The focus here is on the ability of teams to be innovative in creating new and more effective ways of dealing with complexity. *Innovation* means the creation of new ideas and the transformation of those ideas into useful applications. Both are needed to get results, both are difficult, and each requires its own process for success.

As a general rule, teams have a tendency to follow their leader's approach to risk-taking. If the team leader supports new ideas and is willing to take prudent risks, so will the team. Over time teams develop a certain philosophy on creativity. They may spend little time questioning the routine problems and use solid, well-proven approaches. Or they may constantly question all aspects of their work while searching for opportunities to find exceptional solutions, new ways to add value to customers and deal with complex issues. The team leader usually sets the tone for which approach is taken, perhaps without the team even being aware of it.

Senior leadership can also encourage creativity. By follow-up actions like accepting reasonable mistakes and not rejecting new ideas, they demonstrate the acceptability and importance of everyone in the ICAS investigating, evaluating, and proposing creative solutions to problems. Building and sustaining a creative and innovative environment is challenging and difficult. Consistency of senior leadership support helps give all knowledge workers the confidence and incentive for taking risks through creativity and innovation. There are typically four stages in the creative process (Bennet, 1997):

- Stage one is the problem, situation, or opportunity identification where a thorough discussion of the issues and objectives occurs among interested/responsible organizational employees to ensure common understanding of the desired effort.

- Stage two is gathering relevant information needed to limit potential new ideas and to provide stimulation for idea generation.
- Stage three is the actual generation of ideas via brainstorming or some other technique.
- Stage four is the discussion, evaluation, and prioritization of ideas to determine which ones are the best.

Each of these stages is built on social capital, the interaction among individuals, and exchange of ideas, or the idea of flow. In the ICAS setting there is less formality to this process. As people are in close and flexible proximity to each other, with a nomadic flavor, and there is the expectation of responsibility at all levels of the organization, the innovation process occurs and reoccurs throughout the day. The close relationships and rapport of employees, and the non-threatening, supportive organizational climate, provide the opportunity for reaching the level of trust necessary for optimal sharing, and optimal innovation.

Simultaneously, the external environment within which the ICAS operates coupled with the permeable and porous boundaries, where people as well as information flow in and out of teams, communities, and the organization itself, keeps the organization and the individual in a state of flux. Belgian physical chemist Ilya Prigogine (1997), who won the Nobel prize in 1977, believes that this state of flux leads to creative responses. He suggests that people are open systems, and that the internal energy flows and complex connections within each individual maintain a constant state of flux, so to speak. Any additional stress on this state causes a jump to a higher state of creativity. "Experimental evidence supporting Prigogine's theory in chemistry includes molecules cooperating in vast patterns in reaction to a new situation; bacteria that, when placed in a medium that would normally kill them, develop a new interaction that enables them to survive at a higher level; the Belousov-Zhabotinsky reaction, in which beautiful scroll-like forms unfold in a chemical solution in a laboratory dish while the colors of the solution oscillate; and complex patterns occurring in a sudden and nonlinear fashion on the surface of oils when they are heated" (Ray and Myers, 1989, p. 29).

Learning makes creativity easier and creativity reinforces learning. Creativity, learning, and flexibility are closely coupled and, as a group, will significantly improve the ICAS's ability to develop better service and products.

The generation and acceptance of new ideas is hard because of unconscious assumptions that inhibit new ways of seeing things. For example, a typical assumption might be that career success in the ICAS is achieved by playing it safe and not taking any risks. New ideas and innovative approaches may then be rejected as dangerous and risky. On the other hand, if the perception is that career success depends on the overall quality of work, while accepting the need for prudent risk-taking, a different view of creativity and risk would result. Creative ideas would be encouraged and have a much better chance of survival.

Each assumption leads to an entirely different set of ideas that are acceptable for consideration. A useful technique to aid *thinking out of the box* is to first surface the basic assumptions of individuals and teams that may underlie an initial response, then change that set of assumptions and follow the consequences. This frees up the mind to generate more and different ideas.

Brainstorming

Brainstorming is the classical process by which groups of people can generate a large number of new ideas related to some problem facing the group. The process starts with the facilitator describing the sequence of events and the ground rules. There is usually a discussion of the problem, and the context within which the team is trying to develop ideas. However, there are no restrictions on the nature of the ideas so long as they have some relevance. Going around the room, each team member offers one idea to the group while the facilitator writes the idea on a whiteboard in front of the group. No discussion of the idea is permitted other than clarification. This process continues as quickly as possible, continuing around the room several times so that each member has several opportunities to offer ideas.

The result is a large number of ideas generated in a very short time. After they are all on the whiteboard, the ICAS team studies them one at a time. Each idea is discussed in terms of its meaning, application, and potential value in solving the issue at hand. Through this process the best ideas are selected. These can be further analyzed by subgroups or individuals who then make recommendations back to the team. A significant part of this process is the prevention of negative comments when the idea is first offered to the team. It is crucial to first look at how the idea can be made to work before evaluating its negative aspects.

One problem with the above technique is that once the team hears several ideas, their minds may be influenced and thereby focused on the general trend or nature of these ideas. This can subconsciously limit thinking and the ability to be creative. Recent research indicates that the brainstorming approach may be improved by having each person privately write down a short list of their ideas before offering them to the team. After all team members have written these down, they go around the room as before.

In addition to brainstorming, there are other techniques to facilitate creativity. These include the nominal group technique, metaphor/analogies, interrogatories, and problem reversal. Couger (1995) provides a detailed description of these and other insights into the innovation process. Of particular interest to the ICAS is the optimal team size for innovation. Couger addresses this issue as follows: "Most of the creativity techniques described in this book can be used by individuals or groups. However, there are optimal group sizes. Some thirty-three studies of group size have resulted in a data set that shows that the optimal group size is two persons. Dyads were found to be superior because two individuals can achieve rapport more easily, reaching the level of trust necessary for optimal sharing. Stated another way, it is important for you to find a person with whom you have good rapport to facilitate creativity most effectively. Two persons can bounce ideas off each other in a less-threatening, more supportive climate" (p. 262).

Given that Couger's idea has merit, a team might consider dividing into pairs to create innovative ideas prior to bringing the pairs together for group analysis and discussion. On the other hand, note that Couger says that achieving rapport and trust are the determinant factors in generating ideas. An ICAS team that has achieved a high level of collaboration will have the rapport and trust that allows the entire team to be creative as a group.

Getting all knowledge workers to buy into a new idea is a prerequisite for selling and implementing the idea. To achieve team consensus and develop the internal fortitude to try new approaches and take managed risks requires a team with confidence, mutual trust, and a can-do attitude. This spirit of collaborative success, when achieved, can be one of the greatest strengths of the ICAS.

In *The Care and Feeding of Ideas, a Guidebook to Encouraging Creativity,* James Adams (1986) acknowledges that all people are creative and all people change, that "creativity and change are two sides of the same coin" (p. 3). Adams goes on to state that creativity has something to do with being smart and that we all want to express our unique capabilities and feelings, so creativity is important. In the ICAS there is a marriage of creative individuals and a creative organizational culture and structure that provides an idea-nurturing internal environment in response to a turbulent external environment. The emergent flow characteristics make creativity more likely and selectivity and porous boundaries provide plenty of new ideas and challenges to sustain the energy of knowledge workers. While creating and sustaining the right internal environment is challenging and difficult, over time an organizational culture develops around the philosophy of trying out new ideas, and creativity and innovation become the accepted and expected way of doing business.

Generating new ideas is sometimes, but not always, a predecessor to effective problem-solving.

PROBLEM-SOLVING

Problem-solving is one of the most important processes in the organization. Taking inputs from the creative process as needed, the problem-solving process provides the links between ideas, problems, and decisions. The output of the problem-solving team or community is a solution set of alternatives that provide ways to achieve a desired situation or problem solution.

There is no one process for solving problems. Every problem places its own demands on the problem-solver. There are, however, different levels of problems and their associated techniques that improve a team's ability to develop solution alternatives. For example, for even relatively simple situations, it may be difficult to separate the problem from its symptoms. Under such circumstances, the Japanese *five whys* approach (Swanson, 1995) can very effectively and quickly home in on the problem. This approach means asking the question "why?" and when answered asking "why?" of the answer, continuing to dig down in this manner five levels or until the root cause is apparent.

Where people, organizations, and complex relationships exist, it is often impossible to identify causes. There may well be *several or many causes* that have created the situation, or problem. For the most complex problems, identifying the problem or even reaching agreement that a problem exists can be a real challenge to a team. Every team member will see the situation in their own, unique way. In a very real sense, problems exist in the mind of the observer. Before a team can solve a problem, it must first agree on exactly what the problem is, and why it is a problem.

A problem can be viewed as an *undesirable situation.* Ideally, its solution then becomes a new, desirable situation. This process of finding ways to change an undesirable situation into a desirable one is a creative part of problem-solving, or the process of gap analysis. For the most complex problems it will likely be impossible to "change the situation." What is more likely is a solution that includes influencing the problem and changing/adapting the team's actions to accommodate a *mutual* adjustment in the relationships between the team and its environment.

Problem-solving can also be used to find and take advantage of opportunities, with an opportunity defined as a desired situation that is preferable to the current state of affairs. From a classical view, *the more options available to solve a problem, the better the final solution.* This simple heuristic drives the organization to share large problems and issues widely, and to welcome the thinking and passion of those who contribute critical thinking and creative ideas. Dorothy Leonard-Barton (1995) suggests selecting people to participate on problem-solving teams "*because* their ideas, biases, personalities, values, and skills conflict— not in spite of their differences. Why? Because an effective guard against people's considering only a few problem-solving alternatives or, worse, framing problems so that they can be solved only with familiar solutions is to involve a variety of people, with their diverse signature skills, in the task" (p. 63).

For the most complex problems there is rarely enough right information or time to provide a definitive, clean solution. Finding solutions to complex problems is a creative act. Experience, intuition, reflection, and dialogue among all problem-solvers will usually produce a set of sensible alternatives based on the group's collective judgment and *comfort level.*

DECISION-MAKING

Decision-making refers to the selection of one or more alternatives generated by the problem-solving process. In a complex adaptive system agents are purposeful, goal-seeking decision-makers. In the ICAS, decisions are made at all levels, with each level having a band of decision authority commensurate with their experience and scope of responsibilities.

Recognizing that there is no single way to make decisions, we consider some aspects of decision-making that the ICAS teams can use to get results. Every team is unique and lives within a context of internal pressures and goals and external demands and uncertainties; and every team can improve the way it does business, including the way it makes decisions.

Decision-making is both an art and a science and cannot be avoided where responsibility is concerned. Our focus is on the decision-making process as it applies to the complex environment. Routine decisions are usually straightforward, although not always easy. As the world becomes more complex, the ICAS workers' teams will be faced with more and more complicated and fast-moving decisions.

Although team decision-making is more complex and time-consuming than individual decision-making, teams can provide significant advantages by making high-quality decisions, that is, those that can be implemented and contribute to ICAS goals. Teams are particularly effective in making complex decisions that require a balance among functional disciplines and/or between short-term and long-term priorities. An effective team can provide the full range of knowledge and the different perspectives needed to filter out biased views, and to objectively consider all options. Through a collaborative interaction process the team can arrive at balanced, high-quality decisions. But they do not come easily or quickly.

The number and difficulty of decisions will vary widely with the experience, authority, and specific responsibilities of each ICAS team. Having participated in the problem-solving process that leads up to the final decision, team members have a good understanding of the reasons for the decision and its consequences. They are then able to implement the decision and explain the issues and decision to others, both within and external to the ICAS.

Team decision-making also provides team members with the knowledge and understanding that will aid them in the implementation of the decision once this is made. The use of technology—common databases, intelligent algorithms, high-powered three-dimensional visualization, complex display graphics, and modeling and simulation, etc.—helps teams make decisions. However, group-ware technology may also constrain team members and possibly reduce team effectiveness. The Knowledge Center aids teams by supporting and providing a free flow of accurate, real-time data, information, and resource knowledge to all team members. In addition, individual knowledge workers will use their personal networks to get information and suggestions from colleagues.

Some key points to note concerning decisions are:

1. *No decision* is a decision.
2. All complex decisions involve *values and judgments*.
3. No one can *predict* the future.
4. Every decision is a *guess* about the future.
5. The quality of a decision *cannot* be measured by its outcome.

The quality of complex decisions is a major factor in determining the ICAS's ability to survive and grow in its turbulent environment. Decisions, coupled with the effectiveness of their implementation, are the ultimate performance measure on how successfully the ICAS functions. When needed, a robust strategy may be built into major decision options to reduce the risk level. Chapter 22 suggests ways of thinking about the future that may help reduce the inherent risk in forecasting decision consequences through a better understanding of unknowns.

Flow is an important consideration in decision-making. This aspect of flow has to do with the flow of the product and the flow of action across the organization. Stakeholders must be ready to accept and take action on the decision. Also, the political climate must be right. If the results of a decision create political disturbances or major stakeholder opposition that could have long-term negative consequences for the organization, the decision must be very carefully reconsidered. A major decision may require a lot of pre-decision work on the part of the team and their support communities to smooth its implementation.

The Decision Process

There are many ways to make decisions and there are just as many processes. Each process depends largely on the decision to be made, the time allocated to make the decision, or the make-up of the team. But no matter what the process is, there are some questions that should be considered before starting to make the decision.

First, who should make the decision? Then, if it is determined that the team should make the decision, how will the outcome be measured? What is the type and degree of team interaction needed during team decision-making discussions?

Will the decision require creative thinking or analysis and logic? Do all team members need to be present? Should outside experts participate in the process? Is a facilitator needed? Finally, what is the sequence of thinking that the team will go through to arrive at a decision? These questions are addressed throughout the rest of this section.

When should decisions be made by the ICAS team, and when by subgroups, individual experts, or by the team leader? Who makes such decisions and how can significantly impact team collaboration and performance. When the decision requires special expertise the team expert should make the decision and explain the rationale to the team and, if needed, get their concurrence. The team may act as a sounding board and discuss the expert's rationale for the decision, particularly if they have a role in its implementation. This will also expand the team members' knowledge of the expert's discipline and broaden their perspective of the decision consequences.

On the other hand, if the decision space encompasses considerations which include additional experience, other disciplinary knowledge or political and organizational factors, then the team as a whole should become involved and make the decision; preferably by unanimous concurrence, otherwise by consensus.

If the decision has to be made quickly and the team leader has the experience and knowledge, the leader may make the decision and then explain the situation to the team. If the decision needs to be made at a level above the team, the team leader can discuss it with the team and forward it to higher levels. When this happens, the team needs to be kept abreast of the results and the rationale for the final decision. As we have noted before, keeping the team aware of the current context surrounding both the ICAS organization and the team's customers is vital to the team members being able to contribute their knowledge and experience.

Thinking Sequence

Decision-making as used here is the selection of one alternative from a number of options. Looking at the sequence of thinking that a team goes through in hunting for the best alternative, the highest potential for conflict and diversity usually occurs during the analysis and investigation of the alternatives. A good team leader, or facilitator, will ensure divergent thinking by team members so that nothing is overlooked in the evaluation of each alternative. This is when team members are encouraged to express their opinions and analyze others' opinions to create as many possibilities as possible.

Once these ideas are brought forth, the team process moves to convergent thinking. Convergent thinking focuses on the desired results of each decision option. This allows the team to start bringing the previous ideas together to reduce and refine the set of likely choices. This convergence focuses on the strengths, weaknesses, threats, and opportunities related to each choice. In particular, the uncertainties and their related risks are investigated and evaluated. In addition, the factors affecting decision quality are reviewed and used to compare choices.

Decision Quality

The quality of any given decision cannot be determined by its outcome because it is impossible to predict circumstances after the decision is made. Decision quality *does* impact the probability of its outcome, but it *cannot determine it*. Many factors that determine decision quality do so by helping the decision alternative have a better chance of getting the desired results. Complex decisions are far more judgment-driven than data-driven, although data and information are important inputs. This is one reason that ICAS teams can almost always make better decisions than individual knowledge workers can; their collective judgment is most often better than a single individual's judgment.

Those decisions that significantly impact the ICAS decision process need to be thoroughly evaluated to ensure maximum decision quality. Decision quality depends upon a number of factors that have varying degrees of importance, depending upon the particular decision and its context. Additionally, the relative importance of each decision quality factor will change over time. While any given decision may have additional quality factors not described here, some specific factors that may impact decision quality are: shared vision, efficiency, risk, timing, balance, customer impact, political consequences, scope, and worst-case scenario analysis. We will briefly address each of these to provide an idea of their potential value to decision results.

Shared Vision

The importance of a shared vision stems from the need for team members to have a common reference to judge their decision quality. Since every team member brings their own perspective of the problem and its solution to the team, and they have their own language and priorities, good communication among team members may be difficult. A shared vision of what the problem is and what a good solution would look like is imperative for decision success.

Efficiency

The team's local environment can influence how efficiently the decision is made. Good decision-making requires accurate, real-time data, information, and resource knowledge available to all team members. This, coupled with a decision conference center supported by groupware and other facilitation devices, makes for a very efficient support system for decision-making. Variable lighting, table, and seating arrangements, comfortable chairs, and writing supplies can change the professional atmosphere of the room and thereby influence the decision process. Companies such as IBM and Xerox have pioneered such conference rooms as described by Dimancescu et al. (1997). We have noted the importance of a collaborative environment in our discussion of ICAS structure and culture in Chapters 6 and 7.

Team leadership and the team collaboration level also play a big role in team efficiency. While collaborative team members do not always agree with each other and, in fact, may disagree more than ordinary groups do, they are still more efficient because they go through this noisy process with a clear objective in mind. What they *do* is work together to reach the best decision, recognizing that disagreement and discussion are a vital part of bringing out all of the information and knowledge needed for the best decision quality.

Risk

A decision that cannot be implemented is of poor quality because it does not get results. Since every decision is a guess about the future, every decision has inherent risk. However, some decisions have more risk than others, and some have a tendency to hide risks. A high-risk decision may still be of good quality if the risks are planned, prudent, and necessary for getting the desired results. If the risks are not thought through and are not a recognized part of the decision process, the decision will be low quality, no matter what the outcome.

In *The Art of Strategic Planning for Information Technology,* Boar (1993) identifies pivot points that allow for shifts in direction as the future unfolds. By building such a robust strategy into the decision process, risk levels can be reduced. For very important decisions, other possible techniques include parallel action paths, modeling and simulation, continuous environmental scanning, and virtual feedback networks. See Chapter 9 for a further discussion of risk.

Timing

Decision timing is another factor in decision quality. The decision must fit into the program *flow* and the stakeholders must be ready to accept and take action on the decision. Also, the political climate must be right. A major decision may require a lot of pre-decision work on the part of the team to smooth its implementation.

The timing of a decision may be critically dependent upon the context of the situation and the local stakeholder relationships with the team. If the team has developed strong enterprise partnering and feedback programs, they will be able to assess the local environment and make the best timing choice for the decision.

Making a decision before all facts and information are known is another timing issue. For complex decisions there will never be enough information. Yet delaying a decision to continually look for more information can lead to a poor decision or one that comes too late to be effective. This is always a tough

judgment call on the part of the team and is based more on experience, intuition, and gut feel than logic. Understanding complexity, knowing, and deep
knowledge can be helpful here (see Chapters 19 and 20, respectively).

Political Considerations

If the results of the decision create political disturbances or customer concerns that
could have long-term negative consequences, the decision must be very carefully
considered. On the other hand, if a decision encourages stakeholder support and
makes implementation easier, decision quality is enhanced.

Another consequence to consider is whether the decision will limit the ability
of the ICAS or the team to solve future problems. In other words, is the decision
robust enough to provide the team with the needed freedom to make future
decisions? Finally, the major assumptions underlying the decision should be
clearly articulated and evaluated in terms of their validity, life expectancy, and
consistency with the current and anticipated environment.

Scope

A decision intended to solve a particular event or unique problem has a considerably smaller scope in time and space than does a major decision intended to change
the culture or major processes within the organization or have a strong effect on
the external environment of the ICAS. A common error among decision-makers,
as noted by Drucker (1967), is to interpret an event or a pattern of events as a need
for major policy changes. Although this goes primarily to a proper understanding
of the problem, it shows a clear and important connection between understanding
the problem and the scope of the decision intended to resolve the problem.

Systems thinking postulates that it is neither events nor patterns of events
that drive behavior in organizations, but the structure of the organization.
Policies or decisions that are intended to change events or patterns of events will
rarely work because they do not change long-term behavior. These usually result
in a short-term positive impact and, as the organization adapts to the new
policy, long-term negative consequences begin to show up. Thus even if the
causative factors of change are correct, there may be reactive, second order or
non-linear forces that yield undesirable consequences. Morecroft and Sterman
(1994) note in *Modeling for Learning Organizations*: "[...]; we must be alert
to represent properly the—worse before better—sequences that often arise.
The short-term and long-term influences on a decision by a particular input are
often in opposite directions [...]" (p. 67).

Organizations can become rule-bound by a series of top-level policy decisions intended to prevent reoccurrence of specific problems or events without
consideration of their long-term impact. At the organizational level, the ICAS
must constantly guard against this possibility. As different events continue to
occur, new policies must not be generated which begin to stifle the organization

internally or create a negative reaction from external customers. Decisions by the ICAS teams that impact the external environment may also have a long-term negative effect after short-term successes. It is also important to note that policies, and even guidance, needs to be *eliminated–and forgotten–by* the organization when it has served its purpose and is no longer needed.

Worst-Case Scenario

Good decision-making takes into account the worst-case scenario. This acts as a hedge against the future by identifying and clarifying the worst possible outcome if everything goes wrong. Primarily applicable for high-level decisions such as strategic planning or large investments, worst-case scenario development and evaluation may also be useful for decisions dealing with high uncertainty or a rapid pace of events. Where it is very difficult to anticipate, even broadly, the results of a team's decisions, a worst-case scenario may illuminate understanding and create a safety net. If a reasonable worst-case scenario can be generated and its consequences understood, the expected outcome is put in a different light. Knowing the boundaries of the worst case, the decision implementation can proceed with a better appreciation of the risks involved and where the danger areas are located.

In Summary

After reviewing the relevant decision quality factors just described and reaching agreement on a specific alternative/decision, the team may want to hold its final decision in abeyance overnight or over the weekend to allow team members to *sleep on it* and convene one more time for second thoughts. Psychologically, this allows each individual to become *comfortable* with the decision and to utilize their intuition and *gut feel* for the adequacy of the decision. It is important for all team members to feel good about the decision to get their buy-in and full participation during implementation. Objectivity, fairness, equal participation by all members, and a thorough evaluation of each decision alternative leads to team member ownership of the decision.

IMPLEMENTATION

Actions and results make the difference. Making high-quality decisions is essential to getting good results, but it is not enough. Taking good decisions and turning them into actions and changes that solve problems, satisfy customers, take advantage of new opportunities, and enhance the image and value of the ICAS is where the final payoff comes from. Implementation is the most situation-dependent of all of the major processes. The details of the actions required to achieve the desired results cannot be generalized. However, there are a few points to remember.

When individuals who will have responsibility for implementation are aligned with the decision, implementation becomes much more effective. Big decisions that set the fundamental tone and nature of the ICAS require greater understanding and support throughout the organization. Ultimately, implementation is built on relationships and an understanding of the objectives and the environment. Efficiency and clarity of communication, coupled with openness and a sincere concern to share understanding and get participation, is a tenet of the ICAS.

The Knowledge Center of the ICAS keeps a "virtual brain book," a common data package and historical record (complete with context through video clips and special context fields for decision-makers), to ensure consistent presentation and accurate tracking of all of the most important past decisions. Organizations are at their best when they have a common perception of the intent and desired results of the decision and they can communicate these to all concerned.

SUMMARY

These four processes are embedded within the ICAS and under ideal conditions become a natural part of its culture, that is, the expected way of doing things, with each process well organized and formalized—but not bureaucratized. These properties working together within the framework provided in the discussions related to the eight emergent characteristics will create and sustain the ICAS as it maneuvers through change, complexity, and uncertainty to fulfill its mission.

REFERENCES

Adams, J. *The Care and Feeding of Ideas, a Guidebook to Encouraging Creativity.* Reading, MA: Addison-Wesley Publishing Co., 1986.

Axelrod, R. and M. D. Cohen. *Harnessing Complexity: Organizational Implications of a Scientific Frontier.* New York: The Free Press, 1999.

Bennet, D. *IPT Learning Campus: Gaining Acquisition Results Through IPTs.* Alexandria, VA: Bellwether Learning Center, 1997.

Boar, B. H. *The Art of Strategic Planning for Information Technology: Crafting Strategy for the 90's.* New York: John Wiley & Sons, 1993.

Boden, M. *The Creative Mind, Myths & Mechanisms.* London: Basic Books, 1991.

Couger, J. *Creative Problem Solving and Opportunity Finding.* Danvers, MA: Boyd and Fraser Publishing Co. 1995.

Dimancescu, D., P. Hines, and N. Rich. *The Lean Enterprise: Designing and Managing Strategic Processes for Customer-Winning Performance.* New York: AMACOM/American Management Association, 1997.

Drucker, P. "The Effective Decision," *Harvard Business Review,* January–February, 1967, Reprint 67105, pp. 1–8.

Koestler, A. *The Act of Creation*. New York: Dell Publishing Co., 1975.

Leonard-Barton, D. *Wellsprings of Knowledge: Building and Sustaining the Sources of Innovation*. Boston, MA: Harvard Business School Press, 1995.

Morecroft, J. D. W. and J. D. Sterman (eds). *Modeling for Learning Organizations*. Portland, OR: Productivity Press, 1994.

Poincaré, H. *The Foundations of Science: Science and Hypothesis, The Value of Science, Science and Method*. Washington, 1982.

Poincaré, H. *The Foundations of Science: Science and Hypothesis, The Value of Science, Science and Method*. New York: Modern Library, 2001.

Prigogine, I. *The End of Certainty: Time, Chaos and the New Laws of Nature*. New York: The Free Press, 1997.

Ray, M. and R. Myers. *Creativity in Business*. New York: Doubleday, 1989.

Swanson, R. C. *The Quality Improvement Handbook: Team Guide to Tools and Techniques*. Del Ray Beach, FL: St. Lucia Press, 1995.

Warmington, E. H. and P. G. Rouse (eds.) (trans. by W. H. D. Rouse). "Ion," in *Great Dialogues of Plato*. New York: Penguin Books USA, 1984.

Chapter 9

THE ART OF COLLABORATIVE LEADERSHIP

When Sir Isaac Newton discovered the laws of gravitation and developed the mathematics of the calculus in the seventeenth century, he unwittingly set in motion a paradigm of thinking. This paradigm viewed the world as a mechanical system of clocks and levers that obeyed deterministic laws and followed the rules of logic and cause and effect. With the industrial revolution came inventions, technology, and mass production and, most importantly from our perspective, organizations and management based upon the mechanical model of Newton. As described in Chapter 1, this led to the creation of bureaucracy and hierarchical, control-oriented leadership and management. Over the past half-century the industrial age has gradually given way to the information age and we are now entering the age of complexity. Information has exploded to the point where it is often detrimental to decision-making. As we approach a fully networked, dynamic, and turbulent local, national, and global society and business landscape we find that only knowledge can provide the understanding needed to deal with this complexity. Such a milieu demands a different paradigm and new rules and roles for leaders and managers.

The challenge of this new leadership is to create, maintain, and nurture their organization so that it creates and makes the best use of knowledge to achieve sustainable competitive advantage or, in the case of government and not-for-profit organizations, sustainable high performance. Collaboration is such an important part of creating the right environment and leveraging knowledge that we call the type of leaders described in this chapter *collaborative leaders* and the art they practice *collaborative leadership*.

We have previously described the eight emergent characteristics, the structure, culture, and major processes needed to create a successful intelligent complex adaptive system. It is within this context that we now investigate the leadership attributes and behavior that will move the ICAS into the future.

Leadership is probably the most widely studied aspect of organizations. Many thousands of books have been written on the subject over the past century, and undoubtedly many others before that. Continuing interest in leadership is exemplified by the number of edited books with multiple authors offering different views and suggestions on leadership (Spears, 1998; Bennis et al., 2001; Hesselbein and Cohen, 1999; Hesselbein et al., 1996; Shelton, 1997). In general the trend in leadership has been toward more awareness and recognition of the workforce and a concern for the well-being and empowerment of workers.

Is there a leadership style or approach that would meet the needs of the ICAS? The classical autocratic leader would not be successful because no one individual knows enough to second-guess the environment. The charismatic leader would not be, since knowledge workers, while inspired by passion, are rarely taken in by surface glitter. Strong, individualistic leaders want and expect control and visibility, since they lead by personality and image. The ICAS needs leadership throughout its structure to aid in cohesion and rapid adaptability. In addition, the ICAS cannot be designed and constructed; it must be *nurtured* and allowed to *co-evolve* with its environment through self-organization at the local level and iterative interactions with the outside world. This is not something strong, ego-driven leaders are good at, or willing to do.

Since the ICAS is a generic theory of the firm rather than a specific design, its leadership cannot, and should not, be fixed with a great deal of precision. Some of the references above identify a short list of characteristics that leaders should have to be effective. In our view, there is no short list that makes a leader. Leadership is, above all, situational, historical, context-sensitive, a matter of character, and time and space dependent. The work of the collaborative leader is to create, maintain, and nurture the ICAS so that it makes the best use of knowledge and the full competencies of all workers to achieve sustainable competitive advantage while maintaining the values, ethics, and purposes of the organization. Overall, this is the ultimate responsibility of collaborative leadership.

If we are to develop a new concept of leadership we need a theory of leadership upon which attributes, character, and style can be constructed. For the ICAS to be successful, leadership needs to be distributed throughout the organization, from the CEO to senior managers to team leaders to team members to individual knowledge experts. Working with knowledge workers and ensuring they have what they need, collaborative leaders will ensure the ICAS alignment by connecting local work with the Operation Center and other parts of the ICAS. They will set standards, leverage knowledge, reinforce the action culture, interpret and explain the environment, support knowledge worker career growth, and orchestrate disputes and internal problems. Their main work, however, will be to set an example, inspire and energize the workforce, and above all to create more collaborative leaders who can create more collaborative leaders. They will build other leaders through mentoring, staff meetings, role modelling, informal conversations, challenging workers, and insisting on high standards. Many collaborative leaders will serve as team leaders, fostering a collaborative working environment while also serving as a connecting link between the knowledge worker and the higher-level teams and line management hierarchy. The collaborative leader in a knowledge organization operating in a volatile environment must work with other workers as a coequal. Only then will knowledge workers use all of their experience and professional capacity to support the ICAS. Collaborative leaders do not represent positions in the ICAS, they are individuals who have demonstrated their ability and accepted the responsibility of leadership within the ICAS. They are not bosses so much as exemplars, collaborators, and respected colleagues.

Leadership can emerge from the interaction of knowledge workers within the context of the ICAS structure and culture, and the environment. As its environment perturbs the ICAS its knowledge workers perceive, evaluate, learn, make responses, and observe the results. In turn, this process changes the beliefs and assumptions of knowledge workers. Through this continuous, iterative process, knowledge workers create both their reality and their own character. This interactive process is further influenced by structure through its support (or lack thereof) of their responses. Culture helps build the reality and character through its quiet effects on how workers go about their day-to-day efforts. Through this complex set of interactions among the environment, selected responses from ICAS knowledge workers, the structure and culture within which they work, and their own personal needs and goals, emerges a world view and an understanding of who they are and what their purpose is. During this process some individuals change and grow in such a manner that they become respected, admired, and trusted by others. Through this process collaborative leaders emerge who have earned their *right of influence*. These leaders are seen as equals, but equals who help others get their work done, equals who are good role models to mimic, equals who care about others personally and who understand how and why the ICAS is what it is and does what it does, equals who understand how the work gets done and what the knowledge workers need to do their jobs. Others respect the collaborative leader's role, responsibility, and integrity, not because of the position, but because of the leader's character, knowledge, drive, and willingness to work with them as coequals.

The task of the ICAS leader is to guide and nurture the organization so that it makes optimum use of all of its resources. These resources include knowledge workers, their knowledge, their ability to leverage knowledge through relationship networks, and their flexibility through empowerment and self-organization.

Because knowledge workers—with their creativity, initiative, loyalty, and competency—without exception represent the single most valuable resource for the ICAS, leaders must support, challenge, and work with them as coequals and highly respected partners. Knowledge workers need the freedom and responsibility to decide how to organize and complete their assignments, either individually or in teams.

Effective ICAS leaders have some unusual characteristics. Their objective is to *leverage* competency, not direct it. They are participants, not directors. They combine the art of collaboration and the art of leading others. The most senior leaders in the ICAS have responsibilities similar to those of other companies. They are accountable for the health of the organization, overseeing all departments, developing strategic direction, approving high-level policies, making top-level decisions, and allocating resources. While all these actions are normal and necessary, their real value is in inspiring the workforce through their behavior, sensitivity, and support. They are not *per se* the leaders of the ICAS, they are *part* of the leadership of the ICAS. That is the difference that makes the difference.

For leaders to effectively support and nurture the entire workforce, they will be found everywhere in the organization, at all levels and on all teams. These leaders provide their professional expertise and knowledge of the things that make the organization successful—keeping the structure supportive, maintaining the action culture, creating, leveraging, and applying knowledge, and maintaining organizational alignment in the face of multiple, divergent external forces. They are all leaders (in the sense of top-level decision-makers and role models) and collaborators, working with others to accomplish tasks and helping others grow personally and professionally. We now consider what combination of leadership traits, skills, and styles would serve the ICAS organization best.

IMPORTANT ASPECTS OF COLLABORATIVE LEADERSHIP

Some important aspects of collaborative leadership are discussed below. These are: values; trust; empowerment; alignment; communicating vision, purpose, and direction; tasking and evaluation; monitoring and building the culture; integrative competencies; sense-making; and collaboration.

Values

Values and moral principles have always played an important role in the ability of leaders to lead and keep followers. In the ICAS their importance takes on a new level because knowledge workers are independent thinkers and differences in basic values can quickly lead to distrust. In the ICAS, organizational values are made visible, discussed, analyzed, and used as a foundation for organizational behavior, decisions, and performance expectations. At the same time, common values provide a means of relating to each other and a base to build trust and understanding. An important role of organizational values is their contribution to knowledge worker empowerment. If individuals understand and agree with the organization's values, they have created a space for decision-making because they know what kinds of decisions are not acceptable and what kinds are. This information also helps reduce external complexity through filtering by selecting only those opportunities in the environment consistent with their organization's values. Leaders can improve their organization's internal communication and cooperation by talking about personal and organizational values at staff meetings, providing seminars and workshops on their importance and role in organizational performance, and through stories and anecdotes from the organization's history.

Trust

Trust is foundational to the ability of the ICAS to create, share, leverage, and apply knowledge anywhere and anytime it is needed. Trust is notoriously difficult to create and becomes fragile in times of stress. From the ICAS leader's perspective, words and behaviors have to be consistent, objective, and sensitive to all of their coworkers. Individuals perceived to operate from power positions are easily distrusted by their subordinates, who often look for *sub rosa* intentions or goals. A leader who has authority but uses that authority only when absolutely necessary—most of the time working with others in a collaborative, coequal way—is in a position to gain the trust and cooperation of others.

This trust has to be mutual to be effective. A leader who does not trust his or her people will not be able to treat them as equals, openly share information with them, and be fair in their evaluations. For all of these reasons trust needs to be brought into the light and openly discussed, monitored, and quick actions taken when it buckles. Lack of candor, unethical behavior, a non-caring attitude relative to others, egotism, and acrimonious debates all lead down the road of distrust. Collaborative leaders recognize that trust is an emergent property of their organization and pay close attention to the level of trust throughout their three-dimensional network of contacts. Trust is discussed as an example of emergence in Chapter 10.

Empowerment

For the ICAS to have the capability to self-organize, adapt, and respond rapidly to changing events, knowledge workers (and their teams) are empowered to use their knowledge and act, sometimes on their own, more often within teams. Empowerment has become a touchy subject with some organizations who have attempted to use it within a classical hierarchical company. As de Geus (1997) notes, "When push comes to shove, most managers will choose control. In fact, it is emotionally difficult, in most companies, even to *relax* the emphasis on control. Managers who are doers, accustomed to getting things done, will tend to trust themselves more than anybody else" (p. 152).

One issue arises when managers give subordinates more freedom to make decisions without giving them the knowledge, boundaries, or context needed to make good decisions. Subordinates then proceed to make mistakes, feeling frustrated and even betrayed. The manager then withdraws the empowerment, convinced that it cannot work. The problem is that without knowing the limits of their decision space, without having been given the situational context and history of relationships, and without the experience of making decisions, no one can be successful. Knowledge worker empowerment and freedom is a dual responsibility of the manager/leader and the worker. The freedom and capacity to make local decisions is vital to the ICAS and can only be assured through collaborative leaders *working with* their knowledge workers to prepare them for empowerment.

Alignment

Alignment is the process of continually assuring that the activities of all workers are directly or indirectly supporting the organization's common vision and purpose. In a fluctuating environment, where the mosaic of events and tasks continually changes, there has to be a network that maintains awareness and some degree of cohesion among activities even as people and structures change. Recall that the Operations Center has the responsibility for tracking and coordinating these activities. ICAS leaders provide inputs into this nerve center and assist in working out duplication problems or resource shifts to accommodate teams. Many ICAS leaders serve as team leaders and members, and are actively involved in the day-to-day work. Note that in a highly dynamic world, duplication may be needed in some areas to generate more ideas (optimum complexity) or keep options open (risk aversion). Alignment of work efforts is frequently a judgment call and requires seeing the work from the higher perspective of systems thinking or broad experience. ICAS leaders also see alignment as a key part of strategic implementation, managing a dynamic balance and achieving a correlation of forces (see Chapter 19). The degree of responsibility for alignment varies with the level and experience of the leader.

Communicating Vision, Purpose, and Direction

Senior leaders continuously communicate the ICAS vision, purpose, and direction. Vision provides workers with knowledge of what the organization is (ICAS culture, beliefs, and values), and what it should look like (the ICAS persona) to a knowledgeable outsider. This differs from the classical meaning of vision as a clear picture of what the organization is seeking to look like at some point in the future. So long as the environmental parameters of change, uncertainty, and complexity do not drastically change, the vision will remain relatively stable, since the ICAS is designed to match such an environment. Its vision is a broad description of the organization's values, beliefs, what it stands for, and the direction it is going.

Purpose establishes the reason for the ICAS's existence and what it is trying to do. Direction is where it is going within the context of its immediate market and environment. All ICAS leaders understand, agree, and communicate these concepts throughout the organization, using metaphors, analogies, anecdotes, and stories to help employees understand, feel, and share in the importance of what the firm is doing. Empowered knowledge workers making many decisions on their own will understand the larger context, purpose, and direction of their organization. When ICAS leaders meet this responsibility, line-of-sight activities become clear, alignment occurs more easily, and unity of identity can develop. Through collaborative leadership, leaders have the ability to translate corporate-level concepts into terms and activities meaningful to knowledge workers, shifting the center of mass for their maintenance and implementation from top-down driven to one driven by the culture and workforce.

Team Leader

Leading a team is challenging and a quite different role than classical line management. It requires good leadership skills and a flexible style leading to participative and collaborative relationships. Knowledge workers are sensitive to the style, knowledge, and interpersonal skills of their leaders. Teams are a major means for collaborative leaders to interact with, support, and influence ICAS knowledge workers. Establishing and maintaining a team collaborative environment will greatly influence team-member attitudes, expectations, quality of work, and feelings of respect and fair treatment.

Team leaders have many roles: counselor, leader, manager, coworker, skeptic, referee, facilitator, and standard setter, to name a few. The objective of collaborative leadership is to create and maintain a team environment in which knowledge workers are encouraged to give—and are rewarded for giving—their best contribution to the team and to the organization; yet they are also recognized for individual efforts. One of the challenges of collaborative leadership is letting the team self-organize, such as deciding when they should work as a team and when they should operate as a working group, perhaps with strong leadership. When a task needs the collective efforts of all team members, there is time for the team to work together and the team decides for itself how to get the work done, the outcome will surpass any individual working alone. However, some situations may require quick action that does not allow for team deliberation. The team must then decide what makes sense and act accordingly. Perhaps one or two team members will handle the situation and report back to the team. The successful team leader will walk a balance between team self-organization and leadership direction. Being first among equals, collaborative leaders will not exercise authority unless they foresee the team making a fatal error. Experienced ICAS leaders adjust their mode of operation, and sometimes even negotiate their way out of problems in order to maximize overall team performance. This flexibility of operating as a team, a working group, or as individuals is an important strength of the ICAS.

The team leader has great influence over the team in setting performance standards, determining training and development, and developing a strategy for team success. In building team performance, the team leader and the team should determine the appropriateness of each of the key success factors. These factors include team leadership, a common team vision, the ability to collaborate, the degree of freedom and empowerment, technology support, the desired learning rate, collocation and size, and finally the amount of feedback they seek to determine their performance (Bennet, 1997). As the team performs its work, these various success factors and the major processes in Chapter 8 may be used to improve performance and can be acquired through just-in-time development or by individual team member training.

Team leaders play a major role in working with the team to set learning objectives and monitor real-time performance. They should think about the interactions among the key success factors and how to get the team members to balance team development and task work. This tradeoff is always difficult because work demands are immediate and team development has a delayed payoff. Although every team leader is challenged by this dilemma, over time the team can become high performing and will need less and less team development. Ideally, as more knowledge workers learn how to collaborate and optimize team effectiveness, even moving individuals in and out of teams will not hurt performance. Recall that knowledge worker mobility is a basic tenet of the ICAS to provide the flow of knowledge, maintain learning, and keep new ideas and creativity flowing. Team leaders must also understand and manage the forces that make their teams effective and develop the right balance among these forces to optimize the team's relations with customers and other stakeholders while maintaining high moral and personal satisfaction and professional development of team members.

Tasking and Evaluation

Depending on their level within the ICAS, leaders identify objectives and lay out programs and plans of action and milestones, but they do not do these things alone. Using teams or selected groups of experts, leaders set goals, and let their team determine how to organize to accomplish them. In some cases, depending upon the situation, teams themselves select goals and then structure themselves to achieve specific results. Here again we see that good judgment, sound thinking, and clear perception are needed in collaborative leadership. Working with their people rather than over them, ICAS leaders can both liberate and challenge knowledge workers to stretch themselves, grow, and contribute. Evaluations are based on both team and individual performance, as seen by the team members, the team leader, senior management, and other stakeholders. Since knowledge workers have assignments, not jobs or positions, they rarely find themselves competing with each other. Ideally they would be competing only with themselves to improve their own performance and take on more responsibility.

Monitoring and Building the Culture

As trendsetters and role models, ICAS collaborative leaders play a strong role in observing how the work gets done and in influencing the working environment and knowledge worker expectations. Their ability to objectively observe their own actions and those of their coworkers allows them to monitor the morale, frustrations, perceptions, and attitudes of their colleagues. Their sensitivity to informal networks and to cultural changes coupled with their collaborative style and leadership perspective helps them nurture the ICAS culture to sustain the characteristics addressed in Chapter 7.

Integrative Competencies

Through their knowledge of integrative competencies (see Chapters 14–21), ICAS leaders are able to assist knowledge workers in interpreting and understanding the complexities of the environment and making decisions. By applying systems thinking, relationship network management, risk management, and particularly knowing and complexity thinking, leaders and their teams of knowledge workers are better able to anticipate and react to customer behavior and market changes. Information literacy and knowledge management, coupled with the Knowledge Center, enable the knowledge needed to work with complex challenges. Critical thinking helps remove some of the fog and glitter surrounding the confusion and paradox often found in complex environments. Learning prevents repeating mistakes and ensures continuous change and growth of the team.

Sense-Making

Making sense of the myriad, sometimes conflicting, demands of a multitude of fast-paced business endeavors is often considered an intellectual skill. In our view, sense-making is more of an experiential process. Rational thinking is only one mode of understanding and is usually inadequate for complex problems. ICAS leaders need to be able to use their feelings, intuition, insight, judgment, and past experience to extract useful patterns and interpretations out of messy situations. To do this, these leaders develop knowledge about knowledge, learn how to learn, and recognize and respect their gut feelings, leveraging sense-making through techniques like dialogue, brainstorming, knowledge fairs, situation analysis, verication, computer modeling, and scenario development. Reading and learning outside of the leader's immediate work interests creates a wide awareness of perspectives and possibilities that help in making sense of seemingly nonsense phenomena (Wiig, 1993; Weick, 1995).

Collaboration

According to Kayser, collaboration is close communication and the sharing of understanding with no hidden agendas (Kayser, 1994). We broaden his interpretation to include active and willful working together, openly and purposively, to accomplish some task. Collaboration requires a close, open, and trusting relationship where each party contributes their capability and works with others to align and integrate the efforts of all. ICAS leaders use collaborative relationships and interactions to share understanding, get the work done, and guide development of their coworkers. It is through a collaborative approach to relationships that ICAS leaders *earn their leadership rights* while at the same time serving the knowledge workers.

Collaboration often includes play. As team members work a given problem they need to play with it in their minds, then share concepts and ideas and perspectives. These actions are "play" in the sense that different, and sometimes wild things are tried before conclusions are drawn. Such interactions foster mutual respect, active listening, and camaraderie—all valuable for building synergy, excitement, and feelings of accomplishment. When asked to solve a difficult problem, ICAS leaders respond by admitting: "I don't know how to solve this, but if we all work together, I know that we can figure out a good solution." This openness brings others into the challenge, sets the stage for collaborative efforts, and communicates the respect and confidence the leader has in others.

THE LEADER AS FACILITATOR

Facilitation might be considered an advanced form of collaboration; it is clearly an important strength of leaders. An effective facilitator is a leader, a follower, a collaborator, and a servant to the group. Like collaboration, facilitation can be learned only through experience. It is both a behavior and a mental process, demanding parallel monitoring of several different processes occurring simultaneously during teamwork sessions. Experience in processing several streams of data simultaneously helps a leader monitor situations and interactions and adjust their own behavior and responses accordingly. To expand on this consider the following story.

Thoughts of a Facilitator

John had been facilitating a group of business executives all morning but had not been able to get them to communicate very well. They faced a challenging and complex issue that was hard to understand, confusing, and had potentially dangerous consequences to their organization. Everyone took the issue seriously and most of the group had their own quick solutions, but they all seemed to be talking at cross-purposes. There had been many heated discussions and arguments with little listening; some personal animosities had burst forth. Even when they *did* seem to listen they did not get the deeper meaning behind the words. It was a classic case of everyone feeling that they knew the right answer. In frustration, John begged away from lunch and went to his office to think about what he should do. He was a good, proven facilitator, yet nothing he had done seemed to be working that morning. In desperation, he picked up an old sheet of questions he had kept from a seminar years ago. It read:

1. What are "you" doing to make the problem better or worse?
2. Are you enforcing the ground rules?
3. Did you prepare the group for dialogue and inquiry?
4. Is the process appropriate for the objective?
5. Is the problem due to diversity of personalities, language problems because of different disciplines, levels of seniority, competing objectives,

inexperienced participants, organizational loyalties, personal arrogance, or misguided faith in their own knowledge?

John read over the questions carefully and began to realize that the essence behind all of the questions was to prepare the individuals in the group so they were open to *learning and knowing*. Such preparation would help the participants question their own beliefs and knowledge and look carefully at other ideas—and how they were delivered and responded to—in order to see beyond images, hear beyond words, and sense beyond appearances. This was essential to get to the heart of the matter and create an understanding and consensus for the road ahead.

Regarding the first question, John realized that he had become involved in several of the discussions and, although he always tried to be objective, there were probably individuals in the group who felt he was biased. In thinking about his behavior, he recalled the trick of taking himself out of himself and looking at himself from the upper corner of the room. When he reflected on this, he became aware that he had been giving some participants more attention than others and that his mannerisms had shown some of his personal bias.

Regarding the second question, several times John had not enforced the ground rules and allowed some individuals to ramble and talk too long. This had undoubtedly irritated other participants. He recalled his first rule of management, "If you're not getting what you want the first thing that has to change is you."

Regarding the third question, he realized that although he had originally intended to talk about the question "How do we know what we know?" and to do a systems review of the topic, he had let several of the senior participants talk him out of it because they thought it would waste time and they wanted to have more time to resolve the issues. He now realized this had been a serious mistake on his part.

Thinking about the fourth question, John felt certain that all participants were extremely well-qualified, dedicated, and loyal, and trying to do their best in coming up with a good solution. Certainly there were personality differences. The language problem was not too serious, although he knew it would probably have been better had he helped them develop a common perception of the problem. Looking at the other possible problems he concluded that the major issue was that, even though all participants were well intended, they each had a strong belief in their own knowledge and were certain that their answer was the right one. They came from a culture of hierarchy and combativeness. They had proven themselves through their careers, had demonstrated good decision-making capabilities, and firmly believed that their understanding and solution was the best.

Reviewing the last question he concluded that although the group had shown some signs of every possibility in the question, none of their behavior was enough to be the cause of the current problem.

As a final thought, John reviewed in his mind how well he had been able to keep up with the four processes that unfold simultaneously during every team-work session. He felt good about being able to follow the flow of content of the group and to understand the significance of some of the ideas. Monitoring the quality of interpersonal relationships among members and taking early action to prevent disruptions had been straightforward. The third process, the movement of the group toward its objective, is what got stymied and he had not handled it well. He also knew that he had not monitored his own behavior—how he came across to the group—very well. Learning to track all four of these processes in real time while standing in front of a group of well-educated, proactive knowledge workers had not been easy for him. But through experience and the school of hard knocks he had come to feel confident about his abilities as a proactive facilitator.

Reviewing all of these thoughts in his mind, John realized that he had not given enough attention to preparing the group to question their own knowledge, and thereby be open to other ideas and perspectives. He knew this was a critical step in guiding the group through the overall path. Once it is brought to their attention that there is no easy answer to the question, "How do I know what I know?" almost everyone is willing to consider other ideas and try to keep an open mind.

Since it was too late to drastically change the planned process, John decided the best action was to get everyone to step back from the situation and spend time looking at their own belief sets, recognizing and respecting the belief sets of others, and exploring the context within which the task needed to be accomplished. In addition, he wanted to explore the possibility there were no right or wrong answers, only possibilities and probabilities. He really wanted to spend time on complexity thinking to get the group to appreciate the challenges and possibilities of piercing their unknown world of the future. "But there was no time for that," he quietly muttered under his breath as he walked back into the lunchroom. When lunch was over, John began the afternoon session feeling much better about the way ahead. John's experience, here described as a formal facilitation responsibility, is very close to what collaborative leaders do in their interactions with knowledge workers. During their conversations, they continuously monitor and support the content flow, the process and direction of the discussion, the interpersonal relationships being developed, and their own behavior as seen by others—always done within the framework of honesty, openness, values, and integrity. This is one way that collaborative leaders *lead, learn, and build their own character.*

MANAGING RISK

We have frequently mentioned that in the new world the future is unknowable, but perhaps not unfathomable, due to our inability to understand nonlinearity change and complexity. The ICAS, living in this new world, must be able to recognize, understand, and deal with risk in a manner that makes the best use of its strength. Quick response, flexibility, knowledge leveraging, flow, selectivity, and other ICAS characteristics help deal with the risk of a misguided action or wrong interpretation of the external environment. ICAS leaders will know their organization well enough to make good use of its strengths to buffer errors, in terms of poor communication, weak social capital, and workers not having adequate resources, i.e., the risk of poor organization, structure, culture, or leadership. ICAS leaders, in carrying out their responsibilities, are consistently evaluating difficult problems and situations from the viewpoint of what could go wrong, what is the inherent risk, and what can we do now to mitigate any loss.

A common interpretation of risk is the exposure to some chance event or possibility of loss. Looking from a somewhat wider view, we take risk to also mean the chance or possibility of not achieving an intended goal or objective and the consequences associated with the outcome. In other words, there is risk that a decision is not the best one, or that our actions do not lead to the intended consequences. In this sense, an organization runs the risk of non-optimum performance every day. The usefulness of this broader interpretation is that it provides a corollary benefit. In asking the question, "How can we do the best we can?" we push ourselves to learn and improve. In asking the question, "What are the risks in taking this or that action?" we look at a number of possible outcomes from the view of being wrong, that is, worst-case scenarios or the costs of errors. Each question provides important information that may influence the final decision. Both positive and negative thinking are needed for balanced reflection before decisions or actions. While the power of positive thinking and the self-fulfilling prophecy are well known in management, the cautionary reminders of do no harm, and consider the second-order consequences are often forgotten. Both may be equally important.

Leaders and workers in the ICAS have a great deal of freedom, and with that freedom goes the need for a good understanding of the broader ramifications of their work. For convenience we consider three categories of risk: technical risk; the risk of ineffective management; and the risk associated with decisions and actions.

Technical Risk

Technical risk is well known and applies to the engineering, development, and operation of complicated systems ranging from vacuum cleaners to buildings to aircraft carriers. This risk deals with understanding and applying the laws of science and engineering and the capability of engineers and manufacturing personnel to perform their jobs. While very important, it is not the immediate concern in the ICAS, even though it may well apply to some ICAS internal processes.

The second category relates to the risk related to understanding and applying social, management, and leadership skills and procedures within the ICAS organization. The third category relates to the difficulty of anticipating the future impact of decisions and actions in a complex environment. These latter two categories are of particular concern here because in the ICAS world everyone's effectiveness is dependent upon their supportive structure and culture and their capacity to learn, adapt, make decisions, take actions, and work together.

The Risk of Management

Management risk entails recognizing that individual and team performance is heavily influenced by workers, team leaders, the structure and the culture. Performance also depends on communication, systems thinking, and the level of collaboration. The risk of management is very much a social awareness and networking issue. A culture that does not encourage teamwork and learning represents a high risk when knowledge workers are working in a fast-paced, complex, uncertain situation. Without teamwork and communities, workers will not have, nor be able to get, the information and knowledge they need for good decision-making. For example, if leaders delegate responsibility to a team, they must provide the context and resources as well. If these are not provided, the team will experience considerable risk in attempting to meet its objectives, and the chances of team success are lowered, no matter how strong the desire, competency, and intentions of the team members. Another example would be knowledge workers who are unaware of the impact of their activities on other parts of the organization. The amplification effect from the rippling of unintended consequences can seriously degrade the performance of organizations that depend on multiple interconnections for their success.

A third example of risk is a senior person who insists a recalcitrant team member remain on the team for political or organizational reasons. Leaders' behaviors, their roles, the relationships with workers, the clarity of communication, and the technological support provided all influence knowledge worker success and the quality of their work. Each of these factors can be evaluated with respect to their risk, i.e., the probability that they will result in a loss or a less than desirable outcome. Each possible outcome can be reviewed for its consequences and impact on other parts of the ICAS. It is certainly not worth-while to pursue such a procedure for every outcome or aspect of work processes. Where critical leverage points exist in the ICAS or where the cost of mistakes is high, it is incumbent on collaborative leaders to recognize the potential risks and deal with them accordingly. Awareness by all ICAS personnel of the impor-tance and value of recognizing the value of their actions on others' work is essential to achieve cohesion and effectiveness.

The Risk Associated with Decisions and Actions

The third category of risk is associated with making decisions and taking effec-tive action under conditions of rapid change, uncertainty, and complexity. As discussed in Chapter 8, there are certain criteria for making decisions that improve their quality. Every decision envisions some desirable result that the decision-maker hopes to achieve. How good that anticipation is depends upon many things, including the decision-maker's deep knowledge of the situation and the context within which the decision is made. But it is an educated guess at best. We use the term deep knowledge because when faced with an unknow-able future, heuristics, intuition, judgment, and knowing (discussed in Chapter 17) all help decision-makers to make better decisions.

No matter how much knowledge workers try to improve their decisions and actions, uncertainty may still result and with it comes risk—the risk of being wrong, of making situations worse, or of creating additional problems through ripple effects or misunderstandings. Even the risk of not getting accurate and timely feedback on decisions and actions comes into play. As with the previous two risk categories, just being aware of the existence of the risk of a decision is a good start. Careful reflection by leaders and other decision-makers of the magnitude of risk can go a long way toward making those decisions more effective. For decision situations that have a large impact on the ICAS's success, careful risk analysis methodologies can be used to help understand and antici-pate the final effects of the decision. In other words, risk assessment offers one tool for improving organizational effectiveness and for understanding and anticipating the future.

From an organizational perspective, collaborative leaders should be cognizant and competent in understanding and assessing risk as related to the develop-ment and production of engineering systems, to the quality of management, work flow systems, processes, and organizational structures, and to the making of complex decisions and their implementation. Understanding and thinking about risk creates a broad view and an appreciation of the consequences of using any of the four major processes (see Chapter 8).

DESCRIPTION OF COLLABORATIVE LEADERS

To get another perspective on collaborative leadership and how leaders think, act, and relate to knowledge workers we provide a list of brief descriptions that characterize their behavior. These are not so much traits of leaders as a characterization of the kinds of actions they would take.

- Insist that everyone always be treated with respect, fairness, and equality.
- Reward sustainable high performance, not quick fixes.
- Maintain strong moral and ethical values and apply them to all areas of their working life.
- Treat people as individuals and professionals, give them the benefit of the doubt until proven otherwise.
- Inspire others through positive thinking with an optimistic but not naive outlook, pursuing appreciative inquiry.
- Understand and actively foster relationships and their role in ICAS operation.
- Ask how and why things happen, and how and why an action is taken.
- Challenge the status quo to prevent stasis and the creation of false realities.
- Use networks to align the organization, leverage knowledge, and support all workers.
- Focus on quality, effectiveness, and organizational health.
- Lead by example and collaboration, not by ego.
- Build other leaders, and leaders who can build other leaders.
- Facilitate loyalty, respect, competence, synergy, and learning among the workforce.
- Do not pretend to know when they don't.
- When confronted with very complex issues, admit they don't know and suggest that "If we work together we can figure this out."
- Challenge all knowledge workers with high standards.
- Change the structure to support the workforce.
- Always share context with team members.
- Leverage knowledge wherever possible.
- Do not tolerate rotten apples, egomaniacs, or the living dead.
- Be a servant and a world-class model for all workers.

As a final note on collaborative leadership, consider that rather than use power or control, these individuals use the seven "Cs" to lay the groundwork for getting knowledge workers to listen and work with them.

- *Compass*—they set a direction to go, not a specific objective. In a turbulent world the best one can do is continue pushing in the right direction, since the future is unknowable.

- *Connect*—they make connections, know who to contact when needed and who to help when asked.
- *Communicate*—they work to *share understanding* with everyone so they can create knowledge and lay the groundwork for collaborating.
- *Collaborate*—they work with others in an open and coequal basis with everyone contributing and helping everyone else.
- *Care*—they really care about people, listening to them, trusting in them, and supporting them.
- *Co-create*—they work with others to create new ideas, build new relationships, and solve problems in new ways.
- *Character*—they demonstrate strong values, moral and ethical strength, and a high respect for others.

REFERENCES

Bennet, D. *IPT Learning Campus: Gaining Acquisition Results Through IPTs.* Alexandria, VA: Bellwether Learning Center, 1997.

Bennis, W., G. M. Spreitzer, and T. G. Cummings (eds). *The Future of Leadership: Today's Top Leadership Thinkers Speak to Tomorrow's Leaders.* San Francisco: Jossey-Bass, 2001.

de Geus, A. *The Living Company: Habits for Survival in a Turbulent Business Environment.* Boston, MA: Harvard Business School Press, 1997.

Hesselbein, F. and P. Cohen (eds). *Leader to Leader: Enduring Insights on Leadership from the Drucker Foundation's Award-Winning Journal.* San Francisco: Jossey-Bass Publishers, 1999.

Hesselbein, F., M. Goldsmith, and R. Beckhard (eds). *The Leader of the Future: New Visions, Strategies, and Practices for the Next Era.* San Francisco: Jossey-Bass Publishers, 1996.

Kayser, T. A. *Building Team Power: How to Unleash the Collaborative Genius of Work Teams.* Burr Ridge, IL: Irwin Professional Publishing, 1994.

Shelton, K. (ed.). *A New Paradigm of Leadership: Visions of Excellence for 21st Century Organizations.* Provo, UT: Executive Excellence Publishing, 1997.

Spears, L. C. (ed.). *Insights on Leadership: Service, Stewardship, Spirit, and Servant-Leadership.* New York: John Wiley & Sons, 1998.

Weick, K. E. *Sensemaking in Organizations.* London: Sage Publications, 1995.

Wiig, K. M. *Knowledge Management Foundations: Thinking about Thinking—How People and Organizations Create, Represent, and Use Knowledge.* Arlington, Texas: Schema Press, 1993.

Chapter 10

CREATING EMERGENCE

This chapter looks at a unique property of complex systems called emergence. We have referred to emergence as a global property of complex adaptive systems that is created through the multiple interactions and reactions of the agents or elements within the system. In the ICAS these elements are primarily people, although technology and other artifacts play a role in how people interact and develop relationships. These interactions among people are frequently nonlinear and through multiple cause-and-effect chains create many feedback paths. Interaction with the external environment also produces feedback that modulates the perceptions, feelings, and behavior of knowledge workers within the ICAS. Over time, the result of all of these relationships, interactions, and feedback loops creates patterns of behavior throughout the organization that we refer to as culture. Other emergent characteristics, flow (patterns of movement of information, knowledge, and people) for example, are also affected by knowledge workers actively and naturally sharing information, and facilitating the movement of ideas, people, and resources in support of the ICAS needs throughout the organization. Again, each individual does things to help others in a manner which, when feedback and individual readjustments are considered, creates patterns of easy movement of information and knowledge around the organization.

Another way of looking at emergence is to ask if a global property can be seen in the individual employees of the organization. If the exact same property can be found in individuals and is not changed by their relationships, then it is not an emergent property of the organization. An example would be that every knowledge worker reads every day. But the property of reading does not emerge from their interactions, although what individuals read on any given day may well be influenced by their interactions.

An emergent property is often said to be greater than the sum of the parts, although perhaps it would be more accurate to consider that an emergent property is different than the sum of parts. For example, each individual can learn and so can the organization. However, organizational learning is different than individual learning. Organizational learning requires multiple individuals to work together to accomplish a task with the results created by combining each individual's own knowledge with the capability gained through their mutual interactions. The same results could not be obtained by adding the contributions of each individual together because the interactions change what each individual knows, learns, and does. It is their interactive gain that provides the synergy. Thus the sum of individual learning and organizational learning becomes the total learning of the organization.

CULTURE AS AN EMERGENT PHENOMENON

As workers go about their daily business of communicating, solving problems, taking action, and reacting to information from others, they modify their own behavior and perception of the work environment until things "settle down" into a normal and expected *way of getting the job done*. Over time the entire organization achieves a consistent way of working together to meet the needs of internal and external customers, although each knowledge worker has their own unique way of behaving, their behavior still falls within cultural expectations. A set of beliefs, feelings, expectations, and norms develops in all employees that provide comfort and stability, allowing them to work with less anxiety and uncertainty. Everyone understands how, when, and with whom they should interact, how to treat each other, and how they are supposed to act as they get their job accomplished. As this atmosphere is created, with its behavior patterns and unstated assumptions, the organization's culture is created. This culture is a global property of organizations and because it emerges out of the interactions, it cannot be traced back to any single cause or individual. New employees may have problems accepting the organization's culture, particularly if it is significantly different from their previous organization. New employees can either adapt to their new organization, get the organization to change, or leave. If they stay and do not adapt to the new culture they will live under continuous stress. Culture, as a global phenomenon of the ICAS, plays a strong role in influencing what people should and should not do, how they see themselves and their role in the organization, and how motivated and loyal they are to the organization.

Since emergent properties of complex organizations arise out of multiple, nonlinear interactions among individuals, is it possible to design an organization that has certain desired emergent characteristics? In principle, the answer is no because you cannot identify or predict the outcome of your actions. While this is correct in the sense of not having control, from another perspective actions may be taken that *influence* the system's behavior in such a way that the desired emergent properties, or something close to them, will emerge. In Chapter 16 we discuss systems and complexity thinking in more detail. As systems become more complex and their behavior becomes less and less predictable, they may still be nurtured to guide their evolution toward some emergent phenomenon. *Emergence is not random, rather it is the result of multiple interactions that settle down to internal coherence and patterns.* While there is no guarantee that the desired patterns will surface, by understanding the key variables within the organization it is possible to take actions that may lead to desirable results. Small, young companies often take on the personality and character of their entrepreneurial founder. Typically the larger the organization the less influence any one individual has, although exceptions such as Henry Ford and Jim Watson are well known.

Complex systems exhibit patterns and forms that may or may not be used for anticipating future behavior. On the other hand, complex adaptive systems are much more difficult (or impossible) to predict because an external action is likely to cause the system to change itself, thereby making prediction very difficult. All of this said, what we are interested in is not prediction so much as being able to create certain emergent characteristics that the ICAS needs to survive and grow in a turbulent environment. If we cannot predetermine the *exact* emergent property, such as a specific culture for example, we may be able to create a culture that is acceptable—or perhaps better—than the one we believe is needed. If we take the right actions we may have a good chance of creating a culture that is somewhere close to our goal.

Recall our overall strategy for creating the ICAS. Survival of the firm depends upon the sum of all of the daily actions of employees. Each of these actions should be consistent with the organization's direction and supportive of local and organizational goals. For these actions to be effective, each worker must have the knowledge, and resources, to determine what the appropriate action is and to carry it out. This may be individual or team knowledge and it may be explicit, tacit, or created on the spot. Since the environment is uncertain and highly complex, it probably will not be possible to predict what will happen next or what the consequences of these actions will be. Experience, intuition, judgment, knowing, and other integrative competencies will help understand a given situation, but rarely will they fully anticipate or explain events or patterns in the environment. Thus, the strategy becomes one of Darwinian survival, where every individual at the organization's boundaries takes the best action possible, carefully observes the results and uses this feedback to adjust their knowledge for follow-on actions. When the action works, feedback then reinforces it and it is continued. If the action fails it is stored in memory for use in another situation. For this strategy to be effective, the structure, culture, and knowledge worker competencies must be in place that fully supports local knowledge and actions.

From a research perspective, much work needs to be done to learn more about emergence and emergent properties in complex adaptive organizations. The following represent some ideas we think are worth considering. In our example below we have omitted the adaptive effects on the process of creating an action culture. This is done to simplify the example. Because each organization and its environment are unique in space and time, the following approach is offered as a guideline with possibilities, *not a recipe*. Hopefully it will raise questions that lead change agents to understand their organization and guide its evolution toward the desired culture.

STEPS TO CREATING AN ACTION CULTURE

Assume that you want to change a typical knowledge organization's culture into something similar to the action culture discussed in Chapter 7. Creating an action culture begins at the top of the organization, with senior leadership's awareness of the need for change. This begins with a thorough review and reflection by all senior managers of their beliefs, assumptions, feelings, and expectations of the environment, their workforce and their own roles and responsibilities. As a minimum this will lead to intensive questioning of their perception of reality and will most likely result in double loop learning coupled with a deeper understanding of themselves, individually and as a leadership team; the creation of a shared understanding of the current and anticipated environment, the history, strengths, weaknesses, opportunities, and threats of the organization, its culture and how the work gets done.

The next step is to take a closer look at the environment including: (1) developing a description of the current and expected market and external environment of the company and its impact on the company's operation; and (2) preparing a strategy for surviving and growing in the anticipated environment. For the turbulent environment of the ICAS, this means that planning is for learning, not doing. Local action coupled with quick feedback that drives changes in actions are the keys to maintaining survival fitness in the unpredictable business ecology. Senior management must develop the strategy so they understand and have ownership in it.

Senior leadership should recognize and accept the fact that for the change to be successful, they, individually and as a group, will have to change their own thinking, perspectives, and behavior. Although their actions alone cannot create the desired culture, those actions can easily derail any new culture formation. For example, after the desired workforce attributes are identified, *every leader and manager* throughout the organization will have to understand, accept, and live those attributes if they expect the workforce to do so. Senior leadership may have to review and revise the organization's structure as well as the culture because structure can support or hinder cultural needs.

As a third step, the major characteristics of the culture need to be identified. For an ICAS with the action culture these would be something like the following:

- Flow—knowledge workers share information and knowledge throughout the organization.
- Collaboration—workers work together in teams and small groups to leverage the knowledge and actions of everyone.
- Creativity—workers have learning conversations, dialogues, open disagreement, throw out ideas, and try new approaches to their tasks.
- Empowerment—knowledge workers have the freedom (and support) to get their work done, understand the context of their work, and are aware of the boundaries of their action space.
- Communication and networking—employees have open communication and there is wide networking throughout the organization and with external stakeholders.
- Adaptability—employees continuously learn, change, and adapt to new circumstances and challenges, with encouragement and support from leaders and managers.
- Action orientation—everyone has the knowledge and motivation to take action, observe the results, get feedback and adjust their behavior as needed.
- Leadership—knowledge workers learn to be leaders by being role models, remaining objective, taking charge when appropriate, and looking out for others.

The above characteristics should become a natural fallout from how the work gets done and what knowledge workers and leaders should expect from, and contribute to, their working environment.

The next step is to determine what knowledge, personal attributes, and behavior ICAS employees need to create and implement the characteristics listed above as they perform their daily work. A sample of individual characteristics that make knowledge workers successful are: trust and trusting, self-confidence and a strong ego, integrity, the motivation and skill to apply their knowledge to new situations, social skills, self-discipline, and leadership potential. Knowledge workers also need to be articulate, continuous learners and team players.

With the above information, the fifth step is to select a set of actions that create and reinforce behavior through the multiple and myriad interactions occurring as the work gets done. These actions will then move the organization toward the desired action culture. In other words, the day-to-day work of the knowledge workers will create customs, norms, and behaviors that help get the job done and are comfortable to the workers. These norms should be close to the desired cultural characteristics developed in the third step. The knowledge worker characteristics suggested above are needed to enable the workers to create these cultural characteristics. Since cultural characteristics cannot be created through policy, rules, or managerial control, it is knowledge worker characteristics, skills, and behaviors that have to be nurtured and reinforced.

For individuals to change their characteristics and behavior, they must understand and agree with the need to change. This is much more that just providing a logical explanation. Reason falls before emotion and experience. Reason also depends on assumptions, context, and the laws of logic. Emotion, experience, personal goals, and the level of acceptable risk all come into play when change is imminent. This is why policies, rules, and memos that declare new processes and changes in behavior will not work by themselves. Individuals must see some personal gain such as improved performance, greater professional rewards, higher efficiency, or some other motivator. Workers also need to feel comfortable in their new roles of behavior. In other words, change must not endanger their self-image or persona. Any major change in the way things are done in an organization shifts roles, relationships, and psychological contracts between the individual and the organization. From the individual's perspective, these are gains and losses in a sea of unknown future relationships. Those who would change a culture must be acutely sensitive to the individual's perceptions, feelings, and expectations about the outcome of the change desired.

In selecting which actions to take, several factors should be kept in mind. One is the concept of leverage points within the organization. For example, some people will have more influence than others and can be very helpful in getting support from other workers. Another leverage point could be new technology that supports the workforce and at the same time requires new ways of doing the work, ways that support the desired action culture. For example, *ba* spaces (von Krogh et al., 2000), knowledge repositories, and yellow pages make sharing knowledge easier, thereby reinforcing other actions to get knowledge workers to communicate and share knowledge.

Another consideration is to look for patterns in the existing culture that help, or harm, the movement toward the action culture. A good place to start is by observing how the work actually gets done and understanding why it is done that way. These patterns of action have been created for good, albeit usually unknown, reasons on the part of the workforce, and wherever possible, actions that encourage the desired culture should be taken to speed up the transformation. For example, if people use friends and certain colleagues to help answer questions or solve problems, then networks can be set up to support these habits. Social network analysis, discussed briefly in Chapter 21, may be helpful to identify the most-used networks among the workforce as well as flow blockage points. A third action would be to review recent significant events and understand how and why they occurred. What, if any, patterns resulted from the events? Did they help or hurt organizational performance? This is another way of understanding the present culture and being able to make better decisions on how to shift to the new culture. A fourth action would be to review all company policies, rules, and processes to ensure that they are consistent with the desired culture, and, in particular, to eliminate contradictory or inhibiting policies wherever possible. An action culture contains risks that senior leadership must understand and accept if it is to be successful.

As we can see, changing a culture involves selecting and implementing many changes at the same time. When many changes happen at the same time, there is a sense of being out of control, a scary feeling to senior managers. This is usually counter to a manager's natural risk aversion behavior, since it exposes them to criticism and there is the difficulty of defending the approach if things do not go well. This is the price for success in the age of complexity. If we cannot predict the future nor control knowledge worker productivity, then the only alternative is to embrace complexity into our organizations and get everyone involved using their best efforts to work together within the uncertainty, change, and complexity that looms over and throughout the organization.

TRUST

As an example of change actions to create an action culture, we consider the need for the action culture to have the characteristic of flow; for workers to communicate, share knowledge, and network with each other. A major determinant of effective communication and sharing is the degree of trust throughout the workforce, of the organization as a whole and particularly of the organization's leadership. If knowledge workers trust each other and their leaders, they are much more apt to help each other and communicate more openly. The question then becomes: What actions would build and improve interpersonal trust throughout the organization?

As De Furia (1997) notes, "Interpersonal trust is present in a situation in which one individual places his or her interests under the control of another individual, with the expectation of gaining a desired outcome for which the potential negative consequences of violated trust are greater than the value of the potential desired outcome" (p. 5). For me to share my knowledge with you, I must believe that you will not misuse that knowledge, will not use that knowledge against me, and that if I need some knowledge from you, you will reciprocate. If I do not believe all of these things, then why should I share my knowledge? Note that *feelings about a person* may have nothing to do with trust. Trust is a cumulative belief that another individual will live up to our expectations, i.e., trust takes time to create, but can be lost in a single event.

De Furia (1997) proposes five behaviors that help build trust: sharing relevant information, reducing controls, allowing for mutual influence, clarifying mutual expectations, and meeting expectations. Now we are in a position to set up actions and encourage behavior throughout the organization that will lead to interpersonal trust. We can explain the importance of sharing information and the responsibilities that go with that sharing. Team leaders can discuss these responsibilities in the teams and communities and over the networks of the organization. They can also make information and knowledge sharing a part of the organization's performance appraisal system. On a one-to-one basis, collaborative leaders can work with team members who provide extraneous, irrelevant, or confusing information and explain how these traits make them appear untrustworthy.

For the organization to gain the trust of its employees, all leaders, managers, and influential workers have to be trustworthy and sensitive to their words and deeds *as seen* by the workforce. For example, senior manager's statements concerning the organization's direction, objectives, and vision should be cohesive and consistent. While differences among senior personnel are often a good thing, workers may interpret those differences to be deceit, defection, or distrust. From an overall organization's view, all communication should be open, honest, and thorough so that context and understanding are shared by all parties. This is not an easy thing to accomplish, yet it is essential for flexibility, collaboration, and fitness for survival.

Managers and team leaders can facilitate staff meeting dialogues on the importance of trust and discuss factors involved in creating and maintaining trust. They can point out daily examples of the need and benefit to individuals and the organization of working together and sharing knowledge, answering WIIFM (what's in it for me) questions in real time. To show that they trust their workers, managers can reduce their own controls by giving more freedom to their workers, letting them self-organize when and where it makes sense, and bringing them into relevant decisions, sharing the context and consequences. This is of immediate importance to an action culture because local self-organization, decision authority at the point of action, and team leveraging of knowledge all call for increased worker participation, authority, and accountability.

By giving up control, managers and team leaders model the trust behavior they want others to exhibit. Clarifying mutual expectations is basically open, honest communication on what each person expects of the others and prevents misunderstandings that can quickly be misinterpreted as a failure of trust by either party. When all parties meet other's expectations over time, trust, collaboration, and camaraderie build up in teams, networks, and organizations. Because of the importance of collaboration and knowledge sharing to an action culture, the level and importance of trust needs to be a continuous item for discussion throughout the organization, at least until it is firmly embedded in the culture. On the down side, if individuals clearly prove that they are untrustworthy and beyond redemption, they cannot remain in the organization. As harsh as this may seem, organizational survival and health cannot tolerate wounds or possible cancers within its body.

Finally, trust is as much a communication problem as an attitudinal problem. Often people do not have the communication skills to clearly signal their intentions or expectations. Good communication skills and the ability to clearly communicate intent are essential for each and every knowledge worker.

We have dwelt on trust because it is a foundation for leveraging knowledge and because it is so fragile. De Furia (1997) offers five "facts" about trust that provide the context for our concern:

- Low trust drives out high trust unless behaviors are corrected.
- Building trust is a slow process.
- Trust can be destroyed by a single event.
- Trust is destroyed by a win–lose mentality.
- Groups with low intermember trust can be so unsuccessful as to self-destruct.

To create an action culture many changes are needed at the same time and many people at several levels should be involved, i.e., creating or changing a culture requires parallel changes applied consistently and cohesively over time. Trust is only one of a number of factors mentioned above that need to be developed. You cannot just tell knowledge workers to share knowledge. Providing only technology and information solutions is never sufficient. These approaches may yield short-term responses but are unlikely to provide the long-term cultural changes intended. To get workers to share knowledge, they cannot just be told to do so, or given some reward. While providing the structures and artifacts that make it easier for knowledge workers to obtain and share information and knowledge will help encourage this behavior, their reasons for not sharing need to be surfaced and the context changed within which they get their work done. Trust needs to emerge from daily interactions and become *the way things are.*

REVIEWING STRUCTURE AND MANAGEMENT

In addition to making changes in individual behavior, the organization's structure can—and should—be analyzed and changes considered that would improve its support of the action culture. One approach is to start by studying recent events and patterns from the viewpoint of the current structure to determine their impact on how the work gets done. As Peter Senge (1990) has noted, structure is a key force in driving organizational events, patterns, and behavior. In Chapter 6 we presented a structure for the ICAS designed to support the action culture. The structure of the organization must be consistent with, and supportive of, the organization's culture. For example, if the IT department sees its role as supporting only senior management, it would be very hard to create a culture where knowledge workers would depend upon that department for either information or technical support.

Another factor in creating emergent properties is the role played by middle management. While it is important for senior management to understand and buy into any strategy for creating an emergent property, senior management will not be able to "sell" the desired changes to the workforce. In general, they do not have the interpersonal relationships with the workers and their context is often not as meaningful as a team leader who is local and close to the team's working world. Given that this is a good assessment of the challenge of creating an emergent property, how do we get senior managers to believe in and support the requisite multiple changes to create a new emergent property with the uncertainty of the outcome? Also, how do we get buy-in from middle managers on the importance and need for this new action culture and for the changes they must personally go through? Without the full understanding and personal enthusiasm of all of the leaders for the new organization, any lasting change or improvement is unlikely.

Considering senior management first, earlier in this chapter we described a process to go through to develop the strategy and approach to building the ICAS organization. An important key to this approach was that every senior manager must participate, learn, challenge, and thoroughly understand, accept, and believe in whatever results the group comes up with. The only way that we know of to achieve this is to have senior managers, working with outside experts as needed, *personally* develop a workshop that thoroughly covers all aspects of the strategy, emphasizing its implementation. The purpose is threefold: first, to ensure that all aspects of the strategy and its implementation have been carefully scrutinized and challenged by the view from the top; second, to get full understanding and buy-in on what will be done and how the process is to be conducted; and, finally, to get senior management participation by requiring every manager to teach/facilitate the workshop to their subordinates. There is no better way to learn (and believe in) a subject than to teach/facilitate the material in front of a group of serious and concerned subordinates. The process of asking and answering questions, generating ideas, and dialoguing about consequences not only creates a common understanding but develops ownership of the need and approach to be implemented. The workshops will also provide valuable feedback and potential problems back to the managers. Ideally each senior would give, or participate in, four workshops. It typically takes four repetitions to learn, develop insights, and make understanding a part of the unconscious beliefs and assumptions. If senior managers *believe* in the change *they will act on those beliefs* and in so doing transmit their beliefs to others in the workshop and to those they work with on a day-to-day basis.

The initial workshop could be developed by senior management with outside support. After the senior managers have completed their workshops each manager would then give the workshop to their immediate subordinates. This roll-down process continues until every employee in the organization has participated and provided inputs on the desired changes. These workshops—in concert with staff meetings, senior management talks, team dialogues, focus group sessions, and the usual corporate communication channels—will explain, reinforce, and support the desired changes. Time-consuming? Yes. Expensive? Yes. Risky? Somewhat. Necessary? Depends on the situation. Cost effective? Depends on the cost of not doing it.

THE ICAS EMERGENT CHARACTERISTICS

We now consider the eight emergent characteristics discussed in Chapter 4 to address some major factors that contribute to each of these characteristics. This process is the same as discussed earlier for flow. The first step is deciding what actions should be taken that would be used to create each characteristic. Recognize that the emergent characteristics are not independent, thus they cannot be treated in isolation, other than for explanation purposes.

The eight ICAS emergent characteristics discussed in Chapter 4 are shown in Figure 10-1. The figure also shows some of the main contributors to the ICAS operation, namely key factors of each emergent characteristic shown influencing the four major processes addressed in Chapter 8. Conceptually, the structure and culture are shown on the left as they support the key aspect of resources,

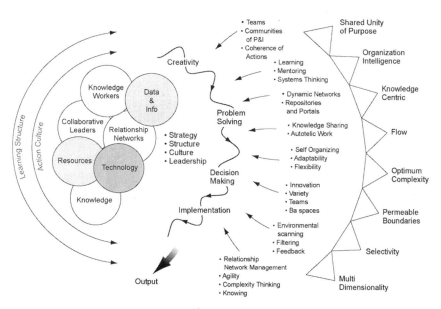

Figure 10-1
Factors Driving Emergence

knowledge, leaders, technology, knowledge workers, data and information, and relationship networks. These aspects, guided by the ICAS strategy, structure, culture, and leadership, also ensure the effectiveness of the four major processes through which all value for the customers is created. At the global level, the output of the four major processes represents the daily actions taken by ICAS knowledge workers. These actions determine the value added to customers and other stakeholders and the sum of all these actions make up overall organizational performance.

To influence each of the emergent characteristics, managers and leaders can take actions that create or modify the key factors shown in the figure. The factors shown may not be the only ones that influence their respective characteristic. Each ICAS-type organization is unique to its own environment and purpose. For example, in our previous treatment of flow we addressed many more factors than are shown in the figure. Whatever the right set of factors is for a given ICAS, recognize that those factors, working through the structure, culture, leadership, and strategy create their emergent characteristic as a global phenomenon that in turn supports and influences the quality of the four major processes.

To achieve a shared unity of purpose consider the following factors: clear and continuous two-way communication throughout the firm; a line of sight between the purpose of the organization and the actions of employees; a purpose that is consistent with organizational strategy and with employee values; the use of teams, communities of practice, and integrators to provide coherence of understanding.

Knowledge centricity requires senior leadership support; an awareness and appreciation for the impact of knowledge in performing work; knowledge repositories and information systems that support the decision and action needs of the knowledge worker; a knowledge taxonomy and ontology that facilitate the storage and retrieval of information; teams, communities, and dynamic networks to encourage the sharing, leveraging, and application of knowledge; and continuous learning.

Selectivity requires an awareness and understanding of the purpose, objectives, and values of the organization; a sensitivity to the competitive environment; the ability of workers to assess situations and their meaning so they can extract information useful to the organization; knowledge workers with the ability to see possibilities within and adjacent to their local domain of work; the skill and capacity to feedback and relay information and understanding to other workers throughout the organization.

Optimum complexity depends upon the organization's ability to generate ideas and responses capable of successfully responding to the events and situations impinging on the firm from the marketplace. It requires that knowledge workers understand complexity and are able to interpret events and patterns in the environment, and that organizational leadership allows and supports the creativity and innovative thinking needed to generate internal possibilities for action. It also requires that managers and team leaders have the ability to keep their people working at the edge of chaos when necessary, without falling into either chaos or stability. The organization must be tolerant of mistakes resulting from the trial-and-error application of new ideas.

There are many recommended approaches in the literature for implementing organizational change. To our knowledge, none of them directly addresses the issue of changing the organization by creating desirable emergent properties through changes in the work processes and workforce behavior. In any case, the creation of emergent properties has no guarantees. Each organization is unique, with its own history, context, culture, and marketplace. There are no silver bullets or panaceas in the world of complex adaptive organizations with their emergent properties. The approach offered here is no exception. As organizations become more and more complex and more adaptive the number of emergent properties is likely to increase and their role may dominate performance in industries operating at the forefront of change. If this happens, the challenge of dealing with emergent properties could inspire both organizational scholars and reflective practitioners in the future. The next chapter provides another perspective and additional ways to change organizations.

REFERENCES

De Furia, G. *Interpersonal Trust Surveys*. San Francisco: Jossey-Bass, 1997.

Senge, P. M. *The Fifth Discipline: The Art and Practice of the Learning Organization*. New York: Doubleday, 1990.

von Krogh, G., K. Ichijo, and I. Nonako. *Enabling Knowledge Creation: How to Unlock the Mystery of Tacit Knowledge and Release the Power of Innovation*. New York: Oxford University Press, 2000.

Chapter 11

THE CHANGE AGENT'S STRATEGY

Surviving and thriving in a multifaceted world requires a multifaceted change strategy. Paraphrasing Ashby's (1964) law of requisite variety, there must be more variety in the change strategy than in the system you are trying to change.

So how do we change a complex organization to meet the challenges of this new world of exploding information, increasing uncertainty, and ever-increasing complexity? While there is certainly no simple answer—since change is situation and time-dependent—the change process for an organization moving toward becoming an intelligent complex adaptive system must engage every individual in the firm as well as external partners. Since organizational networks of people and knowledge have become more and more interconnected and more and more complex as the world has become more global, the larger an organization the more a self-organizing change strategy must come into play.

An ICAS change strategy sets out to achieve what we call a *connectedness of choices*. This means that decisions made at all levels of the organization, while different, are clearly based not only on a clear direction for the future, but made in a cohesive fashion based on an understanding of both why that direction is desirable and the role that individual decisions play with respect to immediate objectives and their support of the shared vision. At the top level, a continuous increase of knowledge and sharing based on a common direction of the organization and a common set of beliefs and values is the theoretical force behind the change strategy.

THE GROWTH PATH OF KNOWLEDGE AND SHARING

Implementing change at every level of the organization follows the growth path of knowledge and sharing. For example, when exploring a new idea whether within an individual or in an organization as a whole—closed structured concepts are first created. As these concepts germinate, some focused but limited sharing of these concepts occurs. Over time, particularly if positive feedback occurs during the limited sharing, there is increased sharing and a deeper awareness and connectedness through sharing occurs, i.e., a common understanding of the concept is shared across a number of people. From this framework, individuals and organizations participating in this sharing create new concepts and from those concepts new innovations, then purposefully share them across and beyond the framework, leading to application of these ideas to everyday work. As connectedness increases, there is also heightened awareness, or consciousness, of the potential value of these concepts to a larger audience, leading motivated individuals and organizations to advance these concepts even further, engendering the rise of social responsibility (see Figure 11-1).

Wisdom occurs when knowledge is integrated with a strong value set and acted upon with courage. Through leading and teaching (leadership and education), this wisdom facilitates the growth of new concepts, and an expanded connectedness with like individuals and organizations around the world. It is at this level in the growth of knowledge and sharing where we have built enough wisdom and knowledge to create and share new thoughts in a fully aware and

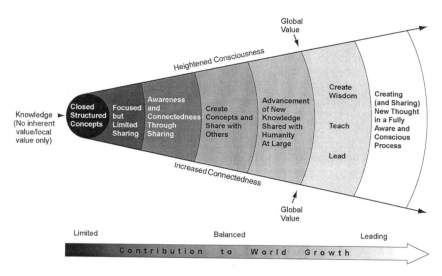

Figure 11-1
The Growth of Knowledge and Sharing

conscious process, i.e., to purposefully strategize what concepts to share and how to share them, consciously contributing to world growth.

The underlying realization in this pattern is that a single individual in an organization (or a single organization in an enterprise, or a single enterprise in a global market) cannot effectively function at a level so far above others that there is a lack of recognition and understanding of the level of that functioning. Historically, there are occurrences where innovators and forward-thinking ideas failed during one period of time only to emerge again during a later period as a leading market product or practice. The old adage "Everything in its own time" has helped explain the earlier failure. In the fast-paced and interconnected world of today, we have the ability to create "its own time," inverting the adage and placing success of forward-thinking ideas squarely in the ability of an organization to create a shared understanding across the global environment. In other words, while ideally the ICAS will stay ahead of competitive organizations, it may want to encourage sharing and the growth of knowledge across its market sector to ensure a wider and deeper understanding by customers of the value of its contribution to the marketplace.

For example, in an organization not built on flow and sharing, a brilliant idea developed before its time, which is so far beyond current thinking that no one recognizes its value, will have little chance of funding and support. In an industry where there is little cross-organizational sharing (other than piracy out of context), when a forward-thinking firm produces a product before its time, the product will have little opportunity for success without the recognition of value, the industry's ability to support and sustain it, and people's ability to use it. The sharing of ideas within and across organizations can plow the ground for receptivity and demand, with initial competitive advantage going to the first product in the field and the long-term competitive advantage going to the best and most continuously improved product.

Using Figure 11-1 as a model, the change agent's strategy suggested here is holistic, and not bounded by the organization. Indeed, it encourages interactions across large relationship networks and sharing and learning across organizational boundaries. As discussed above, while this may at first appear contrary to organizational advantage in a competitive world, having the best information and knowledge is only a first step toward being competitive. The greater value for an organization is how this knowledge is used and the ability of those who are using this knowledge to discern value in it, integrate it, recognize patterns, and adapt it to changing requirements in a turbulent environment. This knowledge can rarely be given away because no other organization would know how to discern value, interpret it, recognize patterns, or adapt it, but other organizations can build on it and, from their different perspectives, create new ideas that, in turn, can be built upon by other organizations.

Since change itself is an emergent characteristic, it is a product of combining, integrating, and correlating elements of the change strategy with the organization's direction, objectives, structure, culture, and leadership. The change strategy must be consistent with the desired organization (ICAS). In the ICAS, the means do not justify the end; they serve as an example of the richness and effectiveness of the end state, of the desired approach for how future work gets done. There is a visible consistency in ICAS theory and actions throughout the strategy suggested below.

The change strategy model can be viewed in terms of orchestrating and implementing *twelve specific elements*. These elements are: creating a shared direction; building the business case; demonstrating leadership commitment; facilitating a common understanding; setting limits; sharing new ideas, words, and behaviors; identifying the strategic approach; developing the structure; measuring and incentivizing; providing tools; promoting learning; and envisioning an even greater future. Each element is detailed below.

CREATE A SHARED VISION

In *The Fifth Discipline*, Peter Senge (1990) emphasizes the importance of a shared vision where employees participate in the development of a corporate vision, and can then make decisions and take actions consistent with the directions set by senior leadership through the shared visioning process. For the ICAS, in an unknowable future, the vision must be more of a direction than an end state. In their research on consciousness, Edelman and Tononi (2000) identify the mechanism that provides unity to consciousness, thereby creating a continuous history of thought and a consistency of identity and action. This ability to maintain different parts of the brain in harmony and to pull them together in an organization is facilitated by constant and widespread communication.

The journey toward becoming an ICAS starts with a shared direction of what the organization will accomplish and *how it will be accomplished*, i.e., how the work gets done. Learning from history, we realize that it is advantageous for an organization to have a strategic plan. What may be different about the ICAS approach is that the plan is a product of the whole organization, with inputs and reviews at every level of, and from every functional area in, the organization. In the development process, goals are worked and reworked to assure the right set of goals addressed at a low enough level to make them real and viable, and a high enough level to provide flexibility and tailoring at the point of action where implementation decisions are made. The plan has the potential to bring the organization's collective vision of its future into clear focus, and communicates leadership's commitment to this vision.

The process of developing the strategic plan is part of the change strategy. The strategic plan as a collective process brings with it a sense of ownership across the organization, and responsibility for the outcome, both laying the groundwork for successful implementation. A way to get even more people involved is to make success stories a part of the plan. Early in the planning cycle, leadership publicizes the desire to locate early successes to serve as examples for each top-level goal or objective of the plan. As the top-level goals/objectives emerge over the course of the planning process, with them emerge examples of innovative thinking that are jumpstarting the organization toward achieving these goals/objectives. Not only does this process identify innovations underway, but it facilitates further ownership of the plan, and encourages organizational units to understand and begin implementation of the plan prior to its publication and distribution. By the time the plan is staffed through the various stakeholders of the organization, the organization is aligned, senior leadership is committed, and implementation has already begun.

BUILD THE BUSINESS CASE

From a corporate view it is essential to have a strong business case for any anticipated change strategy. This business case lays out the current organizational effectiveness level, identifies needed changes and, most importantly, describes the anticipated changes and expected results of those changes in terms that make sense from a business perspective. However, the business perspective is not the only perspective to be considered because it is equally important to have the anticipated changes make sense to the employees and other organizational stakeholders such as customers and the environment and local community as they apply.

Walking through the process, the business case first looks carefully at the anticipated result of changes, the strategic and tactical actions necessary to achieve those changes and the anticipated performance and competitive advantage of the organization assuming those changes are successful. It needs to address those changes in terms of long-term organizational health and competitive advantage, short-term anticipated payoffs, and the various risks arising from the strategic and tactical implementation of the changes. For the business case to make sense, it must also address the current and anticipated environment from marketing and customer viewpoints as well as potential risks relative to government regulations, technology breakthroughs, etc.

The business case should include, wherever possible, quantitative parameters with backup information relative to their reasonableness in terms of investment requirements, return on investment expectations, etc. The reasons for the suggested or needed changes must be identified and thoroughly examined. Ideally, the changes needed at every level of the organization and perhaps with vendors, partners, and even customers are identified. The suggested changes are also looked at carefully relative to the impact on employees, the structure, and the culture. Historically, each employee's silent question will be WIIFM (what's in it for me?) and how will it affect my local work and my local organization, as well as the organization as a whole?

The business case also addresses the feasibility and fundamental approach for the change management recommended. Thus, are the changes consistent with the current structure and culture of the organization, or are both of those going to have to be significantly revamped to achieve the desired end state? What are the financial, managerial, sociological, technological, and political consequences of the recommended changes as seen by both outsiders and insiders?

An examination of basic beliefs and assumptions underlying the recommended changes needs to be performed with the results made part of the business case to ensure that suggested changes are not accidentally biased by antiquated assumptions or belief systems. For a business case to be solid, it also must include some idea of, and characterize in some fashion, the future market within which the organization is going to move.

The strength and thoroughness of the business case will depend heavily on the size of the organization, the nature of its leadership, and the expectations of its customers and other stakeholders. These balances may be large-scale research balances all the way down to individual knowledge worker competencies, attitudes, and decisions on priorities or work or how to approach problems. As always, since everyone is potentially subjected to internal biases, erroneous assumptions, and misplaced beliefs, it is wise to get a second, or perhaps group, opinion to reevaluate how individuals or teams perceive the situation, their most effective aspects of work, or their balance points. From another perspective, all changes in organizations create/demand a change in a number of balance points. While often knowledge workers and leaders do not recognize that they are changing balance points, it is exactly these changes that can be so threatening to individuals if they do not recognize them as balance points and important aspects of the work.

DEMONSTRATE LEADERSHIP COMMITMENT

When a respected senior leader clearly demonstrates commitment to a vision through words and actions, members of the senior leader's relationship network, which includes sub ordinates, quickly follow. In short, there are champions waiting to emerge throughout the organization: champions of theory and action, champions of specific processes or projects who are in fact *already implementing these processes or projects at some level.* In every organization there are forward-thinking individuals who push the edge of change, no matter what name that change is called by. It is the change agent's responsibility to find these individuals and spread the word of their successes, tying them to the vision of the organization. As leader after leader begins to demonstrate and communicate successes, large or small, other leaders recognize potential value to their focus areas of the organization. Interconnected successes quickly spread across the enterprise, proving the old adage "success begets success."

It is appropriate here to discuss the change agent's role in the organization. While the most effective change agent is recognized as organizationally connected to the highest levels of the organization, having free access to senior leadership, a true agent of change cannot be considered a competitive part of the infrastructure, nor can a successful change agent own the change they lead. These people are assigned to act as a funnel for building change across the organization, identifying successes, picking up the ideas behind those successes, and spreading them throughout the organization. The change agent connects people, integrates ideas and actions, and builds visibility of leadership commitment to those ideas and actions. Simple but consistent actions can facilitate this change. Here are some ideas about how to capture and communicate leadership commitment in a large, widely dispersed, global organization:

- Develop a *short* video, beginning with a two-minute opening by the senior leader of the organization, and featuring project leaders talking about their early successes. Have the senior leader hand-write notes to accompany copies of the video to leaders throughout the organization, asking them to ensure that every employee has the opportunity to see the video.

- Develop pass-it-down training, beginning at the very top of the organization. The concept of pass-it-down training is that leaders at all levels have the opportunity to impress on their teams the importance and significance of building the ICAS. This process has the added benefit of ensuring that organizational leadership understands the new organization and how it will operate. Teaching and facilitation are forms of learning and leading.

- Hold a "town hall," featuring senior leadership, virtually supported (television, video) to facilitate geographically dispersed organizations, with live connectivity via telephone and computers. Much like a telethon, this event will offer the opportunity for workers at all levels to interact with senior leadership, voicing their concerns and ideas and receiving an immediate response, albeit "we need to think more about that." This process, called "event intermediation," ensures a point in time where all senior leaders understand the importance of the ICAS, and have an awareness of what their areas of responsibility are doing to move toward becoming an ICAS.

- Capture quotes from early leaders and champions and embed these in presentations, both internal and external, at every level of the organization.

- Hold a "knowledge fair," where every functional and organizational area of the organization is featured showing how they are contributing to achieving the vision. Have senior leadership open the fair, and include enjoyable, memorable events that are centered around the way the organization needs to work, with members of the organization participating in the presentation. Create a groundswell of sharing and understanding by opening the fair to employees, stakeholders, and partners.

- Develop a virtual CD or portal-based reference tool about the knowledge fair capturing people talking about their projects and leaders talking about their organizations, all focused on their contribution to achieving the ICAS vision. Circulate this throughout the organization and the organization's stakeholders.

FACILITATE A COMMON UNDERSTANDING

So often we as human beings leap forward with little thought for the consequences. While a shared vision certainly helps define the direction we are leaping, the larger and more complex an organization the more the imperative to develop a shared understanding of the *reasons behind* the movement toward that vision to ensure a connectedness of choices.

Representations in terms of words and visuals are the tools of trade for facilitating common understanding. Early models should address those areas needing the greatest clarity. Since every organization is at a different stage of development, has a different culture, and may or may not already understand the importance of knowledge and learning to the success of the organization, it is critical to ensure a solid recognition of the power of sharing knowledge, moving the organization from the bureaucratically embedded concept of "knowledge is power" to the emerging concept of "knowledge shared is power squared." For example, the knowledge life cycle model used through the government (Figure 11-2) was intended to generate discussion on the relationship among data, information, and knowledge; the reality of information decay (information has the potential to become less important over time); and the effects as knowledge spreads across the competitive base. Each employee has a story to tell, and the intent of this model was to engage response, to bring out both positive and negative feelings regarding past experiences, clearing the air to move toward a new way of thinking, and build focused thought. Facilitating a common understanding of the knowledge life cycle is so critical that the KMCI organization has spent several years developing a knowledge life cycle model (Firestone and McElroy, 2003).

When Figure 11-2 was used as the Department of the Navy moved toward becoming a knowledge-centric organization, there were common stories that emerged. For example, one explication might go like this: as knowledge is shared across organizations, it becomes more widely used. On the negative side this

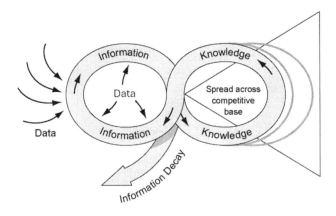

Figure 11-2
The Knowledge Life Cycle Model

means that competitors now have the same opportunities; on the positive side, since ideas generate ideas, everyone has a greater opportunity to build new knowledge. What becomes of paramount importance is how those ideas are used. Another common explication that emerged from looking at the model focused on creativity and went something like this: since all people are creative, and everyone in today's world has access to an almost exponentially increasing amount of information, it is likely that any given creative idea will emerge in more than one place. Once again, what is paramount in a competitive market is *continuous learning* (creation of new ideas) and the *ability to effectively (and quickly) act on those ideas.*

To build a common understanding of "knowledge," a simple visual of a red apple with a bite taken out of it can be used (see Figure 11-3). Within the apple are listed many of the IT advances important to success. The word "knowledge" streams out of the empty space where the bite was taken. The message delivered with this visual is simple and straightforward: while all that we are doing in information technology and information management is critically important, it is not until the bite (of information) is taken, chewed, digested, and acted upon that it becomes knowledge. Knowledge is created within the individual, and it is actionable. While organizational knowledge could certainly be considered an emergent phenomenon, the creation of knowledge and recognition of patterns at the organizational level is through people.

Once again, the process and thinking that goes into developing the models an organization uses to convey the way work gets done are just as important as the outcome. We'll discuss this further in the next change element on setting limits.

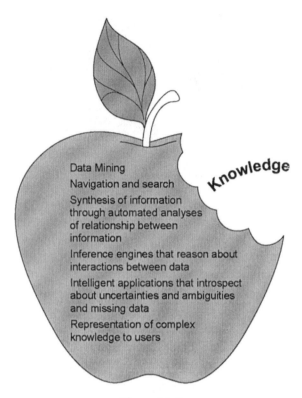

Figure 11-3
The Bite of Knowledge

SET LIMITS

All of the models discussed above limit the field of the possible in order to focus on a concept, facilitate a deeper understanding of that concept, and provide a mechanism for communicating that concept. We also set limits (provide focus) through developing and refining descriptions and definitions. Focusing on a concept in this manner provides the opportunity for developing new ideas, and new thinking. For example, The Federal Chief Information Officer Council invited cross-agency participation, and representatives from the private sector and academia to focus on what knowledge management meant to the Federal government. The results of this partnering were a clearer understanding of the role of Chief Knowledge Officers in the U.S. government, and definition of the fourteen learning objectives for a government certification course. In essence, these learning objectives defined the scope of knowledge management for the Federal government as seen at that point in time. Limiting the scope of what was involved provided the opportunity to focus in these areas to add value to the bottom line of the organization. These learning objectives are detailed in Chapter 15.

A second example is one that might sound familiar; it has occurred in many government and private sector organizations. It is also analogous to any new change effort that the environment dictates—and management agrees—will add value to organizational effectiveness. When e-business became the leading concept of the day, in many organizations money was taken from current change efforts to fund the new idea on the block. When a new concept emerges and is either supported by senior leadership or should be, it is the change agent's task to clearly build the relationship between the new idea and current efforts to harness any synergy between new and current management focus areas. Too often, ongoing change efforts are tossed aside for new ideas before they have a chance to add value to the organization, and, eventually, as this pattern repeats itself, it is difficult for employees to take management change efforts seriously. This results in an organizational culture encouraging a wait-and-see attitude regarding all change strategies. By building on current efforts—and then fading out or merging these efforts with the new as is determined favorable to the organization over time (with employee input)—it is possible to take full advantage of new concepts, approaches, and perceptions.

A potential first step toward achieving this strategy is for the leaders of each change effort to coauthor and publish articles on the focus of each of these efforts, and how they fit together to work toward achieving the organization's mission. This process helps develop agreed-upon definitions, brings about focus, and builds working relationships that will help both efforts succeed. Returning to our example, how would we provide focus and create synergy between e-business (eB) and knowledge management (KM)? The focus of KM is on intellectual capital (with KM viewed as a process for optimizing the effective application of intellectual capital to achieve organizational objectives), and that means people; while eB is the interchange and processing of information via electronic techniques for accomplishing transactions based upon the application of commercial standards and practices. These definitions reflect a common focus viewed through different lenses. Continuing the analogy, both eB and KM bring with them a focus on processes. KM provides a methodology for creating processes within the organization to promote knowledge creation and sharing—processes that build on total quality and business process reengineering concepts. In like manner, an integral part of implementing eB is the application of business process improvement or reengineering to streamline business processes prior to the incorporation of technologies facilitating the electronic exchange of business information. KM, implemented by and at the organizational level, and supporting empowerment and responsibility at the individual level, focuses on understanding the knowledge needs of an organization and the sharing and creation of knowledge through communities and Web-enabled collaboration, connecting people. The knowledge systems supporting these communities, based on interoperability concepts to ensure enterprise-wide sharing, build on information management, taking into account the human factor. While both KM and eB are in the business of information exchange, the KM focus is specifically on the knowledge sharing aspect of this exchange. This focusing of KM and eB—or setting of limits—provides a rich fabric for the two strategic efforts to complement each other and for the organization to recognize that both efforts offer synergistic opportunities for long-term success.

SHARE NEW IDEAS, WORDS, AND BEHAVIORS

Thinking in new ways demands new words, or putting old words together in new ways, to communicate new thinking; and those new words (or combinations of old words) drive new behaviors. In like manner, new behaviors drive new thinking and new words. As early as 1784 Hugh Blair identified a clear, close alliance between thought and language, "Thought and Language act and re-act upon each other mutually" (Erlbaum, 1982, p. 72). Later theorists such as Brown, Black, Bloomfield, Skinner, Quine, Popper, Wittgenstein, and Whorf regarded language as a major form of behavior, a significant entity in its own right. Emig (1983) contended that language is a powerful, if not unique, way of constructing reality and acting on the world. While the theoretical tapestry that builds relationships among thinking, language, and actions is varied and inconclusive, it is clear that there is a relationship, and that effective use of words and understanding the concepts these words represent has the potential to affect thoughts and behaviors.

As an example, take the concepts of clustering and clumping. While these words have long been a part of Webster's collection, the way they are used in forward-thinking organizations today drives a necessary change in behavior. Clustering and clumping define different ways of organizing (and accessing) data and information. Clustering is how data and information are usually organized, bringing together those things that are similar or related. This way of organizing is driven by the content of the data and information itself. Clumping is organizing data and information driven by the decisions that need to be made. At the enterprise level, those authoritative data fields that are needed for decision-making are identified and connected (or clumped together) to provide real-time input to emerging decision-making requirements. In a system, that means linking secondary data and information needed by the individual who will use the primary information for decision-making. For example, if a decision-maker has repeated failure of an engine part that is only periodically used, not only is it important to know how to fix it and have spare parts available if it is a recurring problem, but it might have saved considerable time, effort, and dollars if the decision-maker had the knowledge that the engine was scheduled for replacement six months down the road. There are often pieces of information that if known would change the decisions we make on a daily basis. When a segment of the organization creates a database or information system for the organization or enterprise, it is responsible for thinking through how that information will be used, and what additional known or potentially available information may be required by the decision-maker using the original information. We don't know what we don't know. With knowledge comes the responsibility to use and share it wisely, and to help others use and share it wisely.

A second example is the increasing use of the word *verication*. Verication, not yet discovered by dictionary updaters, is the process of consulting a trusted ally. We as humans do it regularly. When we do not have explicit evidence to verify the correctness of a decision, or question the explicit evidence we do have because of our "gut" feeling, we vericate the decision. This means going to a recognized expert with whom you have a relationship (a trusted ally, often a colleague or friend) to get their opinion, i.e., grounding your decision through implicit data and information. Having a word for this behavior helps leaders and workers to recognize it as an acceptable practice in decision-making, increasing the value of intellectual capital in the organization.

As new ideas, words, and behaviors are shared consistent with the vision of the organization, an aggressive, comprehensive communications strategy, both internal and external, is essential to ensure the connectedness of choices discussed above. Internal successes and external validation provide strong explicit evidence in support of the business case. The use of teams and communities—an important part of the ICAS implementation strategy helps—facilitate the flow of information and knowledge across the organization. Here are a few ideas on how to do that:

- Create a *meme* (an idea that catches on and becomes embedded in the culture). An example of a meme is "change through ex-change" or the famous army slogan, "be all you can be." These are expressions that take on a life of their own. "Knowledge shared is knowledge squared" is also a meme.
- Build a story on the vision of your organization and circulate it widely, using it as a basis for discussions.
- Participate in external studies and research projects with respected, high-name-recognition organizations such as APQC (American Productivity Quality Center). When participating in a study, rotate representatives and create forums for these representatives to share what they are learning.

IDENTIFY THE STRATEGIC APPROACH

There is no substitute for strategic thinking at all levels of the organization. To create an ICAS organization, all knowledge workers need to think strategically as well as locally. The first key to any kind of "thinking" is an understanding of what needs to be thought about. So, develop a draft concept of operations for the new organization and spread it across the organization for response. Put it up on a server and open it up for virtual comment (with ownership of comments). This is an important point. If a knowledge worker has a point to make, it should be a point they will claim, and one the organization will look at and consider. (Another option is to have every leader in the organization read this book.)

Implementation at the organizational level must be discussed in terms of connectivity and flow. See Chapter 10 for a complementary approach to change related to the creation of emergent characteristics of an organization.

A key part of the change strategy is creation of a community of practice to help facilitate change, engaging integrators at all levels of the organization. One person, or one part of the organization, cannot accomplish change; it must come from within at every level of the organization. Integrators (often collaborative leaders) are knowledge workers who are respected, trusted, and regularly communicated with by others in the organization. The integrator role is highly dependent on personality and values, and is a role that emerges over time in relationship networks. These individuals, key to both formal and informal networks, are usually obvious in an organization, but can be identified through social network analysis. (See Chapter 21, "Networking for the Bottom Line.") Develop these integrators into leaders and champions. Implement their good ideas; and, above all, engage them in multiple teams and communities.

DEVELOP THE STRUCTURE

As technology advances, seamless infrastructure is essential to facilitate the collaboration and free flow of information that enables effective decision-making. While short-term change can occur through mandates, unfortunately it is often short-term in effectiveness as well. Long-term change requires embedding the change in the culture of the organization (see Chapters 7 and 10). At the same time, the infrastructure must be put in place to support the vision of how work will be done.

We live in a technology-enabled world with global implications. More and more work will be done at a distance, driving the need for collaboration and knowledge systems that support interoperability. Development and support of, and rewards to, teams and communities ensure *use* of the technology and information infrastructures; education and training of the workforce ensure the *ability* to successfully use it.

The organization's Career Center, in conjunction with the human resources department, can benefit long-term change in a number of areas. Here are some ideas:

- Conduct a gap analysis of the skill sets of the current organization and the desired organization, addressing the competencies necessary to achieve projected missions and strategies and initiatives to help the organization attract new personnel and sustain the capabilities to accomplish its missions.
- Identify the work that will be done within the organization, and that work which will be outsourced to support the organization. For the government, this includes identifying the work that is inherently governmental.
- Develop a Workforce Strategic Plan to develop strategies and specific plans for hiring, training, and professional development, with the goal to promote integrative competencies throughout the workforce. A thoughtful, visionary, and forward-thinking plan can lay the foundation for positive organizational transformation.
- Develop a career path guide to provide individual guidance to employees in meeting the continuing challenges of technological change. The guide should include an explication of roles in the new ICAS organization with related learning objectives and sample assignments.
- Create a virtual tool for individuals to use in developing their personal career paths. The tool could help the workforce assess their current and required competencies, as well as helping them generate a career progression plan to attain competencies needed for future assignments based on individual, long-term goals.
- Embed change elements and future skills needed into all ongoing short and long-term education, and learning training initiatives.

MEASURE AND INCENTIVIZE

In a survey conducted a few years ago in a government organization implementing a KM system pilot, responders identified the most important factors in successful KM implementation in this relative order: culture (29%), processes (21%), metrics (19%), content (17%), leadership (10%) and technology (4%). What is fascinating, and a product of the organization's culture as well as that of many industry organizations, is that metrics (how success is measured and communicated) appeared more important than content (that which is in the system itself). Metrics are critical to most organizations, and have become part of the culture of the organizations as well as their managing system. Recognizing this aspect of your organization from the very beginning of a change approach can mean the difference between success and failure of your change efforts.

Metrics drive behavior, and can be a powerful force of behavioral change. One change approach is to ensure metrics are used that measure the organization's intent for the future—not just measuring past actions. Senior leadership can sponsor a working team focused on developing metrics *guidance* for the organization that includes participation from across functional and organizational units. While metrics must be specifically tailored to the organization, there are three types of specific measures to monitor and guide change initiatives from different perspectives: *outcome metrics* (concerning the overall organization and measuring large-scale characteristics such as increased productivity or revenue for the organization); *output metrics* (measuring project level characteristics such as the effectiveness of lessons learned information to capturing new business); and *system metrics* (monitoring the usefulness and responsiveness of the supporting technology tools). Have your team develop an overall process for developing metrics, including sample metrics and case studies. Again, recall that what you measure should identify what management feels is important, and drives the way work will be done. Measure for the future.

An active and highly visible awards program that rewards both individual and team behaviors draws out successes and involves a larger number of employees in change efforts. Once again, behaviors that are rewarded will become behaviors that are embedded into the infrastructure of the organization and of the organizational culture. Here are some ideas:

- Develop an awards program rewarding teams who are early implementers, with senior leaders presenting the awards. Create events to publicize these awards.
- Sponsor spin-off communities of practice and interest and build-in both individual and group awards. Examples of awards programs would include a monetary award for the individual who is voted (by members of the community) as the most knowledgeable, most accessible, and with the best response rate; and a group award to all members of the community who participate in specific solutions.
- Give promotions in terms of leadership and monetary remuneration to those individuals (and teams!) who best emulate the desired behavior for the future organization.

PROVIDE TOOLS

Buckminster Fuller once said that if you want to change a culture, provide tools. Any change approach can benefit when we recognize the truth of this observation. As guidance and policy is issued, tools that provide approaches to, and resources for, accomplishing that guidance and policy are distributed. As befits the ICAS organization, the tools themselves are a product of subject matter experts across the organization who come together for a period of time to develop these resources, i.e., the process of development as well as the product is part of the change strategy. Virtual toolkits are then made freely available—on the server and/or compact disks—to all employees, stakeholders, and organizational partners, with the understanding that change in a complex organization must be validated externally while driven internally. Change cannot occur in isolation, and with the permeable and porous boundaries necessary for successful organizations in a global world, it is difficult for a single organization, or part of an organization, to move forward when those surrounding them are operating at a stale level of thinking. Areas of initial focus for developing the ICAS include:

- All of the integrative competencies (see Chapters 14 through 19) and any additional ones specifically required for your organization to survive and grow.
- Team and community care and feeding.
- Metrics guidance.
- Security and privacy issues in an open environment.

PROMOTE LEARNING

No organization or individual can change without learning, nor once change is made can any organization or individual continue to function and be of value in a changing environment without continuous learning. Though this important concept emerged over a decade ago in the Total Quality environment, and Senge (1990) pushed the learning organization into higher-level executive thinking, we're just beginning to realize the importance of it, and putting systems in place to help facilitate learning in a virtual world.

A first step is to embed learning into the everyday life of the organization, with the organization and its leaders encouraging and providing opportunities for learning, and every knowledge worker taking responsibility for—and being accountable for—their own learning (see Chapters 14 and 16). Here are several ideas to begin this approach:

- Issue continuous learning guidance for the entire workforce, placing increased responsibility on employees to remain current and expand by taking advantage of new ways of learning. Distributed learning technologies, experiential learning, and other nontraditional approaches to education and training are rapidly supplementing the traditional classroom student/instructor approach. With these new approaches, knowledge workers have the ability to take responsibility for and direct their own learning and development in a variety of ways, and on a continual basis, throughout their careers. The guidance sets the expectation that all knowledge workers participate in a set figure such as 120 hours of continuous learning activities (using organizational toolkits, attending conferences, etc.) each year in addition to the minimum competencies established in their career fields and required for specific workforce assignments.

- Make continuous learning a bullet in every individual's performance appraisal. Taking the ICAS approach, each employee would develop a continuous learning plan in concert with their manager and team leaders, self- certifying completion of this plan during performance appraisals.
- Set the organizational expectation—and validate that expectation by example at the highest levels of the organization—that every leader will be a mentor, and that every learner has the responsibility for horizontal sharing of what they are learning.
- Ensure rotational assignments, allowing individuals to build viable networks based on relationships across the organization (and beyond the organization in their fields of expertise wherever possible).

ENVISION AN EVEN GREATER FUTURE

The place from which we currently act and respond, our point of reference, is reflective of the bureaucratic model upon which our organizational structures were grounded. As a groundswell of change is created through this strategy in conjunction with the creative change ideas that will emerge from within, the organization's point of reference will also change. To ensure this process of continuous improvement, new ideas and new thoughts need to come into focus and enlarge the future vision. This, of course, is the role played by new management movements, as organizations in the Western world moved through total quality management and business process reengineering, then e-business and knowledge management. What is critical for future success is an organization's ability to take the best of each new focus area—each new fad—discern the value, determine fit, and integrate the best of each focus area into the organization in a way that makes sense.

In the complex world in which we live, there is no lack of new management approaches, and assuredly each approach offers potential value. What is difficult to some to achieve is the balance between recognizing and sustaining that which is good in an organization, embedding that which has been determined valuable and is currently being implemented, and embracing the value offered by new management approaches. What is that balance? What are the potential gains and losses from this approach? How do we facilitate the gains and mitigate the losses? Finally, since a complex organization cannot be controlled in the classical meaning of the term—nor should it be—how do we ensure that value, as it emerges, is shared across the organization?

This dilemma of balance extends through every aspect of an organization. A visible example is the insertion of new information technology such as wireless. At what point does the organization wishing to succeed in the future global world embrace wireless technology? How fast should this transition move? What mindsets and strategies (such as moving the security focus from technology to information) need to be changed?

In this new world, many organizations are moving forward at a fast pace, with a vision and strategy, but without a predetermined path. The path has been and will continue to be forged by dedicated professionals in each organization, working individually and collectively, but always aware of the organization's mission and vision. The ICAS vision is to increase the number of dedicated professionals, and to ensure that every single individual in the organization has awareness of—and is committed to achieving—the vision of the organization. As this vision turns and changes in response to the turbulent environment, the understanding of individuals within the organization must turn and change with it.

This focus on people is holistic, ranging from the creation of theory and the building of shared understanding to the development of infrastructure to support individual and organizational learning and development of knowledge centricity. Enterprise-level leadership ranges from promulgating guidance and policy, to providing tools, to rewarding success. Effectively, this complex change strategy cannot help but encourage a natural progression toward the ICAS across and within the organization, contributing to the cultural change essential to take full advantage of the opportunities offered by the ICAS, and facilitating a connectedness of choices through the sharing of new thought in a fully aware and conscious process.

REFERENCES

Ashby, W. R. *An Introduction to Cybernetics*. London: Methuen, 1964.

Edelman, G. and G. Tononi. *A Universe of Consciousness: How Matter Becomes Imagination*. New York: Basic Books, 2000.

Emig, J. *The Web of Meaning: Essays on Writing, Teaching, Learning and Thinking*. New Jersey: Boynton/Cook Publishers, 1983.

Erlbaum, L. *Writing: The Nature, Development and Teaching of Written Communication*, Vol. II. Lawrence Erlbaum Associates, 1982.

Firestone, J. M. and M. W. McElroy. *Key Issues in the New Knowledge Management*. Burlington, MA: KMCI Press/Butterworth-Heinemann, 2003.

Senge, P. *The Fifth Discipline: The Art and Practice of the Learning Organization*. New York: Doubleday, 1990.

Chapter 12

STRATEGY, BALANCE, AND THE CORRELATION OF FORCES

For decades, senior managers have felt compelled to develop detailed plans and strategies to define a vision, objectives, and a pathway to achieve those objectives for their organizations to guide them into the future. The standard procedure is to study the environment, find the major trends, and develop a vision of what the organization should be to achieve a competitive advantage. Then these same senior managers analyze the current status of the organization, lay out the difference between what currently is and the vision (identifying the gap as it is commonly called), and prepare the strategy, tactics, and operational actions to close the gap. The often unstated assumption is that the future will be like the present, or at least that the future is predictable and they have a good idea of what it will be. After decades of thinking efficiency, stability, quality, and optimization, and trying every new idea in management, senior managers look for another new idea, work harder, and continue to do what they have always done: identify the gap, write the strategy, and implement according to plan. This approach worked reasonably well when the environment was stable and the assumptions were right.

During the past decade this approach has come into question. Strategies are often shelved and ignored, or revised so often that they become irrelevant, other than as good learning tools. The most common errors that occur are making wrong assumptions about the present, or thinking that they could forecast the future. Recall that with the explosion of computers, communication technology, and the Internet came the acceleration of change, the rise of uncertainty, and the growth of complexity, resulting in the diminishing ability of organizations to anticipate what the future will be (see Chapter 2). For any firm operating in markets that behave this way, classic strategic planning and gap closure management is simply a dangerous way to go.

The questions faced by leading edge corporations operating in a complex environment are not so much what products to make or what processes are the most efficient, although both of these are important. The critical questions become considerations such as:

- How can we keep long-term customer loyalty when we do not know what their wants and needs will be next year?
- How will low-cost production techniques pay off if the product life cycle becomes six months?
- How cost effective is our value chain if it has a half-life of one year?
- How can we afford to develop our people if the turnover rate is 25 percent annually?
- How do we maintain high-quality products and services that have to continually change just to keep up with the market?
- How might we develop smarter products and better services than our competitors before we even know what our customers will want?
- How can we predict the consequences of our actions when we do not understand what is happening in our marketplace?
- Where can we find managers smart enough to run their departments when things are happening so fast that no one can know enough to make effective decisions?

In looking for answers to these critical concerns, managers have tried a full range of solutions, from management by objectives to total quality management to business process reengineering to customer relationship management to the balanced scoreboard to whatever comes next. While each of these can be valuable, and certainly each of these focus areas bring new learning to the workforce and organization, their successful implementation is situationally dependent and far from easy. When understood well and applied appropriately, each idea can contribute to organizational performance. Unfortunately, many application attempts fall short of expectations—not because the ideas are poor, but because they are limited in scope and rarely understood well enough to take into account counter-effects of the organization.

Historically, during times of intense competition and rapid change the corporate response has been to increase control so that the organization can react faster, but this only works where those in control know what the right decisions are. In a fast-paced, confusing, and unpredictable marketplace, how do we know what are the right decisions and actions? What level of decisions is appropriate for senior managers to make? Where do we find the answers to these types of questions?

There is another way to approach the problem of strategy. If we cannot know what the future will bring, then what strategy, if any, will best prepare an organization for surviving and maintaining competitive advantage? With this question the focus now shifts away from how can we do better what we have been doing, to *how can we create an organization that does not need to be able to second guess the future*. We can now escape from our historical assumptions and beliefs about business and start with a new framework for constructing strategy.

A FRAMEWORK FOR CONSTRUCTING STRATEGY

The framework presented here rests on three assumptions. First, the environment is basically unknowable, uncertain, nonlinear, complex, and rapidly changing. This is an extreme version of reality but not unknown. That said, it may be fathomable, that is it may be *possible*, to gain enough experience, knowledge, and insights that permit us to comprehend situations and take effective actions with a reasonable probability of success. We may be able to sense some local patterns and nuances in the environment without being able to predict their behavior; and we may be able to anticipate short-term behavior well enough to open up possibilities and opportunities. Thus we may be able to penetrate to the meaning or nature of the environment.

Second, if no one knows what the right answers are, the person closest to the environment and the specific situation will likely make the best decision, particularly if they are given the freedom, resources, competency, and organizational backing to act. The probability of effective actions can be increased further if individuals work together to sense, interpret, understand, and try to comprehend the environment. While the future may be unknowable, it is not unfathomable.

Finally, the process that has proven successful in unknowable environments is the process of evolution. As Axelrod and Cohen (1999) put it, "From evolutionary biology came the insights of Darwinian evolution, particularly that extraordinary adaptations can come about through the selection and reproduction of successful individuals in populations" (p. xiii). Along with successful individuals, think of successful ideas, knowledge, and actions of the workforce and the power of the ICAS becomes visible.

With these three assumptions in mind, we start at the interface of the organization and its environment. Here is where knowledge, decisions, and actions make the difference. Customers talk and interact with employees, events are seen and experienced by knowledge workers, and value is offered and purchased, or lost, at this interface. It is here that images and reputations are strengthened or tarnished. It is here that experiences (and feelings) are embedded in customer and stakeholder memories, holding the keys to the organization's future. Being close to the events and the patterns and structure of the environment, knowledge workers are in the best position to observe and react to external situations. Even so, they may often be faced with many things that do not make sense—confusing behavior from customers, regulator demands, competitor moves, local and global economic perturbations, and technological surprises—so that they will be continuously challenged to anticipate the results of their actions. To counter this uncertainty, knowledge workers take an educated trial-and-error approach: taking their best, most knowledgeable action, observing the results, studying the feedback, and continuing those actions that work and changing those that do not work. This approach is almost continuous, with workers adapting and readapting to their local situations, amplifying when they are right and quickly correcting actions that do not produce desirable results; always, however, using all of the resources of the organization to find, create, test, amplify, and vericate the best knowledge possible to ensure that the most effective actions are taken.

For this strategy to pay off, the organization must provide knowledge workers with the resources, the information, and the knowledge needed to take the best possible actions. At the same time these actions must be consistent with the local objectives and global direction of the organization. Since effective actions are based on effective decisions, and both depend on the knowledge of the individual (or team), a major part of this strategy is to make knowledge centricity, flow, and collaboration a natural part of the organization's day-to-day operation, i.e., its culture. We now realize how far the ICAS strategy has gone beyond the usual control approach of laying out objectives and assigning individuals the responsibility for them. Instead, we look at the whole organization in terms of its structure, culture, leadership, management, and human resource policies. It is the complete organization, operating more as an organic body than a mechanical system, that has the learning, adaptability, sustainability and synergistic capacity to act intelligently and utilize all available resources, acting through its local teams and individuals, all closely supported by the leadership, structure, and culture of the ICAS.

These characteristics are both local and global, arising from the competency of the knowledge workers combined with enlightened leadership and management. Mid-level managers and team leaders play a vital role in influencing how the work gets done and coordinating the overall day-to-day operations. Senior leadership sets the direction, allocates top-level resources, and nurtures the character and capacity of the organization for survival and success. Their emphasis is not on the historical planning, organizing, staffing, directing, and controlling. Instead, they work to make the firm internally strong and externally smart. Rather than getting things done through others, they get things done with others, taking a collaborative leadership role. Their goal is sustainable competitive advantage; their methodology is internal organizational intelligence and mobility.

To achieve this, senior leadership strategy includes the organization-wide capacity to continuously monitor and adjust the balance of internal forces and resources to match the changing needs of the workforce as it adapts to a changing environment. Organizations have always operated with an internal balance of structure and resources. This balance provides the organization with the strength and stability of equilibrium while maintaining some flexibility for change. To operate in a complex world, effective strategy will include deliberate, consistent, and dynamic management of this internal balance to ensure that the right blend of structure, technology, knowledge, material, and financial resources are available as needed. Classical strategic planning includes the concept of pivot points, the ability of the organization to change its tactics at some point when things are not going as planned (Boar, 1993). The concept of dynamic balance with its practice of real-time adjustment is more effective in a turbulent environment and complements pivot points at the global level.

THE ISSUE OF DYNAMIC BALANCE

When considering a situation, an organization, or a state of affairs, the statement, "Everything is exactly as it should be" has a very interesting interpretation. It can be interpreted as implying that the organization when observed is the result of a balance of forces among many different interacting individuals and artifacts. Clearly, where things are moving and changing within the organization there is an unbalance of forces creating this movement. These forces may come from knowledge workers needing help, customer requests, or a team leader wanting to have a quick meeting. Higher-level examples would be the reallocation of funding to take advantage of a new opportunity or a competitor's recent action that could jeopardize the ICAS market share.

In order to be successful in the turbulent world, the ICAS must be a robust organization capable of changing within itself and being able to respond to many different and surprising events in the environment. At the same time, when things are relatively stable, the ICAS must be capable of maximizing its output performance and maintaining a steady state or system that is pretty much in balance. To be able to handle both of these conditions—relative stability and expected agility, and flexibility and adaptiveness—we introduce the concept of dynamic balance. What dynamic balance means is that leaders and workers throughout the organization will typically have to continuously balance a number of opposing forces or demands. These balances will rarely remain constant for very long. Hence, collaborative leaders and others will be able to change the balance of forces within their area of responsibility to optimize local effectiveness. This dynamic balancing will happen at all levels of the ICAS, with the result of facilitating flexibility, agility, and adaptation.

Below we examine various forces and parameters within the ICAS organization that may be balanced either statically or dynamically. A complex adaptive system strives to co-evolve with its environment by maintaining a close ecological fit with that environment. It responds to changes in the environment by changing its structure, processes, culture, and/or behavior through dynamic balancing of the relevant forces throughout the organization and perhaps throughout the enterprise. This internal rebalancing of various resources, relationship, and needs will be done at the organizational level, the leadership level (that is, team leaders and managers), and the knowledge worker level. We make no attempt to address all possible tradeoffs or balances since they are extremely numerous and depend upon the specific firm considered. Rather, below we will consider some of the more important forces in the organization as follows:

- *Organizational Balancing Needs*
  Resource allocation
  Short-term vs. long-term
  Information vs. knowledge
  Maintaining optimum complexity
  Stakeholder needs
  Corporate alignment vs. local responsiveness
  Cost vs. payoff of global characteristics
- *Leader Balancing Needs*
  Control vs. freedom
  Resource allocation for major processes
- *Knowledge Worker Balancing Needs*
  General vs. individualized learning
  Acquiring vs. contributing to knowledge

For dynamic balancing to work all levels of personnel must accept, support, and implement continuous change through rebalancing for adaptation. The structure, culture, leadership and resources of ICAS must all be capable of consistent change. We start with organizational-level balancing.

Organizational Balancing Needs

One balance that organizations must achieve is that of resource allocation. Here managers and leaders at all levels continually look at resources and their application with respect to the various internal and external needs of the organization. The results of these allocations have a significant impact on where the organization puts it efforts and talent to resolve short-term problems and opportunities as well as looking toward long-term potential payoffs. Since funds are almost always limited, such allocation usually results in specific tradeoffs of one possibility versus another. For the ICAS, where the environment is changing continuously and rapidly, the resource allocation process must be efficient, quick to respond and well balanced. The Operations Center, coupled with the leadership hierarchy, the teams-within-teams concept, and the action culture will allow rapid collaboration. This collaboration, accompanied by a common understanding of the direction of the organization, will provide an agile resource allocation system. One issue flowing from this will be the balance of resources applied to immediate action, such as taking advantage of opportunities and threats versus investment for long-term payoffs. This balance may include considerably more than funding resources since the organization must continually consider immediate organizational and individual learning needs versus long-term learning requirements.

Another short-term versus long-term tradeoff occurs in terms of profitability. Quarterly stock market evaluations and profits can significantly impact the immediate stock value of the company, yet investments in areas that may create higher long-term profitability may lower current profitability. This, of course, is not new with the ICAS. What is different in the new world is the difficulty of anticipating long-term profit investments, except for organizational factors such as learning, competencies, infrastructure, etc.

A third aspect is the learning versus doing balance. For the ICAS to survive over the long term it must become a learning organization both organizationally and individually (see Chapters 16 and 17). To create such a culture requires a certain amount of learning on a continual basis. Therefore, this represents a long-term investment in the future of the organization while reducing short-term profitability.

A fourth tradeoff is that between information versus knowledge. Recall that information is data with some context associated with it, and typically answers the questions of what and who. Knowledge, on the other hand, is the potential and actual ability to take effective action through understanding and the use of judgment, intuition, and experience. In addition, knowledge includes facts, theories, and anticipated results based upon specific actions. As the technology becomes more and more powerful, as information technology becomes cheaper and more sophisticated, and as Internets and other networks grow, more and more information becomes available. However, although accessing the information may be easy, making sense out of it, knowing how to filter it and what information is pertinent to a particular situation or anticipated future becomes harder and harder, and more time-consuming. At the same time information alone is not sufficient to handle complexity. Information cannot create under-standing—only humans can do that. One must be able to transform informa-tion into knowledge through the recognition of patterns and relationships within that information, by personal experience, and the use of teams. Thus getting information and converting it into knowledge represents a balance in terms of time and effort on the part of the organization as a whole as well as individuals. Since information is so easily available and knowledge so hard to create, organizations can easily slip into a high information-to-knowledge ratio, *a dangerous balance in the complexity age.* However, the importance of informa-tion versus the importance of knowledge will depend upon the needs of the customers and marketplace, and each individual ICAS will have to find its own balance. A point to remember, however, is that this balance will vary through-out the ICAS and over time.

A fifth balance is that of maintaining optimum complexity. Recall that optimum complexity is the ability to generate ideas and actions (increase its internal variety) that are creative and innovative and allow the organization to make use of, harness, or overcome comparable complexity in the environment. The idea is that if the ICAS has more options than its environment it will be better able to deal effectively with that environment. This generation of addi-tional variety internal to the ICAS is a cost in terms of time and manpower that has to be traded off against direct application of energy and mental capabilities toward customer needs. Also note that creativity is not an efficient process and it cannot be predetermined. Therefore, there is a cost to creativity that must be understood by the organization as a necessary requirement for long-term business success. The balance is between people, space, and time for creating new ideas and people, space and time applied directly to customers or other direct line-of-sight work.

A sixth challenge that the organization must face is that of balancing its resources and activities among the needs of the stakeholders. These stakeholders typically include the customer, the investors, the employees, the local commu-nity, and the ecological environment. Each of these stakeholders may place different demands upon the organization's time, energy, and capabilities as the environment changes. If any of these stakeholders becomes extremely unhappy, they can do significant damage to the organization's image, reputation, and effectiveness in the marketplace.

A seventh area requiring balance is that of alignment or cohesion of the ICAS as an organization versus responsiveness to customer needs and the market-place. You may recall that a number of capabilities have been designed into the ICAS to support continuous alignment of activities. These include the charac-teristics of collaborative leaders throughout the ICAS, the existence of the Operations Center and its continuous communication with the teams, and the use of teams, communities, and relationship networks, as well as mobility of people and the flow of knowledge. Nevertheless, time, energy, and money put into this alignment part of the organization takes away from direct work for the customers, although in another sense cohesion can significantly improve customer response.

Another organizational challenge is the cost versus benefit balance of the ICAS's global characteristics such as flexibility, agility, and adaptiveness. Having been built into the ICAS structure and culture, it may be relatively difficult to change these capabilities. However, it is essential that some change be possible at all levels. We have discussed earlier the emergent characteristic of the ICAS called flow and, included in that concept, the movement of people within, into, and out of the organization. The movement of people within the ICAS and the flow of new people coming into the organization provide new ideas and stimulate more challenging questions about the organization's operations—leading to improved performance. On the other hand, too much mobility of people can be threatening to other workers and may make it difficult for the ICAS to create and maintain alignment and a single identity. Thus as the environment changes the ICAS must maintain the right balance between the flow of people and the cohesion of the organization.

Leader Balancing Needs

From the collaborative leadership perspective a dynamic balance arises from the issue of how much control versus freedom the teams and knowledge workers should have. We have said earlier that strong control is harmful to an organization such as the ICAS in a dynamic environment because single individuals are not smart enough to be able to interpret all the needs of the marketplace at the local levels. While recognizing that hierarchy, responsibility, and some level of authority is essential to any organization, the issue of the self-organization of teams and the degree of freedom and empowerment of individual knowledge workers and their teams is of constant concern and may well have different levels for different parts of the ICAS. This is a balance that only the leaders and knowledge workers on the scene can make, but clearly the long-term desire would be to maximize the degree of self-organization and freedom within, of course, the constraints of available resources, the experience of the individuals and a full acceptance of the organization's direction and value system.

Another balance that leaders need to consider is the amount of resources put into the four major processes of teams in terms of learning and gaining experience in being able to use those processes efficiently and effectively versus the effectiveness of the teams themselves (see Chapter 8). As in all learning, it typically has a payoff, but the payoff is downstream and sometimes hard to measure. However, where teams are concerned, it doesn't take much to determine whether a team is highly competent in decision-making or problem-solving or creating ideas. The record will often speak for itself. Obviously different teams work in different markets and have different work assignments, resulting in different needs relative to the degree of expertise in a given major process. However, major determinants of team performance are leadership and learning.

Knowledge Worker Balancing Needs

As far as the individual knowledge workers are concerned, there are several areas wherein they have to recognize the need to balance their own time and resources. An example would be that each knowledge worker has their own best style of learning depending upon their experience, education, and natural affinity. Some individuals learn better by reading, some by listening, some by having conversations, some by visual aids versus the written word, some by models and flight simulators. Thus the individual knowledge worker in approaching the challenge of continuous learning and expanding knowledge and competency must match the way they learn with the subject matter. This often requires them to expand their learning styles.

Another balancing issue of the knowledge worker is how much time should be spent in acquiring knowledge through the Knowledge Center, communities, their relationship networks, etc. versus how much time to spend in helping others and providing knowledge to other people. It would be easy to spend more time gathering information and learning to do their own job better than spend time helping others. However, in the long term this typically does not have the best payoff either to the individual or the organization. This is why it is so important for leadership and the knowledge workers together to work toward a collaborative culture that is knowledge centric, supported by a structure that encourages and makes it efficient to create, leverage, share, and apply knowledge. Workers who share their knowledge, expanding their knowledge through that sharing process, make contacts that will help them later, and help the organization while enhancing their own reputation.

In summary, it is important to recognize that the ICAS organization operates in a continual state of flux in the sense that there are many, many dynamic balancing decisions made on a daily basis that allow the organization to stay flexible and robust enough to adjust to the needs of customers within and external to the organization. This requires ICAS employees to work effectively in a changing environment. Such a demand may be difficult for some individuals who need stability and continuity in their work life. Such stability can be found in the ICAS in terms of the high level of trust, the camaraderie, and collaboration, coupled with the recognition of the alignment and direction of the organization. The reference point in the ICAS does not lie at the local level only as it does in most organizations. Rather, individual and organizational identity lies with the sense of belonging, trust, spirit, and pride throughout the organization. These characteristics represent one of the major responsibilities of all collaborative leaders throughout the ICAS.

When implementing a dynamic balancing approach to organizational management, recognize that there is a possibility that if care is not taken, a drifting balance may occur. What drifting balance means is that when an individual knowledge worker or collaborative leader changes the balance in a particular factor and finds a positive result, the tendency will be to continue moving that balance in the same direction, rewarded by the excitement and satisfaction of seeing a positive result. While this in itself is not bad, one has to be careful of the tendency to leave the balance as such or let it continue to drift in that direction. Eventually things will change and the gain will be lost. An example would be a leader who has learned nurturing and strong empowerment in the past and finds an emergency situation or special circumstance where it is very important that the leader apply more control over the team. When this happens and the results are positive, the team leader may want to continue that control under the misapprehension that it was the control that did it and that control is a good long-term thing to do for all situations.

Now consider when the team has a great deal of empowerment and makes a mistake that creates a strong negative result. The team leader then might have a tendency to tighten the controls, recognizing that more control could have prevented the error. While in fact the team leader may be absolutely right in that particular situation, there can easily be a tendency to continue maintaining more control because of the fear that if the controls are moved another mistake will be made. If this is done for very long, the team leader will believe that things are going well now *because* the leader has taken control. When this happens the balance will significantly drift toward the control side and it will be very hard to reverse the direction. At the same time morale with the team will usually fall considerably; they will feel that they can no longer be trusted to do the job. It is because of the potential for balance drift to occur that networking, strong feedback, open communication, and the mobility of individuals are so useful in the ICAS in terms of continuing to challenge the status quo wherever the balance points are set and forcing all concerned to reevaluate the efficacy of the current situation from an objective viewpoint.

Because the balance points throughout the ICAS significantly impact its overall effectiveness, it behooves team leaders and senior leadership to consistently remind all ICAS personnel that they should recognize and identify those key aspects of their work that make the difference in their effectiveness. Once these factors are identified, they can ask what causes them to have the levels of effectiveness they do and then identify the balancing forces involved. It is these balances that the best knowledge workers and team leaders must recognize, continuously monitor, and treat as a management responsibility. These balances may be large-scale resource balances all the way down to individual knowledge worker competencies, attitudes, and decisions on priorities at work or problem approaches. As always, since everyone is subjected to internal biases, erroneous assumptions, and misplaced beliefs, it is wise to get a second or, perhaps, group opinion to reevaluate how workers or teams perceive situations, the most effective aspects of their work, or their balance level.

A CONCEPTUAL OVERVIEW OF THE ICAS STRATEGY

Figure 12-1 provides a visual conceptual overview of the strategy of the ICAS. The arrow represents the ICAS organization itself including its major characteristics. The region outside the arrow represents the highly uncertain, nonlinear, rapidly changing complex environment. The tip of the arrow labeled "Sustainable Competitive Advantage" indicates the movement of the organization through the complex environment. The arrows coming back toward the left both above and below the cylindrical arrow indicate various feedback mechanisms and impacts that the environment has on the ICAS organization.

The broadest strategic approach is to align the organizational resources so they can support the structure, providing the formal relationships, hierarchical chain, and organizational framework within which knowledge workers operate, and through that operation build their culture. The culture, coming out of

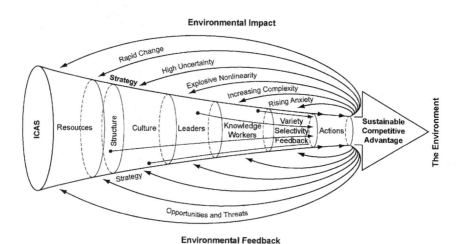

Figure 12-1
The ICAS Strategy Model

the structure, is used by ICAS leaders to work with knowledge workers in a collaborative manner to gather information, develop knowledge, make decisions, and take actions. These actions are then taken within a framework of specific focus based on the overall strategic direction of the ICAS. These actions are developed through multiple and creative relationships among the knowledge workers and include both the Knowledge Center and its supporting technology. The diversity of actions is ensured through the creative and collaborative interactions of team leaders, individual knowledge workers, teams, and meshes. Effectiveness of the final actions, shown just before the tip of the arrow, is dependent upon the knowledge that can be brought to bear on the action as well as the specific aspect of the environment that is expected to respond to the action.

The figure also shows the general direction of flow in terms of each ellipse such as resources, structure, culture, leaders, and knowledge workers each supporting the one to the right and through that support providing a line of sight to the final action. For example, the structure must facilitate learning throughout the ICAS and it must ensure that adequate resources can be placed where needed in an efficient way. At the same time the action culture depends upon the structure in terms of which relationships are formal, which ones are informal, and what resources are available. The culture depends upon the collaborative leaders and knowledge workers and their perception of how the work gets done. Collaborative leaders, shown between culture and knowledge workers on the diagram, must operate to work with knowledge workers within the action culture. The knowledge workers are the ultimate goal of the ICAS organization in terms of performance because it is their actions on a day-to-day basis that make the difference. These knowledge workers—working with their leaders and through the culture—generate ideas and create new understanding of the environment and what needs to be done to meet the overall ICAS direction and objectives. Their approach is to create a variety of ideas, select the best ones, try them, and continue or change them based on feedback. The end result on the right represents the desired sustainable high performance and growth capability of the ICAS.

THE CORRELATION OF FORCES

Another aspect of strategy is that known as the correlation of forces. A good strategy identifies the major strengths, or forces within the organization, and those that meet day-to-day changing external threats and opportunities. Senior management should recognize and monitor the fundamental forces within the organization to ensure that these forces are aligned to maximize their effectiveness in creating sustainable competitive advantage. This alignment means that the forces are moving the organization in the same direction and they are coordinated so that together they reinforce each other.

In a complex organization there are many forces at work. By harnessing, directing, and/or nurturing the major forces, the organization can correlate its major resources to achieve maximum effectiveness. The correlated organization may perform at a point on the operational spectrum that utilizes less of one resource and more of another, achieving a higher gain than if these resources were added separately. This is what could be called organizational synergy through the correlation of resources. This correlation is not static, but may be responsive to external pressures.

The forces the ICAS needs to correlate are considered in light of the following:

1. The short-term effectiveness of an organization depends on the actions of all of its employees.
2. The long-term health (sustainability) of an organization is partially determined by the same set of actions of all employees seen from their downstream consequences and implications for the future.

Being able to take effective actions every day is a function of the knowledge and intent of knowledge workers. The environment and the organization's knowledge would be correlated when that knowledge as applied by the workforce is directly related to those areas in the environment consistent with the organization's direction. That is, knowledge created and used by knowledge workers is within the knowledge space of the organization as influenced by the environment.

THE FORCES

The strength of the ICAS organization is a combination of four forces that directly influence the organization's success. These four forces are the force of direction, the force of intent, the force of knowledge, and the force of knowing.

- *Force of direction.* Direction serves as the compass for the organization as it moves into an uncharted and uncharitable future. It both limits ICAS activities within some action space surrounding the chosen direction and conserves energy by defining what areas the ICAS is not interested in. With any direction comes a purpose and a vision of what is required to make the journey. In that regard direction acts on organizational reason for being and provides spirit and purpose to all employees. It also is used to explain why the ICAS must be as it is—providing sound reasons for collaboration, empowerment, etc. The strength of the force of direction is measured by organizational cohesion, the line of sight, and the connectedness of choices. The level of communication, the alignment of work activities, and the effectiveness of the Operations Center all impact the force of direction. Are the organization's resource allocations consistent with the mission? Do knowledge workers have access and two-way communication with leaders? Are decisions at every level geared toward achieving a common direction? Why are we going in this direction? Why do *we* think this is the best direction? What happens to us if the environment drastically changes? Does our direction include my own pet idea? Is everyone expected to go in that direction? What about new ideas and opportunities? What do we need to learn to contribute to the direction? What could happen that will make us change direction?

- *Force of intent.* Intention is an act or instance of determining mentally upon some action or result. It includes the purpose and attitude toward the *effect* of one's action, the outcome, with purpose implying having a goal or the determination to achieve something and attitude encompassing loyalty and dedication. Intent focuses the energy and knowledge of the organization. It is the power and consistency that overwhelms competitors and gains the admiration of the marketplace. Knowledge is the "know how"; intent is the power to focus the knowledge and maintain the direction. The strength of the force of intent is measured by the desire, willingness, and energy of every member of the organization. How does the work get done? Where do people focus their attention? Are knowledge workers excited about their work? Is there strong competition among team leaders that weakens intent and drains energy? Does senior leadership act consistently with the stated direction and value set of the organization?

- *Force of knowledge.* This is the fundamental force of the organization, consisting of the creation, sharing, dissemination, leveraging, and application of knowledge. The strength of the force of knowledge is measured by capacity, competency, connectivity, and flow. What is the knowledge capacity of the organization? What abilities does the organization have to create, leverage, and apply knowledge? How do technology, structure, culture, and leadership support this force? How does the organization ensure connectivity of its knowledge workers with each other and with the external environment? How does the organizational structure and culture facilitate flow in terms of data, information, and knowledge; in terms of people; and in terms of autotelic work? Does the hiring, movement, and learning of workers support the long-term needs of the ICAS? Is knowledge recognized for its strong role in the ICAS's success? Are decision feedback loops in place?

- *Force of knowing.* Knowing is a blending of the cognitive capabilities of observing and perceiving a situation, the cognitive processing that must occur to understand the external world and make maximum use of our intuition and experiences, and the faculty for creating deep knowledge and acting on that knowledge. It can be elevated to the organizational level by using and combining the insights and experiences of individuals through dialogue and collaboration within teams, groups, and communities. Such efforts significantly improve the quality of understanding and responsiveness of actions of the organization. It also greatly expands the scope of complex situations that can be handled through knowing because of the great resources brought to bear. Knowing is the tip of the ICAS spear, penetrating the haze of complexity by allowing workers to think beyond normal perception and dig into the meaning and hidden patterns in a complex world. Knowing represents the fog lights into the future. The strength of the force of knowing is measured by the organization's ability to perceive, interpret, and make sense of the environment and take actions. How is the organization supporting learning? Are teams and communities supported and rewarded? Are knowledge workers achieving integrative competencies? Do knowledge workers trust their intuition and act accordingly? Are decision feedback loops in place? (See Chapter 20.)

Figure 12-2 represents a graphic display of the various aspects of the correlation of forces. At the top is represented the complex environment and within that environment there are certain areas that represent opportunity spaces for the ICAS, depending of course on the direction the ICAS is evolving and on the local capability of ICAS employees to identify these opportunities. The four major forces discussed in this section are represented by arrows. Below these are shown circles that represent a set of particular success factors that are significant in driving the four major forces. The diagram shows general characteristics because each specific ICAS organization embedded in a unique environment will, of course, have different critical success factors, with some more important than others.

The objective of the strategy of correlation of forces, however, is to create a specific organization with its unique environment in which the right set of critical success factors are managed so that each of the four forces (knowledge, intent, direction, and knowing) are maximized to support the organizational goals and objectives through the individual knowledge workers. In addition, these four forces should work together in a synergistic manner so they can mutually support each other through the critical success factors and the day-to-day operations of the collaborative leaders and the knowledge workers. When this occurs, the ICAS has its maximum probability of marching through the environment, surviving, and creating a sustainable competitive advantage over its competitors. We have talked before about leveraging knowledge for the ICAS because of the great importance of knowledge in

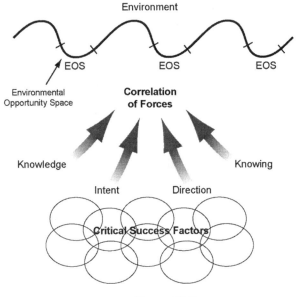

Figure 12-2
The Correlation of Forces

understanding the environment. In the correlation of forces we are referring to the capability to leverage these forces to maximize the effectiveness of the ICAS organization.

Consider the four forces: direction, intent, knowledge, and knowing. Direction sets the compass, gives meaning to the trip and offers a vision of what to strive for. Intent provides the energy and consistency of movement. Knowledge provides the competency to take the right actions. Knowing provides a deeper understanding of the environment and how to deal with it over the long term. These forces are aligned when:

- Direction is set and understood.
- Intent moves the organization in the desired direction.
- Knowledge ensures actions follow intent and direction.
- Knowing improves knowledge, bolsters intent, and signals the ICAS whether the actions and directions are on track.

THE ENVIRONMENTAL OPPORTUNITY SPACE

In a turbulent environment there are holes that offer opportunities, what we call the environmental opportunity space, a window of opportunity in terms of space and time. A correlated organization has a consistent direction and a comprehension from what knowing has provided about the environment.

While the company may not be able to define this space, nor can it go there before it exists, the organization's direction is such that it can take advantage of the environmental opportunity space as it emerges, and does so. Intuition, judgment, and insight do not just happen in particular minds. They can be studied, developed, and practiced over time and within domains of interest.

Here is where the organizational forces come into play. Most opportunities and threats in the environment are "sensed" (through the sense of knowing) prior to actuality. Defining and understanding the environmental landscape is necessary before the organization can set its direction to move in. Success is then dependent on employees having the intention to take advantage of that window, and creating, leveraging, and applying the right knowledge to do so. Knowledge enables workers to continuously make sense of and track the window. Learning (open system) and knowledge provide the flexibility to keep up with (or ahead of) changes inside the window. Knowing creates the opportunity to see beyond the window.

CRITICAL SUCCESS FACTORS

Even in an evolving organizational structure that is flexible to emerging needs, there are boundless factors that influence organizational success. These critical success factors are major characteristics and factors working at the tactical level of the organization, enabling the forces of the organization to operate at the highest level of effectiveness. They deal as much with the way specific initiatives are implemented as the content of the initiatives themselves.

Since organizations begin their journey toward becoming intelligent complex adaptive systems with different missions, cultures, and environments, critical success factors are somewhat organization dependent. However, there are critical success factors that are indeed essential to the success of the ICAS organization. These include a team approach, a systems approach, continuous learning, sharing, freedom and flexibility, creativity and innovation, and managing change.

- *Team approach.* Because of the complexity of the challenge facing organizations in a new world and the speed of change, it is essential to take a team approach to achieve organizational objectives. Teams, communities, task-forces, and other vehicles of collaboration encourage knowledge workers to work together, solve problems, and share experiences.
- *Systems approach.* A broad systems view allows the organization to focus on the most important issues while understanding differing views on many issues and problems. It also recognizes the payoff of a long-term view of desired results, and encourages balanced understanding of the overall needs of the organization.

- *Continuous learning.* Continuous learning must become a daily routine for knowledge workers. As environmental change accelerates, there is need for new workforce skills and capabilities. New challenges require new ideas, solutions, and approaches.
- *Creativity and innovation.* Meeting new challenges in a dynamic, uncertain, and complex environment requires the continuous insertion and implementation of new ideas. These ideas emerge from within and without the organizational frame work. Teams and communities play a major catalyst role in the stimulation and integration of these ideas.
- *Sharing.* The widespread sharing of ideas, opinions, information, and issues facilitates learning and creates organizational coherence in responding to new threats and opportunities.
- *Freedom and flexibility.* Providing resources and facilitating the skills to support new ways of doing business helps empower decision-makers at every level of the organization. Effective strategy implementation requires many rapid, complex decisions that can only be made locally. Knowledge workers have the freedom to make decisions and take the actions needed to do their jobs within the context of local needs. Such freedom and rapid actions greatly enhance the organization's ability to effect change and respond to the environmental opportunities and threats.
- *Managing change.* Every organization must adapt to its changing environment. New technology, new missions, and new global political situations demand the organization's culture, capabilities, and processes be continuously reviewed and recreated as needed. Thus, the ability to identify and overcome barriers to change, coupled with an effective change management program becomes critical to the organization.

It is assumed that every organization understands the importance of quality and hard work. However, just as it is a good idea to periodically review organizational values and ethics, it may serve an organization well to add quality and hard work to the list of critical success factors (Porter et al., 2003). They would look something like this:

- *Quality.* The ICAS organization adheres to a high quality of products and services. A significant part of the organization's change strategy deals with recognizing quality throughout the organization, rewarding that quality, and diffusing it throughout the organization.
- *Hard work.* As always, hard work and dedication, backed by integrity and a strong value set, serve as the foundation for internal and external credibility and trust: the two essential characteristics for influencing others and managing change.

Many of the critical success factors cited here are mutually supportive. For example, freedom, flexibility, continuous learning, working in teams, and sharing, taken together, form an interconnected system that generates trust, motivation, and hard work, which cannot help but lead to success. High-quality standards, and a systems perspective, coupled with collaborative leadership, create an image to the outside world of a positive, dedicated, rational, and competent organization. This image goes a long way toward cooperation and collaboration with customers. Of course, the critical success factors that an organization identifies as important to success are, like all things in a turbulent world, highly dependent on the culture, vision, and mission of the organization, as well as the place from which the organization starts its change movement.

In summary, the ICAS strategy focuses on the knowledge worker and how they can best be supported through effective structure, culture, dynamic balance, and correlation of forces.

REFERENCES

Axelrod, R. and M. D. Cohen. Harnessing Complexity: Organizational Implications of a Scientific Frontier. New York: The Free Press, 1999.

Boar, B. H. The Art of Strategic Planning for Information Technology: Crafting Strategy for the 90's. New York: John Wiley & Sons, 1993.

Porter, D., A. Bennet, R. Turner, and D. Wennergren. The Power of Team: The Making of a CIO. Alexandria, VA: Department of the Navy, 2003.

Chapter 13

A Tale of Two Firms

As Joe looked out over the river at the end of a long day, he pondered the current situation and how his company was progressing. He and his friend and ex-schoolmate, Mary, had both started companies about eight years ago in this Midwestern city where a lot of engineering and management talent grew locally through the excellent universities in the area. Joe felt tired, somewhat perplexed, and concerned over recent events both in his company and in the market. He wondered if his dream of building a billion dollar company would ever come true.

At that time Reliable Systems, Inc. had close to a thousand employees, a good reputation, and a 20 percent per year growth rate. Joe had deliberately chosen to build a systems integration firm because he wanted to offer full-spectrum support to major customers. This included providing the software and hardware, basic systems design, installation, and then follow-on maintenance. His value added was the increased efficiency that his integrated systems offered to clients, and being a technologist by nature, he loved to see the extra value obtained from a well-integrated technology system. Although he was more of an engineer and entrepreneur than an executive, he had good, strong knowledgeable people working for him and together they had designed an organization that had worked very well during their growth period over the last eight years.

Reliable Systems, Inc. was pretty much a standard organization with a control-oriented hierarchy, support departments such as contracting and human resources, and a matrix structure where program managers ran individual contracts for particular customers supported by a set of functional departments providing specialized expertise to the program managers. The whole system was smooth running, very conscious of efficiency and cost reductions as well as customer satisfaction, and the organization had developed a good reputation and image in the marketplace. Their hiring policies had been directed toward identifying and hiring the technical and managerial expertise necessary to perform specific jobs, and their long-term strategy was to continue their growth rate of between 10 and 25 percent per year by providing well-proven, reliable systems. Decision-making was done at the supervisory and executive level, although managers had good working relationships with their knowledge workers and specialists. Learning was focused on immediate needs relative to specific systems being installed and to respond to customer needs.

Over the past few months, Joe and his board had spent time thinking about the environment because of recent events that might be part of a larger pattern, a pattern that gave him an uneasy feeling. On the other hand, he knew that profitability was good, growth seemed to be continuing and he would have trouble with his board of directors if he tried to make too many changes. Besides that, he really didn't know what needed to be done since his organization was operating so well. Thoughts about Mary and how she would look at this situation passed through his mind. From past experience he knew she would always be an entrepreneur and an out-of-the-box thinker more willing to take risks than himself.

Perhaps it was synchronicity—or more likely, just coincidence—but it just so happened that across the river Mary was also thinking about the environment and what Joe would do. She recalled that she and Joe had started their companies at about the same time, during the period when technology was flying and companies begged to get the latest IM and IT systems. They were even in the same business, but the market had expanded so quickly that neither one of them felt they were competing with each other. Mary's company had also been growing at about 20 percent per year. However, over the past 18 months its growth had slowed to the point where it was now flat. Intelligent Systems, Inc., the love of Mary's life, had done a great job early on after it was formed and was pretty much a systems integration firm similar to Joe's. The only difference was that Mary, because of her nature and interest in new technology, had put more emphasis on advanced systems, new ideas, and looking for the potential added value to customers. Her organizational structure was not much different from Joe's. It was also hierarchal, emphasizing efficiency and effectiveness. She had also hired specialists who could provide the expertise to complete the systems integration and satisfy customers.

Over the years she and Joe had maintained their relationship by getting together for lunch every couple of months just to talk about how things were going. While it was true that in one sense they were competitors, it was also true that neither company had a large market share. Their real competition was national, not local. Of more interest to Mary was how to grow a business in the market as it stands and as it would become.

As one would expect, Mary had become very concerned over the flattening of her company's growth rate, even though profitability still looked as good as it was before. She had done a great deal of soul searching with others whom she respected, including her board of directors, to try to understand why Intelligent Systems had stopped growing. Was it a temporary statistical phenomenon because they had lost a couple of contracts or was it perhaps caused by something deeper, like the way they were doing business or a change in their customer's reaction to their product? She really didn't know the right answer, but she knew she had to find out. Now was the time to put some serious thought into how the organization was operating, what the environment was like and what it would be like in the future. She had learned from too many colleagues that a CEO never waits until things are heading south before taking action; that was the way companies went bankrupt or were bought out. Deep within, she feared that she may have waited too late.

While she hesitated a bit, Mary knew she needed to call Joe for lunch to see what he thought about the current environment and how his business was going. Her hesitation, of course, was that from all indications his company was continuing to grow while, as she mulled again through her mind, hers had flattened. Before setting up the lunch, she must put a lot of time into thinking about what her company was doing and how it compared to what she knew of his.

At lunch Mary and Joe had both been open about their companies with Joe agreeing with Mary's views on the market. Joe was providing standard state-of-the-art hardware, software, and systems integration, whereas Mary was dealing with more advanced technology. So her customers were slightly different than Joe's. But it seemed to Mary that customers might be looking more for reliable, well-proven technology that did not have the capabilities that her products offered. Her costs had always been higher than Joe's because of the initial cost of the technology and the learning necessary for her knowledge workers to keep up with that technology.

Mary came away from her lunch with Joe somewhat puzzled, because Joe seemed to be satisfied with his company's operation and had even suggested that perhaps Mary's people were not satisfying customers well enough, or perhaps the apparent problem was just in response to a temporary drop in the market. Joe had always been conservative and was satisfied with any steady growth so long as it was profitable. Still, Mary thought, there has to be something happening that was causing Intelligent Systems, Inc. to stop growing. If it was just economic conditions, why wasn't Joe facing the same problem? If it was something internal to the company, her own leadership perhaps, or her supervisors' and managers' inability to keep up the high-quality work and responsiveness, then she must find out and find out quickly.

It had in fact hurt her a little bit at lunch when Joe made the rather flippant comment that perhaps the problem was leadership. But she passed it off as a friendly joke and didn't think about it any more. After giving the meeting more thought, she came back to her office and made a quick and strong decision.

Her company would not try to wait out some "economic slump." She identified five key individuals within her company whom she knew quite well to be intelligent, objective, and very different thinkers than herself. She knew that these five individuals knew the views of employees at all levels and that she could count on them for being honest in their communication and in their assessments. She then called them together, explained to them the context of the situation and her concerns. After answering their questions—followed by a lot of dialogue—they committed to working with her as an action team chartered to take a thorough look at the environment and all internal operations of the company. However, Mary intuitively knew a single team looking at the organization could not solve her problem, and might even create more irritation and concern on the part of employees. So her approach was to charter ten teams throughout the organization, represented by all levels and areas of expertise, to take their own look and assess how the organization was doing and what areas of improvement could be identified. At the same time, the action team would do a detailed study of the environment and their own markets to better understand what was happening and what to expect in the future.

Six months later, Mary, her team, and the teams chartered throughout the organization were prepared to provide their results to all employees to generate a dialogue on the situation, the company, and the future. The ten teams chartered to investigate the internal effectiveness of Intelligent Systems, Inc. came up with a large number of ideas for change and a number of concerns on the part of the workers. Many of these concerns had never surfaced before or, if they had, middle managers had not passed them up the chain, or perhaps had not understood the depth or seriousness of the concerns. In any case, Mary was interested in "what do we do now" not "why aren't things better."

Mary's group, looking at the environment and marketplace, came to the conclusion that the environment was becoming unpredictable due to advances in technology, new product entry rates, the explosion of new software, and the saturation of computers. At the same time nanotechnology was beginning to grow rapidly, biological systems were within distant sight and artificial intelligence was continuing to improve. It appeared that high tech was losing its aura even under these conditions and many companies were becoming unhappy with the lower than expected value added from integrated and powerful hardware systems. Uncertainties in the economy and stock market, and continuous international political unrest, together with the terrorist cloud, all seemed to make it impossible to predict the future, although there were always articles in the papers and pundits everywhere that willingly offered their own predictions. Even at the local level where Mary's company worked with customers no one had a good feel for what was happening. Feedback had indicated that the company's customers were equally concerned and confused over what they should do in the current environment in order to grow and remain profitable.

After much heated discussion, dialogue, soul searching, and brainstorming, their choice was to either put the future in some soothsayer's hands or create a company that had the health and capacity to sustain itself even if it could not know what the future would be like. Mary and her staff decided that the time was now to re-create Intelligent Systems, Inc. and make it more viable for the future. Starting with their customer base, they decided that Intelligent Systems, Inc. should look beyond adding value and efficiency to the customer's operation through integrated systems. They would also look at their customer's customer and see how the once removed customer value could be enhanced, not just by supplying and maintaining integrated systems but by also providing professional services to help their customers grow. It became clear to the action team that although the key to their customers' success was situational and depended on the nature of their business, there was a generic potential of value improvement through knowledge and information. This line of thought caused the team to look carefully into the potential returns from the creation and application of knowledge. To take advantage of this, the team decided that Intelligent Systems, Inc. must first become a knowledge-based organization, building in the capability to help its customers beyond its integrated systems. To do this, Mary started to quickly invest first in the technology to support knowledge creation, sharing, etc., and then in developing the networks and relationships among her workers to ensure that everyone would benefit from this knowledge transformation.

Several of the study teams had reported back that many knowledge workers felt that they were limited by the company's tendency to control. They wanted more freedom to do their jobs, and wanted to work together more often and more effectively. In response to this, Mary created a number of working teams with team leaders who were given line responsibility for customer support. The team leader's responsibility was equally shared by every member on the team. This gave the teams and the knowledge workers much more freedom in dealing with customers, identifying problems and opportunities, and in being creative to find better and more effective solutions for their customers.

Mary's own team had concluded that the real value to most organizations in their world and marketplace came from increased understanding of the value and application of their technology. It had also become clear that many of their customers' businesses were knowledge dependent and that efficiency and lowest cost was not necessarily a winning combination. Thus, Mary decided that one of the focus areas of Intelligence Systems, Inc. would be to find new ways that the company could add value to their customers through their integrated systems, their knowledge of their customers' needs, and through the professional services that their own knowledge workers could provide. With this in mind, Mary got the concurrence of her board of directors to begin a massive rebuilding process within the organization to reorient its direction, structure, culture, and leadership approach. This would enable knowledge workers throughout Intelligent Systems, Inc. to make the maximum use of their experience and learning to the benefit of both their company and their customers.

Mary knew this change would be difficult and risky. If she was going to bet the survival of her company on its employees, then she had to make sure those employees had what it takes. This meant new learning programs, changing hiring and termination practices, and revamping personnel policies to match a knowledge-centric culture; and that was only part of the changes.

Mary heard through the grapevine that Joe's company, Reliable Systems, Inc., had lost several new contracts and the rumor mill had it that his growth rate had turned downward. A quick phone call to him verified the truth of the rumors. Joe mentioned that in response to the recent environmental pressures he had reduced staff, eliminated some inefficiencies, and was having his people work harder than before. He could not accept that the direction, strategy, and management approach of his company were the problem; his company had been too successful the past few years. Besides, his board had agreed with his recommendation to hang in there and wait the economy out. Things would soon return to normal and his company would be back on the growth track. To his old friend, Joe admitted he had some doubts about this strategy, but he really didn't know what else to do. He didn't want to risk making things worse by disrupting his people at this time. Besides, the market value of Reliable Systems had dropped and he could not afford for it to go down any more—at least not if he could help it.

After the phone call, Mary thought carefully about the changes she was making and recognized the risk involved and the long-term consequences if she was wrong. After further reflection, she decided to go with her intuition and gut feel: the best long-term solution for the growth and health of Intelligent Systems was to build a robust, flexible, agile corporation that understood their customers and their customer's customers, one that would provide value added to those customers through integrated systems and their applications coupled with the information and knowledge that would help those customers grow and succeed. To do this, Intelligent Systems had to become competent to deal with the increasing speed of change. Employees had to trust each other, make good decisions, and work collaboratively while supporting the values and direction of the company. The company had to develop a capability to understand and deal with the environment. If prediction was not possible, then there were a number of ways the company could improve its ability to deal with uncertainty and unknowns, not the least of which was—borrowing from Darwinian fitness—the intelligent use of a trial-and-error basis. Mary knew that her company had a tremendous amount of brainpower and competency. She had to find ways of pulling that competency and knowledge out and motivating employees to create ideas and apply them wherever appropriate. She was convinced that the employees, if they had the support of their managers and accepted responsibility, would work wonders with the customers. With the company, its leaders, and the workers working together and moving in the same direction, they could leverage knowledge and improve decisions and actions everywhere in the organization. The simple truth was that every action and every relationship made the difference, because that was where organizational performance was created or destroyed.

Mary's philosophy of dealing with the market was to work with it, not against it. While there was always a concern and danger of giving up secrets and silver bullets, she had never really believed in that too much. Her approach was to insist that everyone do their best to work with and help their customers and count on the results to help the company grow. Relationships were more important and more valuable than momentary financial gain.

As Mary went about implementing these changes she found it quite difficult at times. Many employees were not willing to accept the changes, did not understand nor believe in them, and simply would not share knowledge, collaborate effectively, or go the second step for coworkers or customers. Mary had always known change was hard, but until now she had never realized just how hard it was. Nevertheless, she was stubborn. Once she made up her mind, she kept her direction and did not waver. Mary knew that for the company to change, all levels had to cooperate and work toward a new vision of the organization and their role in it. As preparation for the changes, she had her ten study teams prepare one-day workshops on each of their areas. These workshops were taught by leaders and other study team members within the company and were designed to get feedback and to stimulate thinking, questioning, and ideas to help the company transform itself. They were to be honest and open, and to encourage dialogue and discussion on any topic of relevance. These sessions strove to transfer understanding of what, why, and how Intelligent Systems was transforming itself to match the environment and create a sustainable competitive advantage.

Within six months—to Mary's own surprise—the company had already made significant improvements. Their customer base was increasing as word about their new mode of operation and the value added to customers spread across the marketplace. As always, success begets success. As the company grew, its employees recognized the value of cooperation, collaboration, learning, and knowledge leveraging. There were still problems: the structure was not fully supportive of the knowledge workers, the culture was different, but not optimum, and some managers had to be *reconditioned*, and some left.

Nevertheless, Mary felt comfortable with their progress because her fundamental assumptions were proving to be good. Her people *were* the ones that would make the difference. They *did* know more about their work than anyone else. They *would* work together if they trusted each other and the company. The structure, culture, and leadership *did* play a big role—but that role was in *supporting* the workers, not in directing or controlling them. Knowledge *did* seem to be the key to the future and to *understanding* the environment—if not understanding then being able to *live* with it. Flexibility, agility, and adaptability *were* becoming the hallmark of Intelligent Systems, Inc. and employees and stakeholders *were* proud of being identified with an organization that seemed able to *work and co-evolve* with its marketplace and *maintain* its high values and integrity. But we live in an uncertain and sometimes nefarious world, Mary thought to herself as she relaxed with a cup of coffee over the latest sales and profit curves. She wondered how Joe was doing, and could not help but wonder how she would feel a year from now. It never pays to gloat or slow down—she had learned that things are never as good as they seem or as bad as they seem. "Everything is exactly as it should be," she muttered to herself as she picked up the phone to see if Joe was available for lunch—perhaps she could help him?

———————

We leave it to the reader to speculate on the future of the two companies. Clearly, a future scenario could be developed which would prove Mary right and Joe wrong, or perhaps both would survive in their slightly different markets, or perhaps Reliable Systems could in fact wait the problem out. More important, the story is a means of contrasting two fundamentally different approaches to business. The one strives for efficiency, customer satisfaction, stability, and clear, clean decision chains and quick results. The other looks toward the organization, its structure, culture, and leadership in terms of how organic and robust it is and how well it can make the maximum use of knowledge and the workforce.

Both could be right, both could be wrong. It depends completely on what the environment is like and what it will become over the next five, ten, twenty, or thirty years. As we enter the age of complexity—and recognizing that a social complex adaptive system cannot ignore its environment—we leave it for each reader and for each organization to decide for themselves which direction (or what direction?) makes the most sense.

Is it better to develop an all-around, strong, healthy body or to be the fastest runner in the world? Perhaps it depends on the landscape, the weather, and where you want to go!

PART IV

THE KNOWLEDGE SOLUTION*

At the forefront of the ICAS organization is the knowledge worker, the individual whose work is centered around creating, using, and sharing knowledge. Chapter 14 explores ways that knowledge workers direct their learning and manage their knowledge to best prepare them for present and future challenges. This chapter includes an introduction to what we call integrative competencies. Chapters 15 and 16 focus on knowledge management and the learning organization, respectively, with Chapter 17 bringing it all together in a discussion of learning, knowledge management, and knowledge workers.

Chapters 18 and 19 rethink thinking, specifically in the areas of systems and complexity, offering new ways of thinking about the world in which we work and live. Systems thinking allows us to step out of our organizations and see them from a more objective and

*Sections on integrative competencies are built on material developed for the Department of the Navy. Several concepts presented in Chapters 14–17 were published as "Learning and the Knowledge Worker" in Koenig, M. and K. Srikantaiah (eds.), *Knowledge Management Lessons Learned: What Works and What Doesn't*, Oxford, NJ: Plexus Books, 2003. Several concepts also appeared in "The Partnership between Organizational Learning and Knowledge Management" contributed to Holsapple, C. (ed.), *Handbook on Knowledge Management 1: Knowledge Matters*, New York: Springer-Verlag, 2003.

insightful perspective. Complexity thinking suggests ways to understand and deal with our current and future complex organizations. Chapter 20 focuses on "knowing," methods to increase individual sensory capabilities while increasing the ability to consciously integrate these sensory inputs with that knowledge within each of us that is created by past learning and experiences but cannot be put into words.

Chapter 21 introduces an old concept in a new light, offering approaches each of us can use to manage our network relationships. In a connected world, relationship network management is a skill none of us can live without.

Chapter 14

THE NEW KNOWLEDGE WORKER

The knowledge worker is now recognized as a major part of the workforce; that is, those workers who use their experience, education, and mental capacity to deal with the problems and opportunities arising from complexity, uncertainty, and rapid change (Drucker, 1989). As denoted by the name, knowledge workers are individuals whose work effort is centered around creating, using, and sharing knowledge. Over the past decade the focus on knowledge management has caused organizations and workers alike to recognize how important knowledge has become to the workplace, and to search for new capabilities and processes to ensure the increase and best use of this resource for the organization.

In the days of the assembly line a worker could learn one process, acquire one skill, and spend a lifetime being paid for doing it. For those who compete in the global knowledge world, this is no longer possible. The value of each employee goes far beyond a single capability or skill. In the ICAS organization significant changes happen at the collective level. The ICAS is a high-synergy organization not limited by the constraints of any single individual's mind, but with individuals working together naturally and easily, with a day-after-day spontaneity, recombining and refocusing in response to new challenges and opportunities.

The knowledge worker of the ICAS relates in a new way to the organization and other knowledge workers. The organization provides strong motivations to protect and nourish individualism, for it is the knowledge worker who is the ultimate source of knowledge, and each and every worker is an integral part of the organization. The individual brings personal experience, uniqueness, and diverse perceptions, capabilities, and opportunities to the organization. A strong sense of self is essential for productive interactions, open communication and self-improvement, and when accompanied by a willingness to learn and collaborate provides the foundation for organizational flexibility and growth. Simultaneously, the organization supports a culture of sharing, the way work gets done, because it is the exchange of knowledge that leverages knowledge and produces intelligent behavior as an organization.

The multidimensionality of the organization is dependent on its knowledge workers. One aspect of that multidimensionality is the knowledge worker's capability to work in multiple domains simultaneously, moving in and out of those domains as needed, combining the physical, the mental, the intuitive, and the emotional to continuously expand their knowledge, capabilities, capacity, networks, and perceptions (see Figure 14-1).

We will focus on several areas important to the knowledge worker in achieving this continuous expansion: having knowledge about knowledge, learning and learning how to learn, collaborating with others, building new skills sets and what we call integrative competencies, and developing peripheral discipline awareness. We begin with the need for a clear line of sight.

CLEAR LINE OF SIGHT

Knowledge workers do not always work in organizations that recognize the value of knowledge and have processes and technology that support and leverage the creation and application of their work. Often, organizations need to be reminded that their performance is determined by the day-to-day actions of all employees. If a clear line of sight from these actions to the mission and purpose of the firm can be made visible, the value and contribution of knowledge workers can be understood and guided. This line of sight is best seen as the interplay between knowledge management, learning, and knowledge workers (see Chapter 17). Knowledge workers take action because someone (perhaps themselves) makes a

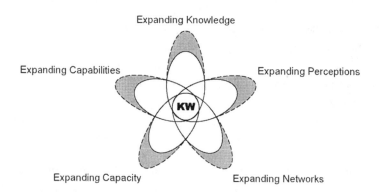

Figure 14-1
The Continuously Expanding Multidimensionality of the Knowledge Worker

decision to do so. That decision, in turn, is the result of some existing situation that needs to be changed. For nontrivial situations, problem-solving can become challenging and generate alternative options often as the result of creative thinking and innovative ways of viewing a situation. Knowledge management provides the environment, learning keeps the knowledge up to date, and the knowledge worker both creates and acts on that knowledge.

HAVING KNOWLEDGE ABOUT KNOWLEDGE

The best knowledge workers learn and apply their knowledge in collaboration with others, while simultaneously recognizing the breadth of information and knowledge needed to comprehend and resolve complex problems and situations. To be successful, they have the ability to manage knowledge in the sense of recognizing, creating, finding, and moving knowledge that is valid, useful, and applicable to the issue at hand. Beyond this, knowledge workers need the foresight to sense their future knowledge needs and acquire that knowledge to handle challenging problems well before the problems arise. Even though they may not know the specific problems that will be faced, they are aware of the *types* of issues and challenges that may occur. Using capabilities to be discussed in the following chapters, knowledge workers will be able to sense the direction and pattern of their customers and work progress. Understanding systems and complexity will help them identify possible knowledge needs, needs that they and their colleagues can then learn to handle and watch out for.

Each of the four major processes used in knowledge organizations—creating ideas, solving problems, making decisions, and taking effective actions—can be implemented by each individual knowledge worker or by teams or groups of workers. Each process presents an opportunity for knowledge workers to learn and increase both their knowledge and experience.

THE KNOWLEDGE WORKER AS A TEAM PLAYER

Teams have proven their ability to improve decision-making and enhance learning (Katzenbach and Smith, 1993). Knowledge workers can improve their learning during team problem-solving and decision-making by withholding their own beliefs and opinions until late in the dialogue process. A position stated quickly becomes a position defended. When this occurs, the conversation moves from open inquiry to a debate or face-saving challenge. Much learning is lost when debate replaces inquiry. Although debates can certainly be learning experiences, much more learning can occur during deeper levels of thought where assumptions, context, patterns, relationships, and expectations of the future are reflected upon rather than the higher levels of thought such as beliefs, events, and opinions. These beliefs, events, and opinions are more like surface phenomena that usually represent information, that is, they do not necessarily increase understanding or provide meaning in situations. Keeping group discussions at deeper levels requires an open and supportive organizational culture (KM) and continuous team-member attention to learning, inquiry, and self-reflection (Bennet, 1998).

Teams and communities can be particularly effective as learning experiences because many ideas and viewpoints are shared, and dialogue and discussion help clarify questions and misunderstandings that participants may have, often leading to "a-ha" experiences. To get the maximum learning from group meetings, the knowledge worker can take a number of actions. These actions include: keeping an open mind, not taking sides quickly, and always remembering that knowledge is never absolute. Even scientific knowledge, such as the law of conservation of energy, is not always true. The efficacy of knowledge depends on its situational context and the future flow of events. The former is never completely known and the latter is often contingent upon many unpredictable interactions.

The knowledge worker who actively listens and reflects on multiple views not only achieves broader understanding and insights that leverage and modulate his/her own knowledge but also develops an objective, systems-oriented perspective that significantly contributes to problem-solving and cognitive growth. For example, if a team is interdisciplinary, the awareness and appreciation of other modes of thinking and fields of learning will significantly enhance the knowledge worker's ability to integrate information and balance priorities, thereby preventing the hardening of sides and viewpoints during team discussions. It also helps maintain rapport and trust with other team members. The ability to remain objective and still actively participate in the discussion is a mark of leadership that helps both the knowledge worker and the organization. In the best case, knowledge workers direct their learning and manage their knowledge so they are well prepared for both present and future challenges. This is the payoff from learning how and when to learn and from treating their knowledge as a manageable asset that greatly influences career success and organizational performance. Since their competency is the source of the organization's performance, KM and learning become everyone's responsibility and everyone's gain.

Physical environment, culture, and interpersonal relationships must be taken into account for a team to achieve learning and high performance. The use of groupware, such as whiteboards and computer systems that allow input from every team member and real-time integration and display of ideas, can be very helpful. The physical layout of working spaces also influences the way knowledge workers think and feel during meetings. Good facilitation is essential for productive and open communication among diverse knowledge workers. Individual empowerment of team members gives them confidence and strength of resources. Many of the KM strategies—such as knowledge sharing, knowledge repositories, knowledge systems, storytelling, knowledge flow channels, and communities of practice—provide strong support for team performance and individual learning.

THE KNOWLEDGE WORKER AS A LEARNER

Classical research in adult learning has two primary foundations: Malcolm Knowles (1998) research in adult learning and David Kolb's (1984) research in experiential learning. Knowles identifies the conditions in which adults learn best and the human characteristics that drive those conditions. For example, adults are usually driven by real-world problems and learn best from solving problems that are directly related to their current work. They are self-directed and each individual, usually without conscious awareness, has developed a comfortable way of learning that is unique and maximizes his/her ability to take in information and create understanding. Although there are many individual learning "styles," a given worker will usually have one particular style that is most effective and most personally satisfying. A knowledge worker who takes time to "learn how to learn" will be able to learn via several styles. Since much learning takes place in situations that are not within the learner's control, being able to learn through images, lectures, reading, dialogue, debate, computers, and so forth will be very helpful over the long term.

Another challenge for the learning knowledge worker is the increasing number of situations in which learning can take place. As the Internet grows, there will be more learning through browsers, chat rooms, and communities of practice. Normal classroom education will still count, as will conferences, retreats, and other off-site experiences. An often neglected, yet most important source of learning, is the casual conversation that occurs around the coffee pot. An informal question-and-answer exchange concerning issues at work between two colleagues of differing experiences can lead to significant growth in the knowledge of both workers. Organizations that are aware of these gains make special efforts to design their facilities and the knowledge workers' spaces so that they may take advantage of these natural cross-fertilizing opportunities. They often provide the information technology that supports learning and knowledge sharing (Coleman, 1997). While no one can "order" a knowledge worker to learn or share knowledge, the smart organizations nurture and create environments within which learning and sharing occur naturally.

The exponential increase in available and accessible data and information—and the mounting pressure for the workforce to identify, assimilate, understand, and act upon it—has led to the need to develop new capabilities and methods to handle this information. We call these skills integrative competencies.

INTEGRATIVE COMPETENCIES

Integrative competencies provide connective tissue, creating the knowledge, skills, abilities, and behaviors that support and enhance other competencies. They have a multiplier effect through their capacity to enrich the individual's cognitive abilities while enabling integration of other competencies, leading to improved understanding, performance, and decisions (see Figure 14-2).

Integrative competencies can be understood from two perspectives. The first is from the individual's viewpoint. Here the competencies help the individual to deal with the larger, more complex aspects of their organization and its environment. They either integrate data, information, or knowledge to give the individual more capability or they help the individual perceive and comprehend the complexity around them by integrating and clarifying events, patterns, and structures in their environment. From the organization's view the integrative competencies help strengthen the organization's capacity to deal with its environment by creating programs, networks, and cultures that pull together capabilities that can more effectively handle uncertainty and complexity.

A number of what could be considered integrative competencies are discussed in this book. Knowledge management and learning make up the content of Chapters 15–17. Systems thinking and complexity thinking are addressed in Chapters 18 and 19, respectively; Chapter 20 introduces knowing; and Chapter 21 lays the groundwork for relationship network management. Each of these

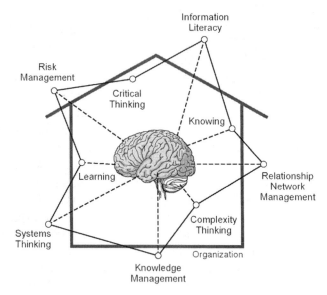

Figure 14-2
The Integrative Competencies

contributes to the capacity of the organization to sense, interpret, and take effective action within the ever-challenging, fast-paced, uncertain, and complex environment. Knowledge management supports both individuals and organizations in their need for, and application of, knowledge to handle uncertainty and complexity. It also improves the robustness, response time, and adaptability of the ICAS. Learning helps both individuals and organizations "learn how to learn" and serves as the foundation for change and adaptation. Systems thinking provides a broader perspective from which individuals can understand their own systems and what is happening in the environment. Complexity thinking provides individuals with an awareness of what complexity is and how it can best be interpreted, understood, and acted upon. Knowing helps individuals recognize the true potential of their experience, judgment, and intuition in understanding, finding meaning, and acting upon complex problems and situations. Relationship network management creates and uses personal networks to leverage knowledge and actions to respond to the new environment.

Critical thinking, always important to decision-makers, and information literacy, an important integrative competency since the advent of the Internet, help individuals and organizations find and select data and information needed to deal with the coming environment.

CRITICAL THINKING

Critical thinking, which includes the integrative competencies of systems thinking, complexity thinking, and knowing, explicated in Chapters 18, 19, and 20, is the process individuals use to make sense of and evaluate data and information, whether informational or opinion-based. Reconstruction, assessment, and evaluation are used to discern the information; to determine its status as deductive, inductive, or irrational; and to judge its accuracy and reliability.

The intent of critical thinking is to allow individuals to form their own opinions of information resources based on an open-minded evaluation of the features and components of those resources by using, for example, problem-solving skills such as listening, considering other points of view, negotiating, and evaluating one's own mental models. Critical thinkers consider not only the data and information, but the context of the resource, questioning the clarity and strength of reasoning behind the resource, identifying assumptions and values, recognizing points of view and attitudes, and evaluating conclusions and actions.

Critical thinking includes, but is not limited to:

- Open-mindedness.
- An awareness that groups and other individuals can shape issues and may have their own agendas and interests in mind, and the ability to identify those agendas and interests.

- The ability to make detailed observations, question, analyze, make connections, and try to make sense of a situation, a set of behaviors, or a single piece of information that may be out of context.
- Recognition that there is no single right or wrong way to interpret information, but many different ways, and the ability to explore each of these interpretations for is strengths and weaknesses.

With the advent of the Internet, and the increase in the amount of data and information available to knowledge workers, critical thinking becomes essential to function in the ICAS to increase the probability of desirable outcomes. Halpern (1996) states: "[Critical thinking] is used to describe thinking that is purposeful, reasoned and goal directed—the kind of thinking involved in solving problems, formulating inferences, calculating likelihoods, and making decisions when the thinker is using skills that are thoughtful and effective for the particular context and type of thinking task" (p. 117). This includes meta-thinking, or thinking about our own thinking and decision processes in order to continually improve them. The processes of problem-solving and decision-making are addressed in detail in Chapter 8.

INFORMATION LITERACY

Responding to the information and knowledge age, information literacy (IL) is a set of skills that enable individuals to recognize when information is and is not needed, and how to locate, evaluate, integrate, use, and effectively communicate information (Department of the Navy, 2000). These skills are critical in dealing with the daily barrage of information, and in using the broad array of available tools to search, organize, and analyze results, and communicate and integrate them for decision-making. As early as 1989, a Presidential Committee on Information Literacy identified IL as a survival skill in the information age. The study found that instead of drowning in the abundance of information that floods their lives, information-literate people know how to find, evaluate, and use information effectively to solve a particular problem or make a decision. In the U.S. Department of Labor's 1991 Commission on Achieving Necessary Skills, IL was called out as one of the five essential competencies necessary for solid job performance. Since this early identification of the need for IL, academic institutions have been the leaders in understanding IL issues and working to facilitate the growth of IL in the United States.

A simple analogy points out the importance of IL. In 1855, pulp papermaking was discovered, providing the opportunity to create paper that was both scalable (in the sense of having the ability to produce both small and large amounts of paper) and economical. But only 5 percent of the U.S. population could read or write. The impact of the invention could not be fully realized until the level of reading proficiency in the United States increased. From 1858 through 1899 systemic schooling raised the level of reading proficiency in the United States to 85 percent of the population. Continuing the analogy, the late twentieth century ushered in technologies such as the Web, and broadband and wireless communications. Individuals now have the ability to access information from anywhere in the world, but what percentage of people have the personal capabilities to do so, and to assess the value of and use the information they access? What percentage of people is information literate?

There is a gap (see Figure 14-3) between individuals' understanding and their ability to access what they need from the external environment. Information literacy, providing what we could refer to as meta-information (or knowledge about information), helps close that gap and provides ways of increasing the knowledge worker's ability to access what they need from the external information environment. Information literacy skills help knowledge workers: determine the nature and extent of the information needed; access needed information effectively and efficiently; evaluate information and its sources critically; use information effectively to accomplish a specific purpose; and understand the economic, legal, social, and ethical issues surrounding the use of information in a virtual world.

The first step to becoming information literate is to do a self-assessment to learn what areas should be targeted for further study. Each knowledge worker can assess their own strengths and weaknesses in IL, build on existing strengths, and correct weaknesses on the road to becoming information literate. For example, consider the following questions:

- Do you recognize when you need information? All the time?
- Can you name at least two search engines?
- Can you find basic facts on the Internet?
- Can you analyze the data you get on the Internet for validity and reliability? Are you always sure where the information comes from?
- Do you know how to identify a computer hoax or urban legend?
- Do you know how to request permission to use information under copyright?
- Do you know basic steps to ensure your online privacy?
- Do you know what browser you are using?
- Do you know what the deep Web is and that it has 500 times more information than the surface Web we usually surf?

These are only a few of the questions addressed by the Department of the Navy (2000) Information Literacy Toolkit, the first virtual tool developed for the government and its support team on IL. These questions begin to provide a flavor of what it means to become information literate.

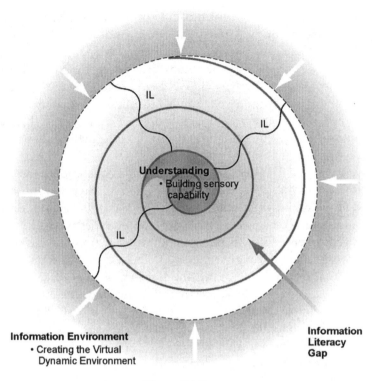

Figure 14-3
The Information Literacy Gap

Information literacy can be talked about in terms of learning how to use the Internet, selecting resources, searching resources, evaluating information, using information, and information ethics. For example, using the Internet would include common terms and explore the different types of search tools available and methods for searching. Selecting resources digs deeper in tying specific types of searching to specific information, including use of the deep Web. Searching resources is a strategy for understanding and planning a search approach. Evaluating information can be difficult in a world where anyone can put anything up on the Web. There is a great deal of information on the Web, but not all of it is accurate, up to date, or even true. Critical thinking is one approach to discerning the value of information resources. With the advent of the Internet, a new set of information ethics has emerged in the areas of intellectual property rights, privacy of information, copyright, plagiarism, filtering or restricting access to Internet content, and the privacy of users. Information literacy also includes skills in virtual communicating. ICAS knowledge workers will need to be well trained in all areas of information literacy to optimize their own knowledge and to take full advantage of knowledge management.

LEARNING HOW TO LEARN

While knowledge workers must know their professional field and learn how to continuously keep up with that field, as the world moves into the age of complexity and events become more difficult to predict, there are certain areas of knowledge that are becoming essential for career success and maintaining organizational performance. Because technology and the pace of change will almost surely continue accelerating, successful knowledge workers must be able to learn rapidly, continuously, and flexibly to fulfill their work responsibilities and maintain employability, as well as employment. This means that they must learn how to learn in a variety of situations and in many different ways. Rarely, if ever, do we reflect on how we learn and consciously try to expand the ways we learn. Living in the world of the future, where professionals often deal with five to ten subject areas in the course of an hour, requires the ability to communicate and share understanding with professionals from other disciplines, and make decisions and solve problems that entail multiple subjects.

From an external perspective, we believe others have learned when they demonstrate changes in behavior that produce effective results. In exploring learning how to learn, we will consider learning in the context of acquiring complex concepts and deep knowledge as distinct from simple data and information. Because of our individually unique genetics, personal growth, experience, and cognitive and emotional characteristics, there is no single process that accurately describes the best way to learn. Some people learn best from reading, some from listening to lectures, some from teaching, some from dialogue, social conversation, or listening to stories, some from visual displays, some from internal reflection, some from intense debate, and some from rituals and repetition. Any one or combination of these learning methods may work best at any given time and situation.

For the sake of this discussion, we take as an axiom that *the responsibility for learning, and learning how to learn, falls on the individual professional, and that self-directed learning is usually the best.* Any general theory of learning cannot take into account individual characteristics. Unfortunately, "It has been found enormously difficult to apply laboratory derived principles of learning to the improvement of efficiency in tasks with clear and relatively simple objectives. We may infer that it will be even more difficult to apply laboratory-derived principles of learning to the improvements of efficient learning in tasks with more complex objectives" (Hilgard and Bower, 1966, p. 542).

Another axiom offered is that *proactive learning is better than reactive learning.* Academic institutions, training programs, and other adult educational programs that offer or facilitate learning are useful, but in general they produce students that are passive learners. Yet for most situations passive learning is inadequate; only the adult learner knows what knowledge is needed, when it is needed, how it will be used, and possibly how best they can learn.

As knowledge workers move through the phases of their professional life, their local environment will change significantly. In school they learned from lectures and self-study, with this learning dealing mostly with theory and tractable problems. In real life, knowledge workers now must learn to deal with ambiguity, no-win problems and messy situations. They also have to learn in a wide variety of local environments, some of which will be difficult or even offensive. In other words, to maintain learning over time and in a wide variety of situations, knowledge workers must *learn how to learn*—a subject that is rarely discussed in academia or in the corporate world.

Since each of us is unique, with our own history, motivations, and cognitive skills and preferences, we take as a premise that our ability to learn will also be unique to each of us. It then follows that learning how to learn will be a personal journey, undoubtedly with help from others, but the brunt of the work must be done by each of us. If we consider the need to learn deep knowledge as noted above, then the normal academic approach of lectures and self-study may well be inadequate. If x is some challenging, complex subject, we may learn about x but we must *live* with x to make x a part of us; that is, to get the "feel of x," to be able to anticipate the consequences of our decisions and actions, and by doing so achieve effective results. Only experience coupled with practice, thinking, questioning, challenging, guessing, and trial-and-error creates the insights and "a-ha" experiences that lead to real understanding, comprehension, and meaning.

A most important question is: How do we learn how to learn from all of these ways of gaining data, information, and knowledge? The starting point is to know ourselves: our own strengths, weaknesses, feelings, and likes and dislikes relative to the acquisition and assimilation of new information and knowledge; how we have learnt best in the past, what our preferences for receiving new information are, and, most important, can we learn how to learn from all of the various techniques and artifacts of learning situations. As professionals we will continue to be exposed to a wide variety of learning situations such as those mentioned above. If we dislike learning from lectures, we should make an effort to expand our learning capacity to include learning from lectures. Every process for learning can contribute to our stores of knowledge. To ignore some methods by "turning off" is to lose opportunities. Each individual can look at a given situation and reflect on how to learn from that situation. Two perspectives are helpful. One is to look at the situation and ask: What is in the situation that I can learn from? The second and more difficult is to ask: What do I need to do to get the maximum learning out of this system (composed of the situation, me, and the interaction between us)? Answers to such questions will encourage everyone to learn how to learn in many situations. Let's take a couple of examples—storytelling and reading.

Storytelling and Reading

Most people are aware of the power of stories to communicate understanding, values, and guidelines. They are easily remembered and recalled when needed and may even serve as internal mentors that offer guidance to the person when they find themselves in a situation related to the lessons of the story. Storytelling could be looked at as a way of teaching; and while teaching, the storyteller can learn from listening to the comments and observing the reactions of the audience. Any forthcoming dialogue will give the storyteller much greater insight into the levels of meaning within a good story. However, to learn from such an experience the storyteller must consciously ask questions, listen carefully, and be open to different interpretations of their story. Just as good teachers learn much from their students, every professional can learn from helping others learn.

Many people consider reading a book a passive activity. It doesn't have to be. Since we all learn from an interaction and a dialogue on a given subject, we can interact with a book by highlighting or underlining passages we believe are important. This simple process gives the unconscious mind more time to absorb the meaning of the sentences and think about them. By prioritizing ideas and concepts by putting crosses or stars next to important passages in the book, we can easily return to the book and pick out areas that were most interesting and informative, thereby reviewing and reinforcing our earlier thoughts—again increasing learning. Another technique is to challenge statements believed to be untrue, thereby creating action items for our own further research. Or we add our own thoughts and questions in the margins where the author made statements that trigger our own knowledge.

In other words, we can become active participants with the book and use it as a vehicle for creating and pulling information and knowledge from our own experience and unconscious mind. There is an old saying that is very appropriate: "We don't know what we know until we say it, write it, or think it." Thus if a book is read not just as a source of someone else's ideas, but as a tool to leverage and surface our own experience, emotions, intuitions, and creative powers, we can amplify our learning from every book we read. To do this takes patience, practice, and time. It is an example of learning how to learn and each reader will have to develop his/her own techniques that are comfortable and fit individual learning preferences and needs.

The above examples are not meant to be definitive. They hope to suggest the sometime invisible situations that can be used by knowledge workers who seriously want to maximize learning and are willing to put personal effort into answering the question: "How can I gain the maximum knowledge from this specific situation?" In the ICAS world, knowledge workers will face this dilemma many times every day.

In the best case, knowledge workers direct their learning and manage their knowledge so they are well prepared for both present and future challenges. This is the payoff from learning how and when to learn and from treating their knowledge as a manageable asset that greatly influences career success. Since their competency is the source of the organization's performance, KM and learning become everyone's responsibility and everyone's gain.

Keeping up with a discipline or profession has always been a challenge. Most businesses today produce products and services that encompass many disciplines with customers demanding rapid, full-service support of those products. These factors, coupled with a changing marketplace, create a need for Knowledge Workers who have both strong discipline knowledge and a broad competency that covers many dimensions.

Learning new disciplines requires a new language, different assumptions, rules, and perspectives. For a Knowledge Worker to become knowledgable in several fields may mean giving up valued beliefs, adopting new ways of thinking, and a motivation to start over on the learning curve. This necessitates a strong ego, a clear acceptance of our limitations, and a willingness to step down from our self-image as an "expert".

The challenge to meet these requirements will tax many professionals and their organizations. The successful Knowledge Worker of the future will spend more time learning, thinking and collaborating and less time applying what they already know.

REFERENCES

Bennet, D. *IPT Learning Campus: Gaining Acquisition Results Through IPTs.* Alexandria, VA: Bellwether Learning Center, 1997.

Coleman, D. *Groupware: Collaborative Strategies for Corporate LANs and Intranets.* Englewood Cliffs, NJ: Prentice-Hall, 1997.

Department of the Navy. *Information Literacy Toolkit.* Washington, DC: DON, 2000.

Drucker, P. F. *The New Realities: In Government and Politics/In Economics and Business/In Society and World View.* New York: Harper & Row, 1989.

Halpern, D. F. *Thought and Knowledge: An Introduction to Critical Thinking,* 4th ed. Mahwah, NJ: Lawrence Erlbaum Associates, 2003.

Hilgard, E. R. and G. H. Bower. *Theories of Learning.* New York: Appleton-Century-Crofts, 1966. As quoted in Knowles, M. S. *The Adult Learner: A Neglected Species.* Houston: Gulf Publishing Company, 1998.

Katzenbach, J. R. and D. K. Smith. *The Wisdom of Teams: Creating the High-Performance Organization.* New York: HarperCollins Publishers, 1993.

Knowles, M. S. *The Adult Learner: A Neglected Species.* Houston, TX: Gulf Publishing Company, 1998.

Kolb, D. A. Experiential Learning: *Experience as the Source of Learning and Development.* Englewood Cliffs, NJ: Prentice-Hall, 1984.

Chapter 15

KNOWLEDGE MANAGEMENT

Knowledge management is a systematic approach to getting an organization to make the best possible use of knowledge in implementing its mission, broadly viewed as either sustainable competitive advantage or long-term high performance. The goal is for an organization to become aware of its knowledge, individually and collectively, and to shape itself so that it makes the most effective and efficient use of the knowledge it has or can obtain. By management we do not mean control in the sense of strong authority and direction. This style of management fails with knowledge because no one can control another person's mind—where the knowledge is. Instead, managers must first set examples through leadership, management, and personal behavior. Then they must strive to create and nurture a culture and an infrastructure that stimulates workers to create, use, and share their knowledge and that also supports their freedom to self-organize and to act effectively over a broad range of situations. When an organization lives in a turbulent, unpredictable, and challenging world, it must be a learning organization, capable of handling change, uncertainty, and complexity. That is, the culture and infrastructure must be such that individuals and groups of individuals can and will continuously question and if needed, change their beliefs in order to create and apply new knowledge to achieve desired goals and objectives.

At the manager level, knowledge management (often seen with both terms capitalized, but hereafter referred to in lower case or as KM) can be viewed as a process for optimizing the effective application of intellectual capital to achieve organizational objectives. *Intellectual capital* covers the broad spectrum from tacit to explicit knowledge loosely framed through a discussion of human capital, social capital, and corporate capital. *Human capital*, a company's greatest resource, is made up of every individual's past and present knowledge and competency, and their *future potential*. Each person brings a unique set of characteristics and values from the past, including expertise, education, and experience. Built on these characteristics and values are a set of capabilities and ways of seeing and living in the world (such as creativity and adaptability). Just as important is a person's future potential. Part of the success of the ICAS is for leaders and knowledge workers at all levels to have the capacity to learn and quickly respond to emerging challenges.

Social capital includes human and virtual networks, relationships, and the interactions across these networks built on those relationships. (See the discussion of relationship network management in Chapter 21.) Social capital also takes into account all the aspects of language, including context and culture, formal and informal language, and verbal and nonverbal communication. Added to this grouping is an element of patterning that deals with timing and sequencing of exchange, as well as the density and diversity of the content. This includes the number of interactions between individuals in a relationship network, the length and depth of those interactions, and the frequency of those interactions in short, how much, how often, and how intense.

Corporate capital, sometimes called organizational capital or structural capital, includes all the content in databases and information that employees can visibly get their hands around, everything that has been made explicit. The challenge is for an organization to fully leverage its intellectual capital through sharing, collaborating, innovating, and learning within the framework of its needs for security and information assurance in achieving competitive advantage.

Building on good information management, the ongoing process of KM is the final element in Figure 15-1 of an effective information technology (IT) strategy, focusing on people and their ability to use information in decision-making. It provides a methodology to achieve the knowledge centricity essential to the effective ICAS. Information technology, information management, and knowledge management are connected layers built upon a strong, supportive infrastructure. Each successive layer must be in place to successfully implement the next layer, yet the full value of the any layer cannot be achieved in today's knowledge economy without success throughout all four levels. That means that organizations need to have good information management (IM) to effect good knowledge management, and good information management, in turn, is dependent on the right technology investment. Intuitively, most organizations have recognized that using information to help create knowledge to drive improved decision-making was the ultimate IT goal. Knowledge management has provided the framework to make that intuitive awareness explicit.

As demonstrated in Figure 15-1, the capital elements that drive the definition of KM can be traced through IM, IT and the infrastructure. For example, social capital aspects of IM would focus around relationships; social capital aspects of IT center around connectivity (software and hardware); and the social capital

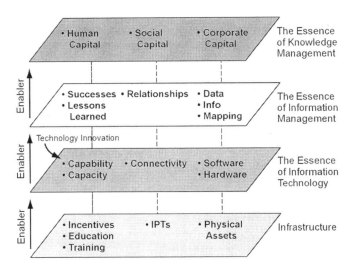

Figure 15-1
The Relationships Between IT, IM, and KM

aspects within the infrastructure are very much concerned with the use of teams and groups. Following the KM concept through these four layers surfaces critical focus areas that individually and collectively affect the success of the ICAS.

MANAGING KNOWLEDGE

While intellectual capital in terms of an individual's thoughts can certainly not be "managed," the term knowledge management has come to include those elements of information management that increase the opportunity for an individual to use information to create knowledge and to share that knowledge. An example is the use of meta-information, or the importance of transmitting the context of information along with the information. It may be critical for a decision-maker to know whether information was the product of a single expert or a group of practitioners, how information was used and with what results, and how recent this information is.

A second example is development of the knowledge taxonomy, the classification scheme used to categorize a set of information items. This scheme represents an agreed-upon vocabulary of topics arranged around a particular theme. Effective use of an enterprise taxonomy enables a common language that engineers and logisticians (for example) can use to access needed information and communicate and understand each other no matter who has stored it. While technically a taxonomy is an "information taxonomy," the term "knowledge taxonomy" is used to stress that this scheme helps users organize and find information and build understanding based on their own education and experience. Classifying information becomes more important as the number of items increases and people have more and more trouble remembering what they have and where to find it. A taxonomy becomes crucial as we buckle under the immense volume of information available to everyone by global electronic networking. Creating an orderly method of classifying human knowledge and writing is tremendously complex. People use the same words to convey different concepts depending upon the context of the exchange, what we think other people already know or don't know, and how it relates to other activities and thoughts. Built on ontologies—the conceptual framework in a classification scheme—the knowledge taxonomy enables the efficient and interoperable retrieval and sharing of data, information, and knowledge across the organization based on natural workflow and knowledge needs (Malafsky, 2003).

UNDERSTANDING THE BREADTH OF KNOWLEDGE MANAGEMENT

As an example of the application of KM, consider the U.S. government and its use of KM in moving towards an *enabled* government, or eGoverment, largely defined as government of the people, by the people, and for the people in a virtual world, a collaborative government where technology meets human creativity, and where government manages and shares its vast stores of knowledge with, and for the benefit of, the citizen. In the late 1990s, the Federal Chief Information Officer Council sponsored development of a Federal Knowledge Management Working Group dedicated to fostering interagency collaboration, interagency communities of practice, and the sharing of knowledge throughout the government. Starting from small beginnings, this group began to grow as more and more government agencies and organizations realized the potential of KM, albeit each defined KM in a different fashion.

Although this was at first confusing, this learning community eventually realized that the true value of KM was both what it held for each of their organizations *and* that it was bringing them together to build a connected and sharing government. Still, it was realized that if KM was defined as everything it would, of course, fall short. In 1998, the government sponsored a partnering session with academia and industry associations offering KM certifications to figure out what those things were in KM that government knowledge workers wanted and needed to know.

This approach defined a conceptual framework for KM through developing criteria for accredited government certification programs. The result was a draft set of learning objectives for government employees attending certification courses. While these learning objectives cover the *breadth* of what is needed to implement knowledge management successfully in the federal sector, it was determined that the depth of knowledge and ability needed in each area was highly dependent on the specific job that needs to be done. Half of the learning objectives identified through the above process were concerned with the specific knowledge a knowledge worker needs to work effectively in the area of knowledge management. The second half of the KM learning objectives deals with specific abilities, or skills. The fourteen objectives and their explication as prepared for the Federal KM Working Group are discussed briefly below. While perhaps not encompassing the full scope of KM as it is emerging today, this well-rounded set of learning objectives provides a robust way of understanding knowledge management. While reviewing these objectives, keep in mind their applicability to bringing KM into an ICAS organization and their potential contribution to the bottom line. From an ICAS viewpoint, many of the following learning objectives could easily apply to every ICAS collaborative leader and to many ICAS knowledge workers.

Learning Objective 1

Have knowledge of the value added by Knowledge Management to the business proposition, including the return on investment, performance measures, and the ability to develop a business case. Though knowledge management is capitalized in the above sentence, knowledge management is best considered as having a small "k" and a small "m." The intent is that knowledge management is not an initiative in and of itself, but supports the mission and business objectives of the ICAS. This positions KM as a strategic enabler for the organization. Fundamental in this objective is a tie-in to ICAS strategic business. KM is an extremely broad discipline and using metrics brings solid management practices to the forefront of decision-makers, thereby enabling choices. Since knowledge is at the foundation of the ICAS, it should be built into the business proposition and the business case. Each ICAS business proposition would have a specific end objective with measurable outcomes to guide decisions and evaluate success. In this book we focus on the broader ICAS characteristics that give it the capacity to deal with its environment. Nevertheless, knowledge would play a large role in almost all ICAS business propositions.

Performance measures are the essence of good management practices. KM initiatives need to be continually monitored to ensure progress toward their goals. Given the complex and dynamic nature of modern organizations, KM— or any other organizational initiative—cannot guarantee that plans and strategies will succeed. Well-designed performance measures provide indications of the efficiency and effectiveness of people, processes, and programs, which in turn help leaders understand and adapt their organizations. Indeed, performance measures are so integral to organizational success in the Federal government that several pieces of legislation have been passed specifically calling for formal metrics. These include the Government Performance and Results Act (GPRA) of 1993, the Government Management Reform Act of 1994, and the Information Technology Management Reform Act of 1996. The government, of course, is primarily a hierarchical, control-oriented organization.

Performance measures are necessary but different for the ICAS. They would have to have a longer timeframe and deal primarily with organizational characteristics such as health, flexibility, and strategy, that is, ecological mating, or how well they merge with their environment. You might use as a measurement the ratio of success ventures versus unsuccessful ventures since the ICAS uses a trial-and-error approach because of its inability to predict the future.

Learning Objective 2

Have knowledge of the strategies and processes to transfer explicit and tacit knowledge across time, space, and organizational boundaries, including retrieval of critical archived information enabling ideas to build upon ideas. Since Nonaka and Takeuchi (1995) first explored the interaction between tacit and explicit knowledge in *The Knowledge-Creating Company,* there has been a steady growth of interest on the capture of tacit knowledge. Aging workforce issues in the public sector have served as a catalyst for the development of processes and systems that facilitate understanding the role and importance of context in decision-making.

But this objective goes even further. Transfer is the focus rather than just understanding the nature of tacit and explicit knowledge. Increasing the dynamics of transfer by itself moves knowledge through the organization at an increased rate. The more knowledge is being transferred, the more it is available to the organization as a resource.

Understanding the relationship between tacit and explicit knowledge and its impact on the organization leads to informed decisions on an organization's KM approach. A high ratio of *tacit* knowledge (knowledge held by individuals in their heads that cannot be verbalized as information that others can re-create as knowledge) leads to a strong dependence on the individual and reliance on the connectivity between individuals for knowledge flow. The loss of individuals and their knowledge can have a serious effect on the organization. A high ratio of *explicit* knowledge (knowledge that is or can be verbalized as information and is readily available for others to re-create as knowledge) requires an investment in the transfer of knowledge from tacit to explicit and may present issues regarding context, currency, and accuracy. However, a high amount of explicit knowledge leads to less dependence on the individual, and explicit knowledge can be stored and easily moved around. The use of teams, communities, mentors, and dialogues coupled with widespread organizational trust greatly assists the ICAS in sharing knowledge.

Learning Objective 3

Have knowledge of state-of-the-art and evolving technology solutions that promote KM, including portals and collaborative and distributed learning technologies. We live in a world of technology. The exponential increase in data and information is both driven and enabled by information technology. We have the ability to reach further and further *within* domains and *across* domains for ideas and solutions. Knowledge repositories, automated libraries, computer services, databases, etc. offer the capability for not only storing large amounts of data and information, but also efficient and intelligent retrieval and assemblage capability. Powerful search algorithms, intelligent agents, and semantic interpreters allow employees to rapidly retrieve information needed for problem-solving and decision-making. Knowledge managers and leaders need to be aware of these capabilities, how they are used, and how to integrate their operation with people to ensure knowledge availability and application.

In the ICAS organizations, portals are one delivery mechanism for knowledge sharing. Collaborative systems range from intranets to video teleconferencing to whiteboards and are used extensively throughout the ICAS. Their purpose is to aid groups of individuals, either co-located or dispersed, to work more effectively together to foster innovations, solve problems, and make better decisions. For example, distributed learning uses information technology to facilitate learning without having the instructor co-located. Knowledge workers at different locations, using their own PCs, can learn via the Internet or computer-based training. The increasing rate of environmental change necessitates faster learning, forcing all organizations to change traditional learning approaches. Classroom-based learning will be supplemented or complemented with new virtual capabilities.

Learning Objective 4

Have knowledge of and the ability to facilitate knowledge creation, sharing, and reuse including developing partnerships and alliances, designing creative knowledge spaces, and using incentive structures. Knowledge creation, sharing, and reuse are the heart of KM programs and the knowledge-centric organization. As people share knowledge within the ICAS, and other knowledge workers use that knowledge and find new ways to improve on it and innovate, its value increases for all of the ICAS. This process also provides the opportunity to identify integrators (knowledge leaders who connect people and ideas together) and subject matter experts (who provide depth of thinking in specific areas). In turn, those involved in exchanges benefit from the exchange through a more complete understanding of the area addressed, thereby becoming a more valuable resource to the organization.

Three examples of facilitating knowledge creation, sharing and reuse are included to facilitate an understanding of the eclectic nature of KM. Partnerships and alliances are means by which the ICAS can share information and knowledge with others while working together toward mutual goals. Knowledge spaces build on the concept of "open space," providing space and time for people to mentally explore events or thoughts and formulate ways in which to proceed. Open space, whether physical or virtual, provides a place to brainstorm and be creative. It comes in many forms: online chat rooms, threaded e-mail discussions, weekly in-person discussion forums, communities, discussion groups, coffee rooms, and water cooler encounters. Here knowledge workers can sort out complexities and receive feedback from others, resulting in new ideas and improved decision-making capabilities (See Chapter 17).

Senior leaders and managers will have to create incentive and reward structures and performance measures to help promote the creation, sharing, and reuse of knowledge. Some organizations provide bonuses and other rewards to individuals who go out of their way to share knowledge with others. Event intermediations such as knowledge fairs have been successfully held in such organizations as The World Bank and the Department of the Navy.

Learning Objective 5

Have knowledge of learning styles and behaviors, strive for continuous improvement, and be actively engaged in exploring new ideas and concepts. People learn differently. Some learn through reading, others through lectures or visual or graphic representations, while still others learn by doing. Effective transfer of information requires understanding different learning styles and how people learn. Since adults learn best from direct experience with real-world problems, how can this be extrapolated across a virtual environment? (Knowles, 1998.) As learning becomes the mutual responsibility of leaders and workers, knowledge professionals must be constant learners, seeking new information and exhibiting behavior for others to model by continuously striving to improve the organization's use of information and knowledge.

This objective also sets the stage for capitalizing on new learning approaches including broadband Web-based multimedia. As new concepts unfold, models and theories for learning will evolve. A foundation in this area will prepare the ICAS and its knowledge workers for the future.

Learning Objective 6

Have working knowledge of state-of-the-art research and implementation strategies for knowledge management, information management, document and records management, and data management. This includes project management of knowledge initiatives and retrieval of critical archived information. Knowledge leaders and workers need to understand the conceptual linkages between knowledge management, information management, and data and records management. KM is part of a larger movement enabled by information technology, a movement that has brought us into the information age and is rapidly propelling us toward an age of increasing complexity where knowledge appears to be the only thing that can deal with complexity. There are continuing advances in data management, document and records management, and information management that will make information technology infrastructures more effective in supporting know ledge workers as they make their organization more effective through the intelligent management of knowledge. The ICAS, through knowledge centricity, will make maximum use of technology and the latest research findings related to information and knowledge management.

Learning Objective 7

Have understanding of the global and economic importance of developing knowledge-based organizations to meet the challenges of the knowledge era. We live in an omni-linked world. Anyone in the world can talk to almost anyone else in the world in real time. Technology has provided totally new ways of moving and transferring data, information, and knowledge among indivi duals, organizations, and governments. The results of these interactions are increased communication, and a corresponding increase in the flow of ideas and the making of decisions. Organizations are forced to scan, select, and quickly respond to the increased flow of Web-based exchanges and actions. Moreover, as the number of nodes in networks increase, the number of links increase, and as the links and their consequent relationships increase, so does the complexity. Critical thinking, the possession of deep knowledge, and the ability to work collaboratively with others who think differently may help address issues of increasing complexity. Knowledge-based organizations such as the ICAS need to provide time and space for critical thinking.

Learning Objective 8

Have the ability to use systems thinking in implementing solutions. KM addresses powerful activities throughout environments, organizations, cultures, and economies. As one considers the relevant issues and opportunities, systems thinking provides a means for looking at the "big" picture while examining the component parts.

Systems thinking assumes that almost everything is a system, made up of connecting elements and their relationships. Systems thinking is one of the ICAS integrative competencies that knowledge workers need to work effectively in a complex environment (see Chapter 19). Systems have boundaries and behaviors that are different from their individual elements. Systems thinking emphasizes the importance of relationships and structure within the organization and makes individuals aware of the effects of their efforts on others in the organization, permitting them to understand and perform their roles more effectively.

The Learning Organization work coming out of the Massachusetts Institute of Technology (Senge, 1990) includes a systems thinking approach to improve decision-makers' strategic thinking skills. Systems thinking helps manage complexity by providing a tool for decision-makers to map and understand cause-and-effect relationships among data, information, and events in an organization. This is done through a process of identifying patterns that repeat themselves over and over again in decision-making and organizational life. This process forces decision-makers to consider the consequences of their actions and their impact on, and relationship to, other organizational functions. Systems thinking not only helps increase an individual's critical thinking skills, but also enhances collaboration and serves as a basis for collective inquiry by providing a common language and perspective for dialogue and understanding.

Learning Objective 9

Have the ability to design, develop, and sustain communities of interest and practice. Communities are social constructs. In a primarily virtual world, communities provide a fundamental capability for developing and sharing expertise throughout the workforce. Communities of practice share a domain of practice, crossing operational, functional, and organizational boundaries, and defining themselves by knowledge areas, not tasks. In like manner, communities of interest share a domain of interest. Communities are managed by establishing and developing connections between individuals and organizations, and focusing on value added, mutual exchange, and continuous learning. They have an evolving agenda as participant knowledge builds and related areas of exchange emerge.

Collaboration, innovation, learning, and knowledge sharing are at the core of communities of practice and interest. Communities increase information flows in order to maximize knowledge, and exploit existing competencies to achieve maximum return. They also facilitate the transfer of best practices and lessons learned between organizational content centers, thus creating efficiencies while improving effectiveness. And communities fill in the gaps where organizational knowledge falls short and where enterprise information is underexploited. In short, sometimes we do not know what we do not know. Communities encourage personnel to access key resources and build new knowledge to complete tasks faster, better, and easier. All of these attributes are designed into the ICAS.

Learning Objective 10

Have the ability to create, develop, and sustain the flow of knowledge. This includes understanding the skills needed to leverage virtual teamwork and social networks. The flow of data, information, and knowledge moves around in the networks of systems and people. It is shared through team interaction, communities, and events, and is facilitated through knowledge repositories and portals. This flow is both horizontal and vertical, including the continuous, rapid two-way communication between key components of the organization and top-level decision-makers.

With increased connectivity, we reach further and further across organizations, communities, industries, and the globe to tap resources. Virtual teamwork requires new skills of leadership, management, and facilitation to create and maintain the trust, open communication, and interdependencies needed for physically separated individuals to collaborate effectively.

Many companies and organizations invest a considerable amount of money in restructuring organizational charts and reengineering business processes only to be disappointed with the results. That is because much of the work happens *outside* the formal organizational structure. Often what needs attention is the informal organization, the networks of relationships that employees form across functions and divisions need to quickly accomplish tasks. These informal relationships can cut through formal reporting procedures to jump-start stalled initiatives and meet extraordinary deadlines. However, information networks can just as easily sabotage the best-laid plans of companies by blocking communication and fomenting opposition to change unless leaders know how to identify and direct them. Learning how to map these social links can help harness the real power of organizations. It is easy to see the importance of knowledge described here and its application to the ICAS.

Learning Objective 11

Have the ability to perform cultural and ethnographic analyses, develop knowledge taxonomies, facilitate knowledge audits, and perform knowledge mapping and needs assessments. As the amount of information and knowledge increases, tools such as taxonomies, audits, and maps help organize information for decision-making. While search engines and agents keep improving, the bottom line is that the human brain is the final arbiter of effective relationships and patterns. Analytic techniques such as cultural and ethnographic analyses help leaders understand organizational cultures and their characteristics. Culture is often cited as one of the main barriers to successful implementation of KM.

As discussed earlier, a taxonomy is a framework for arranging or categorizing information and knowledge so that people can find and use it effectively. This is applicable when designing a knowledge base, but also applies to the wider knowledge system. For example, if knowledge is organized into groupings based upon a community of interest (or practice) on a website or knowledge base, then mentoring programs, training, and other knowledge transfer processes should support these same groupings to facilitate knowledge flow. It is not necessary to pick just one way of arranging information and knowledge, but it is important to evaluate the many different ways before beginning any kind of knowledge base design.

Conducting a "knowledge audit" to find out how information is collected, stored, and reported, and how the reports are used (if at all) can be beneficial in streamlining the information flow within an organization, saving time and effort. A knowledge audit examines what information is available and whether it is used. Simply put, the purpose of a knowledge audit is to help the organization "know what it knows" and then measure the quantity and usefulness of that knowledge base. All of these have relevance to a knowledge organization operating in an ICAS environment. This is why the ICAS places so much emphasis on knowledge management.

Learning Objective 12

Have the ability to capture, evaluate, and use best-known practices, including the use of storytelling to transfer these best practices. The use of best practices across industry and government can provide efficiencies and increase effectiveness, if they are indeed best practices for the organization implementing them. How is the applicability of a best practice determined? How do you understand the context of the best practice, the simple rules that made it successful in some organizations?

Storytelling, the construction of examples to illustrate a point, can be used to effectively transfer knowledge and best practices. An organizational story is a detailed narrative of management actions, employee interactions, or other intra-organizational events that are communicated informally within the organization. A variety of story forms exist and will arise naturally throughout organizations, including scenarios and anecdotes. Scenarios are the articulation of possible future states, constructed within the imaginative limits of the author. While scenarios provide an awareness of alternatives—of value in and of itself—they are often used as planning tools for possible future situations. The plan becomes a vehicle to respond to recognized key elements in each scenario. An anecdote is a brief sequence of events experienced in the field or arising from a brainstorming session. To reinforce positive behavior, sensitive managers can seek out and disseminate anecdotes that embody the value desired in the organization. The capture and distribution of anecdotes across organizations carries high value. Dave Snowden (1999a), a consultant and author in Europe who has investigated the use of storytelling in organizations for over a decade, has discovered that once a critical number of anecdotes are captured from a community, the value set or rules underlying the behavior of that community can be determined. Understanding these values allows the use of informal as well as formal aspects of the organization.

Conveying information in a story provides a rich context. Context remains in memory longer and creates more memory traces than random information bites. Therefore, a story is more likely to be acted upon than other means of communication. Storytelling connects people, develops creativity, and increases confidence. The appeal of stories in organizations helps build descriptive capabilities, increase organizational learning, convey complex meaning, and communicate common values and rule sets. There is little doubt that stories apply directly to the ICAS. On the other hand, best practices may not apply or be appropriate because of the difficulty of transference or the rapid change of events. It depends heavily on the pace of events faced by the ICAS. Note that there is a natural sharing of best practices through the use of teams and communities.

Learning Objective 13

Have the ability to manage change and complex knowledge projects. Management concepts, whether old or new, are about change management, and in today's world where complexity is increasing, according to Ashby's law of requisite variety there must be as many or more ways to change a system as those things in a system that need to be changed.

Cultural change of any kind is a long, slow process. Accomplishing change requires daily support of sharing knowledge openly throughout the entire organization. KM initiatives are particularly challenging to change agents because of the uncertainty of outcome. Most managers like to change only one or two things at a time to mitigate against unintended consequences. When many factors within the organization are simultaneously changed, communicating, coordination, and leadership become important in reducing resistance to change and maintaining motivation. We have already discussed these aspects in Chapters 7 and 10 and they clearly apply to the ICAS.

Learning Objective 14

Have the ability to identify customers and stakeholders and tie organizational goals to the needs and requirements of those customers and stakeholders. Total quality management brought to the forefront the tried and true values successful organizations have used for years, a focus on customers and stakeholders. No matter what new approach or initiative is popular, the government must keep a focused eye on the needs of their constituents, and ensure all efforts underway contribute to fulfilling their needs. This makes good business sense and would certainly apply to the ICAS. For the ICAS, the goals may be local goals tied to local customers because of the possible variety of customer needs.

KNOWLEDGE MANAGEMENT PRINCIPLES

Just as there are many definitions of KM, there are many sets of KM principles in print. Some of them remind us in somewhat humorous terms such things as "KM is expensive (but so is stupidity)" or "Sharing is an unnatural act." The set below is drawn from our experience in implementing KM in a number of public and private organizations ranging from a professional services firm to the Department of the Navy.

- Information technology and information management without knowledge management are necessary but not sufficient.
- Knowledge management focuses management attention on the value of intellectual capital, and that's all about people.
- Ideas beget ideas; ideas shared provide the opportunity to develop new and better ideas.
- Sharing knowledge and expertise is key to organizational flexibility, agility, responsiveness, and success.
- Some explicit knowledge and its context can be represented digitally, and can be stored, shared, and effectively applied across the enterprise.
- It is not enough to develop information systems, or even knowledge systems. A successful organization addresses issues of flow: the flow of data, information, and knowledge; the flow of people in and out and across organizations; and flow in terms of individual achievement.
- Transferring valuable tacit knowledge is a systems issue dealing with information, context, relationships, and culture.
- Effective knowledge systems, processes, and taxonomies focus on user effectiveness.

BUILDING THE KNOWLEDGE MANAGEMENT FRAMEWORK

One model used in the author's work with the Department of the Navy—a model that was adopted by a number of other government and industry organizations— emphasizes a balanced approach addressing technology, process, content, culture, and learning. This balance is necessary to ensure that one facet doesn't dominate the KM program, since the processes and technology must work in concert, i.e., technology alone is not sufficient. It is critical to locate and achieve the point of equilibrium for the dynamic tensions arising through implementation of KM systems. How much risk are we willing to take to achieve leverage and, conversely, how much leveraging are we willing to do despite the risk? How much data and information should be left at the local level, and how much should be available globally? How much data and information and what data and information should be made explicit? How much data and information and what data and information should be captured in a formal system? In this world of access and excess, the answer is not automatically "more."

In each of the five areas of the implementation framework, a few key words are included to stimulate thinking. We have previously addressed many of the key words shown in Figure 15-2 as they would apply to the ICAS. For example, Chapter 7 looks at culture, Chapter 21 covers relationship networks, Chapter 6 addresses teams, and Chapter 16 discusses learning. Chapter 9 on leadership discusses the importance of empowerment. While the ideas and importance of KM occur through this book, the detailed application of KM is highly dependent on the specific organization and its environment.

Figure 15-2 can be used as a template to impose over a KM system or process. In this manner, it suggests the questions that need to be asked to achieve success. Questions can be asked at the key word level, or, ultimately the key concept level: How does this system/process fully exploit technology? How does it ensure the right content? Who knows what the right content is? Who should provide that content? How does this system/process streamline current processes? How does it facilitate individual, team, and organizational learning? How does it enable culture change? Asking and answering these questions will help develop a true knowledge system.

Several emerging concepts represented in this figure bear a short discussion.

Context

Knowledge management has focused attention on the importance of capturing the context along with information and knowledge artifacts (information that has supported the creation of knowledge but is stored as information). Context is unique at any given point in time. It is based on environmental factors, human interactions, recent events, and potential future actions. Knowledge

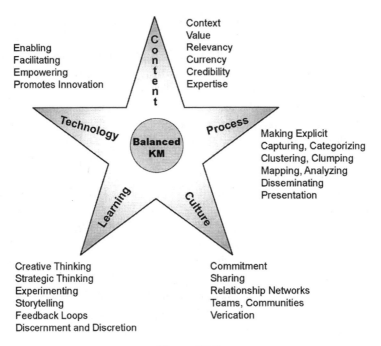

Figure 15-2
The KM Implementation Framework

systems must capture the context along with decisions. This can be done in a number of ways. For instance, a special context field in a database can record important environmental factors that might easily be lost when the decision is looked at down the road. Or, a short video clip of the decision-maker talking about the reasons a decision was made could be included with support material. A dialogue among team members may surface an even richer context to build understanding since it represents several different perspectives.

Clumping and Clustering

Clustering is when you bring data and information together that is similar or related, i.e., first- and second-cousin organization. This process of categorization by similarities is the current popular approach to organization of data and information. It supports ease of locating specific data, and can lead to innovation and insights. Clumping is driven by decision-making. You figure out the decisions you need to make at the top levels and dig out, down, and around to find the authoritative data fields you need from disparate locations. Then you link directly to those fields for continuous real-time feed to support emerging decision-making requirements. An example of application at the tactical level would be a database field providing information that the owners of that information realized was insufficient for the best decision, i.e., the suppliers of the information recognizing the need for additional information and supplying that additional information connected to the original information, *even though the decision-maker may not know such information exists*. The organization of information and knowledge around key decision points, closer to that of the human brain, can increase the efficiency and effectiveness of decision-making.

Decision Grounding

Historically, managers have placed significant emphasis on grounding decisions with explicit data, and verifying those decisions through evidence, documents, and references to prove truth and accuracy. Yet, in the complex world of today, captains of ships and managers of support organizations are often called upon to rely on their "gut" feelings. For this reason, grounding decisions on implicit data has become more important. This grounding is achieved through *verication*, the process of consulting a trusted ally to ensure the reasonableness or soundness of a decision. Using a team or staff group to explore alternatives and reflect on a potential decision is another way to ground the decision, or vericate.

Discernment and Discretion

If only two words come to the fore in implementation of knowledge management, they are discernment and discretion. Taken together, these terms address the concept of selection, valuing, and laying aside, i.e., the ability to identify and choose what is of value, and the equally difficult ability to toss aside that which is not of value. With the continuous increase of available information comes the need to quickly discern what information is of value to the organization, and what information can be considered "noise," and of no consequence to the organization. The intent of integrative competencies (Chapters 14–21) is to increase the discernment and discretion capabilities of knowledge workers.

Storytelling

The construction of fictional examples (or of true experiences) to illustrate a point, can be used to effectively transfer knowledge. When well constructed, stories can convey a high level of complex meaning. The use of subtext—an unstated message not explicit in the dialogue of the story—can convey this meaning without making it obvious. Additionally, stories have the capacity to increase an individual's descriptive capabilities, a strength in this age of uncertainty where knowledge workers must be able to describe their environment and have the self-awareness to describe their capabilities. Description capabilities are essential in strategic thinking and planning, and create a greater awareness of what can be achieved.

Because stories communicate common values and rule systems, they provide a mechanism to build organic organizational response to emerging requirements, what is required in the ICAS organization. This means that as new situations and new challenges arise in response to an ever-changing world, a common set of values will drive that response at every level of the organization. As Snowden (1999b) has found, "The higher the level of uncertainty at which we either have to operate, or more beneficially at which we choose to operate, requires a concentration on common values and rule systems that allow the network of communities from which our organization is formed to self-organize around a common purpose. In this world, old skills such as story and other models drawn from organic rather than mechanical thinking are survival skills, not nice to haves" (from reprint).

A variety of story forms exist naturally throughout every organization, including scenarios—the articulation of possible future states, constructed within the imaginative limits of the author, and anecdotes—brief sequences captured in the field or arising from brainstorming sessions. While scenarios provide awareness of alternatives—of value in and of itself—they are also often used as planning tools for possible future situations. The plan becomes a vehicle to respond to recognized objectives in each scenario. Anecdotes can be used to reinforce positive behavior; leaders can seek out and disseminate true anecdotes that embody the value desired in the organization. Healthy organizations are filled with anecdotes. "If there are none, this tells the manager a lot about the socialization and internalization going on in the organization!" (Swap et al., 2001, p. 6).

Organizational storytelling seeks to create purposeful and goal-directed activity. An example is the springboard stories used by The World Bank to move that organization into a knowledge organization. The springboard story is a type of transformational story intended to generate imitative examples so that listeners can discover new knowledge and capabilities that they possess but do not use. As Denning (2001) discovered, these stories have proved a powerful method of communicating knowledge about norms and values. Since conveying information in a story provides a rich and quickly understood context, stories remain in the conscious memory longer and create more memory traces than information alone. Therefore, a story is more likely to be acted upon than normal means of communication.

THINKING KNOWLEDGE SHARING IN SYSTEMS TERMS

In the ICAS, effective storytelling is an important tool for knowledge sharing, supporting learning, knowledge centricity, and flow. Figure 15-3 presents a systems approach to knowledge sharing. Knowledge workers recognize that sharing knowledge goes far beyond picking up the telephone or sending an e-mail. As shown in Figure 15-3, the capture of explicit knowledge can be thought of in terms of developing context-rich information systems that include such things as video clips, community dialogues, and stories. Flow is facilitated through teams, communities, and relationship networks and is increased by such things as providing virtual collaboration systems, building-in *ba* spaces and sponsoring knowledge fairs. Both formal and informal mentoring is a way of life in the ICAS, with every leader and knowledge worker developing and continuing learning and teaching relationships to ensure growth of the organization, the cross-fertilization of ideas, and the generation of new ideas. This is the concept behind a true learning organization; in order to become knowledge centric, the ICAS must be a learning organization. Boundary management contributes to developing the characteristic of permeable and porous boundaries, with the organization purposefully developing partnering relationships, building a reserve workforce composed of former employees and known sources of special expertise, and expanding the boundaries of communities to include external resources. Subconscious access refers to developing the intuitive and building the individual sense of knowing, i.e., seeing beyond images, hearing beyond words, and sensing beyond appearances (see Chapter 20). The major focus points here are that sharing

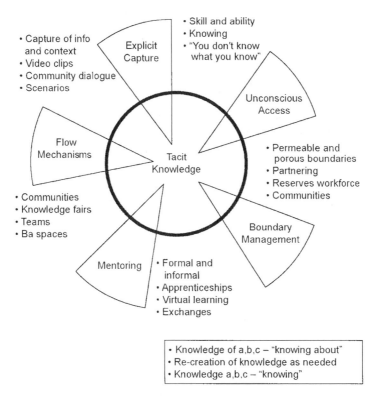

Figure 15-3
The Systems Approach to Sharing Knowledge

knowledge requires a systems approach and is a continuous process that takes many forms, and that there are still untapped resources within each individual that can contribute to organizational knowledge.

COMMUNITIES OF PRACTICE

Communities of practice (CoPs) and interest (CoIs) are built into the structure of the ICAS (see Chapter 6). Communities are built on the tradition of professionals joining together to share skills and resources, and are vibrant learning centers and rich marketplaces for knowledge sharing. Communities of practice have a shared domain of practice, howbeit that practice may be focused in different functional areas of the organization. The use and understanding of common terms in the domain, and many similar experiences related to their domain, help create an ease of communication and level of appreciation for and trust of other community members. By virtue of being communities of *practice*, these communities are focused on and around knowledge areas that are of concern to the organization, and are clearly aligned with the organization's strategic direction. Communities have an evolving agenda, with the migration of focus areas driven by a fluctuating environment, the changing needs of the organization, and the passions of its knowledge workers. Critical factors for community success include a sense of urgency, trust, personal passion, respect, key thought leader involvement and open communications (Wenger, 1998).

At the heart of CoPs are new ways of recognizing and leveraging employees and the relationships they establish. For leaders and knowledge workers engaged in CoPs and CoIs, community benefits are at a higher level and more readily available than for employees not engaged in CoPs and CoIs but indirectly benefiting from their existence. For knowledge workers depending upon CoPs, the quality of available expertise is higher, and the mode of interchange is ubiquitous (available from anywhere 24/7) and virtual in that the expertise may be accessed at the actual location of work performance. The use of communities in the ICAS is discussed in Chapter 6.

While new management fads may come and go, what they bring to the table becomes embedded in the leading organizations of the day, creating new forms of operation and response. The rise of knowledge management over the past decade, building on the early work accomplished through a focus on total quality management and thought leaders like Karl Wiig (1993), has brought organizational focus on the value of intellectual capital, and how to leverage that intellectual capital across the organization. Communities of practice and interest, an old form of practice but bringing with the terminology a new focus on that form and how to use it to the organization's benefit, offer a powerful way to connect people and ideas. The concepts, forms, and processes emerging through the focus on knowledge management and communities are paving the way for the ICAS.

REFERENCES

Denning, S. *The Springboard: How Storytelling Ignites Action in Knowledge-Era Organizations*. Boston, MA: Butterworth-Heinemann, 2001.

Knowles, M. *The Adult Learner*. Houston, TX: Gulf Publishing Company, 1998.

Malafsky, G. P. "Technology for Acquiring and Sharing Knowledge Assets," in C. W. Holsapple (ed.), *Handbook on Knowledge Management 1: Knowledge Matters*. Lexington, KY: Springer-Verlag, 2003.

Nonaka, I. and H. Takeuchi. *The Knowledge-Creating Company: How Japanese Companies Create the Dynamics of Innovation*. New York: Oxford University Press, 1995.

Senge, P. *The Fifth Discipline: The Art and Practice of the Learning Organization*. New York: Doubleday, 1990.

Snowden, D. "The Paradox of Story: Simplicity and Complexity in Strategy," *Journal of Strategy and Scenario Planning*, November 1999a, reprint, 1–8.

Snowden, D. "Liberating Knowledge," in *Liberating Knowledge*. London: Caspian Publishing, 1999b.

Swap, W., D. Leonard, M. Shields, and L. Abrams. "Transferring Tacit Knowledge Assets: Mentoring and Storytelling in the Workplace," *Journal of Management and Information Systems*, Vol.18, 95–114, Summer 2001.

Wenger, E. *Communities of Practice*. New York: Cambridge University Press, 1998.

Wiig, K. *Knowledge Management Foundations—Thinking about Thinking—How People and Organizations Create, Represent, and Use Knowledge*. Arlington, TX: Schema Press, 1993.

Chapter 16

THE LEARNING ORGANIZATION

Recall that knowledge has been defined as the human capacity (both potential and actual) to take *effective* action. We have chosen the definition for reasons similar to those explained by Sveiby (1997) in *The New Organizational Wealth*, "Based on Michael Polanyi and Ludwig Wittgenstein [...]; I define knowledge as a capacity to act. This is not an all-encompassing definition but rather a practical notion for managers to keep in mind as they read the rest of the book. One's capacity to act is created continuously by a process-of-knowing. In other words, it is contextual. Knowledge cannot be separated from its context. The notion also implies a teleological purpose. I believe that the human process-of-knowing is designed by nature to help us survive in an often hostile environment" (p. 37). Since individuals, teams, and organizations all may have the capacity to take effective action, they can all possess knowledge. Teams and organizations may have collective knowledge (both potential and actual) and therefore are capable of taking actions that an individual could not take.

Learning is considered to be the creation and acquisition of potential and actual ability to take effective action, or in other words the creation of knowledge. Allee (1997), in her discussion of the new knowledge era, suggests that, "Against this backdrop we are seeing the resurgence of an ancient quest: The quest for knowledge. We are stretched to the limits in our ability to integrate, synthesize, incorporate, and adapt [...]; the ability to learn is becoming the new 'core competency' for all of us participating in this quest. We find that the greater our capacity for learning and building knowledge, the greater our likelihood of enjoying continuing success. This is now not only true for individuals, it is also a basic principle for successful enterprise" (p. 8).

Learning is the *process* of acquiring new information or knowledge so that individuals can change their understanding and behavior to successfully adapt or influence their environment. Thus, learning and knowledge are closely related but not identical. Learning is a process that creates new meaning from experience and new capabilities for action. Knowledge may be a process (taking action) or an asset (capacity) residing in the minds of knowledge workers. Often, we do not know what we know until we say or do something. Knowledge, like memory and how to ride a bicycle, is often created and brought forth from the unconscious mind when we need it.

To put learning in perspective, consider several other closely related concepts: training, teaching, education, and what is called acquiring deep knowledge. All of these are forms of learning, each emphasizing a different goal with varying processes used for each one. Training normally deals with developing skills and abilities that do not require abstract concepts or a great deal of experience, and usually has a narrow focus and results in achieving a specific capability. Education is usually thought of as a process of learning about things that provide the learner with a broad, balanced perspective on the world and the ability to understand and deal with many areas of life.

Learning is a dynamic process that manifests itself in the continually changing nature of organizations, as exemplified by innovation, collaboration, and culture shifts, especially during times of change, uncertainty, and external challenge. Social learning most often occurs when individuals with experience and knowledge share their understanding with each other through conversation, storytelling, or dialogue, either formally or casually. Deep learning refers to the acquisition and understanding of highly abstract and complex concepts and information. For example, knowledge of calculus would be the ability to solve calculus problems. A deep knowledge of calculus would be the ability to understand the foundations of the theory, its limitations, and domain of application. Deep knowledge is created by study, reflection, assimilation, practice, and simply "living with the subject." Deep learning brings objective knowledge (knowledge about something) into the learner and through study, practice, and experience melds the objective knowledge with the learner's internal subconscious world such that the learner owns and lives the knowledge. This may produce the capacity to know, as discussed in Chapter 20. All of the above forms of learning (and others) can occur within individuals, teams, and organizations, with training and social learning being the predominant modes.

The term *organizational learning* may refer to individual learning within the organization, the entire organization learning as a collective body, or anywhere in between these extremes. However, most organizational learning refers to either group learning or the entire organization learning. Of course, all of these modes of learning are needed for the firm to possess the requisite knowledge to take effective action. From a knowledge management perspective, all levels of learning are important and all must be nurtured to become a natural part of the culture. Firms implementing KM usually put their emphasis on locating, creating, and sharing individual knowledge. For this reason, we consider organizational learning to refer to the capacity of the organization to acquire the knowledge necessary to survive and compete in its environment. However, there is an important distinction between individual learning and group-/organizational-level learning. Individual learning is a cognitive or behavioral activity between an individual and their environment, whereas in groups or organizations, learning is a collective process dependent upon relationships and interactions among individuals such that learning occurs primarily through the interaction of the participants and creates an understanding that is larger than any single individual process can.

While individual learning is achieved by study, observation, cognition, experience, practice, and developing effective mental models in the mind, organizational learning, being as much a social as a cognitive activity, occurs when groups learn to interact, share their knowledge, and act collectively in a manner that maximizes their combined capacity and ability to understand and take effective action.

Organizational learning requires a sharing of language, meaning, objectives, and standards that may be significantly different from individual learning. When the organization learns, it generates a social synergy that creates a global knowledge, adding value to the firm's knowledge workers and to its overall performance. When such a capability becomes embedded within the organization's culture, the organization may have what is called a core competency. These are usually unique to each organization and can rarely be replicated by other firms. The knowledge behind a core competency is built up over time through experiences and successes. It rests as much in the relationships and spirit among the knowledge workers as in the sum of each worker's knowledge.

Since individuals create organizations, it is they who establish the standards, processes, and relationships that enable group and organizational learning. But organizational learning is more than the sum of the parts of individual learning. For example, when individuals leave, effective KM can help enable the organization to retain its corporate knowledge, that is, the knowledge that comes from the experience, cooperation and collaboration of its employees. In the ICAS there is a high degree of organizational learning resulting from the flow of knowledge through teams and communities and the support centers tasked to facilitate this flow.

Some of the specific ways that organizations learn include single-loop, double-loop, deutero, and strategic learning. Single-loop learning (SLL) occurs when mistakes are detected and corrected by changing their actions. The organization then continues on with its present policies, strategies, and goals. Double-loop learning (DLL) occurs when, in addition to detection and correction of errors, the organization actively questions and modifies its existing underlying assumptions, beliefs, norms, procedures, policies, and objectives. DLL involves changing the organization's knowledge base or organization-specific competencies or routines (Argyris and Schön, 1978).

Deutero learning (DL) occurs when organizations learn how to carry out single-loop and double-loop learning. DLL and DL are concerned with the why and how of changing the organization, while SLL is concerned with correcting errors without questioning underlying assumptions and core beliefs. SLL is a surface solution and works only if the mistakes are surface errors. It looks good because it shows visible, quick actions and usually implies or identifies someone who is at fault. SLL may prevent DLL from occurring. In order to encourage the deeper learning, organizations must move away from mechanistic structures and adopt flexible and organic structures. This requires a new philosophy of management, which encourages openness, self-reflection, and the acceptance of error and uncertainty. That is the ICAS approach.

MODES OF LEARNING

There are many ways to discuss learning in terms of both individuals and organizations. Because of their significance in supporting the ICAS, several modes are explicated below. These are: strategic learning, e-learning, action learning, accelerated learning, and mindful learning.

Strategic Learning

Strategic learning is the continuous process of expanding the future possibility space of the organization as well as identifying the resources and actions needed to respond to unpredictable and surprising events. The objective is to develop a robust set of opportunities, resources, and consequent actions. This is seeking to increase internal complexity to take advantage of Ashby's law of requisite variety as addressed in Chapters 5 and 20.

Cunningham (1994) cites twelve factors that he considers important to achieving strategic learning. These are organization-wide commitment, support of top management, learning linked to organizational direction and cultural change, full participation of all leaders, a full-blown program (not a pilot, or at least a full-blown program to follow the pilot), development of an organizational capability to support and foster learning, multifunctional learning (crossing organizational functional boundaries), long-term commitment, the cascading of learning down the organization, making learning part of the organization's competitive advantage, giving it high visibility, and integrating strategy and tactics. In the ICAS, learning is a strategic enabler for individuals, teams, communities, and the organization as a whole. Supported and encouraged by the organization, each knowledge worker and leader takes on the responsibility of their own learning, and sharing this learning across the organization.

In scanning the environment, strategic learning looks for adjacent events, patterns and trends, that is, those that are close to the immediate events and patterns dealt with every day. This strategy for selection provides the ICAS with a broader knowledge of the environment. We call this a deliberate expansion of the possibility space. When we look backward we can almost always understand the flow of history, however erratic it may seem at the time it occurred. But when we try to look into the future, it is very difficult to forecast and impossible to predict with any reasonable accuracy. Yet events are connected in some way and these relationships, although numerous and often confusing, do influence the forward flow of the environment. By taking events and patterns that are our primary interest and studying those closely related events and patterns, we can become cognizant of other possible-if-not-probable possibilities. See Chapter 22 for additional discussion on exploring the future.

e-Learning

In the systems sense, e-learning is any virtual act or process used to acquire data, information, skills, or knowledge. Rosenberg (2001) refers to e-learning as the use of Internet technologies to provide many types of solutions to enhance knowledge and performance. Note that this definition focuses on the Internet but allows a wide variety of possibilities for learning, creating, and changing knowledge. We prefer thinking about e-learning as *enabled learning,* learning in a virtual world where technology merges with human creativity to accelerate and leverage the rapid development and application of knowledge.

The advantages of e-learning include reduced cost and time of both instructors and students. Once an e-learning course has been developed, it can be given to a large number of people with minimum expense. The material can be updated at one time and all students can quickly be notified. Changes and new ideas can be easily inserted into the material. Discussion groups operating in conjunction with e-learning courses allow students and instructors to dialogue and expand upon the material as needed. The main thing missing is the interpersonal interactions that allow in-depth exchange of ideas and insights through real-time conversations with facial and other nonverbal communications gained through teams and communities. While e-learning may not work for learning deep knowledge about complex subjects, it is well structured for many knowledge worker needs.

Action Learning

Another form of learning, known as action learning, uses a team or group to solve real, practical problems while deliberately emphasizing learning as they do. The action-learning group takes a systems approach to solutions, since their actions are designed to affect all parts of the organization necessary to ensure long-term (and widespread) problem resolution. Thus, action learning enhances individual and group learning, facilitates organizational change, and solves real-world problems.

Action learning is a special form of team learning, problem-solving, and implementation. The group has a facilitator, and learns through questioning and reflecting, clarified via group dialogue. True to the concept of knowledge, an action-learning group is committed to taking action but only after considerable time is spent in understanding the problem, the situation, and the ramifications of potential actions. In effect, an action-learning group becomes a knowledge-creating (learning) team. This process not only improves decision-making, it also achieves buy-in by team participants and creates a learning environment within which team members and their organization learn and share their own knowledge. This learning occurs when the group is open to new ideas, questions old and current assumptions, and works collaboratively toward a common interpretation of the problem based on their collective understanding and experience. Rather than rush toward a solution an action-learning team meanders to a thorough understanding of the situation, the problem, a solution set, and possible consequences. They are learning and taking action. The organization's role, through KM, is to provide action-learning teams with workspaces that are conducive to open conversation and honest inquiry, effective information technology support and information repositories, and a culture that rewards knowledge sharing (See Chapter 8).

Although the concept originated many years ago, action learning has now come to the forefront as an effective way to meet the demands of the new world (Marquardt, 1999). There are recognized successes throughout the current literature.

A great deal of personal development occurs when a team learns to work together, dissect, and understand major facets of the organization and then bring them back together into a complex system that produces a desired product. Put another way, an individual's domain of action and sources of knowledge expand as a result of solving real-world problems that are of high interest and importance to them. Not only have they made useful contacts and learn from those contacts, they see the enterprise in a new light and understand their own work within a broader context.

Accelerated Learning

Accelerated learning is a systematic process designed to take advantage of our brain's full capabilities through the use of findings in recent research in neuroscience. Recognizing that our brains are highly complex—with five types of memory; right and left hemispheres that specialize in different capabilities; three major parts (the brainstem, limbic system, and neocortex) each with different functions; and eight intelligences (language, logic, visual-spatial, musical, kinesthetic, social, interpersonal, and naturalistic) (Gardner, 1993)—accelerated learning is an approach designed to take advantage of the whole brain's capability to learn. Briefly, the process consists of six phases: motivation, getting information, finding meaning or sense-making, committing to memory, practicing what you have learned, and reflecting on how you have learned. The techniques used in each of these phases could best be considered as meta-learning, since their purpose is to help one learn how to learn. Each of Gardner's eight intelligences is inherent in everyone to varying degrees, and they all can be improved through learning and practice.

While individuals can personally make good use of the ideas and practices of accelerated learning, the best learning often occurs in a low-stress, small-group environment that is positively reinforcing, with some enthusiasm and humor (Rose and Nicholl, 1997). In addition, the knowledge worker must want to learn, that is, the material must be relevant, needed, and applicable. It helps to deliberately involve as many senses as possible. Studying and exploring a problem from each of the eight intelligence areas provides viewpoints, insights, and solutions that may not otherwise surface. Another useful technique is to search for good metaphors and analogies that provide windows to better understand the problem.

Mindful Learning

Perhaps one of the most useful approaches to learning for the ICAS is based on the work done by Ellen Langer (1997) on mindfulness. Mindful learning is based on an understanding of context and the recognition of the ever-changing nature of information. This approach, also referred to as conditional learning, surfaces the myths, or mindsets, of individuals. "Wherever learning takes place—in school, on the job, in the home—these myths are also at work and the opportunity for mindful learning is present. Whether the learning is practical or theoretical, personal or interpersonal; whether it involves abstract concepts, such as physics, or concrete skills, such as how to play a sport, the way the information is learned will determine how, why, and when it is used" (Langer, 1997, p. 3).

The mindful learner stays open to new ideas; looks for similarities, differences, and patterns (discernment and discretion); seeks to understand the context of what is learned; and looks at what is learned from different perspectives. There is also the realization that what is memorized today may be of little value in tomorrow's world, so it is the patterns of the learning that may hold deeper value for the future. This realization leads to questioning what Langer (1997) refers to as the "illusion of right answers" (p. 117). Indeed, the knowledge workers of the ICAS are on a continuous search for the "best" answers in terms of time and place, then moving forward to quickly discover the next "best" answer for a new time and place.

THE LEARNING CONTINUUM

John Seely Brown and Paul Duguid (2000) view learning as a social phenomenon. Certainly looking at "social" as of, relating to, or occupied with, matters affecting interactions, discourse, and human welfare, we agree fully. The social phenomenon of learning is not only among individuals, but among an individual and the environment, whether that environment consists of people, places, processes, or things; whether it is silent or active; or whether it is defined in terms of learning from a negative or positive influence.

As we have discussed learning throughout this chapter, we glide in and out of the concept of knowledge management. Indeed, knowledge on the subjects of organizational learning and knowledge management has become increasingly important as a point of focus for the business world driven by the development of the Internet and virtual worldwide access to the exponentially increasing amount of data and information. Since knowledge is situationally dependent, i.e., what is understood as knowledge relates to some specific domain, situation, and context, a changing environment insinuates changing knowledge needs. Learning is the individual and organizational process for creating new knowledge to meet changing environments. The points of intersection between learning and knowledge management are discussed in depth in Chapter 17.

Figure 16-1 explores the learning continuum from an individual or organization highly interactive with its environment, in the flow state, to an individual or organization whose thinking and actions have become locked, or static, and therefore continuously diminishes in effectiveness as the environment changes. For ease of explanation, the model will be discussed in terms of organizational learning. As an organization realizes the value of a product or process, it tends to freeze that process or product in time. This occurs for a number of reasons such as the need to train, limited funding, or temporary success. Perceived competitive advantage also causes a locking-in as new products/processes move into a mature phase where the focus is on sales and/or implementation.

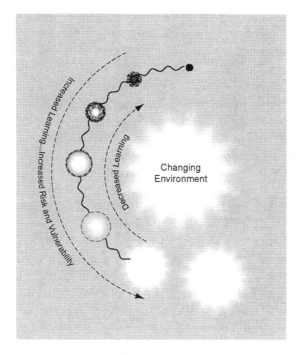

Changing
Environment

Figure 16-1
The Learning Continuum

If the organization has healthy feedback loops in place and responds to this feedback, it can move in and out of learning cycles to periodically develop and produce new versions of the product/process.

The organization just described sits in the middle of the learning continuum as it markets and implements its process/product, and moves down along the continuum as it receives feedback from the environment, learns from that feedback, and creates an improved version of its product/process. The innovative development environment, discussed in case studies of Apple Computer, lies further down along the learning continuum (Drucker, 1985). The Apple organization was highly open and interactive with its environment, with minimal locking-in of products/processes. The furthest learning point along this continuum represents the state of flow introduced by Csikszentmihalyi, where there is a fluid exchange among the environment, the organization and individuals within that organization. In the flow state, autotelic work, work whose purpose lies within the individual and is done for its own sake, is both a goal and a reality.

Moving upward along the continuum, still using an organizational scenario, the organization is achieving enough continuing success with its product/process that it does not recognize the need for change and remains locked into that product/process. In fact, in a large customer base, this success may continue for a number of years, dependent on how rapidly the organization's areas of focus or customer needs are changing. As front-runners move on to new and better processes and products, followers move in behind them to continue purchasing/using the offered product/process. However, over time, the product/process will diminish in value and the market will look to new ideas and products/processes for satisfaction. When this happens it is usually too late to catch up with alert and more nimble competitors who have continued growing themselves and their products/processes.

Another way to use the learning continuum model is to reflect on the fit between individuals and the organization within which they work. If an organization is locked into a product/process and in the distribution mode, it would be difficult for an individual who operates near a state of flow to flourish. In like manner, for an individual who has locked onto a specific set of beliefs and work habits, it would be difficult to succeed in a learning organization that fluctuates and bounces in response to the environment.

Taking a systems view of relationships among organizations and the people who work within those organizations, to succeed in organizational structures built on the bureaucratic model, it is necessary to have the ability to solidify ideas and slowly work them into the system. Simultaneously, to respond to the fluctuating environment, it is necessary to have the ability to be open to interact with that environment, and learn from it. This points to the need for individuals and organizations to develop a capability to move in and out of learning modes, although that movement along the continuum will be burdened by capacity and culture. Still, the ideal condition is the ability of individuals and organizations to choose where to function on the continuum at a specific time and in a specific situation. It must be noted, however, that there is a limit to the amount of flexibility an individual or organization can achieve. The further an individual or organization moves to either end of the continuum, and the longer he/she/it remains in that mode, achieving a comfort level, the more difficult it becomes to move away from that comfort level, the irony of a learner being unable to learn how to learn. In all things there is a balance, a region within which movement assures strength and stability without rigidity or undue risk.

On the other hand, while an organization (or individual) is in an increased learning mode, there is also increased risk and vulnerability. This is due to the large amount of interaction with the environment that provides both negative and positive data and information, and the increased need for greater discernment and discretion. In organizational terms, this may be thought of as the need for increased discrimination capability in a world with porous and permeable boundaries, where a large amount of data and information flows into the organization and much of it is irrelevant or false. *What* the organization learns may be more important than how fast it learns. In fact, an organization may become saturated with learning and fall into the trap of always trying something new without discerning the learning that is applicable to its immediate needs. Another danger is when an organization or individual becomes obsessed with learning it may fall into the trap of being unable to make a decision or take action because it never has all of the information it wants. This is often called educated incapacity.

Discretion and discernment, the selection and validation competency developed by a high-quality knowledge organization, can focus learning in the right directions to reduce error signals, confusion, and wasted effort. Recall that knowledge is the capacity to take *effective* action. The word effective is significant because of the inundation of possibilities and the chaotic nature of events in the environment of many extant firms. To learn to take effective action means to learn the relevant things, to unlearn those things that hide the right actions, and not fall prey to educated incapacity. Since knowledge is the capacity to take effective action and learning provides the continuous creation and updating of knowledge, knowledge management, and organizational learning, taken together, provide the foundation for leveraging the full value of the organization's human resources. The relationship of the knowledge worker, learning, and knowledge management is further explored in Chapter 17.

REFERENCES

Allee, V. *The Knowledge Evolution: Expanding Organizational Intelligence.* Newton, MA: Butterworth-Heinemann, 1997.

Argyris, C. and D. A. Schön. *Organizational Learning: A Theory of Action Perspective.* Philippines: Addison-Wesley Publishing Co., 1978.

Brown, J. S. and P. Duguid. *The Social Life of Information.* Boston: Harvard Business School Press, 2000.

Cunningham, I. *The Wisdom of Strategic Learning.* New York: McGraw-Hill Book Company, 1994.

Drucker, P. *Innovation and Entrepreneurship: Practice and Principles* (Special Edition for the President's Association). New York: Harper & Row Publishers, 1985.

Gardner, H. *Frames of Mind: The Theory of Multiple Intelligences* (10th Anniversary Edition). New York: Basic Books, 1993.

Langer, E. J. *The Power of Mindful Learning.* New York: Addison-Wesley Publishing Co., 1997.

Marquardt, M. J. *Action Learning in Action.* Palo Alto, CA: Davis-Black Publishing, 1999.

Rose, C. and M. J. Nicholl. *Accelerated Learning for the 21st Century.* New York: Delacorte Press, 1997.

Rosenberg, M. J. *e-Learning: Strategies for Delivering Knowledge in the Digital Age.* New York: McGraw-Hill, 2001.

Sveiby, K. *The New Organizational Wealth: Managing & Measuring Knowledge-Based Assets.* San Francisco: Berrett-Koehler Publishers, 1997.

Chapter 17

LEARNING, KNOWLEDGE MANAGEMENT, AND KNOWLEDGE WORKERS

Learning and knowledge go hand in hand. It took several hundred years for the most advanced nations of the world to move from agricultural to industrial to information-driven economies that continue to challenge organizations to improve performance. During the past decade the new field of knowledge management (KM) has generated excitement and achieved increased visibility for its potential to leverage the newly recognized asset we call knowledge and, by doing so, bootstrap organizational effectiveness. During this same decade, the notion emerged that organizations can learn and from that learning create competencies that lead to competitive advantage and agility. As introduced in Chapter 16, KM and learning form a powerful force for improving organizational performance and accelerating the career growth of individuals who work primarily with knowledge knowledge workers.

Learning, both organizational and individual, has seen a resurgence in popularity, driven by the accelerating pace of market changes, the Internet, the opportunities offered by virtual learning, and books such as *The Fifth Discipline: The Art and Practice of the Learning Organization* (Senge, 1990). The new knowledge worker (see Chapter 14) is now recognized as a major part of the workforce; that is, those workers that use their experience, education, and mental capacity to deal with the problems and opportunities arising from complexity, uncertainty, and rapid change (Drucker, 1989). Understanding complexity places great demands on knowledge. Making decisions under conditions of uncertainty requires a KM approach to ensure organizational agility and knowledge sharing. Rapid change places high priority on learning and flexibility. Many companies living at the forefront of the emerging landscape are recognizing the importance of the relationship between knowledge workers, KM, and learning. Each of these factors is interdependent with the others, and they are all consistent and synergistic with each other. In a culture that needs workforce competency and empowerment, the growth of KM provides a foundation to leverage and accelerate the improvement of both learning and knowledge worker performance.

Learning, individual and organizational, serves to keep knowledge workers and their organization up to date with changes in the external environment while creating energy, enthusiasm, flexibility, and collaboration among knowledge workers. It is with the knowledge worker that both innovation and action occur. Working in a knowledge-centric and learning culture, knowledge workers, individually and in groups, can create, leverage, and apply knowledge to meet changing needs. Knowledge management provides the emphasis, the enabling information technology, the processes, and the attention to help knowledge workers learn, collaborate, and implement the four major processes creativity, problem-solving, decision-making, and taking action. Conversely, knowledge workers can support the objectives of KM and actively increase their own performance by sharing their knowledge and facilitating organizational learning.

Each of these three aspects of the knowledge organization KM, learning, and the knowledge worker both support and need the other two. Over the past decade, KM has grown up and is now a significant part of many knowledge organizations. The partnership of KM, learning, and the knowledge worker is coming into its own and is foundational for the ICAS.

THE COMMON GROUND: KNOWLEDGE MANAGEMENT AND ORGANIZATIONAL LEARNING

In an organization where understanding and the ability to take effective actions are major challenges because of the organization's environment or the nature of its work, both knowledge management and organizational learning become critical factors in its long-term survival. In fact, these two fields are so important that they must become embedded within the ICAS philosophy and culture such that they are continuous, widespread, and mostly invisible; that is, such that they are found in the habits, norms, and expectations of the workforce, managers, and leaders of the organization. As introduced in Chapter 16 and to the extent that such an ideal can be achieved, knowledge management and organizational learning are interdependent and inseparable, but not identical. To understand this relationship we explore a number of characteristics of organizational learning and knowledge management and see how they naturally complement and reinforce each other.

In the current and future environment of business, the major challenge relates to finding, creating, or developing understanding and meaning of the complex events, situations, and patterns arising from an uncertain, complicated, and rapidly changing world. When major paradigm shifts occur in an organization's environment, or within its own strategy or vision, the organization may face its ultimate challenge: finding a new self-image, giving up current doctrine, and replacing strongly held beliefs with ones that more accurately represent the new reality may well be too much for an organization. Thomas Kuhn (1970), Chris Argyris et al. (1985), and others have noted the great difficulty organizations have when confronted with the need to rethink their basic assumptions and beliefs because of rapid shifts in their landscape. This is precisely where organizational learning is put to its greatest test and where knowledge management finds its reason for being. It is not easy to share knowledge; but it is even harder to give up old practices and beliefs that have worked well in the past. Organizational learning, then, has the challenge of identifying the new learning that will succeed and of replacing the old knowledge with the new.

Ideally, one would like to embed organizational learning within a knowledge management program in support of KM processes. To achieve this there would need to be a knowledge network of workers, and collaborative leaders supported by an infrastructure of technology and processes, with an organizational structure of collaborating teams and a culture of learning and sharing. This combination would significantly improve the organization's ability to change its learning (and unlearning) rate. The result would be an organization that can provide rapid internal adjustments that allow it to quickly change in response to external demands. Such an organizational agility is the result of close collaboration between knowledge management and organizational learning efforts.

Organizational memory can be made of both hard data (such as numbers, facts, figures, reports, and other documents and rules) and soft information and knowledge (such as expertise, experiences, anecdotes, critical incidents, stories, artifacts, context information, details about strategic decisions, and tacit knowledge). Most firms have information systems such as inventory control, budgetary, and administrative systems that store and retrieve hard data or facts, but many do not capture the softer information. Ideas generated by employees in the course of their work are often quickly forgotten, yet they can be captured through explicit narratives stored electronically for future reference.

Firms are increasingly focusing on the concept of organizational learning to increase their competitive advantage, innovation, and effectiveness. Organizational learning is accelerated when a firm, through knowledge management, creates a common knowledge repository, and identifies and codifies competencies and routines, including acquiring, storing, interpreting, and manipulating information from within and external to the organization. Knowledge management, through knowledge sharing processes, leverages both individual and organizational learning. By improving the quality and speed of communication and the understanding of problems and changes surrounding the organization, organizational learning, and knowledge management jointly increase the quality of decisions of the organization and the effectiveness of their implementation.

Organizations learn to increase their adaptability and efficiency during times of change. Learning is a dynamic process that manifests itself in the continually changing nature of organizations, as exemplified by innovation, collaboration, culture shifts, and high morale, especially during times of uncertainty and external challenge. Both knowledge management and organizational learning use knowledge generation and sharing as foundation processes. To be successful, these capabilities require a high level of attention to human factors: roles and responsibilities, experience, motivation, self-image, respect and trust, honesty and integrity, and the quality of interpersonal relationships throughout the firm. Since much of our knowledge is tacit, existing within memories and unconscious minds and not easily articulated, its development and sharing is very much a social process (Nonaka and Takeuchi, 1995).

In today's rapidly changing, erratic, and increasingly complex environment, knowledge creation, acquisition, and application through continuous learning are likely to be the only solution to survival and excellence. Organizational learning is contingent upon a number of factors such as leadership, structure, strategy, environment, technology, and culture. Knowledge management helps to create and nurture these factors to make optimum use of the organization's knowledge. Looking at several of these factors will allow us to see the close relationship between knowledge management and organizational learning.

Structure

Structure represents the set of arrangements among the resources of the organization. The resources may be people, facilities, technological, financial, or conceptual. How these resources are related to each other, and especially their influence on human culture and human relationships, influences a firm's self-image, its beliefs about the external world, and its ability to learn and change. Whether a firm lives in denial of external change or embraces that change and, through learning, strives to adapt or influence those changes is heavily influenced by both structure and culture. The increasing emphasis of many firms on information management rather than classical capital management can be seen as an indicator of the movement from industrial to service and knowledge work.

Hierarchical, controlling structures by their very nature tend to prefer stability and minimize the learning and close collaboration needed to meet significant change or paradigm shifts. Loose structures (even hierarchical) that have a culture of sharing and collaboration can often facilitate learning and allow the freedom to change. However, they must also have clear direction and coordination, otherwise the resulting actions will be diverse and the lack of focus may make them unable to support major organizational objectives. Organizational learning can occur for all the wrong reasons. When this occurs, learning may be incapable of providing the needed value to the firm. Here is where a knowledge management effort that creates and manages a structure to correlate the learning and concomitantly focus the application of that learning can pay big dividends. KM can do this by integrating corporate strategy, direction, and structure, using knowledge as the common denominator and corporate direction as the guidepost. However, too narrow a knowledge focus can create an inability to respond to surprises and major environmental paradigm shifts.

Unless deliberately provoked, most organizational structures tend to become rigid over time. To prevent such inertia, and to keep the workforce flexible and open to personal and professional change, organizational learning and knowledge management need to encourage and make use of flexible and changing structures, while retaining the capacity to focus and integrate local knowledge and activities. Policies such as moving people around to broaden their experience and revitalize their challenges, continuously bringing new people into the organization at all levels, and deliberately changing organizational relationships catalyze and perpetuate both individual and organizational learning. Encouraging open communications, getting both managers and workers to constantly challenge their own basic assumptions and support prudent risk-taking, and team collaboration encourages a culture that nourishes and updates the organization's knowledge, ergo its effectiveness. From a measurement view, the only true measure of effectiveness of organizational learning and knowledge management is how well the organization meets its current and strategic objectives the true bottom line of the firm. This requires a line of sight from the organization's policies, decisions, and actions to its organizational learning and knowledge management efforts to its overall performance (See Chapter 6).

Strategy

Strategic applications of information systems for knowledge acquisition can take two forms: capabilities for assimilating knowledge from the outside (such as competitive intelligence systems acquiring information about other companies in the same industry) and capabilities for creating new knowledge from the reinterpretation and reformulation of existing and newly acquired information (such as executive information systems or decision-support systems). They can also be environmental scanning and notification systems and intelligent and adaptive filters.

Learning is stimulated both by environmental changes and internal factors in a complex and iterative manner. An organization's strategy influences learning by providing a limit, or focus to the decision-making space and a framework for perceiving and interpreting the environment. In turn, the strategic options chosen will depend on the unique history, culture, and learning capacity of the organization. Such causal feedback loops are widespread within organizations, demonstrating why it is so difficult to change organizational behavior and mindset. Knowledge management, by providing a systems-wide perspective that can affect all parts of the firm, may initiate change in the perception of knowledge and learning and in their role in improving organizational performance and support organizational strategy. By making multiple changes throughout a firm, it is possible, but never certain, that the above-mentioned closed causal loops can be modified in such a way that employee behavior becomes redirected toward learning and knowledge application. For example, a knowledge management effort might change the technology, the communication networks, the physical spaces, the questions asked by policy-makers, and the expectations of employees, all changed in a way that would encourage and facilitate learning, collaboration, and the awareness and respect for knowledge and its role in the organization (See Chapter 15).

Technology

The influence of information systems, in particular, can be considered twofold: direct influence and indirect influence. Information systems can indirectly influence organizational learning by affecting contextual factors such as structure and environment, which in turn influence learning. They can also directly influence the organizational learning process. The introduction of information systems flattens the structure of relationships within the organization and promotes greater dissemination of information to all individuals. Through the Internet, intranets, communities of practice, communities of interest, groupware, etc., anyone in the corporation can talk to anyone else, almost at any time. These open, informal networks and multipaths serve to partially equalize positional influence and emphasize the value of information and knowledge. These equalizers, if used effectively, will facilitate the evolution of the organization's culture toward learning and knowledge management objectives. The information technology should be low-cost, support low-friction information and knowledge transfer, and, over time, become an invisible part of the infrastructure.

Through the increased availability of information and the sharing of that information, the organization becomes more informed, flexible, and organic. Information systems go beyond automating to "infomating" (Zuboff, 1984). In an infomated organization, the focus of control shifts from managers to workers, who are now empowered with all the information required for their effective performance. A number of current technology trends will help the organizational discernment and discrimination problem. As discussed earlier, discernment is the ability to differentiate the meaning and value among multidimensional concepts; and discrimination is the ability to choose those things upon which the organization needs to focus. Discernment and discrimination are key elements of the organization's filtering process.

Technology is moving beyond expert systems (which make logical inferences based on a fixed set of rules) to systems that combine the use of embedded textual information with human cognition and inference to improve the decision-making and interpretation processes needed to understand and act upon messy, complex situations. Technologies such as network publishing on the Internet and the information superhighway can facilitate the creation of organizational repositories. These repositories not only capture formal documents such as training manuals, employee handbooks, training material, etc., but also informal experience such as tacit know-how, expertise, experiences, stories, etc., often ignored in organizations. The use of such information systems to support and enhance organizational memory (and learning) by improving the precision, recall, completeness, accuracy, feedback, and review of informal knowledge complements well the human contribution to decision-making creativity, rational thinking, intuition, emotion, and social synergy.

Leadership

The essential function of senior leadership is to provide direction, build an organization's culture and spirit, and shape its evolution. Senior leaders must also shape the design of the organization's structure and policies to best fulfill its corporate mission. To do this, they must model desired behavior, communicate the organizations direction and strategy, and insist on effective implementation of requisite policies and procedures. Organizational learning also requires commitment from executives for a long-term process with adequate budget and resources. Organizational culture (beliefs, ideologies, values, and norms) and the amount of resources (money, facilities, people, and ideas) heavily influence the quality and quantity of learning. In the ICAS, collaborative leaders are found at all levels throughout the organization and foster learning and knowledge sharing by example, by encouragement of all knowledge workers, and through facilitation and dialogue (see Chapter 9).

Environment

Learning organizations treat competition as a means of learning, since competition enables organizations to compare their own performance with others in the industry and learn from that exercise. Through knowledge sharing, learning results as the organization interacts with its environment. Knowledge management looks to the external environment as a source of knowledge and as a testing ground for its understanding and interpretation of itself and the outside world. As part of a major feedback loop, the environment presents a standard for measuring the organizations learning; unfortunately, it can also be a harsh taskmaster for organizational mistakes.

AREAS OF INTERSECTION

Having addressed the broad areas of structure, strategy, technology, and the environment, we now look at a number of specific areas where knowledge management and organizational learning intersect: individual learning and KM, learning and communities of practice, learning and systems thinking, and learning and flow.

Individual Learning and KM

Organizational learning is greatly dependent upon individual learning and the competency of the workforce. If the firm has a culture and leadership conducive to organizational learning, chances are that that same environment will also support individual learning. It is not so clear that KM facilitates individual learning, since to date many KM efforts have emphasized technology and knowledge sharing rather than individual development. However, the culture of KM closely matches that needed for individual learning. Borrowing heavily from adult learning expert Malcolm Knowles, the main characteristics of adult learners are summarized below (Knowles et al., 1998).

Adults want to learn more than just data and facts, they are interested in understanding "the why and how" of their information. Since most adults (or knowledge workers) are not closely supervised, they see themselves as autonomous and self-directing. This same self-image becomes particularly strong when they are in a learning environment. Feeling that only they know how they best understand something, knowledge workers do not want to be told what they need to know and how to learn it in a pedagogical manner, they want to take ownership of their learning. They use their prior experience and their mental models to make sense of new information and knowledge. This may prove beneficial or detrimental, depending on the relevance of these past experiences. Spending much of their time solving problems at work, knowledge workers tend to prefer practical, goal-oriented problem-solving in a realistic context versus textbook solutions. Preferably, these problems should relate directly to their current work and interests. Comfortable with workplace conversations, they tend to prefer learning through group discussions and dialogue rather than self-study. Seashore et al. (1992) point out that a problem with learning arises when people have difficulty listening and giving feedback.

From these learning characteristics it is clear that a successful knowledge management program would provide many of the conditions desired by knowledge workers, and by doing so greatly leverage learning throughout the organization. For example, KM builds a culture of knowledge sharing and open communication, both leading to an environment conducive to adult learning. Communities of practice, teams, knowledge repositories, inter mediaries, yellow pages, etc., all support the autonomous worker to meet their own learning needs. A somewhat surprising consequence of KM is the awareness and instantiation of the importance and payoff of learning and knowledge in the minds of the organization's knowledge workers.

Learning and Communities of Practice

Communities of practice accelerate learning. The practice of CoPs denotes a group with the same work focus, and therefore a group that has much in common in their everyday work life, including a common language. The community part of CoPs denotes a group that has a relationship built on trust and a focus on the open sharing of ideas and best practices. In CoPs the creating, learning, sharing, and using of knowledge are almost indivisible. John Seely Brown and Paul Duguid (2000) explain this phenomenon: "[...]; talk without the work, communication without practice is if not unintelligible, at least unusable. Become a member of a community, engage in its practices, and you can acquire and make use of its knowledge and information. Remain an outsider, and these will remain indigestible" (p. 126).

Etienne Wenger, a thought leader in communities of practice and formerly of the Institute for Research on Learning, found that the group was important to both what people learn and how they learn. Within the group setting of claims processors, Wenger (1998) discovered that knowledge, traveling on the back of practice, was readily shared. This same pattern was found from shop floors to professional fields, where scientists, doctors, architects, or lawyers, after years of classroom training, learn their craft with professional mentors. Brown and Duguid agree: "[...]; the value of communities of practice to creating and sharing knowledge is as evident in the labs of particle physicists and biotechnologists as in the claims processing unit" (Brown and Duguid, 2000, p. 126).

Communities have an advantage when the organization needs to question its own beliefs and assumptions. Communities encourage the exchange of ideas, assumptions, and theories that open their members to new ways of seeing situations. The continuous, rapid feedback system of a community provides the opportunity to tie discussions and dialogues to decision results, generating new ways of understanding the system. Within the trusting framework of communities, individuals can observe other's results and rethink their assumptions and theories (See also Chapter 15).

The value of learning in general, and double-loop learning in particular, will be to speed up the acceptance and application of new ideas, techniques, methods, and tools that provide themselves in the workplace. Of special importance is the full acceptance of new ways of doing business that change roles and relationships among organizations and individuals. Relationships among team leaders–team members, colleague–colleague, community–community members, government–industry, headquarters–field activities, buyers–users will all change in one form or another. How effective these changes will be depends on the beliefs and actions of the individuals in each area. Learning and change are the primary forces for success because they are absolutely essential for adaptation, experimentation, and innovation. In today's world, every decade and every year we find new technologies, new rules, and new environments that demand new perspectives, new insights, new behaviors, and new actions.

Learning and Systems Thinking

Systems thinking and system dynamics facilitate both individual and organizational learning. Systems thinking, according to Peter Senge (1990), is an approach to understanding complex systems (such as organizations) that have many elements and relationships. As discussed in Chapter 18, systems thinking provides a conceptual process and a visual way of describing multiple causality relationships that include both positive and negative feedback loops, as well as time delays and nonlinear influences.

Systems thinking encourages groups to dialogue and develop a common understanding of a complex problem within the organization, and thereby learn from each other and thereby develop a much better understanding of how their organization really works. They are then in a position to solve problems, make decisions, and implement actions that improve organizational performance. Systems thinking also helps restructure views of reality by identifying and challenging prevailing mental models and fundamental assumptions and by promoting double-loop learning. In the process of understanding how organizations work, systems thinking encourages exploration of multiple viewpoints on any problem through dialogue and discussion. It is via such knowledge sharing and creation processes that knowledge management and organizational learning benefit each other.

There is another interpretation of systems thinking: being aware of what systems are, what characterizes them, and their general properties. Perspective and viewpoint are often critical to solving problems and understanding situations. A systems perspective permits one to see the organization, external threats, or internal processes as systems with boundaries, elements, relationships, and networks of influence that provide insight and understanding of how the system works and how it will respond to a specific action. Learning by using the system perspective greatly facilitates the development of knowledge of both individuals and groups. It also puts each situation in its true place relative to other systems, permitting more effective priority setting and prediction of knowledge application.

The best organizational learning is distributed throughout the firm such that from a backdrop of continuous learning to meet routine challenges, teams and processes can, when called upon, rise to anticipate and meet fundamental threats and opportunities that challenge the organization. This means that learning must be local and distributed, and it must be both continuous and episodic. These demands may strain knowledge workers and their leaders, since they require living with change and uncertainty relative to both what needs to be learned, how fast it must be learned, and how to apply such new knowledge. This highlights the difference between learning and knowledge processes. While there are generic knowledge processes such as knowledge creation, sharing, and storing that may be described in general with some assurance, successful learning processes are mostly local and depend upon the history, nature, local culture, and leadership needs of the firm, and on the learning styles and recent experience of both its knowledge workers and the teams they make up. Successful knowledge managers are sensitive to the locality of effective learning and to the unpredictable nature of many learning situations.

A fundamental requisite to learning is the attitude and motivation of the individual knowledge worker. While collaborative leaders may influence individual attitude and motivation, the amount of such influence is limited. Given this limitation, what knowledge managers can do is to support individual learning and organizational learning through the effective nurturing of culture, infrastructure, technology, policies, and personal behavior. In today's changing, uncertain, and complex business environ ment, knowledge organizations must be learning organizations and all ICAS leaders must therefore recognize and accept the responsibility of building and maintaining an organization that treats learning as a key success factor and as an integral part of the normal KM areas of concern. Leaders must also be sensitive to the individual and group needs and capabilities of knowledge workers as they relate to learning, changing, risk-taking, innovation, and courage (see Chapter 9).

Learning and Flow

Organizations flourish with the flow of data, information, and knowledge; the flow of people across and in and out of the organization; and flow in terms of the optimal human experience. In a learning-centric organization, learning and knowledge that is core to the business of the organization are captured and shared. The more learning is valued in the organization, the better its core knowledge flows and grows through innovation, mission performance, and the creation of new knowledge. While each individual is important to this process, it is the continuous movement of knowledge and learning among people that keeps organizational learning going. This continuous flow is facilitated through the movement of people in and out of networks, communities of practice, and workgroups as they change jobs, change their priorities, and interests, and grow in new areas of thought. Perhaps even better than the use of teams, this fluid movement of people in and out of communities of practice and networks creates diversity of perspectives and ideas, bringing together new combinations of knowledge and learning that offer ever increasing opportunities for discovering better ways of taking action and achieving their organizational mission.

Considerable work is emerging on the science of knowledge flow within organizations. Nonaka (1994) considers knowledge flow through four steps. Since he states new knowledge is created only by individuals and is necessarily tacit in nature, this flow occurs through a process of *socialization*, with members of a community sharing their experiences and perspectives through apprenticeships and mentoring. A second flow occurs through *externalization*, where the use of metaphors, stories, and dialogue leads to the articulation of tacit knowledge, converting it to explicit knowledge. A third flow occurs through *combination*, where community members interact with other groups across the organization to share and move explicit knowledge around the organization. A fourth flow occurs through *internalization*, where individuals throughout the organization learn by doing and perhaps even through listening to stories are able to create knowledge, usually in tacit form. When all four of these processes coexist, they produce knowledge spirals which result in accelerated organizational learning (Nonaka and Takeuchi, 1995).

Optimal flow is a psychological state identified by Csikszentmihalyi (1990) as one in which an individual, while actively performing some task, loses track of time and easily and naturally makes use of all of their experience and knowledge to achieve some goal. Within an organization, these three forms of flow can work together to activate and accelerate both creativity and cohesion of action. High personal productivity, useful dialogue, and knowledge sharing, when coupled with new employees having different perspectives and asking challenging questions, will create an organizational synergy and dynamic that moves the knowledge-based organization to achieve its best performance.

Although flow and knowledge spirals are knowledge management concepts, one can easily appreciate their power to support and facilitate organizational learning. Although learning is inherently an individual experience, that experience can be significantly influenced and leveraged to help the individual and the organization learn and create knowledge.

CONCLUDING THOUGHTS

As uncertainty and complexity increase in the future, and decisions become more challenging, individual, group, and organizational learning, coupled with a strong knowledge management program offers the best capability an organization can have to change, adapt, and influence its environment in a way that maximizes its performance over time. Thus, within the ICAS, focused, flexible, and friendly communities will help knowledge workers continually learn and change. By combining the strengths of organizational learning and knowledge management, the ICAS will create cultures, structures, and leadership styles that enable it to scan, perceive, evaluate, anticipate, and take effective action on new, ambiguous, unexpected, and complex threats and opportunities. Achieving such an ideal is as challenging as it is productive.

REFERENCES

Argyris, C., R. Putnam, and D. McLain Smith. *Action Science.* San Francisco: Jossey-Bass Publishers, 1985.

Brown, J. S. and P. Duguid. *The Social Life of Information.* Boston: Harvard Business School Press, 2000.

Csikszentmihalyi, M. *Flow: The Psychology of Optimal Experience.* New York: Harper & Row, 1990.

Drucker, P. F. *The New Realities: In Government and Politics/In Economics and Business/In Society and World View.* New York: Harper & Row Publishers, 1989.

Knowles, M. S., E. F. Holton III, and R. A. Swanson. *The Adult Learner.* Houston: Gulf Publishing Company, 1998.

Kuhn, T. *The Structure of Scientific Revolution.* Chicago: The University of Chicago Press, 1970.

Nonaka, I. "A Dynamic Theory of Organizational Knowledge Creation," *Organization Science,* 5, No. 1, 1994, 14–37.

Nonaka, I. and H. Takeuchi. *The Knowledge-Creating Company: How Japanese Companies Create the Dynamics of Innovation.* New York: Oxford University Press, 1995.

Seashore, C., E. W. Seashore, and G. M. Weinberg. *What Did You Say? The Art of Giving and Receiving Feedback.* Columbia: Bingham House Books, 1992.

Senge, P. *The Fifth Discipline: The Art and Practice of the Learning Organization.* New York: Doubleday, 1990.

Wenger, E. *Communities of Practice.* New York: Cambridge University Press, 1998.

Zuboff, S. *In the Age of the Smart Machine: The Future of Work and Power.* New York: Basic Books, 1984.

Chapter 18

RETHINKING THINKING: SYSTEMS

Systems thinking is a conceptual framework, or body of knowledge and tools, that has been developed over the past 50 years to make the structure of systems and patterns of change clearer so we can better understand their behavior and solve problems more effectively. The term is often used to describe a new way of interpreting the world and our work in it. This new way of thinking began in the 1950s and was known as General Systems Theory (GST). GST studied many systems to see if they had common underlying principles of operation. While only moderately successful, GST was able to identify many insights and observations that help understand how systems work. In the 1960s, Systems Dynamics was introduced by J. W. Forrester (1971) at MIT as a way of analyzing systems by finding their influence elements and feedback loops and modeling them on computers to simulate the systems behavior. Then in early 1991, MIT's Peter Senge (1990) published his seminal book The Fifth Discipline that made systems thinking a popular subject with managers throughout the world. Systems thinking is now widely used in management and organizations to understand how things interact and affect each other and to provide a broader perspective of work and organizations that improves problem-solving, decision-making, and overall performance.

As professionals and knowledge workers, we all strive to become knowledgeable and competent. In our schooling, training, and on-the-job experience we typically concentrate on the immediate task. Our world is sometimes seen as a never-ending sequence of surprising and seemingly random events that demand our immediate attention and resolution.

Systems thinking offers a new way to see the world. First is its ability to broaden an individual's perspective. Second is the understanding of what systems are and how they work. Third is the ability to model a system to better understand the key forces and the effect of major relationships within the system. Using sensitivity analysis, a systems thinking model can clarify relationships and often pinpoint problem areas and suggest solutions (Morecroft and Sterman, 1994). Finally, systems thinking offers a way of understanding the environment, allowing us to see our own work as it relates to the larger organization, and guiding decisions for improving operational effectiveness in a complex world. As an integrative competency (IC), systems thinking provides a prolific way of improving performance through the integration of work and the understanding of relationships.

Some specifics of how systems thinking (ST) adds value are noted below:

- ST expands the individual's critical thinking skills and provides a framework for understanding and analyzing situations and organizations.
- ST identifies parameters that play a crucial role in system performance and can be used as guides for taking corrective action in a given situation.
- Adopting a top-level systems perspective encourages individual managers and teams to develop and implement balanced decisions that optimize the entire system instead of the common suboptimization action that so often occurs.
- ST can provide a basis for filtering information applicable for a subsystem while keeping the total system in balance. It can also help set relative priorities in an organization by offering an objective and agreed-upon framework.
- When applied to specific problems, ST offers causal loop analysis to bring out the major causes and identify their relationships, thereby making possible solutions clear. It provides a set of twelve archetypes (or patterns of relationships) that occur over and over again in organizations.
- ST provides an approach for managing complicated situations by helping decision-makers recognize and understand the cause-and-effect relationships among organizational parameters.
- ST expands individuals' thinking skills and changes their perception and interpretation of the world around them. Systems thinking enables a clearer perception of the full patterns of change and the structure of systems to better comprehend their behavior.
- ST suggests the usefulness of using metaphors and analogies for problem-solving through the areas of commonality of all systems from physical to biological to social to psychological to organizational.

DEFINITION OF TERMS

With a new way of perceiving the world comes a new way of talking about it. While the language of systems thinking uses many familiar words, they have new meanings. Definition of terms is a good place to start our discussion.

System

A system is a group of elements or objects, the relationships among them, their attributes, and some boundary that allows one to distinguish whether an element is inside or outside the system. Elements may be almost anything: parts of a TV set, computers in a network, people in an organization, ideas in a system of thought, etc. The number of elements and their relationships to each other are very important in determining system behavior. Almost everything can be viewed as a system. The following are all systems because they have many parts and relationships: automobiles, ER teams in a hospital, cities, organizations, pipes on a submarine, integrated product teams, and individuals. It is normal to find systems within systems within systems. This can easily be seen in the hierarchy of organization–department–division–branch–section–individual. Systems can evolve in time and they can change size and space. Processes are often seen as systems moving through time. Several experts have noted that "everything is a system," it just depends on where you define the boundaries and from which perspective you are looking.

System Boundaries

All systems have boundaries that separate them in some way from the environment or other systems. Organizations have people and facilities that are in the organization and there are customers, etc. that are outside the organization. Typically lines of authority, policies, technology, and many processes and functions lie within the organization, but not always. The boundary may be highly permeable or insulated. Boundaries may be open or closed. Completely closed systems are rare; gas in a closed bottle would be an example. There are degrees of openness in systems, some have boundaries that are very open to interaction with the outside world, others very controlling. The ICAS is an example of the former and the Berlin wall of the latter.

Environment

The region outside the boundary of a system is referred to as its environment. Since the environment may also be considered as a system, it is sometimes referred to as the suprasystem. The ICAS also has an internal environment that consists of many subsystems such as technology, meshes, teams, networks, and Knowledge Workers.

Inputs and Outputs

Every system has inputs (energy, information, people, or material) from the environment and provides outputs (energy, information, people, or material) to its environment. To continue existing, organizations, particularly companies, must transform their inputs into outputs that add value to their environment. Without this value added, no company can stay in business and no government organization can justify its existence. In our world of information and knowledge, many organizations add value through the creation or leveraging of information and knowledge.

Feedback and Regulation

Systems, particularly organizations, contain many causal relationships within them. Some of these may be positive, reinforcing feedback loops and some will be negative, balancing feedback loops needed to perform their mission during stable times. Positive feedback loops create new ideas, products, and energy to try new ways of getting the job done—all needed during times of uncertainty and change. Sometimes, of course, positive loops can lead to disasters, such as when large funds are invested in new technology without a full understanding of the limitations of the technology. Often the idea of having the latest and greatest technology, the wonderful promises of vendors, and the need to improve organizational performance form a positive, reinforcing loop that can be very costly to an organization.

Purpose

There are two uses/meanings of the idea of purpose in systems thinking. The first is the stated intention of the organization, its official goal or purpose. For technological systems purpose would be the use of the system intended by the system designers. The second interpretation of purpose in systems thinking is the set of interactions between the system and its environment; in other words, what the system does, not necessarily what is officially stated, or what is intended. Where a system has a mission or purpose, the individuals within that system adjust their relationships and their individual actions so that the sum of those actions achieves the desired purpose.

Structure

Systems that survive over time usually have some form of hierarchical structure. The reason for this is that subsystems within a hierarchy tend to be more stable and able to withstand shocks from outside, thereby permitting the entire organization to survive (Simon, 1984). This said, there are also detrimental side-effects of too strict a hierarchy. Flexibility, adaptation, empowerment of individuals, creativity, and innovation are all essential when the external environment is rapidly changing and threatens or offers opportunities to the system. Strong hierarchies are power driven and rarely tolerate these characteristics. Weak hierarchies that work with and through teams have recently been very successful.

PRINCIPLES OF SYSTEMS THINKING

There are rules, or principles, that not only provide a basic understanding of systems but help us put this thinking to use as we begin to see the ICAS as a living system (de Geus, 1997). Note that these are more like guidelines that are useful but not always appropriate for a given situation.

Principle 1: Structure Is Key to System Behavior

In addition to observing and reacting to events and patterns in the system, a useful insight and understanding of how organizations, i.e., systems, behave is found in their structure. The nature of the elements of a system and their function is derived from their position in the whole and their behavior is influenced by the whole to part relation. In other words, recognize that relationships and structure play a large role in driving individual and team behavior. Thus while it is normal to watch for and react to events that impact our work, we should be wary of reacting to events without being conscious of the context and system within which these events occur. We often react to events when patterns of events are the more important. When we observe patterns of events, we should look at the underlying structure of the system for root causes and possible leverage points for problem solutions. Systems thinking suggests that when we understand the structure of a system, we are in a much better position to understand and predict the behavior of the individual elements (people) and their relationships and can therefore make better decisions.

Principle 2: Systems That Survive Tend to Become More Complex

This usually is a result of the system's external environment becoming more complex. The interactions of systems that are competing in some way drives each to try to control or dominate the other. The system with the most options, variety and flexibility is the one most likely to dominate and survive. Thus the passage of time results in surviving systems being more complex. For example, if you normally receive 30 e-mails a day and you start getting 300, the natural reaction would be to quickly scan and ignore all but 30. You have simplified your own system at the risk of overlooking something that might be very important. Another approach is to assign another person the responsibility for reviewing and responding to the e-mails. This has increased the complexity of your system (you and now the other person) but it also has given you more options and possibilities for expanding business, etc. There is some danger in oversimplifying organizational complexity. For instance, it is easy to assume that people will work harder if they are paid more salary. With the modern workforce, individual needs vary drastically and are usually quite complex. Often it is the challenge of contributing to a worthwhile cause and of working with others whom they respect and can learn from that motivates them. These drivers—worthy cause, respect and learning, etc.—frequently come from the entire system, that is, they are a result of the culture, the structure, and the individuals involved and they cannot be decreed by any single manager. An understanding of the organization as a system of relationships and patterns helps managers to recognize that they do not control the system but rather must learn how to nurture and influence the organization to achieve desired ends.

Principle 3: Boundaries Can Be Barriers

It takes more energy and time to send information or products through a boundary than within the system. Most organizations require some form of approval for formal letters, products, etc. that go out of the firm to another organization. In a dynamic environment such policies can slow down the organization's reaction time. While open-door policies, empowerment, e-mails, communities of practice, etc. are opening organizational boundaries, systems thinking recognizes that boundary protection is a natural phenomenon of systems and must be managed carefully. The ICAS minimizes boundary protection by trust, knowledge sharing, learning, empowerment, and self-organizing teams. All of these give knowledge workers at the boundary the competency to make good decisions while simultaneously keeping the boundary porous.

Principle 4: Systems Can Have Many Structures

Systems often exist within systems and each level usually has a different purpose or objective. Given the hierarchical structure of some systems in their organizations, senior leaders select and integrate the information and knowledge needed to make decisions that optimize the right system-level objectives. By recognizing the long-term consequences of those decisions, they can optimize the desired results over time. This is the classical control-type of system. However, as discussed in Chapter 6, the ICAS is a system that consists of a combination of hierarchy and nested teams with a superimposed layer of networks for coordination and flexible response.

Principle 5: Be Extra Careful When Intervening in a System

To minimize the unintended consequences of intervening in a system, consider the impact of second-order and long-term effects and the power of informal networks. Many experts suggest that the first rule of management in decision-making is to do no harm. This means thinking about the possible consequences of the decision from a systems perspective, not only first-order effects but second and third orders as well. Here is where knowledge of key causal paths, feedback loops, and how the organization will react to the decision implementation becomes significant. A corollary is to beware of unintended consequences. Here again systems thinking helps in recognizing potential results of decisions. Sometimes small changes can create big results (leveraging or positive feedback loops), and more often seemingly big changes have very little impact (damping or negative feedback loops) on organizational performance. The key is to separate the formal rules, policies, and directives of the organization from how the work gets done. The work usually gets done through the informal network, giving it a vital role in the organization's performance. This informal system should always be taken into account when making changes within the organization. In the ICAS these changes would be made by collaborative team leaders, in concert with their team members, ensuring that the informal networks had buy-in.

GUIDELINES FOR USE

Since everything can be viewed as a system, it would seem that systems thinking would apply everywhere. While this may be true, it does not always prove productive to do so. For example, if your objective is to focus and produce a product and not be concerned with broader implications, this is not the time for systems thinking. A good time for systems thinking is when you become concerned about everyone doing their own thing when they should be communicating their actions to others, or an issue is hard to resolve because it impacts many people or groups. Or when things become uncertain, people become protective and parochial and no one knows what to do. When any of these things happens, a shift to a higher perspective can illuminate and clarify the real problems and open the window of perception to allow new solutions to emerge. When communicating your thinking to others, make sure they understand the language of systems thinking. It is often difficult to grasp the meaning and insights gained without some familiarity with the systems approach. Do not confuse systems thinking with systems engineering or systems analysis. These latter two are well-defined disciplines that are very effective in their domain of applicability; however, they are very different from the systems thinking addressed here.

One very effective way for groups to apply systems thinking to organizations is to first get the participants to write down and agree on the mission, vision, or purpose of the organization. Then prepare a high-level diagram of the organization, showing boundaries, inputs, outputs, internal structure, and key processes. Next identify the environment together with its major characteristics that impact the organization. Be sure to include all major stakeholders and external constraints. Go as deep or as shallow as desired. At this point you are ready to ask many questions about the relationships that exist, those that should exist, and to find the key factors that make the organization successful. The diagram may also be useful for locating problems and identifying their causes. A most important benefit will be the group's agreement on what the organization is and what its environment is like. This will then serve as a common artifact for discussion, problem identification, idea generation, and even decision-making. Individuals can perform this same process to create a systems view of their own organization or of their local work environment. Remember, even a branch or a small team can be considered a system.

A second way to use systems thinking is to make use of the balancing and reinforcing feedback loops of MIT's J. W. Forrester (1961) and Peter Senge (1990). Senge's approach is to develop feedback loops that represent complex situations and use these loops to understand the way the system works. As an illustration, consider Figure 18-1, which shows the relationships among a number of factors that influence decision-making relative to information technology and the information explosion. The top loop, marked "R" for reinforcing, tells us that as more funds are put into IT the result is an increase in the amount of data, information, and knowledge. This has the effect of making

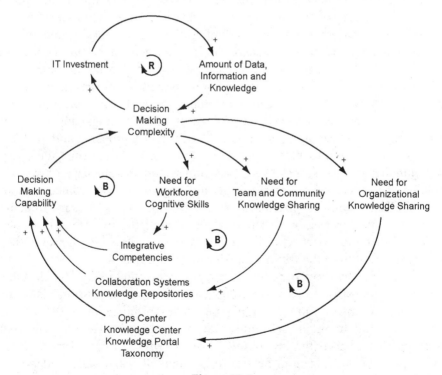

Figure 18-1
A Systems Thinking Model

decision-making more difficult or complex because of the saturation effect of information. To reduce decision-making complexity, managers spend more funds on IT, anticipating that it will help them make better decisions. It is clear that this loop will escalate the problem, not help it.

The solution lies in the lower three loops where other ways of solving the decision-making problem are addressed. These solutions improve workforce cognitive skills (e.g., the integrative competencies), and use team and community knowledge sharing (e.g., collaboration systems and knowledge repositories) and organizational knowledge sharing (e.g., the ICAS Ops and Knowledge Centers and a knowledge portal and taxonomy) to improve the decision-making capability of managers. By laying out the loops and understanding their relationships to each other and to the problem of decision-making complexity, it becomes clear that the three balancing loops will reduce the decision-making complexity and at the same time the organization's investment in IT can continue to provide more information and knowledge. In other words, the best solution is to improve the decision-making ability of leaders, knowledge workers, and the organization rather than cut back on technological applications, clearly not a viable alternative (Senge, 1990).

By getting a group of managers from the same organization together to develop the major causal forces and loops within their organization, they can develop a common framework and language, which will allow them to solve problems and make decisions. This can be done by developing feedback loops on paper and interpreting their effects or by programming the results in a computer with numerical values and functional relations.

Forrester (1961) took this latter approach, creating computer models of these loops using mathematical equations and quantitative parameters. The field is called system dynamics and there are several modern software programs that support the modeling effort. Once the model is developed for a specific organization or system, it can be run to simulate time and show the results of the interactions and relationships modeled. These computer predictions can then be compared with, and if need be, adjusted to match the real systems behavior. After agreement is reached, suggested ideas to improve the real system can first be made in the computer model and evaluated for their effect, prior to real-world implementation. The computer model can also be used for sensitivity analyses to explore "what if" questions. These exercises, done by groups of managers who work in the organization, serve as an excellent process for learning and bringing the group into agreement about how their organization really works (Morecroft and Sterman, 1994; Vennix, 1996). For a specific example of this modeling see Bennet (1998). In this case, one of the authors developed a flight simulator of a team responsible for developing a major product, given a budget, schedule, and milestones. As the team leader, you have ten different decisions that impact team performance. These decisions range from level of team training, degree of collaboration, type of leadership, and team size to co-location and workload. The simulator stops every six months so you can change your decisions. Meanwhile, the program shows graphs that indicate over time how well the team is meeting its cost, schedule, and milestone objectives. The model was developed using system dynamics feedback loops and causal relationships among the relevant factors that influence a team's ability to develop a product.

You can use your own organization as a tool for explaining and understanding organizations as systems. For example, take your own division, or a division you are extremely familiar with, and prepare a system drawing showing inputs, outputs, boundaries, structure, any emergent properties, stakeholders, key relationships, and major dependencies. Now draw the environment and highlight the key characteristics of it that impact your division's success. After describing its purpose or mission, try to trace the relationship of your past week's activities to that purpose or mission. How many other people were involved in using or contributing to your own activities? Identify the people who get the most work done and their relationships to each other and others in the organization. Why are they so productive? How much networking do they do? Remember the last time someone suggested a new idea at a staff meeting. What was the reaction of the group (or of the boss)? Did the reaction spur more ideas and exploration of how the idea could be used? In other words was it a positive reinforcing feedback loop, or did the response stifle the idea without further thought, signifying a negative feedback loop?

REFERENCES

Bennet, D. *IPT Learning Campus: Gaining Acquisition Results Through IPTs.* Alexandria VA: Bellwether Learning Center, 1997.

de Geus, A. *The Living Company: Habits for Survival in a Turbulent Business Environment.* Boston, MA: Harvard Business School Press, 1997.

Forrester, J. W. *Industrial Dynamics.* Portland, OR: Productivity Press, 1961.

Morecroft, J. D. W. and J. D. Sterman, (eds). *Modeling for Learning Organizations.* Portland, OR: Productivity Press, 1994.

Senge, P. M. *The Fifth Discipline: The Art and Practice of the Learning Organization.* New York: Currency/Doubleday, 1990.

Simon, H. A. *The Sciences of the Artificial.* Cambridge, MA: The MIT Press, 1984.

Vennix, J. A. M. *Group Model Building: Facilitating Team Learning Using System Dynamics.* Chichester, England: John Wiley & Sons, 1996.

Chapter 19

RETHINKING THINKING: COMPLEXITY

While complexity theory has been studied in the sciences for several decades, it has recently been expanded to apply what has been learned to current organizational and management issues. But do not be misled, complexity is a young field searching for laws, theories, and principles that can be used to build a structure and a discipline. Even the definition of complexity is not widely agreed upon. Nevertheless, most organizations today can be considered as some form of a complex adaptive system and as such, complexity theory provides useful metaphors, analogies, and insights into their operation.

To survive the increasing complexity emerging throughout the world most organizations will have to become more knowledgeable and complex. The ICAS, operating at the leading edge of the age of complexity, will likely be a prototype of increasing knowledge and complexity. Some basic concepts, definitions, ideas, strategies, and examples of complexity as they apply to present-day problems and organizational challenges will be considered in this chapter. Our objective is to make the reader aware of what complexity is and why it is important. In addition, we want to provide ideas and principles that will help knowledge workers recognize, assess, understand, and interact with complex organizations. There are no cookbook solutions; every complex situation is unique, context dependent, and inherently difficult to understand. Although there are very few "laws" of complexity theory, there are guidelines and principles that, when coupled with the right questions and perspective, may lead to insights, understanding, and solutions.

Lest we think that complexity is a fad, note that both evolution in general and human history in particular have repeatedly shown that systems that survive over time do so by becoming more and more complex. The problem of dealing with complexity is both formidable and long term, challenging enterprises, companies, government organizations, teams, and most professionals and knowledge workers. In simple terms, complexity describes a system or organization that has so many parts (people) and relationships that it is not possible to take into account all of the causal relations underlying its behavior. In the last chapter we discussed Forrester's system dynamics with its causal relationships; in complex systems it is often not possible to clarify, or even identify, the specific causal phenomena. Understanding organizations, their environment, or even individual work tasks is becoming increasingly difficult as situations and issues become highly dynamic, less predictable, more confusing, and often paradoxical. Surprises seem to increase exponentially with expanding time horizons and increasing complexity.

The word "complexity" often comes up when people are discussing the problems and challenges of today's fast paced, day-to-day activities. Our daily work may present us with 200 e-mails a day, 10 action items to be done "now," a decision needed when no one knows whether a right decision even exists, much less what that decision should be, or our bosses insisting on solutions where no solution seems possible. Many of today's problems are what Russel Ackoff (1978) termed "messes." A mess is a situation where you know there is a problem but you don't even know what that problem is. Examples of messes that have occurred throughout industry and the government would include:

- Poor communication throughout the organizations.
- Isolation of individual departments within organizations.
- Cultures that perpetuate processes rather than adapt to changing needs.
- Retirees and employees leaving who take critical knowledge with them.
- The changing nature of the economy, technology, and warfare and the organizational changes needed to maintain effectiveness.
- Rapidly changing leadership preventing long-term consistent organizational improvement to meet an ever-changing customer base.
- Emphasis on efficiency, productivity, and working harder and longer instead of working smarter and more effectively.

Just as being able to recognize, understand, and think about systems has become a hallmark of many of today's successful professionals, being able to recognize, understand, and deal with complexity is the challenge of the immediate future. The purpose of this chapter is to provide a brief introduction of this relatively new field of complexity theory.

Although complexity theory is still in its early stages of growth, using biological metaphors and insights from computer modeling suggests new ways of seeing organizations that provide insight into why they operate as they do and how they can improve performance in complex environments. Complexity thinking suggests that leaders and knowledge workers should take a new perspective on their organizations, develop new competencies, and take different actions to create and maintain high-performing organizations.

Although all organizations are complex (and adaptive) to some degree, from our perspective complexity thinking applies particularly to those firms (such as the ICAS) that are living at the leading edge of change and must deal with an increasingly complex environment. These organizations have to manage their own internal complexity while concomitantly coexisting with an increasingly messy and complex environment. Within this context, what value can complexity thinking add to organizational performance and survival?

Since complexity thinking is first a new perspective or way of looking at organizations, its largest contribution is found in the new questions it raises and the possibilities they create. Recall Einstein's famous quote, "*The significant problems we face cannot be solved at the same level of thinking we were at when we created them*" (Calaprice, 2000, p. 317). Complexity thinking (CT) helps leaders, knowledge workers, and organizations. For organizations,

- CT increases awareness and understanding of the importance and necessity of facing the oncoming problems of uncertainty, rapid change, and complexity.
- Events, patterns, and structure are better understood in terms that make decisions more effective.
- CT provides a rationale and a path to building a flexible and adaptive organization better able to achieve sustainable high performance in a complex environment.
- CT suggests an entirely new set of questions relative to organizational problems and management issues.
- CT improves organizational performance by suggesting a new approach to the efficiency–effectiveness problem.

For leaders and managers,

- CT provides a broad context within which leaders and managers can understand and improve their decisions relative to organizational strategies and performance improvement.
- The value of structure and relationships is made visible and gives managers more options and ideas for reorganizing and solving problems.

- CT encourages leaders to rethink and consider other options to their past approaches to organizational structure and leadership and management.
- Leaders better understand the importance and advantage of diversity, empowerment, and self-organization.

For knowledge workers,

- CT provides an understanding of complexity and techniques to deal with complex problems.
- CT makes visible the value of divergent thinking and the need to create new ideas and options for action.
- CT puts complex adaptive systems in perspective relative to chaos and complex systems and explains the need for KM, knowledge leveraging, and learning.

COMPLEXITY THINKING AS AN INTEGRATIVE COMPETENCY

Complex systems are different from simple or complicated systems. Complex systems are difficult to predict and control, and continuously change and interact with their environment. These changes occur over time, are often unpredictable, and are heavily driven by relationships and distributed autonomy. The bottom line is that to understand and deal with such systems requires new ways of thinking and new competencies. Integrative competencies bring cohesion into critical areas that are needed by workers who live in the middle of complexity or perhaps, using the popular quip, "near the edge of chaos."

One such competency is the capacity to think about complexity, complex systems, and your own complex organization in a way that creates insights and understanding of how these systems work and respond to their environments. Complexity thinking is a shift in the way we understand our world and how we relate to it. It changes the context within which learning occurs by encouraging us to observe differently and perceive intrinsically by combining rational thought with intuitive understanding, judgment, and experience.

As the world enters the age of complexity, our primary resource is our personal ability to comprehend complex phenomena and devise organizations and strategies for dealing with the uncertainty, nonlinearity, and rapid change that are ubiquitous in our working lives. Just as we learn to understand and deal with simple systems through rational thinking, complexity thinking helps us to understand complex systems and in doing so, increases our capacity to solve problems, make decisions, and take effective actions to improve organizational performance. When we deal with complex situations we need to ask better questions, look for different things, and take multiple perspectives before forming conclusions and taking action.

An apt metaphor would be that organizations living in a world of countless factors and innumerable forces are slowly becoming immersed in a "fog of complexity." We can only lift this fog through collaboration, information, learning, knowing, knowledge, networking, and a good understanding of systems and complexity thinking. While each one of these alone can contribute to our performance, taken together they offer an integrative and synergistic capacity for dealing with complexity; thus the rationale for the development of integrative competencies.

At the forefront of organizational actions, complexity thinking makes use of the other integrative competencies. For example, information literacy helps us to efficiently locate and validate information needed to solve complex problems. Relationship network management (Chapter 21) provides a platform for interactions that helps us leverage the knowledge needed to perceive, interpret, and act effectively in complex situations. The systems thinking competency is essential for recognizing and understanding systems, clearly a prerequisite for complexity thinking. Knowledge management tells us how to create, store, share, leverage, and apply the knowledge so essential for handling complex issues. The knowing competency (Chapter 20) addresses the application of intuition and judgment utilizing experience to better understand and deal with situations. The learning competency helps us learn how to learn and makes the case for lifelong learning, the secret of keeping up with change and staying open to the growth of complexity and the changing nature of the working environment. Thus, assuming that the hallmark of organizations is the set of actions they take to meet their mission responsibilities, complexity thinking is directly in the line of action, and uses all of the integrative competencies to help decide what action will work best.

DEFINITION OF TERMS

Much like systems thinking, scholars, researchers, and practitioners have begun to develop a common language to talk about complexity, combining new words with new interpretations of well-known words. For purposes of this discussion we offer the following definitions.

Context
The set of circumstances or facts that surround a particular situation, the totality of features having relevance to the causation, meaning, or effect of an event or situation.

Patterns
Sets of elements (people, events, objects), their attributes and their relationships in space and time that are stable or slow to change over time. Patterns are usually observed within some situation or background, i.e., there is some context associated with the pattern.

Complexity

Conceptually, complexity is the condition of a system, situation, or organization that is integrated with some degree of order but has too many elements and relationships to understand in simple analytic or logical ways. Examples are a team of people, an individual, a city, an ant colony. Internal complexity, from an organization's viewpoint, is its ability to exhibit or contain a large number of states or behaviors.

Adaptation

The process by which an organization improves its ability to survive and grow through internal adjustments. Adaptation may be responsive, internally adjusting to external forces, or it may be proactive, internally changing so that it can influence the external environment.

Chaos

The condition of a system exhibiting disorganized behavior with little or no predictability; a system that appears to behave randomly, with little or no underlying coherence in its local interactions. Typically chaos is a state of bounded instability, where high nonlinear feedback exists but is not so high as to create explosions. Examples are turbulent streams, the weather, a sand pile, some organizations.

Internal Complexity

The complexity of a system as seen from within the system. It is measured by its *variety*, the number of possible states that the system can have. A state is a specific configuration of the system. An organization of high variety has a large number of options and choices of actions it can take to adjust itself internally or when responding to or influencing its environment. If its variety becomes too high, the organization may become chaotic, with no coherence of thought or action.

Agent

In the literature the term refers to a semi-autonomous decision-making unit of a complex system that determines its own behavior within general guidelines. We consider individuals to be the agents in the ICAS. Examples are ants in an ant colony, teams or groups in the ICAS, cities in a metropolitan area.

Emergent Characteristic

A global property of a complex system (organization) that results from the interactions and relationships among its agents (people), and between the agents and their environment. These characteristics represent stable patterns of the organization that are qualitative and exert a strong influence back on the individuals and their relationships. Examples are culture, team spirit, attitudes toward customers, trust, consciousness, laughter, and individual emotions.

Nonlinearity

A system possesses nonlinearity when actions within the system generate responses that are not proportional to the action. A small action may generate a very large outcome—or a large action may have very little effect on the system. Examples are: a program office with a budget squeeze eliminates travel budgets, causing increases in contractor costs due to lack of program office oversight; a key individual leaves the organization, resulting in many future, expensive mistakes; a new leader comes in and redirects programs, thus raising costs and slowing down past investments; an influential low-level employee supports a management change effort and by doing so significantly moves the entire organization towards a better future; a butterfly flaps its wings in South America and causes a severe snowstorm in New York (a well-known story from chaos theory).

Self-Organization

A complex system in which the agents (individuals) have a high degree of freedom to organize themselves to better achieve their local objectives. They also determine *how* to accomplish their objectives. Most complex systems found in nature are self-organizing, though human organizations are often the exception due to a human tendency to control. Current organizations exhibit a range of self-organization, from little or no control at the top to autocratic leadership. Self-organization provides the organization with robustness and resiliency. According to Wheatley (1999), "Prigogine's work [on the evolution of dynamic systems] demonstrated that disequilibrium is the necessary condition for a system's growth. He named these systems *dissipative structures* [...]; they dissipate or give up their form in order to recreate themselves into new forms. Faced with increasing levels of disturbance, these systems possess the innate ability to reorganize themselves to deal with the new information. For this reason, they are called self-organizing systems. They are adaptive and resilient rather than rigid and stable" (pp. 79–80).

SYSTEM TYPES IN TERMS OF COMPLEXITY

Systems range on a continuum from simple to chaotic, with complicated, complex and complex adaptive systems in between. There is increasing complexity as you move along the continuum from simple to chaotic systems (see Table 19-1). Recognize that these categories are a convenience of language. Nature does not separate systems into different types. So the description of each type represents an ideal state to facilitate differentiation.

Simple systems remain the same or change very little over time. There is very little or no change in the elements, relationships, or their attributes. They have few states, are typically non-organic and exhibit predictable behavior. Examples are an air conditioning system, a light switch, and a calculator.

Table 19-1
Systems in Terms of Complexity

Simple	Complicated	Complex	Complex Adaptive	Chaotic
■ Little change over time	■ Large number of interrelated parts	■ Large number of interrelated parts	■ Large number of semi-autonomous agents that interact	■ Large number of parts that interact
■ Few elements	■ Connections between parts are fixed	■ Nonlinear relationships and feedback loops	■ Co-evolves with environment through adaptation	■ Behavior independent of environment
■ Simple relationships	■ Non-organic	■ Emergent properties different than sum of parts	■ Varying levels of self-organization	■ Minimal coherence
■ Non-organic	■ Whole equal to sum of its parts	■ May be organic or non-organic	■ Partially ordered systems that evolve over time	■ Emergent behavior dependent on chance
■ No emergent properties	■ No emergent properties		■ Operates in perpetual disequilibrium ■ Observable aggregate behavior ■ Creates new emergent properties	
■ Knowable and predictable patterns of behavior	■ Knowable and predictable patterns of behavior	■ Patterns of behavior difficult to understand and predict	■ Patterns of behavior may be unknowable but possibly fathomable	■ Random patterns of behavior

Complicated systems contain a large number of interrelated parts and the connections between the parts are fixed. They are non-organic systems in which the whole is equal to the sum of its parts; that is, they do not create emergent properties. Examples are a Boeing 777, an automobile, a computer, and an electrical power system.

Complex systems, as distinguished from complicated systems, while consisting of a large number of interrelated elements, have nonlinear relationships, feedback loops, and dynamic uncertainties very difficult to understand and predict. Complex systems have the ability to create global emergent properties that come from their elements and interactions but these characteristics cannot be traced back to the connections because of the nonlinearity and unpredictability of the elements and relationships. These emergent properties make the whole of the system very different than just the sum of the parts. Examples of complex systems include organizations (with culture being an emergent property), teams (with *esprit-de-corps* being an emergent property) and a dialogue relationship between two knowledge workers (with an increase in knowledge and understanding being an emergent result).

Complex adaptive systems: complex systems contain many agents (people) that interact with each other. In organizations the people are semi-autonomous and have varying levels of self-organization. They operate and direct their own behavior based on rules and a common vision of the organization's direction, working in small groups to take advantage of the local knowledge and experience of coworkers. It is the aggregate behavior of all knowledge workers that we can observe. We call this top-level characteristic organizational performance. The interactions that create this performance are numerous, complex, and often nonlinear, making it impossible to derive global behavior from local interactions.

In the ICAS, where the attributes, experiences, attitudes, personalities, and goals of leaders and knowledge workers significantly impact their relationships with each other, the global emergent characteristics such as trust, flow, intelligent behavior, etc. will arise if—and only if—many employees work hard to create them. The variety and diversity of individuals also contributes to the creation and characteristics of the aggregate behavior. If one person leaves, the ICAS immediately reorganizes to fill the vacuum and the firm internally adapts to its new structure, often with some stress and learning. As people move in and out of the organization, its global behavior may shift and change, adapting to its new internal structure as well as its external environment. This continuous flexing of complex adaptive systems keeps them alive and gives them the capacity to quickly change pace and redirect focus.

Many modern organizations find themselves in a dynamic, uncertain, and complex environment and to survive they must continually reinvent themselves, create, and act on new ideas and knowledge, and take risks. They tend to operate (or oscillate) between stability and chaos. It is that narrow region just before chaos in which creativity, dialogue, and innovation serve to accelerate learning and facilitate adaptation. Complex adaptive systems have the best chance of surviving in environments of rapid change, high uncertainty, and increasing complexity. They have the potential to create new emergent properties that provide the intelligent behavior to adapt to such environments. Examples of complex adaptive organizations can be seen in successful start-up companies, surviving Internet businesses, and government organizations that have recently changed policies, created teams and are empowering employees.

Complex adaptive systems are partially ordered systems that unfold and evolve through time. They are mostly self-organizing, learning, and adaptive. To survive they are always creating new ideas, scanning the environment, trying new approaches, observing the results, and changing the way they operate. To continuously adapt they must operate in perpetual disequilibrium, which results in some unpredictable behavior. Having nonlinear relationships, complex adaptive systems create global properties that are called emergent because they seem to emerge from the multitude of elements and their relationships. They typically cannot be understood through analysis and logic because of the large number of elements and relationships. Examples are Life, ecologies, economies, organizations, and cultures (Axelrod and Cohen, 1999).

It is not just the number of agents involved that creates complexity. For example, a closed bottle full of oxygen contains billions and billions of oxygen molecules but their interactions are simple and predictable in principle, and the system is not complex—it is complicated. Although its agents (molecules) are independent they cannot take individual actions and make decisions. The interaction of the molecules will not create an emergent property.

On the other hand, two individuals interacting to solve a problem may exhibit a high variety of behavior and thoughts during their conversation. This variety will depend, among other things on how they feel about each other as well as their own experience and need to solve the problem. In solving their problem they will have created an emergent phenomenon—the solution—something that came into being from the two individuals *and* their interactions and is different and better than either one could have developed alone. Neither person alone knew the solution. The solution is more than what each person could have developed independently. Clearly this is a complex adaptive system, yet there are only two agents. When two people share their information and knowledge, more knowledge is created, but only if their relationship is up to the task.

Chaotic systems, or more to the point, chaotic organizations, rarely survive because they are unpredictable and independent of their environment. They are complex organizations that have lost much of their coherence and can no longer function through communication and collaboration of people. There is often continual disagreement, poor communication, infighting, and a lack of leadership. Sometimes the chaos can be hard to observe. As Stacey (1992) has pointed out, "[...]; chaos is a state of limited or bounded instability [...]; Chaotic behavior is random and hence unpredictable at the specific or individual level [...]; The particular behavior that emerges is highly sensitive to small changes and therefore depends to some extent upon chance" (p. 76). For example, chaos may exist when firms are going bankrupt or undergoing a merger, when standing down a government office, or when an organization suffers from a repeated change of divergent leadership over a short time. More subtle forms may occur when managers create and use conflict to meet their own agendas, or where small changes escalate and become reinforcing loops, creating a great deal of conflict and misunderstanding.

Figure 19-1 shows the five categories of systems laid out roughly in terms of their difficulty of understanding and predictability. The curve provides a nominal indication of the knowledge required to understand each type of system. In fact, highly complex systems may never be understood by humans; that remains to be seen as research continues to hunt for theories, laws, and underlying principles that would help explain their behavior. The dashed curve at the top demonstrates that the required knowledge increases as you move toward more complex systems. It thus becomes more and more important to encourage individual knowledge sharing as complexity increases.

COMPLEXITY AND THE ART OF WAR

Warfare has long been recognized as a complex activity. Military experts from Sun Tzu to Carl von Clausewitz to General A. M. Gray, Commandant of the U.S.

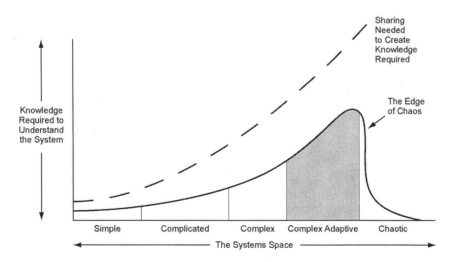

Figure 19-1
The Systems Space

Marine Corps have written on the complex nature of war. The well-known metaphor "the fog of war" is famous for its descriptive accuracy of the friction, uncertainty, fluidity, and disorder of battles. Von Clausewitz noted that: "Everything in war is simple, but the simplest thing is difficult. The difficulties accumulate and end by producing a kind of friction that is inconceivable unless one has experienced war" (von Clausewitz, 1984, p. 119).

General Gray, former Commandant of the U.S. Marine Corps, in his fore-word to the U.S. Marine Corps Book of Strategy, entitled *Warfighting*, wrote: "You will notice that this book does not contain specific techniques and proce-dures for conduct. Rather, it provides broad guidance in the form of concepts and values. It requires judgment in application" (The United States Marine Corps, 1994, p. xv). What better advice could a CEO or senior government executive give to their people as their organization enters the twenty-first century of uncertainty and complexity?

Below are additional phrases from the Marine Corps book that will ring familiar as you read more about complex adaptive organizations. They are listed to highlight the similarity between two very different worlds—warfighting and business—yet with the commonality of operating in an uncertain, rapidly changing, complex environment.

- "In an environment of friction, uncertainty, and fluidity, war gravitates naturally toward disorder" (p. 10).
- "As the situation changes continuously, we are forced to improvise again and again until finally our actions have little, if any, resemblance to the original scheme" (p. 11).
- "War is shaped by human nature and is subject to the complexities, inconsistencies, and peculiarities which characterize human behavior" (p. 13).
- "[...]; command must be decentralized. That is, subordinate commanders must make decisions on their own initiative, based on their understand-ing of their senior's intent, rather than passing information up the chain of command and waiting for the decision to be passed down" (p. 79).
- "In practical terms this means that we must not strive for certainty before we act for in so doing we will surrender the initiative and pass up opportunities. We must not try to maintain positive control over subordinates since this will necessarily slow our tempo and inhibit initiative" (p. 83).

These comments are enough to suggest the complexities of warfare and, as we will see below, many of these same ideas are useful in working and leading complex adaptive organizations.

GUIDING PRINCIPLES

The following principles are presented to give the reader a flavor of the nature and behavior of complex systems. Each must be treated as a rule-of-thumb that may or may not apply in any given situation.

Guiding Principle 1

The future is truly unknowable and therefore we must learn to live and deal with uncertainty, surprise, paradox, and complexity.

Guiding Principle 2

Over time complexity increases in complex adaptive systems. Complex adaptive systems evolve and survive by learning, adapting, and influencing their environment, thereby increasing their own complexity.

Guiding Principle 3

Complex systems generate emergent characteristics through the rich and myriad relationships among their agents. These emergent properties may be volatile and hard to control because a few agents can make changes that may propagate through the structure via nonlinear reinforcing feedback loops. Relatively stable emergent patterns such as cultures may also arise. The way to influence complex systems is to create, nurture, and modify their emergent phenomena.

Guiding Principle 4

Complex adaptive systems cannot be controlled, they can only be nurtured. Control stifles creativity, minimizes interactions, and only works under stable situations. It is not possible to control a worker's thinking, feeling, creativity, or trust.

Guiding Principle 5

When two complex adaptive systems are interacting, the one with the greatest variety will dominate. However, too much variety may lead to chaos.

Guiding Principle 6

Diversity, innovation, selection, interaction, and self-organization are critical for the evolution and adaptation of complex systems.

Guiding Principle 7

Complex adaptive systems cannot be highly efficient and survive in a complex, dynamic environment. High efficiency leaves no room for creativity, learning, or exploration. A certain level of noise is needed to maintain the system's ability to learn, change, and adapt.

Guiding Principle 8

Effective structures are essential to a complex adaptive system that can survive in a complex environment. Structures influence relationships. Relationships determine interactions, patterns and actions. Actions create events.

Guiding Principle 9

Self-organization encourages a diversity of patterns to develop, optimizing the interactions among people (as perceived by themselves) and creating more options for action.

GUIDELINES FOR USE

The following ideas are provided to suggest ways of looking, thinking, and evaluating complex adaptive systems that will help decision-makers understand and deal with their uncertainty and complexity. They are heuristic and suggestive rather than definitive. These guidelines also suggest a process for applying complexity thinking. The steps of this process include:

- Understand complex adaptive systems.
- Review history and context.
- Look for emergent characteristics.
- Analyze the networks.
- Remember knowledge is king.
- More nurturing, less control.
- Use all available mental resources.

- Seek optimum complexity.
- Beware simplicity.
- Self-organize your own learning.
- Expect mistakes.
- Amplify what works and change what does not work.

These steps are explicated below.

Understand Complex Adaptive Systems

Observe, study, reflect, and use your intuition to develop a "feeling" for the key relationships and patterns of behavior in the system. Think how and why something happened, not just what and when. Look for the structural sources of actions, events, and patterns. Talk to people in the system about how the work really gets done and who influences what goes on, asking questions and dialoguing with others. Learning to feel the organization's pulse comes only through close attention, listening, experience, and reflection. Trial-and-error and living with the organization over time can develop a deep knowledge and understanding of how the organization functions and what it takes to correct problems. Unfortunately, we frequently tend to simplify by finding what we believe is the cause of events or patterns and taking action to correct that "cause." While sometimes this is right, often the action does not change the system and the problem resurfaces at another location or time. The typical solution to a bad event is to create a policy that prohibits the event in the future. This approach results in so many (often conflicting) policies and rules that the only way that work gets done is by ignoring or working around them.

Remember that analysis and logic produce useful answers *only if their assumptions are correct, and if every material causal relationship can be taken into account*—a difficult task at best in an organization. When you are in a position to manage or impact an organization that operates in a dynamic, complex environment, do not try to control its operation, rather nurture the people, systems, relationships, and processes. This approach will encourage them to think for themselves, feel empowered, and create solutions at the local level. Encourage many simultaneous small changes if needed, just be sure that your organization knows where it is going and people know what values are important.

Review History and Context

History gives us a perspective on the past and what might continue into the future. It can provide the past context and major forces influencing the complex system.

Patterns are usually easier to find in history than in the present, yet they may extend into the future. The present context illuminates what the present situation looks like and what forces are currently in play. Context may indicate emergent characteristics that will extend into the future. Each of these perspectives provides insights into the workings of the organization and why it behaves as it does. This may also bring out past trends and events that help in understanding the future.

Look for Emergent Characteristics

Emergent properties are meaningful, qualitative, global, and can be very informative. To find out what integrates and creates these emergent characteristics, reflect on the systems behavior, history, patterns, and flows. Patterns are composed of relatively stable sets of relationships and events that occur throughout the organization. Look for the properties created from the interrelation of all of the parts—the networks, teams, structure, hierarchy, technology, and individuals. These properties can rarely be reduced to single causes and therefore must be observed and understood as broad, qualitative phenomena. Their source may be a particularly creative team, a disgruntled employee who is successfully spreading rumors and discontent, or from nowhere that can be identified. Some events result from single causes and others come from multiple sequential or simultaneous causes throughout the organization. Try to understand how and why the event happened, any related patterns, and what structural aspects could be involved. Ask yourself the following:

- Am I looking at the problem or a broader situation?
- Is the formal or informal structure causing this property?
- What can be controlled?
- What can be influenced?
- What may be nurtured to emerge?

Analyze the Networks

Knowledge is created and embedded in individuals and their relationships. Networks—formal, informal, social, and technological—leverage the creation, sharing, and application of the ideas and knowledge of individuals and their relationships. Observe and study the networks in your organization. These networks, as an important part of the overall structure, play a significant role in creating the culture and other emergent properties of the organization. In addition, they can create ideas and new ways of getting the work done, thereby increasing the variety of the organization. Study your own internal networks and those in the external world; they have a significant influence on the complexity of both systems. (See the Chapter 21 discussion on relationship network management.)

Remember Knowledge is King

Knowledge consists of facts, laws, data, information, intuition, judgment, insight, prediction, and experience and understanding. We consider knowledge to be defined as the actual and potential ability to take effective actions. Complexity can be considered as a measure of how difficult it is to predict the systems behavior. We can easily explain the past, but have a hard time predicting the future. Although we may or may not understand the present, we have great difficulty seeing the flow from the present to the future. There are just too many possibilities and too many interactive causal forces. Complex systems may have some degree of continuity to the flow of events, but only in hindsight does the continuity become clear, especially for complex adaptive systems. In a sense, complexity is in the eyes of the individual because individuals vary in their capacity to understand complex systems. If we understand something well we do not consider it complex. Whenever a system exhibits global, qualitative properties that cannot be traced to its elements, we usually have great difficulty in understanding it. However, the more knowledge we can pull together about the system, the better we can understand its behavior, and make good decisions.

More Nurturing, Less Control

Considering the management of a complex adaptive system operating in a complex environment, no one is in control in the sense of setting goals *and* making employees follow a specific regime to achieve those goals. While leadership can set the goals, direction, vision, and structural form of the organization, it is the knowledge workers and their relationships that primarily drive how the work gets done and often even what gets done. What leaders and managers can do is make decisions and establish relationships that open the organization to change, and then guide and nurture that change to keep it moving in the desired direction. In the ICAS it is critical to bring employees into the decision-making process *whenever possible*. This gives employees context for their own work, adds value to the decision quality, and aids employees in better understanding and supporting implementation because of their involvement and ownership. It also encourages more ideas and options for actions to respond to external demands.

In most organizations today, the *certainties of command and control are myths.* To the extent that current organizations are complex and adaptive, they exhibit various degrees of unpredictability and no one fully understands, nor can predict, their behavior. This observation says much about the future of autocratic leadership and the importance of nurturing and collaborative leadership, and of the positive effects of the growth and empowerment of employees. Leaders do not understand complex systems any more than workers, but if the environment is open and conducive to collaboration and inquiry, solutions can be found through leveraging the knowledge of the right people, wherever they are in the organization. This is not to imply that hierarchical structures will go away, nor that they should. Chains of command, responsibility, and accountability are needed in all organizations; they just play a different role in complex adaptive systems. The hierarchy maintains the administrative oversight and its communication channels help ensure the coherence of direction of the subunits. It also supplies resources and knowledge support where needed. What it cannot do is dictate local tactics, schedules, and responses. By setting basic rules of operation and guidelines for decisions, leaders can free workers at the lower levels to empower and figure out for themselves how to work together and achieve their goals. Such freedom is, of course, situational and dependent on the task, the environment, and the individuals involved.

Use All Available Mental Resources

In complex systems there may be times when a small number of dominant causes drive the system. Under these circumstances logic and analysis can be used to identify, study, and understand how the system works. Causal feedback loops can be described and modeled to predict the system's behavior. MIT's systems thinking and J. W. Forrester's system dynamics are representative of this approach. Unfortunately, we are often unable to trace the cause-and-effect paths within the system because they are too numerous, nonlinear, and have too many connections. These complex systems unfold and evolve through multiple interactions and feedback loops; there is no small number of causes behind their movement. Because of this fundamental behavior, we cannot understand them by using logic, analysis, and the reductionist approach. Under these situations, complex systems can only be understood by holistic thinking.

Experts who understand certain complex systems use their experience, intuition, and judgment to solve problems. They know, but are often unable to explain how they know. When dealing with complexity, we need to actively learn from experience, deliberately develop our intuition, build our judgment, and play with the system in our minds and especially in group dialogues. It is through these activities that our experience and intuition become capable of recognizing the unfolding of patterns and the flow of activities in the complex system or situation. Such recognition leads to intuitive understanding and a sense of what the primary drivers are in the system. Sometimes a combination of analysis and educated intuition work best. For example, with practice a leader can learn to "sense" how well the structure, culture, processes, and customer relationships are going. To resolve problems or make changes in their organization, they can combine a systematic analysis with their intuition and emotion by looking for leverage points, patterns, and key relationships in all of the following: structure, culture, processes, customers, technology and knowledge systems, leadership, management, knowledge workers, meshes, and the Centers. Asking how one feels about an event, pattern, or situation provides another perspective with attendant insights. In summary, complex systems can best be understood holistically; they take on a life of their own and often a speed of their own. To be prepared to deal with complexity we need to develop and use all of our mental capabilities: logic, analysis, intuition, judgment, and emotion.

Seek Optimum Complexity

Variety is a measure of complexity and represents the number of possible states that a complex system can have. The law of requisite variety, also known as Ashby's law (1964), says that for a complex system to survive in a complex environment, it must have greater variety than the environment (in areas that are relevant to the organization's health). Too much variety can waste resources and lead to chaos and incoherence. Too little variety may mean an inability to respond to complex situations. Optimum complexity is that level of variety needed to manage the complexity of the present and deal with the anticipated future level. Being able to provide creative, agile, and flexible responses to increasingly complex demands requires preparation and cannot happen instantaneously.

Beware Simplicity

Simplification reduces our own uncertainty, makes decisions easier, and allows easy, logical explanations of those decisions. Simplicity captivates the mind; complexity confuses us and forces us to use intuition and judgment, both difficult to explain to others. We continuously simplify to avoid being overwhelmed, to hide confusion, and to become focused and efficient. In a simple, predictable world this is rational and generally works well. It is easy to ignore many incoming signals, knowing that they are not important to our work. Unfortunately, in a complex world this can become dangerous, and even disastrous. Where complexity lives, it is hard to separate the unimportant from the critical information, events, or signals. It is under these latter conditions that teams, networking, contingency planning, experience, and deep knowledge become so essential.

The hardest thing of all is for a leader to admit, "I don't understand this and need help in making this decision." Sometimes the hardest way is the only way!

Self-Organize Your Own Learning

Accept full responsibility for your own learning and use problems and complex systems as opportunities to learn how you learn (see Chapter 14) and improve your judgment and intuition. Develop your listening capacity by thinking about the above ideas and practice in all conversations. Enter into dialogues more often than discussions. Spend time reflecting, asking yourself difficult questions, and deliberately shifting your perspective on topics of importance. Always strive for insight, understanding, and balanced decisions. With complexity, logic and rational thought have their place and their limitations. Do not hesitate to ask unreasonable or irrational questions, make guesses, and speculate with metaphors when trying to comprehend a complex situation.

Expect Mistakes

Mistakes are a necessary part of interacting with complex adaptive systems. Anyone attempting to change a CAS from within, or trying to understand and deal with an external CAS, is bound to make mistakes during the process. Every CAS is unique and to deal effectively with them requires experience, intuition, judgment, innovation, trial-and-error, testing, and feedback. Since no one has total control in a CAS, it is not possible to completely understand and predict the behavior. Complex adaptive systems are by their very nature unpredictable—recall that they operate close to the boundary between complexity and chaos, with their behavior contingent upon a large number of semi-autonomous individuals. Thus, mistakes are to be anticipated as part of the learning, understanding, and intervention process. However, prudent risk assessment should always be considered prior to any intervention. Clearly a good risk assessment of the unintended consequences is difficult for complex adaptive systems. By mobilizing the energy and knowledge of teams within the CAS, most unintended consequences can be prevented.

Amplify What Works and Change What Does Not Work

Where the system under study is highly complex and adaptive, it will be impossible to know how it will respond to some action. Evolutionary biology has dealt with this problem throughout the evolution of life. It appears that the standard solution is to create a variety of reasonable actions, try some of them, and use feedback to find out which ones succeed. The successful actions are then used over and over in similar situations as long as they yield the desired results, i.e. survival. When actions fail they are stopped and new actions are used. It is important not to continue with an action that is not working. Time is unlikely to help failed actions work because in a complex environment the only future is the present; many actions will have a short half-life. This is not completely trial-and-error since learning continuously occurs and judgement, experience, and deep knowledge may create levels of understanding and knowing that result in more effective actions. In other words, "trial-and-error" used both as a decision strategy and learning tool—coupled with a knowledge of complex adaptive systems, the use of teams, and the deliberate development of intuition—appears to be the best approach to dealing with complex systems. See Axelrod and Cohen (1999) for an extensive treatment of the role of variation, interaction, and selection in dealing with external complexity by creating internal complexity within your own organization.

A BRIEF REMINDER

The complexity era creates situations with the following possibilities:

- The capacity to learn may be more important than experience.
- Leadership may be more important than the knowledge one possesses.
- Effectiveness may be more important than efficiency.
- Teams may be more effective than individuals.
- Nurturing may be more effective than controlling.
- Intuition is often better than logic.
- Understanding and meaning may be more important than analysis.
- Context may be more important than facts.
- Patterns may be more important than events.
- Structures may be more important than patterns.

REFERENCES

Ackoff, R. L. *The Art of Problem Solving: Accompanied by Ackoff's Fables*. New York: John Wiley & Sons, 1978.

Ashby, W. R. *An Introduction to Cybernetics*. London: Methuen, 1964.

Axelrod, R. and M. Cohen. *Harnessing Complexity: Organizational Implications of a Scientific Frontier*. New York: The Free Press, 1999.

Calaprice, A. *The Expanded Quotable Einstein*. Princeton, NJ: Princeton University Press, 2000.

Stacey, R. D. *Managing the Unknowable: Strategic Boundaries Between Order and Chaos in Organizations*. San Francisco: Jossey-Bass, 1992.

The United States Marine Corps. *Warfighting: The U.S. Marine Corps Book of Strategy*. New York: Doubleday, 1994.

von Clausewitz, C. *On War*. Princeton, NJ: Princeton University Press, 1984.

Wheatley, M. J. *Leadership and the New Science: Discovering Order in a Chaotic World*. San Francisco, CA: Berrett-Koehler Publishers, 1999.

Chapter 20

KNOWING

Knowing encompasses three critical areas. The first is a thorough and deep understanding of ourselves, i.e., our beliefs, goals, objectives, values, limitations, internal defenses, and strengths and weaknesses of thought and action. By knowing ourselves we learn to work within and around our limitations and to support our strengths, thus ensuring that the data, information, and knowledge coming to us is properly identified and interpreted. The second critical element is that of knowing others. The third critical area is that of "knowing" the situation in as objective and realistic manner as possible, understanding the situation, problem, or challenge in context. In the military this is called situational awareness and includes areas such as culture, goals and objectives, thinking patterns, internal inconsistencies, capabilities, strategies and tactics, and political motivations. The current dynamics of our environment, the multiple forces involved, the complexity of relationships, the many aspects of events that are governed by human emotion, and the unprecedented amount of available data and information make situational awareness a challenging but essential phenomenon in many aspects of our daily lives.

"Knowing" can be loosely defined as *seeing beyond images, hearing beyond words, sensing beyond appearances, and feeling beyond emotions.* It focuses on methods to increase individual sensory capabilities and increase the ability to consciously integrate these sensory inputs with our tacit knowledge, that knowledge within each of us that is created by past learning and experiences but cannot be put into words. In other words, it is knowledge gained from experience that resides in the unconscious mind. We don't know everything that we know.

The rapid pace and uncertain directions of the fast-changing world can be viewed as a nonlinear, dynamic, complex world in which predictability is rare if existent at all. If we accept this hypothesis, then clearly decision-makers can no longer rely on the logic of the past to make future decisions. As we move away from predictable patterns susceptible to logic, decision-makers must become increasingly reliant on their "gut" instinct, an internal sense of "knowing" combined with high situational awareness. Knowing then becomes key to decision-making. The mental skills honed in knowing help decision-makers identify, interpret, make decisions, and take appropriate action in response to current situational assessments.

This construct of knowing can be elevated to the organizational level by using and combining the insights and experiences of individuals through dialogue and collaboration within teams, groups, and communities. Such efforts significantly improve the quality of understanding and responsiveness of actions of the organization. It also greatly expands the scope of complex situations that can be handled through knowing because of the greater resources brought to bear—all of this significantly supported by technological interoperability.

Organizational knowing is an aspect of organizational intelligence, the capacity of an organization as a whole to gather information, generate knowledge, innovate, and to act effectively. This capacity is the foundation for effective response in a fast-changing and complex world. Increasing our sensory and mental processes contributes to the "positioning" understood by the great strategist Sun Tzu in the year 500 B.C. when he wrote his famous dictum for victory: *Position yourself so there is no battle* (Clavell, 1983). Today in our world of organizations and complex challenges we could say "Position ourselves so there is no confusion."

By exploring our sense of knowing we expand our understanding of ourselves, improve our awareness of the external world, and increase our skills to affect internal and external change. Knowing offers a framework for developing deep knowledge within the self and sharing that knowledge with others to create new levels of understanding. Since each situation and each individual is unique, this framework does not provide specific answers. Rather, it suggests questions and paths to follow to find those answers.

PRINCIPLES OF KNOWING

Along with the changing environment, there were a number of recognized basic truths that drove development of *Knowing: The Art of War 2000* for the Department of the Navy, the first treatment of this concept of knowing (Bennet, 2000). These basic truths became the principles upon which *Knowing* is based.

- Making decisions in an increasingly complex environment requires new ways of thinking and feeling.

- All the information in the world is useless if the decision-maker who needs it cannot process it and connect it to that decision-maker's own internal values, knowledge, and wisdom.
- We don't know what we know. Each of us has knowledge far beyond that which is in our conscious mind. Put another way, we know more than we know we know. (Much of our experience and knowledge resides in the unconscious mind.)
- By exercising our mental and sensory capabilities we can increase those capabilities.
- Support capabilities of organizational knowing include organizational learning, knowledge centricity, common values and language, coherent vision, openness of communications, effective collaboration, and the free flow of ideas and people.

THE COGNITIVE CAPABILITIES

The concept of knowing focuses on the cognitive capabilities of observing and perceiving a situation, the cognitive processing that must occur to understand the external world and make maximum use of our internal cognitive capabilities, and the mechanism for creating deep knowledge and acting on that knowledge, the self as an agent of change. See Figure 20-1 for a visual representation of this process. Each of these core areas will be discussed below in more detail.

The cognitive capabilities include observing, collecting and interpreting data and information, and building knowledge relative to the situation. Figure 20-2 shows the five areas we will address. These are: noticing, scanning, patterning, sensing, and integrating. These areas represent the means by which we perceive the external world and begin to make sense of it.

Noticing

The first area, noticing, represents the ability to observe the world around us and recognize, i.e., identify, those things that are relevant to our immediate needs. We are all familiar with the phenomenon of buying a new car and for the next six months recognizing the large number of similar cars that are on the streets. This is an example of a cognitive process of which we are frequently unaware. We notice those things that are recently in our memory or of emotional or intellectual importance to us. We miss many aspects of our environment if we are not focusing on them. Thus the art of noticing can be considered the art of "knowing" which areas of the environment are important and relevant

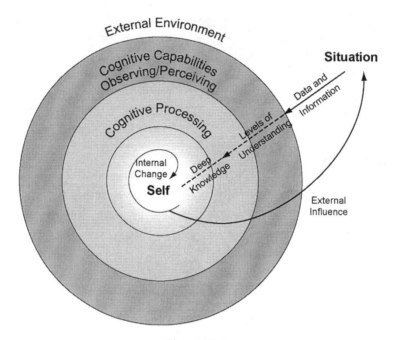

Figure 20-1
Developing the Concept of Knowing

to us at the moment, and focusing in on those elements and the relationships among those elements. It is also embedding a recall capability of those things not necessarily of immediate importance but representing closely related context factors. This noticing is a first step in building deep knowledge, developing a thorough understanding and a systems context awareness of those areas of anticipated interest. This is the start of becoming an expert in a given field of endeavor, or situation.

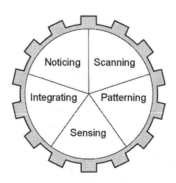

Figure 20-2
The Cognitive Capabilities

A classic example of mental exercises aimed at developing latent noticing skills is repetitive observation and recall. For example, think about a room that you are often in, perhaps a colleague's office or a friend's living room. Try to write down everything you can remember about this room. You will discover that despite the fact you've been in this room often, you can't remember exactly where furniture is located, or what's in the corners or on the walls. When you've completed this exercise, visit the room and write down everything you see, everything you've missed. What pictures are on the walls? Do you like them? What personal things in the room tell you something about your colleague or friend? How does the layout of furniture help define the room? (These kinds of questions build relationships with feelings and other thinking patterns.) Write a detailed map and remember it. A few days later repeat this exercise from the beginning. If you make any mistakes, go back to the room again, and as many times as it takes to get it right. Don't let yourself off the hook. You're telling yourself that when details are important you know how to bring them into your memory. As your ability to recall improves, repeat this exercise focusing on a street, a building, or a city you visit often.

Scanning

The second area, scanning, represents the ability to review and survey a large amount of data and information and selectively identify those areas that may be relevant. Because of the exponential increase in data and information, this ability becomes more and more important as time progresses. In a very real sense, scanning represents the ability to reduce the complexity of a situation or environment by objectively filtering out the irrelevant aspects, or environmental noise. By developing your own system of environmental "speed reading," scanning can provide early indicators of change.

Scanning exercises push the mind to pick up details and, more importantly, patterns of data and information, *in a short timeframe.* This is an important skill that law enforcement officers and investigators nurture. For example, when you visit an office or room that you've never been in before, take a quick look around and record your first strong impressions. What feelings are you getting? Count stuff. Look at patterns, look at contrasts, look at colors. Try to pick up everything in *one or two glances* around the room. Make a mental snapshot of the room and spend a few minutes impressing it in your memory. As you leave, remember the mental picture you've made of the room, the way you feel. Impress upon yourself the importance of remembering this. This picture can last for days, or years, despite the shortness of your visit. Your memory can literally retain an integrated *gestalt* of the room. Realize that what you can recall is only a small part of what went into your mind.

Patterning

The third area, patterning, represents the ability to review, study, and interpret large amounts of data/events/information and identify causal or correlative connections that are relatively stable over time or space and may represent patterns driven by underlying phenomena. These hidden drivers can become crucial to understanding the situation or a competitor's behavior. This would also include an understanding of rhythm and randomness, flows and trends. Recall the importance of structure, relationships, and culture in creating emergent phenomena (patterns) and in influencing complex systems.

A well-known example of the use of patterning is that of professional card players and successful gamblers, who have trained themselves to repeatedly recall complicated patterns found in randomly drawn cards. To learn this skill, and improve your patterning skills, take a deck of cards and quickly flip through the deck three or four at a time. During this process, make a mental picture of the cards that are in your hand, pause, then turn over three or four more. After doing this several times, recall the mental picture of the first set of cards. What were they? Then try to recall the second set, then the third. The secret is not to try and remember the actual cards, but to close your eyes and recall the mental picture of the cards. Patterns will emerge. After practicing for awhile, you will discover your ability to recall the patterns—as well as your ability to recall larger numbers of patterns—will steadily increase. As you increase the number of groups of cards you can recall, and increase the number of cards within each group, you are increasing your ability to recall complex patterns.

Study many patterns found in nature, art, science, and other areas of human endeavor. These patterns will provide you with a "mental reference library" that your mind can use to detect patterns in new situations.

Sensing

The fourth area, sensing, represents the ability to take inputs from the external world through our five senses and ensure the translation of those inputs into our mind to represent as accurate a transduction process (the transfer of energy from one form to another) as possible. The human ability to collect information through sensors is limited because of our physiological limitations. For example, we only see a very small part of the electromagnetic spectrum in terms of light, yet with technology we can tremendously expand the sensing capability. As humans we often take our senses for granted, yet they are highly sensitized, complex detection systems that cause immediate response without conscious thought! An example most everyone has experienced or observed is a mother's sensitivity to any discomfort of her young child. The relevance to "knowing" is, recognizing the importance of our sensory inputs, to learn how to fine tune these inputs to the highest possible level, then use discernment and discretion to interpret them.

Exercise examples cited above to increase noticing, scanning, and patterning skills will also enhance the sense of sight, which is far more than just looking at things. It includes locating yourself in position to things. For example, when you're away from city lights look up on a starry night and explore your way around the heavens. Try to identify the main constellations. By knowing their relative position, you know where you are, what month it is, and can even approximate the time of day. The stars and planets provide context for positioning yourself on the earth.

Here are a few exercise examples for other senses. Hearing relates to comprehension. Sit on a park bench, close your eyes and relax, quieting your mind. Start by listening to what is going on around you—conversations of passersby, cars on a nearby causeway, the birds chattering, the wind rustling leaves, water trickling down a nearby drain. Now stretch beyond these nearby sounds. Imagine you have the hearing of a panther, only multidirectional, because you can move your ears every direction and search for sounds. Focus on a faint sound in the distance, then ask your auditory systems to bring it closer. Drag that sound toward you mentally. It gets louder. If you cup one hand behind one ear and cup the other hand in front of the opposite ear, you can actually improve your hearing, focusing on noises from the back with one ear and noises from the front with the other. How does that change what you are hearing?

Next time you are in a conversation with someone, focus your eyes and concentrate on the tip of their nose or the point of their chin. Listen carefully to every word they say, to the pause between their words, to their breathing and sighs, the rise and fall of their voice. Search for the inflections and subtle feelings being communicated behind what is actually being said. When people are talking, much of the meaning behind the information they impart is in their feelings. The words they say are only a representation, a descriptive code that communicates thought, interacting electrical pulses and flows influenced by an emotion or subtle feeling. By listening in this way, with your visual focus not distracting your auditory focus, you can build greater understanding of the subtleties behind the words.

There are many games that accentuate the sense of touch. An old favorite is blind man's bluff; more current is the use of blindfolding and walking through the woods used in outdoor management programs. Try this at home by spending three or four hours blindfolded, going about your regular home activities. At first you'll stumble and bump, maybe even become frustrated. But as you continue, your ability to manage your movements and meet your needs using your sense of touch will quickly improve. You will be able to move about your home alone with relative little effort, and you'll know where things are, especially things that are alive, such as plants and pets. You will develop the ability to *feel* their energy. Such exercises as these force your unconscious mind to create, re-create, and surface the imagined physical world. It activates the mind to bring out into the open its sensitivity to the physical context in which we live.

Integrating

The last area in the cognitive capabilities is integration. This represents the top-level capacity to take large amounts of data and information and pull them together to create meaning; this is frequently called sense-making. This capability, to pull together the major aspects of a complex situation and create patterns, relationships, models, and meaning that represent reality and allow us to make decisions, is one of the most valuable cognitive capabilities for leaders in the ICAS. This capability also applies to the ability to integrate internal organization capabilities and systems.

In Summary

These five ways of observing represent the front line of cognitive capabilities needed to assist all of us in creative and accurate situational awareness and building a valid understanding of situations. To support these cognitive capabilities, we then need processes that transform these observations and this first-level knowledge into a deeper level of comprehension and understanding.

THE COGNITIVE PROCESSES

Internal cognitive processes that support the capabilities discussed above are presented in Figure 20-3. These include visualizing, intuiting, valuing, and judging. These four internal cognitive processes greatly improve our power to understand the external world and to make maximum use of our internal thinking capabilities, transforming our observations into understanding.

Visualizing

The first of these processes, visualizing, represents the methodology of focusing attention on a given area and through imagination and logic creating an internal vision and scenario for success. In developing a successful vision, one must frequently take several different perspectives of the situation, play with a

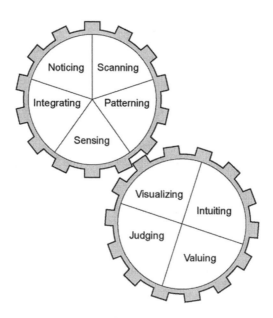

Figure 20-3
Adding the Cognitive Processes

number of assumptions underlying these perspectives, and through a playful trial-and-error, come up with potential visions. This process is more creative than logical, more intuitive than rational, and wherever possible should be challenged, filtered, and constructed in collaboration with other competent individuals. Often this is done between two trusting colleagues or perhaps within a small team. While there is never absolute assurance that visualizing accurately represents reality, there are probabilities or degrees of success that can be recognized and developed.

Intuiting

The second supporting area is that of intuiting. By this we mean the art of making maximum use of our own intuition developed carefully through experience, trial-and-error, and deliberate internal questioning and application. There are standard processes available for training oneself to surface intuition. Recognize that intuition is typically understood as being the ability to access our unconscious mind and thereby make effective use of its very large storeroom of observations, experiences, and knowledge.

Empathy represents another aspect of intuition. Empathy is interpreted as the ability to take oneself out of oneself and put oneself into another person's world; in other words, as the old Native American saying goes, "Until you walk a mile in his moccasins, you will never understand the person." The ability to empathize permits us to translate our personal perspective into that of another, thereby understanding their interpretation of the situation. Such intelligence is clearly advantageous in warfare. An aspect of intuition is "mind mapping." This is a tool to visually recognize relationships from discrete and diverse pieces of information and data. In addition to providing a systems interpretation as discussed earlier, mind mapping can also be used to trigger ideas and dig deeper into one's intuitive capability to bring out additional insights.

Valuing

Valuing represents the capacity to observe situations and recognize the value underlying their various aspects and concomitantly be fully aware of your own values and beliefs. A major part of valuing is the ability to align your vision, mission, and goals to focus attention on the immediate situation at hand. A second aspect represents the ability to identify the relevant but unknown aspects of a situation or competitor's behavior. Of course, the problem of unknown unknowns always exists in a turbulent environment and, while logically they are impossible to identify because by definition they are unknown, there are techniques available that help one expand the area of known unknowns and hence reduce the probability of them adversely affecting the organization (see Chapter 22).

A third aspect of valuing is that of meaning, that is, understanding the important aspects of the situation and being able to prioritize them to antici-pate potential consequences. Meaning is contingent upon the goals and aspira-tions of the individual. It also relies on the history of both the individual's experience and the context of the situation. Determining the meaning of a situation allows us to understand its impact on our own objectives and those of our organization. Knowing the meaning of something lets us prioritize our actions and estimate the resources we may need to deal with it.

Judging

The fourth supporting area is that of judging. Judgments are conclusions and interpretations developed through the use of rules-of-thumb, facts, knowledge and experiences, and intuition. While not necessarily widely recognized, judgments are used far more than logic or rational thinking in making decisions. This is because all but the simplest decisions occur in a context in which there is insufficient, noisy, or perhaps too much information to make rational conclusions. Judgment makes maximum use of heuristics, meta-knowing, and verication. Heuristics represent the rules-of-thumb developed over time and through experience in a given field. They are shortcuts to thinking that are applicable to specific situations. Their value is speed of conclusions and their usefulness rests on consistency of the environment and repeatability of situations. Thus, they are both powerful and dangerous. Dangerous because the situation or environment, when changing, may quickly invalidate former reliable heuristics and historically create the phenomenon of always solving the last problem; powerful because they represent efficient and rapid ways of making decisions where the situation is known and the heuristics apply.

A related aspect of judgment is that of meta-knowing. Meta-knowing is knowing about knowing, that is, understanding how we know things and how we go about knowing things. With this knowledge, one can then go about learning and knowing in new situations as they evolve over time. Such power and flexibility greatly improves the final judgment and decisions made. Meta-knowing is closely tied to our natural internal processes of learning and behaving as well as knowing how to make the most effective use of available external data, information, and knowledge and intuit that which is not available. An interesting aspect of meta-knowing is the way that certain errors in judgment are common to many people. Just being aware of these mistakes can reduce their occurrence. For example, we tend to give much more weight to specific, concrete information than to conceptual or abstract information. (See Kahneman et al. (1982) for details.)

A third aspect of judgment is verication. This is the process by which we can improve the probability of making correct judgments by working with others and using their experience and "knowing" to validate and improve the level of judgmental effectiveness. Again, this could be done via a trusted colleague or through effective team creativity and decision-making. (An additional explication of verication is included in Chapter 11.)

In Summary

These four internal cognitive processes—visualizing, intuiting, valuing, and judging—work with the five cognitive capabilities—noticing, scanning, patterning, sensing, and integrating—to process data and information and create knowledge within the context of the environment and the situation. However, this knowledge must always be suspect because of our own self-limitations, internal inconsistencies, historical biases, and emotional distortions, all of which are discussed in the third area of knowing: the self as an agent of change.

THE SELF AS AN AGENT OF CHANGE

The third area of knowing—the self as an agent of change—is the mechanism for creating deep knowledge, a level of understanding consistent with the external world and our internal framework. The self as an agent of change also takes this deep knowledge and uses it for the dual purpose of our own individual learning and growth and for making changes in the external world (see Figure 20-4).

Deep knowledge consists of beliefs, facts, truths, assumptions, and understanding of an area that is so deeply embedded in the mind that we are often not consciously aware of the knowledge. To create deep knowledge an individual has to "live" with it, continuously interacting, thinking, learning, and experiencing that part of the world until the knowledge truly becomes a natural part of the inner being. An example would be that a person who has a good knowledge of a foreign language can speak it fluently; a person with a deep knowledge would be able to think in the language without any internal translation and would not need their native language to understand that internal thinking. There are ten elements we will discuss here. Five of them are internal: know thyself, mental

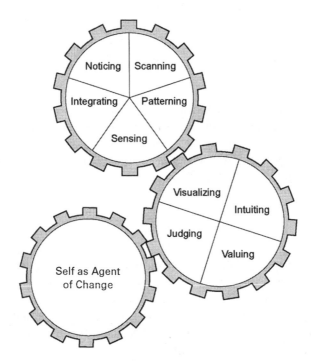

Figure 20-4
The Self as an Agent of Change

models, emotional intelligence, learning and forgetting, and mental defenses; and five of them are external: modeling behaviors, knowledge sharing, dialogue, storytelling, and the art of persuasion.

Internal Elements

Alexander Pope, in his essay on man, noted that: "Know then thyself, presume not God to scan; the proper study of mankind is man" (Daintith et al., 1989, p. 438). We often think we know ourselves, but we rarely do. To really understand our own biases, perceptions, capabilities, etc., each of us must look inside and, as objectively as possible, ask ourselves, who are we, what are our limitations, what are our strengths, and what jewels and baggage do we carry from our years of experience. Rarely do we *take ourselves out of ourselves and look at ourselves*. But without an objective understanding of our own values, beliefs, and biases, we are continually in danger of misunderstanding the interpretation we apply to the external world. Our motives, expectations, decisions, and beliefs are frequently driven by internal forces of which we are completely unaware. For example, our emotional state plays a strong role in determining how we make decisions and what we decide.

The first step in knowing ourselves is awareness of the fact that we cannot assume we are what our conscious mind thinks we are. Two examples that most of us have experienced come to mind. The first is that we frequently do not know what we think until we hear what we say. Our biases, prejudices, and even brilliant ideas frequently remain unknown to us until pointed out by others or through conversations. The second example is the recognition that every act of writing is an act of creativity. Consciousness is our window to the world, but it is clouded by an internal history, experiences, feelings, memories, and desires.

After awareness comes the need to constantly monitor ourselves for undesirable traits or biases in our thinking, feeling, and processing. Seeking observations from others and carefully analyzing our individual experiences are both useful in understanding ourselves. We all have limitations and strengths, and even hidden agendas, that we must be aware of and build upon or control.

Part of knowing ourselves is the understanding of what mental models we have formed in specific areas of the external world. Mental models are the models we use to represent our own picture of reality. They are built up over time and through experience and represent our beliefs, assumptions, and ways of interpreting the outside world. They are efficient in that they allow us to react quickly to changing conditions and make rapid decisions based upon our presupposed model. Concomitantly, they are dangerous if the model is inaccurate or misleading.

Because of the current rapidly changing environment, many of our models quickly become outdated. It is important to continuously review our perceptions and assumptions of the external world and question our own mental models to ensure they are consistent with reality (Senge, 1990). Since this is done continuously in our subconscious, we must continuously question ourselves as to our real, versus stated, motives, goals and feelings. Only then can we *know* who we are, only then can we *change* who we will be.

The art of knowing not only includes understanding our own mental models, but the ability to recognize and deal with the mental models of others. Mental models frequently serve as drivers for our actions as well as our interpretations. When creating deep knowledge or taking action, the use of small groups, dialogue, etc. to normalize mental models with respected colleagues provides somewhat of a safeguard against the use of incomplete or erroneous mental models.

A subtle but powerful factor underlying mental models is the role of emotions in influencing our perception of reality. This has been extensively explored by Daniel Goleman (1995) in his seminal book *Emotional Intelligence*. Emotional intelligence is the ability to sense, understand, and effectively apply the power and acumen of emotions as a source of human energy, information, connection, and influence. It includes self-control, zeal and persistence, and the ability to motivate oneself. To understand emotional intelligence, we study how emotions affect behavior, influence decisions, motivate people to action, and impact their ability to interrelate. Emotions play a much larger role in our lives than previously understood, including a strong role in decision-making. For years it was widely held that rationality was the way of the executive. Now it is becoming clear that the rational and the emotional parts of the mind must be used together to get the best performance in organizations.

Much of emotional life is unconscious. Awareness of emotions occurs when the emotions enter the frontal cortex. Subconscious emotions play a powerful role in how we perceive and act, and hence in our decision-making. Feelings come from the limbic part of the brain and come forth before any related experiences that created them. They represent a signal that a given potential action may be wrong, or right, or that an external event signals danger. Emotions assign values to options or alternatives, sometimes without our knowing it. There is growing evidence that fundamental ethical stances in life stem from underlying emotional capacities. These stances create the basic belief system, the values, and often the underlying assumptions that are used to see the world—our mental model. From this short treatment of the concept, it is clear that emotional intelligence is interwoven across the ten elements of the self as an agent of change.

Creating the deep knowledge of knowing through the effective use of emotional intelligence opens the door to two other equally important factors: learning and forgetting. Learning and letting go—in terms of "filing" away or putting away on the bookshelf—are critical elements of the self as an agent of change because they are the primary processes through which we change and grow. They are also the prerequisite for continuous learning, so essential for developing competencies representing all of the processes and capabilities discussed previously. Because the environment is highly dynamic and will continue to become more complex, learning will be more and more essential and critical in keeping up with the world.

Since humans have limited processing capability and the mind is easily overloaded and clings to its past experience and knowledge, "letting go" becomes as important as learning. Letting go is the art of being able to let go what was known and true in the past. Being able to recognize the limitations and inappropriateness of past assumptions, beliefs, and knowledge is essential before creating new mental models and for understanding ourselves as we grow. It is one of the hardest acts of the human mind because it threatens our self-image and may shake even our core belief systems.

The biggest barrier to learning and letting go arises from our own individual ability to develop invisible defenses against changing our beliefs. These self-imposed mental defenses have been eloquently described by Chris Argyris (1990). The essence of his conclusion is that the mind creates built-in defense mechanisms to support belief systems and experience. These defense mechanisms are invisible to the individual and may be quite difficult to expose in a real-world situation. They are a widespread example of not knowing what we know, thus representing invisible barriers to change. Several authors have estimated that information and knowledge double approximately every nine months. If this estimate is even close, the problems of saturation will continue to make our ability to acquire deep knowledge even more challenging. We must learn how to filter data and information through vision, values, goals, and purposes using intuition and judgment as our tools. This discernment and discretion within the deepest level of our minds provides a proactive aspect of filtering, thereby setting up purposeful mental defenses that reduce complexity and provide conditional safeguards to an otherwise open system. This is a fundamental way in which the self can simplify a situation by eliminating extraneous and undesirable information and knowledge coming from the external world.

The above discussion has identified a number of factors that can help us achieve an appropriate balance between change and our resistance to change. This is an important balance: not all change is for the best, yet rigidity begets antiquity. This balance is situational and comes only from experience, learning, and a deep sense of knowing when to change and when not to change the self.

This section has addressed the self as an agent of change through internal recognition of certain factors that can influence self-change. Another aspect of change is the ability of the self to influence or change the external world. This is the active part of knowing. Once the self has attained deep knowledge and understanding of the situation and external environment, this must be shared with others, accompanied by the right actions to achieve success.

External Elements

The challenge becomes that of translating knowledge into behavior, thus creating the ability to model that behavior and influence others toward taking requisite actions. Role-modeling has always been a prime responsibility of leadership in the government as well as the civilian world. Having deep knowledge of the situation the individual must then translate that into personal behavior that becomes a role model for others to follow and become motivated and knowledgeable about how to act. Effective role-modeling does not require the learner to have the same deep knowledge as the role model, yet the actions and behaviors that result may reflect the equivalent deep knowledge and over time create deep knowledge in the learner—but only in specific situations. This is how you share the effectiveness from learning and thereby transfer implicit knowledge.

Wherever possible, of course, it is preferable to develop and share as much knowledge as possible so that others can act independently and develop their own internally and situation-driven behavior. This is the reason knowledge management and communities of practice and interest require management attention. Since most deep knowledge is tacit, knowledge sharing can become a real challenge.

A third technique for orchestrating external change is through the use of dialogue. Dialogue is a process first originated by David Bohm (1992) to create a situation in which a group participates as coequals in inquiring and learning about some specific topic. In essence, the group creates a common understanding and shared perception of a given situation or topic. Dialogue is frequently viewed as the collaborative sharing and development of understanding. It can include both inquiry and discussions, but all participants must suspend judgment and not seek specific outcomes and answers. The process stresses the examination of underlying assumptions and listening deeply to the self and others to develop a collective meaning. This collective meaning is perhaps the best way in which a common understanding of a situation may be developed as a group and understood by others.

Another way of creating change and sharing understanding is through the effective use of the time-honored process of storytelling. Storytelling is a valuable tool in helping to build a common understanding of our current situation in anticipating possible futures and preparing to act on those possible futures. Stories tap into a universal consciousness that is natural to all human communities. Repetition of common story forms carries a subliminal message, a subtext that can help convey a deep level of complex meaning. Since common values enable consistent action, story in this sense provides a framework that aids decision-making under conditions of uncertainty. (See Chapter 15 for a discussion of storytelling.)

Modeling behavior, knowledge sharing, dialogue, and storytelling are all forms of building understanding and knowledge. Persuasion, our fifth technique, serves to communicate and share understanding with others a specific conviction or belief and/or to get them to act upon it. To change the external environment we need to be persuasive and to communicate the importance and need for others to take appropriate action. The question arises: When you have deep knowledge, what aspects of this can be used to effectively influence others' behavior? Since deep knowledge is tacit knowledge, we must learn how to transfer this to explicit knowledge. Nonaka and Takeuchi (1995) and Polyani (1958) have done seminal work in this area. Persuasion, as seen from the perspective of the self, gets us back to the importance of using all of our fundamental values, such as personal example, integrity, honesty, and openness to help transfer our knowing to others.

APPLICATION

Knowing is an aspect of the self that we need and use every day of our lives as well as in nebulous, complex situations that are not easy to understand. Such a situation is that of competition. In preparing for competition, senior leaders spend a great deal of time understanding the psychology of the competitor, their strengths and weaknesses, and potential opportunities and threats. At the same time, leaders carefully consider the strengths and weaknesses of their own company forces and, from the competitor's viewpoint, the potential opportunities and threats they may recognize and take advantage of. Another way of looking at this is that the senior leaders try to develop context empathy of the marketplace. By this is meant an empathetic understanding of the context in which the competition will be waged to allow the use of intuition, insight, and feelings to better anticipate potential market situations. Leaders often listen to subject matter experts, have dialogues with research consultants and use computer modeling with sensitivity analysis to better understand the possible strategies and outcomes of the competition. Through such processes they develop specific strategies for using their own strengths to overwhelm the competitor's weaknesses while protecting their own weaknesses, all the while studying the customer and the marketplace.

In today's world, scenarios could be developed with worst-case situations analyzed from the perspective of what could go wrong. In the most thorough preparation, a focus search for known unknowns during the competition evolution and contingency planning for possible unknown unknowns would be investigated (See Chapter 22). This preparation obviously includes training, exploration, feedback, and learning both about the objective context and evolution of the competition and the subjective development of the leaders' perception and development of their emotional and unconscious capability for effective decision-making. While rarely thought of in this context, such preparation as just described in fact prepares them for the art of knowing. A very important feature of anticipating and "knowing" the competitor is a deliberate review and questioning of the major beliefs, assumptions, biases, conclusions, defense mechanisms, and feelings that went into the preparation for their market thrust. This introspection provides insight into how leaders might have distorted their own understanding and perceptions of the anticipated situation.

In essence, the preparation for competition starts early so that its anticipated evolution cannot only be reviewed and anticipated, but there is time for the leaders themselves to personally live through the evolution of anticipated events. This act of living through the process before it begins allows internal development in each leader of the knowing, intuitive competency, building the unconscious capacity to make quick decisions during the fog of complexity and competition.

VALUE ADDED

Taken together, the five observables, four processes, and ten elements of the self as an agent of change, represent the factors that can create deep knowledge, understanding, and effective actions, all necessary to obtain the real benefits of *knowing*. Each of these factors is related to many of the others, and hence it is the integrated capability built up over time through learning, awareness, and constant self-change that creates the power of knowing so important to decision-making in a turbulent business environment. In summary, knowing:

- Builds situational awareness through deep understanding, having a large insight into the situation and its implications in a turbulent environment.
- Reduces complexity by developing defenses against information and knowledge saturation and by being able to identify leverage points in the situation.
- Cultivates discernment and discretion to enable one to prioritize information and take appropriate action.
- Empowers decision-making through improved knowledge, a clear focus on the objectives, and the recognition of alternatives at the point of action.
- Supports knowledge superiority in terms of competitive advantage through building the individual's capabilities to create deep knowledge and share it with others.

REFERENCES

Argyris, C. "Teaching Smart People How to Learn," in Howard, R. (ed.), *The Learning Imperative: Managing People for Continuous Innovation.* Boston, MA: Harvard Business School Publishing Corp., 1990, 177–194.

Bennet, A. *Knowing: The Art of War 2000.* Washington, DC: Department of the Navy, 2000.

Bohm, D. *Thought as a System.* New York: Routledge, 1992.

Clavell, J. (ed.) *The Art of War: Sun Tzu.* New York: Dell Publishing, 1983.

Daintith, J., H. Egerton, R. Fergusson, A. Stibbs, and E. Wright (eds). *The Macmillan Dictionary of Quotations.* Edison, NJ: Chartwell Books, 1989.

Goleman, D. *Emotional Intelligence: Why It Can Matter More Than IQ.* New York: Bantam Books, 1995.

Kahneman, D., P. Slovic, and A. Tversky. *Judgment Under Uncertainty: Heuristics and Biases.* New York: Cambridge University Press, 1982.

Nonaka, I. and H. Takeuchi. *The Knowledge-Creating Company: How Japanese Companies Create the Dynamics of Innovation.* New York: Oxford University Press, 1995.

Polyani, M. *Personal Knowledge: Towards a Post-Critical Philosophy.* Chicago: The University of Chicago Press, 1958.

Senge, P. M. *The Fifth Discipline: The Art and Practice of the Learning Organization.* New York: Doubleday, 1990.

Chapter 21

NETWORKING FOR THE BOTTOM LINE

In today's world the term networking is used in a variety of ways. It can mean connecting hardware (computer, audio, or video), utilizing software for exchange, or it can be used to describe the weaving together of people. The last concept is decidedly the most difficult, and holds the greatest rewards when accomplished. In the ICAS, everyone, leaders and knowledge workers, has the responsibility of connecting to others, whether through teams, communities, or one-on-one relationships. This is the networking, together with the relationships it is built upon, that directly impacts the bottom line of the organization.

Although successful businesses have always recognized the importance of relationships, it was through the total quality leadership focus on teams and the knowledge management focus on communities that the value of social capital has finally been tied to the organizational bottom line: sustainable competitive advantage (for industry) and sustainable high performance (for non-profits and government). The social capital of an organization is the total value of all personal relationships within the organization plus the value of the relationships between the organization and its environment. Cohen and Prusak (2001) define social capital as "the stock of active connections among people: the trust, mutual understanding, and shared values and behaviors that bind the members of human networks and communities and make cooperative action possible" (p. 4).

Relationship network management focuses on fully using and increasing the social capital of an organization. *The relationship network is a matrix of people that consists of the sum of a knowledge worker's relationships, those individuals with whom the knowledge worker interacts, or has interacted with in the past, and has a connection or significant association.* The relationship network is both horizontal, in terms of colleagues and peers, and vertical, in terms of bosses and employees and mentors and mentees. Relationship network management occurs when we recognize the potential of these relationships and use them to share and learn, creating and sustaining a conscious give and take movement, or flow, across the network.

Organizational structures (as depicted on organizational charts), teams, and communities are units for managing relationships. Teams and communities are a central and fundamental element of organizational design. They have the ability to integrate and enhance cross-functional knowledge and cross-organizational perspectives to provide faster and more effective decision-making, problem-solving, and implementation. The use of teams and communities in organizations can be likened to the industrial revolution, when the assembly line replaced the craft shops where craftsmen individually made the whole product. The assembly line sped up production by moving the products around and having different elements of the products added by different individuals in order to achieve the whole. These individuals, then, became highly efficient in a small part of the process. On the negative side, this process reduced the amount of learning each individual needed, limiting their view and ability, and removing ownership of the whole product.

Today, where we have achieved a high degree of specialization in our career fields, teams and communities move information around much like the assembly line, with individuals adding their experience and perspective. The difference is that teams and communities provide a way to *integrate* individual pockets of knowledge. As information flows among members of a team or community, the individual has not lost it. Rather, an individual's knowledge is increased as each member contributes to, and gains from, the flow of thought, spreading ownership among all members of the team and/or community.

As we become a global world and the amount of available information increases, decisions are becoming increasingly more complex while simultaneously they must be made faster to ensure sustainable competitive advantage. It is impossible for a single individual to know everything needed to make the most challenging decisions. While our knowledge systems provide better information in terms of quality and currency, it is difficult to capture the context of this information without interjecting the human factor. In short, information (and information technology) is necessary but not sufficient to create knowledge.

How are most good decisions really made? The decision-maker pulls together all the information readily available on the subject, considers (either consciously or unconsciously) their own personal experience, and then, if their own experience is insufficient in the area of the decision, consults a trusted source. This consulting of a trusted source of information is the process of verication, where a decision is grounded by the implicit knowledge of another. An active relationship network provides a source for getting one or more opinions in a trusted environment, whether it is achieved through consulting a boss or employee, a mentor or pupil, or a knowledgeable member of a team or community.

Active relationship networks criss-crossing the organization increase organizational awareness, provide redundancies, and, in turn, affect organizational responsiveness in terms of agility and flexibility. An organization can react faster when information around key areas of concern is flowing freely. For example, the concept of the "mesh" (described in Chapter 7) has emerged in response to the events of September 11, 2001.

An active relationship network also provides a monitoring and scanning system for problems and opportunities. If a line of thinking gets off track, it is easy to expose the problem and correct the course through an open dialogue, where individuals share their thoughts and stories in a comfortable and trusted environment. Simultaneously, an increase in the exchange of ideas resulting from relationship network management also increases the number of new ideas. Creativity is an attribute that resides in all individuals. The more an individual learns and understands, the more opportunity to build on that learning and understanding. The concept of "learning" includes the attribute of openness. Unfortunately, creativity can be limited by rigidity or the belief that there is only one answer to every question.

Another benefit is that of ownership. When a group of individuals contribute to a decision there is broader ownership of that decision, providing a number of people who are already committed to it. This commitment is particularly significant when decisions require broad support in order to be successfully implemented.

On the individual side, the networks we belong to help define who we are, contributing to our self-confidence, purpose, and identity. Affiliation with a team or community that is actively contributing to the organization, and is recognized for its contributions, can produce a high degree of collegial synergy and self-satisfaction.

Relationships are ultimately about people and the way they interact with each other over long periods of time. Ironically, the fundamental principle of success in relationships parallels Sun Tzu's fundamental principle of success in warfare, i.e., know thyself, know thy enemy (the other), and know the situation. Principles of relationship network management start with the individual (know thyself): what the individual brings to a relationship in terms of values, ability to communicate, expertise and experience, and willingness to share and learn. Second, the culture of an organization and the environment in terms of place and time (the situation) significantly impact relationship building and sustainability. For example, are people promoted for their personal knowledge, or for their ability to share and problem solve in a team environment, creating systems solutions instead of individual solutions? Third, what do others (partners and competitors) bring to the relationship in terms of values, ability to communicate, expertise and experience, and willingness to share and learn? For a relationship to last, both parties must gain and give.

BASIC CONCEPTS

Taking the above into account, there are several basic concepts that successful relationship network management is built upon. These will be discussed in terms of interdependency, trust, common framework, openness, flow, and equitability. Collectively, these key success factors support the team's, community's, or organization's ability to successfully take collaborative, cohesive action.

Interdependency is a state of mutual reliance, confidence, and trust. It connotes a two-way relationship with both parties taking responsibility for nurturing and sustaining the relationship. Each party depends on the other for their own success.

Trust is based on integrity and consistency over time, saying what you mean, and following through on what you say. Trust is directly tied to individual and organizational value sets and is measured only by proven behavior. As the old adage says, "To be trusted one must be trustworthy." Respect and reputation also contribute to the perception of trust across teams, communities, and organizations. Trust always takes time to build, yet can be lost in a second.

In this context, there must be a *common framework* upon which the exchange of information can lead to the creation of knowledge. This framework could include: a common language (cultural, functional, organizational); common stories; shared values (the ground truth); shared moral standards; or a shared vision and mission. This is not to say that *all* of these need to be in place. Diversity of ideas and thinking styles can add value in a trusting environment where differences are clearly and openly handled.

Openness is directly related to trust and a willingness to share. Without initial trust, it is difficult to have openness; yet openness contributes to the spread of trust and cooperation. When the organization rewards knowledge sharing it is easier to be open with our thoughts and ideas. Nonetheless, recognition that (1) in today's environment it is important to stay at the front of ideas, not to hold on to the old ones, and (2) value is in how these ideas are used, has moved knowledge professionals from the concept of "knowledge is power" to "knowledge shared is power squared."

A relationship cannot exist without interactions, without the *flow* of information and knowledge. The flow of data, information, and knowledge moves around in the networks of systems and people, is shared through team interaction, communities, and events, and is facilitated through knowledge repositories and portals. This free flow is mutually dependent on both the individual and the organization. It is each individual's responsibility to assure that they have what they need when they need it to make the best decisions (in alignment with the strategy and vision of the organization). This flow is both horizontal and vertical, and includes the continuous, rapid two-way communication between key components of the organization and top-level decision-makers that is essential to mission success, all part of an individual's relationship network.

Equitability in a relationship is characterized by fairness and reasonableness. When used in law, the concept includes the application of the dictates of conscience or the principles of natural justice. The intent of an equitable relationship is that both sides get something out of the relationship. In reality, both sides often gain more than either contributes, since relationships often produce synergy and ideas shared beget new ideas.

None of these six concepts can be created by directing or controlling. They all arise from the sequence of interactions among the individuals involved and depend upon each person's perception and feelings about the other. Effective relationships evolve over time and are created by interacting, testing, questioning, and carefully building an image of and belief about the other person. Good relationships *emerge* from a history of interactions, and as such must be nurtured and protected to be sustained.

MANAGING YOUR RELATIONSHIP NETWORK

How do you manage relationships? The individual's ability to manage their relationship network is based on (1) recognizing the value of relationship networks; (2) identifying their personal network of relationships; (3) consciously choosing to develop, expand, and actively sustain these relationships through continuing interactions; and (4) staying open to sharing and learning through this relationship network.

Recognizing the Value of Relationship Networks

In the beginning of this chapter we talked about the value of using relationship networks, of knowing our own value and limitations, and of valuing the expertise and "know how" of others. In the day-to-day world, as we interact face-to-face and virtually with others, as we move in and out of meetings and teleconferences, it is easy to take those interactions for granted. *Yet these interactions are the foundation of doing business.* The nature of these interactions determines the type and value of the relationships that exist. Generally, how we value an interaction is directly proportional to our short-term decision-making process driven by need, situation, and time. However, every interaction embeds information and understanding in our subconscious, information that can emerge as it is needed, often without reference to where it was obtained.

As organizations move into and function in a more complex environment, management concepts that developed with the bureaucratic model—so successful in the past—lose their effectiveness. Over the long term, knowledge cannot be controlled and people cannot be controlled. As information moves in, around, and out of organizations, and as people move in, around, and out of organizations, it is difficult to identify the origin of a new idea. Indeed, ideas are the product of multiple processing in terms of people and over time. Ideas beget ideas, and grow and mature through interactions with others and time. This is the power that permeable and porous boundaries bring to the organization.

The bottom line is that our interactions with others affect the way we think, feel, and make decisions, over both the short and the long term. When we recognize relationships as a scarce commodity and that how we interact is more important than how often we interact, we begin to realize the importance of building relationship networks and choosing our interactions carefully.

Identifying Your Personal Network of Relationships

The first step in managing your relationship network is awareness of who is (or should be) in your network. This will take time to build, since our networks encompass past and present relationships, are not instantly available in our conscious mind, and are subject to continuous change. Developing a simple relationship network chart is a good start. The chart begins with an individual's name and organizational affiliation, followed by the length of relationship (how long you have interacted with this individual). The information entered in the next six columns is based on your experience with this individual and personal judgment. These columns are: (the individual's) expertise and knowledge; accessibility; willingness to share; tendency to follow through on commitments; your feeling about this relationship; and your contributions to this relationship. This last column is critical because it is important to recognize that we do not necessarily enter into relationships strictly because of what we get out of them. Humans are social animals; interactions are an integral part of our life activity and growth. For those who love people, connection can be its own reward (Cohen and Prusak, 2001). Add a final column entitled "frequency of exchange" to your relationship network chart, leaving space below to record dates of future interactions and one-liners about the content of that interaction.

Recalling that successful relationship network management requires two-way responsibility, fill out a chart on yourself from the perspective of individuals in your network. Periodically repeating this process can serve as a check for your contributions to others in your relationship network.

Actively Developing and Sustaining Relationships

Understanding the make-up and nature of our relationship network provides the opportunity to assess its strengths and weaknesses. Consider these questions:

- Do you have active exchanges with individuals who are knowledgeable in your area of work?
- Do you belong to a team or community that is accessible and available when you have a problem to solve?
- Do you share regularly your ideas, learning, and successes with other members of your organization? How?

It is imperative in this age of increasing information and complexity that every knowledge worker has access to a trusted network of thought leaders in their area of concern. If your personal relationship network is not robust enough to serve your knowledge and decision-making needs, it is your responsibility to develop a relationship network that is. With the ever-increasing number of communities emerging across organizations and around the world, there is ample opportunity to develop collegial exchanges with knowledgeable coworkers and experts in government and industry alike. Conferences, seminars, the Internet, and professional associations are all likely sources for new network members.

Somewhat more difficult is sustaining the relationship network. It is easy to dialogue on an issue when we are on the hook to make the best possible decision. It is more difficult to take the time to respond to others who are working toward making their best possible decisions. It is far more difficult to take the time to dialogue when there is no immediate decision to be made. However, this is often when the greatest headway can be made, i.e., when the innovative idea emerges, because we are not focused on one issue, on one decision, but open to exploring.

Relationships of any nature need to be nurtured. What exactly that entails is relationship dependent. For example, a problem-solving team that convenes once a month will expect participation at least once a month. An active community may encourage weekly interactions. A dialogue on a critical issue that is time sensitive may require three or four exchanges in a single day, with a follow-up in a week or so, then fall off to "keeping in touch" every month or six weeks until another critical issue arises. The nature of nurturing is to support, to care for, and to provide sustenance.

The quality of both intellectual and emotional exchange is of primary consideration. When connecting virtually, there is an entirely new set of communication rules. The ability to communicate virtually is an essential integrative competency, and supports all other integrative competencies.

The very characteristics of relationship networks that make them cohesive, effective partners for decision-makers can become a problem if they become closed, dominated, controlled, or corrupt. Take for example the emotion and temper that may emerge during a football game when two colleagues are rooting for different teams. A mutual love of football can bring people together, while passion and loyalty to different teams may pull them apart. In organizational terms, in a relationship network it is critical to have different thinking, which promotes creativity, yet essential to have agreement on the mission of the team or community, and always respect for the other person.

Staying Open to Sharing and Learning

Receptivity to new ideas is affected by a combination of internal and external information and current beliefs, all of which are subject to continuous examination and update, i.e., all incoming information is colored by an individual's current beliefs and feelings. This means that all incoming information, whether originating from the external environment or the unconscious mind of the individual, is under continuous examination and, as a result, the individual's beliefs themselves are also subject to continuous reexamination. This powerful process goes on at various levels within all learning individuals.

A first step to receptivity is gaining attention. As the environment bombards the senses, attention itself rapidly becomes a scarce resource. Since the perceived trustworthiness of information is highly dependent on the sender, information from a network built on strong, trusting relationships has high value, and is more apt to gain attention. A second step to receptivity is listening. "Listening" is far more than an aural sense; it is the mental act of engaging and reflecting on incoming information and is highly dependent on the perceived value of that information. The subtext of incoming information is in the form of questions being answered by the subconscious:

- Is the sender trustworthy?
- Is the information I am receiving worth my time to think about?

When the answers to these questions are positive, a transformation occurs as we move from listening to thinking and understanding, considering the information, its context (our context) and its meaning, driving the question: What does this information mean to me? Our understanding relates to what we already know. We build relationships with not only people, but with things and situations, and these relationships are largely based on the past, what we have learned and what we have experienced. There is no separate entity called "understanding." Understanding is a state of the mind related to some situation, problem, or set of concepts. Our understanding—

filtered through our own consciousness in light of what we know and believe—is ever changing and unique to each interaction. In dynamic relationship networks, where a dialogue pursues, different forms and perspectives of the information emerge that facilitate a shared understanding and new, innovative ideas.

A study of Bell Laboratory's most successful scientists found that they spent more time developing personal and professional relationships with other researchers than the other laboratory scientists. A spin-off gain from communities of practice and interest is the private relationship network that can develop. Task forces and integrated product teams often give birth to spin-off relationship networks because during the formal work sessions the members have met and learned to respect the value of other opinions and backgrounds.

SOCIAL NETWORK ANALYSIS

Social network analysis (SNA) is a process for mapping the relationships among people, teams, or across organizations. SNA is particularly effective in assessing the flow of information through communication and collaboration. It also identifies people who are central (overly central?) and peripheral (underutilized?) to an organization. The extent to which a group is connected, or the extent to which it is split into subgroups, can be an indicator of a problem, difficulty, or strength in moving information from one area of the network to another.

The process of SNA begins by collecting data through interviews or surveys. Examples of questions asked would be:

1. From whom do you seek work-related information?
2. To whom do you give work-related information?
3. When you need information or advice, is this person accessible to you?
4. When you need information or advice, does this person respond within a sufficient amount of time to help you solve your problem?
5. How frequently have you received work-related information from this person in the past month?

From the answers to these or similar questions a map is created that connects people who receive information with people who have provided that information. Arrowheads indicate the direction of that relationship. For example, in Figure 21-1 we see the analysis of question 1 above. It appears that Rob is central to the group, indicating that he might be either a critical knowledge resource *or* a bottleneck to communications. The questions then become: Has the group become too reliant on this individual? What would happen if this individual left? Or, is this individual hoarding information and bottlenecking knowledge sharing and creation? Or, should this individual be rewarded for the important

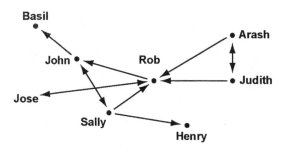

Figure 21-1
Simple Example of Social Network Analysis

role they are playing in supporting the group? (Cross et al., 2002a.) It also appears that Basil, Jose, and Henry might be underutilized resources. When responses to the other questions are combined with this response, other scenarios may arise. The bottom line is that the process of SNA allows organizations to assess their ability to create and share knowledge, and once their current state is recognized, it becomes an enabler for improving these abilities (Cross and Prusack, 2002; Cross et al., 2002b).

There are several software products available to do SNA mapping. These programs use simple screen-oriented interfaces, allowing the user to drag nodes with the mouse and click to add new modes. Each node is assigned a number of attributes, which are highlighted using color and shape. There are also several tools for automatic layout of the network. Once the mapping is complete, analysis of this structure of connections can provide information on relationships that facilitate or impede work, offering intervention opportunities.

VALUE ADDED

In summary, discussions above indicate that good individual relationship network management contributes the following value to an individual and organization:

- Provides a vehicle for sharing knowledge and taking actions.
- Enhances the transfer of tacit knowledge.
- Facilitates knowledge flow throughout the organization.
- Increases the number of new ideas available.
- Provides a source for decision-makers to get a second opinion in a trusted environment.
- Improves organizational responsiveness in terms of agility and flexibility.
- Provides a monitoring and scanning system.
- Contributes broader ownership of decisions and decision implementation.

- Produces collegial synergy and self-satisfaction.
- Directly impacts the bottom line of the organization.

REFERENCES

Cohen, D. and L. Prusak (2001). *In Good Company: How Social Capital Makes Organizations Work.* Boston: Harvard Business School Press.

Cross, R. and L. Prusak. "The People That Make Organizations Stop—or Go," *Harvard Business Review,* 80, No. 6, 2002, 104–112.

Cross, R., S. Borgatti, and A. Parker. "Making Invisible Work Visible: Using Social Network Analysis to Support Human Networks," *California Management Review,* 44, No. 2, 2002a, 25–46.

Cross, R., N. Nohria, and A. Parker. "Six Myths About Informal Networks—and How to Overcome Them," *Sloan Management Review,* 43, No. 3, 2002b, 67–76.

PART V

THE PROBABLE FUTURE

Since to our knowledge no one has ever lived in the future, all conversation and writing concerning the future must be considered as speculative—varying only in degree, not in category. We take no exception to this belief.

Chapter 22 begins by identifying four challenges related to the application of complex adaptive systems to human endeavors that are likely to have a high payoff from research and experience. Following a discussion on the nature of forecasting, the question is asked: How do we know what we know? Methods and processes are presented to assist individuals and organizations in identifying unknown unknowns.

Chapter 23 provides a systems-level summary of the ICAS organization, beginning with the major elements of the ICAS, touching on the integrative competencies, then reviewing the ICAS strategy and change approach. Finally, we continue the "Tale of Two Firms" begun in Chapter 13, moving toward the probable future for successful organizations.

Chapter 22

EXPLORING THE UNKNOWN

In this chapter we address several topics that are significant to the future effectiveness of organizations. The purpose is not to provide answers to some very important questions, but to stimulate thinking in these areas and begin a search for solutions that will be applicable in the near term and possibly directions for the long term. First, the world of the future—from a corporate viewpoint, or looking at the market, environment, or landscape—is a system of systems that possesses all of the attributes of the age of complexity. Accelerating change, non-linearity, increasing uncertainty, and growing complexity are apt descriptors that fit many parts of the world we work and live in. Organizations that survive in such a world will clearly become some form of a complex adaptive system.

As we learn more about the application of complex adaptive systems to human endeavors, the following four areas are likely to have a high payoff from research and experience. The first area is outdated structures and cultures that cannot keep up with the dynamics of their markets. The ICAS is one answer to achieving flexibility, agility, and adaptability.

The second area is the critical importance of knowledge workers and their future role in the new environment. Few workers, and many organizations, seem to recognize that their primary value is in their knowledge and how they can create, leverage, and apply it for the organization's benefit *and* their own growth. Yet knowledge workers are the main source of ideas and actions in the age of complexity. Each individual can manage their own knowledge, can learn how they learn and know how to leverage their own and other's knowledge to create new ideas, solve problems, make decisions, and take effective actions.

Complexity demands understanding and meaning, which can come only through the deliberate development of knowledge. Given a supportive

341

organizational structure and culture, the greatest payoff for the future is having knowledge workers who know how to manage their own knowledge, have knowledge about knowledge and become career experts at learning, sharing, leveraging, and applying their and their colleagues' knowledge. We have identified some integrative competencies that are needed to work effectively in complex situations—many others will undoubtedly surface in the future. Just as research in complexity theory is beginning to be applied to organizational effectiveness, research in neuroscience, learning, psychology, evolution, linguistics, artificial intelligence, and spiritual practices may provide better understanding of intuition, judgment, meta-knowledge, knowing, deep knowledge, etc. In the meantime, technology and knowledge management research are developing taxonomies, ontologies, data warehouses, knowledge systems, and advanced networks that will support knowledge workers.

The third area of need is the characterization of new forms of leadership that will work *with* knowledge workers while creating an environment of change, learning, collaboration, and cohesion throughout their organization. It is not natural for individuals with authority and responsibility to willingly keep responsibility while giving authority to others. Yet, without self-organization, empowerment, and the freedom to use their on-the-scene expertise, knowledge workers will not be able to deal effectively with complex situations and an unknowable future. Much work needs to be done before leadership authority will be shared with workers through collaboration, trust, and self-organization. Leaders are needed that have strong egos, but not big egos; leaders that lead by collaboration, compassion, communication, and values, *not by planning, organizing, directing, staffing, and controlling;* leaders capable of bringing energy and understanding to the local challenges and at the same time integrating those local actions with the organization's purpose and direction. To do this, leadership must be embedded throughout the organization. While this book outlines some desirable behaviors and roles that leaders could play, specific leadership styles, traits, characteristics, experience, and development needs have not been addressed.

Fourth, there is the fundamental challenge of understanding and anticipating the behavior of any complex adaptive organization. This challenge has two dimensions. The first dimension is that of leaders, change agents, and many knowledge workers who must understand their own organization so they can continuously fine-tune them to match the dynamics of the environment. The second dimension—applying to everyone in the organization—is the ability to understand and anticipate the external environment to the maximum extent possible so that, individually and collectively, their actions will be effective. While slightly different, both challenges rest on the ability to anticipate what will happen within a complex adaptive system as the future unfolds.

The past is explainable because we can identify (to varying degrees) causal events and relationships. The future is unknowable if we cannot discover, before the fact, those causes and relationships that will dominate and create the present as the future unfolds. All of this is a function of the level of complexity of the system. For a social complex adaptive system like the ICAS, or an environment that is changing rapidly, nonlinear, highly uncertain, and very complex, predication or forecasting is difficult at best and most probably impossible. But all organizations and environments are not that complex. If we surveyed all organizations and their environments we would certainly find a continuum of levels of complexity of both. So, what can we do to better understand and antici-pate the future environment as it becomes more complex? This is the problem we now turn to.

FORECASTING

For an environment operating close to chaos, predicting or forecasting its future would seem to be an insurmountable task. Or is it? Environments and organi-zations are systems and as such contain subsystems that may have differing levels of complexity. Each subsystem will then have many levels, some compre-hensible, some not. Thus for some areas at some scale prediction may well be possible—even if only over the short term.

Every day, millions and millions of people make decisions and take actions in organizations and other highly complex adaptive systems. Most of these decisions and actions work, and some don't. In most ordinary interactions the anticipated results meet expectations; that is how work gets done and people are able to communicate and collaborate. At the other end of the spectrum there are many people who face difficult, challenging, confusing, and chaotic situations in which decisions must be made. They do their best using their intuition, judgment, friends, and colleagues for support, justifying their decisions using logic and the facts at hand, and hoping for the best. However, as situations become more complex, they are wrong more than they are right, although this often goes undetected due to the confluence of surrounding activities or the time delay before the *real* result shows up.

If, however, you believe as we do that change feeds on itself, nonlinearity prevents backtracking, and complexity begets higher complexity, then the future will not be anything like the present. As a quick mental exercise, go back in your memory and recall what business and work was like in 1994. How many e-mails did you get every day? How much strategic planning was done in your organization? How much shopping did you do over the Internet? How confi-dent were you that you would have the same job a year from then? How does this compare to the results of a survey of knowledge workers taken in 2001, albeit using a limited sample, where 66 percent of them said they were not sure what they would be doing a year from then?

Several times in this book we have indicated that while the future is unknowable it may not be unfathomable. We take this opportunity to interpret that further. By unknowable, we mean that no individual or group of people will be able to predict the behavior of a social complex adaptive system with a high level of probability. Fathomable means to penetrate to the meaning or nature of, or comprehend the environment (*The American Heritage Dictionary,* 1992). In other words, we may be able to comprehend the future system, perhaps to find a set of possible outcomes that have a reasonable probability of coming into existence, though it will take experience, study, knowledge, reflection, knowing, and deep knowledge to understand the most complex of these environments. We also suggest that groups of individuals working together will have an even better chance of successfully anticipating the behavior of such systems. Add then Aristotelian logic, deduction, induction, abduction, critical thinking, dialogue, Delphi, brainstorming, and other creative thinking techniques and one can begin to appreciate the extent of ideas, processes, and cognitive efforts available.

Both individual and group approaches run the danger of invisible internal biases, bad assumptions, and false beliefs related to the specific environment being considered. While this danger can be reduced by taking the time to question oneself, it can never be removed. However, groups can do such cleansing better than individuals if they do not get locked into a *groupthink* situation where everybody agrees that their assumptions and beliefs are right without serious questioning (Janis, 1982).

No matter how good we become at comprehending these systems, surprises will always occur. By their very nature, the environment and organizations are highly complex adaptive systems with areas of chaos scattered throughout. Thus the challenge for knowledge workers and their organization is to develop the capacity to know and possess a deep knowledge of the nature, behavior, and continuity of specific areas of the environment that interest them. Through this deep knowledge and knowing, individuals and groups will have a better chance of recognizing patterns, structural leverage points, key cultural conditions, feedback loops, local and global sources of emergent characteristics, and perhaps the phenomena that create conditions giving rise to surprises. In addition to anticipating what will happen in the external environment, it is useful to contemplate the environment's response to external perturbations. Where the system is not highly complex and adaptive, systems thinking and modeling may unravel the system and allow comprehension as well as some level of prediction.

The field of study of social complex adaptive systems (organizations and environments) is still in its early stages and much work needs to be done before reliable techniques and methods will provide good insight into the nature of their behavior. The search for underlying principles, rules, and laws that govern social complex adaptive systems is underway; however, it is likely to be a long and rugged path. To the authors' knowledge there is no mathematical approach that is powerful enough to handle highly complex social complex adaptive systems. Computer modeling is beginning to make progress. Although highly simplified, such models can be useful learning tools.

We suggest that the best approach is to use the maximum capacity of the human mind through its ability to sense, interpret, understand, and make sense out of its environment. This challenge will require the full use of all of the experience, intuition, and judgment developed by an individual to make effective use of their conscious and unconscious mental capacities. There seems little doubt that the focus of experience and study on particular types of social complex adaptive systems will yield improved understanding and increased ability to anticipate the results of various stimulations. Thus it appears that this field may have a good payoff in terms of understanding organizations and their interactions with the environment and among each other.

Futurists have for years dealt with the problem of prediction by forecasting the future, not predicting it. They generally consider three categories of forecasting: possible futures, probable futures, and preferable futures. These approaches can lead to the creation of imaginative descriptions of possibilities of the future, and can be very useful in bounding a specific problem. Unfortunately, they are usually too general to base a business decision on. At best they provide forecasts that give some idea of what to expect. Other closely related approaches that have found some success are scenario development, Delphi panels, and system dynamics modeling.

Another aspect of the problem of anticipating the behavior of a complex environment is created by our limited ability to sense and interpret the external environment because of our personal histories, experiences, biases, and physiological, psychological, and emotional conditions created throughout our lives. Thus the fields of research related to human consciousness, emotion, psychological states of mind, judgment errors, and neuroscience all contribute to a better understanding of the limitations we each have as we look out at the world through our personal *window of consciousness.*

KNOWING WHAT WE KNOW

A question of extreme importance, although rarely asked, relates directly to our understanding of the environment. *How do we know what we know?* In other words, when an organization (or individual) thinks it understands something such as the future or a specific aspect of its environment, how do they *know that it is right?* What is the basis for this belief? From our previous discussion it is clear that we cannot be assured that any anticipated knowledge of the future will accurately predict what happens next. However, as noted above, there are probabilities of being correct and possibilities for bounding the future in ways that can help organizations survive. By bounding the environment's future we strive to eliminate perceived possibilities that are impossible, highly improbable, or will have little impact on our organization. Recognize, of course, that even these three limits are best guesses or judgment calls and as such they can and should be investigated carefully for their internal consistency, legitimacy, foundational assumptions, beliefs, and completeness. This approach simplifies the complex environment by ignoring or filtering states that cannot come into being, are unlikely to come into being, or can do no harm if they do come into being.

This problem of human biases and limitations is also observable in organizations that operate within paradigms that they have generated through their history or culture. In a turbulent world, these paradigms may no longer apply. To better understand the problem of knowing what we know, consider the following Sufi tale. A father and his young son were sitting outside on a hill looking up at the clear sky on a moonlit night. After some casual conversation, the father turned to his son and remarked: "Son, I think that you see double." The son looked up at the moon, studied it for a while and said: "How can that be father, if I saw double I would see four moons instead of two."

When considering the problem of dealing with unknowns, every organization needs to first evaluate its internal self—its assumptions, beliefs attitudes, decisions, and preferences—and then compare them to the current external environment as seen by both themselves and others. Through this comparison it may be possible to identify gaps or holes in the paradigms, or even dangerous conclusions.

Once a paradigm is cleansed of its failures and rebuilt to be consistent with the current situation, then and only then will an organization be in a position to ask itself the questions: What do I know? What do I know that I don't know? What do I not know that I know? And what are my unknown unknowns? The answer to each of these questions will depend heavily on the organization's paradigms, operations, and the marketplace. In other words, before bounding the known/unknown space, the organization must first know itself and bound its own space. Those boundaries will then limit its areas of interest and concern, its methods of analysis, and its biases and prejudices.

The Domain of Knowns and Unknowns

Referring to Figure 22-1, if we consider the problem of knowns and unknowns, we have four generic categories. At the lower left of the box we have things, information, and knowledge that we know and we know that we know (rightfully or wrongfully). In a sense, this represents the paradigms that we have developed to survive in the world of the past. When working in this box, as

Unknown Knowns	Unknown Unknowns
Known Knowns	Known Unknowns

Figure 22-1
The Domain of Knowns and Unknowns

discussed above, we must be careful to revisit the basis for our belief in what we know and challenge the assumptions and sources of that belief. When our behaviors and actions tend to be successful over time, we tend to think that our belief system is strong, stable, and long-term. However, the environment may have changed yet the momentary success of our belief system may continue until a point is reached where the environment no longer tolerates such actions. When this happens, we tend to become confused, disbelieve what we see, blame it on bad luck, and try to find peripheral reasons why our actions are no longer working rather than giving serious introspection into our assumptions and beliefs.

The box at the upper left of Figure 22-1 presents things that we do not realize that we know but, in fact, we do know. Although frequently unaware of it, we continuously live with this inability to know what we know. For example, often when asked a question we can provide an answer without realizing before the question was asked that we even know the answer. A common trick for writers is to start writing something about a given subject and then, as the writing continues, the unconscious mind will participate in the thinking activity, actually providing information and knowledge the writer was unaware of before the writing started. As we go through life, we gain a huge amount of data, information, understanding, intuition, and insights on things of which we are not consciously aware. Many of these things have been forgotten, but may come to the surface and be quite valuable when needed. There is a theory that the mind re-creates memories and knowledge when needed rather that storing it in memory as a computer does (Edelman and Tononi, 1989). If this is true, the challenge is to learn how to *retrieve and re-create* the knowledge existing in our unconscious mind. Teams and groups often do this frequently through conversation and dialogue. There are also techniques such as those presented in Chapter 20 (Knowing), and such approaches as HemiSync developed through years of research by The Monroe Institute in Virginia that can help individuals or groups move through various processes designed to gain greater access to the unconscious.

Moving now to the lower right-hand corner of the box in Figure 22-1, we see the area identified as known unknowns. This area represents the view from the boundary of our known knowledge. From that position we can easily recognize a number of areas that we perhaps would like to understand, but know that we don't understand them, since we know the boundaries of our knowledge. The known area can usually be expanded by simply identifying those unknown areas and applying learning and studying to them. This is how we normally expand our domain of knowledge.

Moving now to the upper right-hand corner entitled unknown unknowns, we address the most potentially serious problem of all, that is, how do we identify things that we don't know we don't know? Another way of visualizing these areas is presented in Figure 22-2.

In the paragraphs above we discussed methods of identifying possible future events and scenarios. Assume you want to identify potential future events or situations in the environment that could be harmful to your organization. Before studying the environment, carefully bound the future space of interest by identifying those areas in your organization that are vulnerable to environmental perturbations. This limits your area of concern relative to predicting the environment. Looking within your own organization, identify the ways in which the organization could be harmed. This list then narrows your search for possible future environmental scenarios. Each of these future possibilities can then be analyzed for plausibility, consistency, and probability. Also, the forces, events, or patterns necessary for the occurrence of a given scenario can be developed and investigated. Essentially we are simplifying the complexity of the environment's future by filtering out all possibilities that will not harm our organizations and determining the possibility/probability of the dangerous scenarios. Some scenarios may be impossible or have a low probability of occurrence within a specific environment. These can be removed from consideration—a second filtering process. But what if we are wrong? What about the unknowns within the environment that are unknown to us and we do not know it?

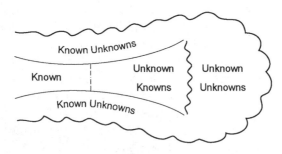

Figure 22-2
Unknown Unknowns

SEARCHING FOR UNKNOWN UNKNOWNS

Once again, our aim is to find those unknown unknowns that can be potentially fatal or near-fatal to the organization. Start with a foundation description of the environment. Look for the environment's fundamental characteristics: things that change slowly and things that change quickly, major patterns from history, processes, and global emergent characteristics. These help you understand local behavior and can be useful in anticipating the system's reaction.

Next, review the slow-changing patterns within the environment and see if they are amenable to surprises or unusual events. If so, those events could be considered unknown unknowns or generators of them. For rapidly changing patterns there is a much higher likelihood that surprises will occur. Many large accidents are the result of a sequence and coincidence of many small errors or actions. Environmental surprises that are truly surprising may come from the same process. On the other hand, a single powerful individual within the system may be unpredictable and drive the system to surprising behavior.

Next, look at known unknowns and identify those, turning those unknowns into knowns. We have now *expanded our known space*. The new known unknowns surrounding this new, expanded known space were originally unknown unknowns. We have thus *reduced our original unknown unknown space*. This process is simply that of digging deeper and deeper into the complex system. At each level one can ask what could possibly happen and what is likely to happen, using these as filters to determine most probable scenarios of the environment's future. As you dig deeper, use creative thinking techniques to generate new and innovative possibilities to see if they are plausible outcomes of the system's future behavior.

The purpose of this very brief and oversimplified discussion is to make the reader aware of the challenges, possibilities, and importance of studying and understanding social complex adaptive systems from a broader perspective than is usually applied. We try to understand things by creating mental models of them and then take action based on those models. This works well most of the time, unless the system is so complex we cannot construct a mental model by the ordinary means of learning and using artifacts such as computer models as aids. In the age of complexity, we must look for new ways of understanding and learning. The above ideas are offered as a stimulus, not a solution to the challenges lying ahead.

It has often been said that the past is easy to understand and the future is perplexing, yet in the present everything is exactly as it should be! How do we reconcile these three statements? In the ICAS we have sidestepped the problem, just as evolution has, by creating an organization that is robust, flexible, agile, and can influence and adapt to a complex, unknowable world. Ecologically speaking, it would be better to say that the ICAS must be able to co-evolve with its environment. In this new world of complexity, we can only offer concepts and ideas and relationships that seem to make sense and have worked in many situations. Time doth make fools of us all, but better a fool than a bystander be.

REFERENCES

The American Heritage Dictionary of the English Language. New York: Houghton Mifflin Company, 1992.

Edelman, G. M. and G. Tononi. *The Remembered Present: A Biological Theory of Consciousness.* New York: Basic Books, 1989.

Janis, I. L. *Groupthink: Psychological Studies of Policy Decisions and Fiascoes,* 2nd ed. Boston: Houghton Mifflin Company, 1982.

Chapter 23

SUMMARY: AND THEN THERE WAS THE ICAS

The Introduction began by asking: How well will your organization perform over the next two decades, and how do you know? We responded by exploring the present and future organizational environment, and building the theoretical and pragmatic groundwork for an organizational system that can enter into a symbiotic relationship with the external environment while retaining its own unity of purpose and selectivity of incoming threats and opportunities, an organization that can turn the *living system* metaphor into a reality. Since the ICAS is, out of necessity, complex, it would be difficult to cull all the elements of the ICAS in a few pages. Nonetheless, there are a number of ideas that are central to the success of the organization and, when taken together, suggest a whole new theory of the firm.

THE MAJOR ELEMENTS OF THE ICAS

Initial development of the ICAS model identified eight emergent characteristics necessary to support its need for flexibility, robustness, agility, and adaptability. These characteristics consisted of:

- *Organizational intelligence,* representing the ability of the ICAS to perceive, interpret, and respond to its environment and meet its organizational goals.
- *Unity and shared purpose,* representing the ability of the ICAS organization to integrate and mobilize resources to (1) provide a continuous line of focus and attention and (2) pull together the relevant parts of the organization when and where they are needed.

351

- *Optimum complexity*, representing the level of complexity of the ICAS sufficient to effectively respond to the complexity in the environment.
- *Selectivity*, indicating the ability of the ICAS to filter the large amount of incoming information from the outside world so that it can deal only with those external events that impact its organizational effectiveness.
- *Knowledge centricity*, representing the focus on and management of knowledge as a critical factor in the operation of the ICAS.
- *Flow*, representing the flow of data, information, and knowledge, the movement of people in and out of organizational settings, and the optimal human experience.
- *Permeable boundaries*, describing the high degree of relationships through boundaries of the ICAS.
- *Multidimensionality*, identifying a specific set of competencies needed by knowledge workers in the ICAS to support organizational flexibility and adaptation.

The above characteristics cannot be decreed by management, but rather will emerge in the organization as a result of the day-to-day leadership, management, and working environment. These characteristics, taken together, are mutually supportive in creating and maintaining the ICAS organization as a complex adaptive system. To facilitate the emergence of these characteristics requires a new way of thinking about structure, culture, major processes, and leadership.

The learning structure was designed to ensure continuous learning and rapid response to external events. The basic structure consists of the use of teams within teams and communities to facilitate collaboration and leverage knowledge. The existence of an Operations Center—together with a Knowledge Center, Learning Center, and Career Management Center—helps ensure unity of the ICAS actions, effective use of knowledge and continuous learning. Action teams, communities, and networks are embedded throughout the structure to provide rapid and diverse response, assisted by meshes as needed. Meshes are special groups of individuals drawn out of ongoing communities and teams that have a deep knowledge in specific areas and are available on short notice. The levels and balance of authority, responsibility, and accountability given to leaders, managers, and workers is designed to provide the right balance between the occasional need for hierarchical decision-making and the continuous need for collaboration and local empowerment and decision-making.

The action culture is the invisible medium through which the ICAS knowledge worker seeks, interprets, and analyzes information, creates and shares knowledge, makes decisions, and takes action on issues and market opportunities. This culture plays a significant role in energizing and helping each worker make the right decisions and take the best actions. The action culture has the characteristics of widespread trust, continuous learning, high integrity, and fair treatment of all workers. In addition, it encourages creativity, allows a high degree of self-determination, and supports knowledge sharing and collaboration, all within an equalitarian base. The culture is action oriented, flexible, and responsive to surprises. Since all cultures emerge from their organizations and cannot be predetermined, the action culture is nurtured, guided, and supported in a manner that will push it in the right direction.

The four major organizational processes—creativity, problem-solving, decision-making, and implementation—are embedded within the ICAS culture and become a natural part of how the work gets done. By formalizing and inculcating these processes throughout the ICAS, knowledge workers and teams are able to leverage knowledge quickly and efficiently and greatly improve their adaptivity and response.

To ensure that the ICAS workforce possesses the knowledge, experience, freedom, and self-confidence to identify problems and take effective action in their area of responsibility, leadership must take on a significantly different role than that presented in classical organizational theory. Two major differences are: (1) leadership cannot be controlling, but rather must be nurturing, supportive, and collaborative and (2) leadership must be implemented at all levels throughout the organization. This *collaborative leadership*, while maintaining accountability and responsibility, shares authority with knowledge workers and, through fostering a collaborative workplace, ensures the ability to make decisions and quickly respond at the point of action.

At the forefront of the ICAS organization is the *knowledge worker*, the individual whose work is centered around creating, sharing and using knowledge. Each and every worker is an integral part of the organization. It is the knowledge worker, moving in and out of teams and communities as needed by the organization and for their career enhancement, who is the ultimate source of knowledge. The multidimensionality of the organization is dependent on the multidimensionality of its knowledge workers, who have the capability of working in multiple domains simultaneously, refocusing those domains as needed and combining the physical, the mental, the intuitive, and the emotional to continuously expand their knowledge, capabilities, capacity, networks, and perceptions. To be successful in the ICAS, knowledge workers possess a high level of competencies. They:

- Are strong team players and openly share their knowledge
- Make effective use of technology
- Have learned how to learn and are continuously learning
- Develop knowledge about knowledge to enable self-management
- Are proficient in the four major processes
- Develop and effectively use their personal networks
- Are action oriented and proactive self-organizers.

THE INTEGRATIVE COMPETENCIES

To be successful in the new world requires new competencies, competencies that promote collaboration, understanding, and the integration of action. These competencies include knowledge management, learning, critical thinking, risk management, systems thinking, complexity thinking, information literacy, relationship network management, and knowing.

These integrative competencies provide connective tissue, creating the knowledge, skills, abilities, and behaviors that support and enhance other competencies. They have a multiplier effect through their capacity to enrich the individual's cognitive abilities while enabling integration of other competencies, leading to improved understanding, performance, and decisions.

Systems thinking provides a new perspective and attitude on organizations, highlighting the importance and need for community and teamwork, open communications, and the alignment of actions. It offers a way of understanding the environment, allowing us to see our own work as it relates to the larger organization, and guiding decisions for improving operational effectiveness in a complex world.

The ICAS, operating at the leading edge of the age of complexity, will likely be a prototype of increasing knowledge and complexity. Just as being able to recognize, understand, and think about systems has become a hallmark of many of today's successful professionals, being able to recognize, understand, and deal with complexity is the challenge of the immediate future. Complex systems are different from simple or complicated systems. Complex systems are difficult to predict and control, and continuously change and interact with their environment. *Complexity thinking* helps develop a roadmap for the ICAS organization. Complex adaptive systems are partially ordered systems that unfold and evolve through time. They are mostly self-organizing, learning, and adaptive. To survive they are always creating new ideas, scanning the environment, trying new approaches, observing the results, and changing the way they operate. Intelligent complex adaptive systems have the capacity to prepare for the unknown future, act rationally, and make use of all of their cognitive capabilities.

Knowing is seeing beyond images, hearing beyond words, sensing beyond appearances, and feeling beyond emotions. It focuses on methods to increase individual sensory capabilities and increase the ability to consciously integrate these sensory inputs with our tacit knowledge. By exploring our sense of knowing we expand our understanding of ourselves, improve our awareness of the external world, and increase our skills to affect internal and external change. Knowing offers a framework for developing deep knowledge within the self and sharing that knowledge with others to create new levels of understanding.

Relationship network management focuses on fully using and increasing the social capital of an organization. Each relationship network is a matrix of people that consists of the sum of a knowledge worker's relationships, those individuals with whom the knowledge worker interacts, or has interacted with in the past, and has a connection or significant association. Relationship network management occurs when we recognize the potential of these relationships and use them to share and learn, creating and sustaining a conscious give-and-take movement, or flow, across the network. The individual manages their relationship network through: (1) recognizing the value of relationship networks; (2) identifying their personal network of relationships; (3) consciously choosing to develop, expand, and actively sustain these relationships through continuing interactions; and (4) staying open to sharing and learning through this relationship network.

In an organization where understanding and the ability to take effective actions are major challenges because of the organization's environment or the nature of its work, both knowledge management and organizational learning become critical factors in its long-term survival. Organizational learning is contingent upon a number of factors such as leadership, structure, strategy, environment, technology, and culture. Knowledge management helps to create and nurture these factors to make optimum use of the organization's knowledge. In today's rapidly changing, erratic, and increasingly complex environment, knowledge creation, acquisition, and application through continuous learning are likely to be the only solution to survival and excellence.

STRATEGIZING FOR THE ICAS

The ICAS strategy prepares the organization for the complex, unknowable future. The highest-level ICAS strategy is based on three factors. First, because the future is unknowable, knowledge, knowing, and insight become vital to success. Second, those closest to the boundaries and the external environment have the knowledge and capability to make the best decisions. Third, the process of interacting with the environment is a trial-and-error process, with rapid feedback and evaluation providing selection criteria for the next sequence of actions.

The ICAS must be a robust organization capable of changing within itself and responding to many different and surprising events in the environment. Simultaneously, when the environment is relatively stable, it must be capable of maximizing its output performance and maintaining a steady state or system that is in balance. The concept of *dynamic balancing* means that leaders and workers throughout the organization will continuously balance a number of opposing forces or demands such as control versus freedom, short-term versus long-term, information versus knowledge, stakeholder needs, corporate alignment versus local responsiveness, and generic versus individualized learning.

These balances will rarely remain constant for very long, hence leaders will continuously monitor and change the balance of forces in their areas of responsibility to maintain local effectiveness.

A good strategy identifies the major strengths, or forces within the organization, and those that meet day-to-day changing external threats and opportunities. The forces the ICAS needs to correlate are considered in light of the following assumptions:

- The short-term effectiveness of an organization depends on the actions of each of its employees.
- The long-term health (sustainability) of an organization is determined by the same set of actions of employees seen from their consequences and implications for the future.

There are four fundamental forces in the ICAS: the force of direction, force of intent, force of knowledge, and force of knowing. The *force of direction* serves as the compass for the organization as it moves into an uncharted and uncharitable future. It both limits ICAS activities within some action space surrounding the chosen direction and conserves energy by defining what areas the ICAS is not interested in. The *force of intent* is an act or instance of determining mentally upon some action or result, thereby focusing the energy and knowledge of the organization. It is the power and consistency that overwhelms competitors and gains the admiration of the marketplace.

The *force of knowledge* consists of the creation, sharing, dissemination, leveraging, and application of knowledge. In the ICAS it is supported by knowledge centricity and the active implementation of knowledge management. The *force of knowing* is a blending of the cognitive capabilities of observing and perceiving a situation, the cognitive processing that must occur to understand the external world and make maximum use of our intuition and experiences, and the faculty for creating deep knowledge and acting on that knowledge. While knowledge represents the ability to take action on what you can see ahead, knowing represents the fog lights into the future, penetrating the haze of complexity by allowing workers to think beyond normal perception and dig into the meaning and hidden patterns of a complex world.

The four forces are aligned when:

- Direction is set and understood.
- Intent moves the organization in the desired direction.
- Knowledge ensures actions follow intent and direction.
- Knowing improves knowledge, bolsters intent and signals the ICAS whether the actions and directions are on track.

In a turbulent environment there are holes that offer opportunities, what we call the environmental opportunity space, a window of opportunity in terms of space and time. An aligned organization has a consistent direction and a comprehension from what knowledge and knowing have provided about the environment. While the company may not be able to define this space, nor can it go there before it exists, the organization's direction is such that it can take advantage of the environmental opportunity space as it emerges.

RELEASING THE POWER OF THE ICAS

The real power of the ICAS comes from the alignment and integration of its strategy, structure, culture, processes, leadership, and its people and their competencies. ICAS survival depends upon the sum of all of the daily actions of employees, with each of these actions consistent with the organization's direction and supportive of local and organizational goals. Structure, culture, and knowledge worker competencies fully support local knowledge and actions, such that every individual at the organization's boundaries takes the best action possible.

At a global level, this alignment and integration creates the emergence of organizational intelligence, unity and shared purpose, optimum complexity, selectivity, knowledge centricity, flow, permeable boundaries, and multidimensionality. While emergent properties of complex organizations—arising out of multiple, nonlinear interactions—cannot be controlled, actions can be taken to influence the system's behavior in such a way that the desired emergent properties, or something close to them, will emerge. For example, as presented in Chapter 10:

- To achieve a shared unity of purpose consider the following factors: clear and continuous two-way communication throughout the firm; a line of sight between the purpose of the organization and the actions of employees; a purpose that is consistent with organizational strategy and with employee values; the use of teams, communities of practice, and integrators to provide coherence of understanding.
- Knowledge centricity requires senior leadership support; an awareness and appreciation of the impact of knowledge in performing work; knowledge repositories and information systems that support the decision and action needs of the knowledge worker; a knowledge taxonomy and ontology that facilitate the storage and retrieval of information; teams, communities, and dynamic networks to encourage the sharing, leveraging, and application of knowledge; and continuous learning.
- Selectivity requires an awareness and understanding of the purpose, objectives, and values of the organization; a sensitivity to the competitive

environment; the ability of workers to assess situations and their meaning so they can extract information useful to the organization; knowledge workers with the ability to see possibilities within and adjacent to their local domain of work; the skill and capacity to feed back and relay information and understanding to other workers throughout the organization.

- Optimum complexity depends upon the organization's ability to generate ideas and responses capable of successfully responding to the events and situations impinging on the firm from the marketplace. It requires that knowledge workers understand complexity and are able to interpret events and patterns in the environment, and that organizational leadership allows and supports the creativity and innovative thinking needed to generate internal possibilities for action. It also requires that managers and team leaders have the ability to keep their people working at the edge of chaos when necessary, without falling into either chaos or stability.

The approach to changing an organization by creating desirable emergent properties through changes in the work processes and workforce behavior requires the force of a multifaceted change strategy. Since change itself is an emergent characteristic, it is a product of combining, integrating, and correlating elements of the change strategy with the organization's direction, objectives, structure, culture, and leadership. The ICAS change strategy sets out to achieve a *connectedness of choices*, ensuring that decisions made at all levels of the organization, while different, are clearly based not only on a clear direction for the future, but a cohesive understanding of why that direction is desirable and how it supports the shared vision.

Implementing change at every level of the organization follows the growth path of knowledge and sharing, leading to the creation and sharing of new thoughts in a fully aware and conscious process. Because of the importance of porosity and collaboration, the suggested change strategy is holistic, not bounded by organizations and encouraging interactions across large relationship networks and sharing and learning across organizational boundaries. The change strategy model can be viewed in terms of orchestrating and implementing twelve specific elements:

- Create a shared vision.
- Build the business case.
- Demonstrate leadership commitment at all levels.
- Facilitate a common understanding.
- Set limits.
- Share new ideas, words, and behaviors.
- Identify the strategic approach.
- Develop the structure.

- Measure and incentivize.
- Provide tools.
- Promote learning.
- Envision an even greater future.

In the new world, many organizations are moving forward at a fast pace, with a vision and strategy, but without a predetermined path. The path has been and will continue to be forged by dedicated professionals in each organization, working individually and collectively, but always aware of the organization's mission and vision. The ICAS vision is to ensure that every single individual in the organization has awareness of—and is committed to achieving—the vision of the organization. As this vision turns and changes in response to the turbulent environment, the understanding of individuals within the organization will turn and change with it.

This focus on people ranges from the creation of theory and the building of shared understanding to the development of knowledge centricity and the infrastructure to support individual and organizational learning. Enterprise-level leadership ranges from promulgating guidance and policy, to providing tools, to rewarding success. Effectively, this complex change strategy cannot help but encourage a natural progression toward the ICAS across and within the organization, contributing to the cultural change essential to take full advantage of the opportunities offered by the ICAS, and facilitating the *connectedness of choices* through the sharing of new thought in a fully aware and conscious process.

CONTINUING THE "TALE OF TWO FIRMS"

Joe reflected on what he had learned over the past few months through his daily interactions with Mary. He knew he had always had a problem with far-out ideas and new ways of doing things. But, he thought to himself, he had spent his career learning to do things the *right way*, taking risks only when he had to and being able to justify his decisions with logic and data. His past successes and increasing responsibilities had reinforced his assumptions that there was one right way to make decisions, deal with employees, and run an organization. His faith in his management style had been reinforced by past successful decisions—until now. Though everyone in his organization was working harder, things just kept getting worse. His company was faltering.

Listening to Mary over these past months and reading the literature had given Joe an uneasy feeling about his past modes of operation. What if his assumptions were wrong! They had worked well over the past 20 years. How could they be wrong now? As he mulled over these thoughts he recalled a story known as the boiling frog syndrome. As soon as the story came to mind, Joe panicked from fear. Could this be happening to him and his company? If you put a frog in hot water it will immediately jump out. But, so the story goes, if you put the frog in cold water the frog will sit there and, as you slowly increase the temperature of the water—even to the boiling point, the frog will remain in the water and die.

Again Joe thought, could this really have happened to him, his executives, and his company? Could their assumptions, their past successes, and patterns of operation now be leading them astray as the world approaches the boiling point?

Joe saw that his own logic—that he had been successful because his past decisions and actions had been right—had driven him to continue to repeat those same decisions and actions in a rapidly changing and complex environment. It dawned on him that this behavior and thinking was really a box that prevented him from questioning his perceptions of reality and seeing the marketplace as it really was. He realized this was a logic box of success, successful in a stable environment, fatal in a dynamic, unpredictable environment. At that moment he recognized just how self-assured, strong-willed, and certain he had become, and how foolish and dangerous that now was. Did he really know what he thought he knew?

Joe was well aware that it was easy to talk rationally about change and its importance. He had always decided what needed to be done, made a plan and implemented it. But now he was *feeling* the need for deep, personal change. It was scary and uncomfortable, but at least he was aware of the issue, and he knew that awareness was the first step toward successful change. He also knew he had to do it—no superficial talk but serious questioning, reflection, and self-examination.

Reflecting on these thoughts, Joe knew from deep within himself what he had to do. He immediately told his executive assistant to call a board meeting for next week, clear his schedule, and get Mary on the phone. He had a lot to learn, and a company to rebuild. He had not felt such complete intense excitement in years.

And then there was the ICAS.

Appendix

THE EVOLUTION OF THE ORGANIZATION

The progress of humanity over the past 30,000 years has been predominantly due to the effectiveness of the organizations used to achieve human goals. For example, religious goals have been achieved through organizational structures developed by the world's major religions. Economic progress throughout history has been driven by commerce and business organizations. Political organizations have both provided stability and been the catalyst for change. While organizations have been used for purposes damaging to mankind (i.e., the religious crusades during the Middle Ages, the sweat shops in the nineteenth century, and the robber barons in the early twentieth century), in the long view of history, mankind has clearly made progress through the creation and effective implementation of organizations. The early evolution and structure of organizations is the subject of this chapter, laying the groundwork from which the organization of the future must emerge.

Organizations can be considered systems with internal structures that mediate roles and relationships among people who work toward identifiable objectives. Experiences have shown that of the great number of parameters that can be used to measure and/or describe the typical organization, only a small number (à la Pareto's rule that often 20 percent of the workforce contributes 80 percent of the output of an organization) are critical to its success. These "key success factors" (KSF) determine the organization's ability to meet its objectives while operating within some influential environment. This external environment may be characterized by nonlinearity, complexity, rate of change, and frequently unpredictable external forces that are political, sociological, economic, and technological in nature. Organizations often exist at the pleasure of their environment and the boundary between the organization and its environment may be porous, flexible, and foggy. A common thread throughout this appendix will be how organizations have made use of knowledge and one of its offspring, technology, to survive during their hour on the stage of history. Organizations are created to meet local objectives (though these local objectives may have a global nature) and tend to match their environment in a manner that increases their chances of success. In doing this, they create certain internal structures, and cultural, leadership, and management characteristics that provide the ability to effectively interact with their environment and achieve desired goals.

Organizations have also become more complex, more flexible, and more egalitarian in order to achieve their goals as they respond to an environment that throughout history has become increasingly complex, dynamic, and technologically sophisticated. To survive these changes, organizations must make optimum use of all available information and knowledge. Since the classic bureaucracy represents the most enduring organizational structure known throughout history, our considerations will take the bureaucratic organization as the baseline.

In our broad brush of the evolution of the organization, realize that the dates used are approximate and the types of organizations considered have lifetimes from decades to centuries. Also, even though many forms of organizational structures coexist at any given time in history, we focus on the dominant form recorded in that era.

Recognizing the recent explosive increase in worldwide communications and technology, and the likely continued world economic growth, we offer as metaphor the growth of the butterfly as representative of the long-term transformation of organizations. Recalling from chaos theory the popular idea that by flapping its wings in Brazil, a butterfly may create a snowstorm in New York, it is not too difficult to imagine that the birth of the butterfly long ago in history is now causing the storm that today is overtaking the world through organizational expansion and effectiveness. In short, about 20,000 years ago the egg was laid for the butterfly that is now flapping its wings, and in the next 10 to 20 years will fly powerfully and freely throughout the world. The butterfly is, of course, the organization that mankind created and has used to accelerate human destiny throughout history.

THE EGG IS FERTILIZED

Organizations have a much longer history than is usually recognized. While a study of evolution demonstrates the ubiquitous role of interactions and relationships among all life, the beginnings of structure and dedicated efforts to meet objectives through intention, planned action, and individual roles had to wait until *Homo sapiens* reached the hunter gatherer/agriculture transition.

Since the early hunter gatherer, circa 35,000 B.C., the success of small bands of humans gathering berries, leaves, and grubs and occasionally hunting larger animals is clear from the world-wide distribution of archeological sites where human colonies lived. Environmental forces demanded specific actions for survival, leading to the development of culture via the need and propensity to cooperate and propelled by Darwinian variation and selection of the fittest. Thus began the first attempts at structure and organization, driven by the same forces that drive organizations 37,000 years later: threats and opportunities in the environment and a strong desire to survive and achieve goals.

About 12,000 years ago, as the sea level rose due to the end of the ice age, *Homo sapiens* found a new way to get food (Roaf, 1999). By cultivating plants and domesticating animals, humans could, and did for the most part, stop their ceaseless roaming, build shelters, and, with the development of language, settle into more long-term social and cultural relationships. With the delineation of geographical boundaries came the building of more permanent relationships that required individual self-control and opened the door to the creation of leaders and followers. This permanent settling, with its attendant relative stability, also spurred the need for learning and the use of new materials and technologies resulting in pottery-making, stone-carving, and metalworking.

Beginning in the fertile ground between the Euphrates and Tigris rivers in Mesopotamia, the spread of farming throughout the world was quickly followed by the first Neolithic villages and then (in 4000–3000 B.C.) by the urban explosion. This transition involved the development of cities, with large numbers of people living in small areas, many of whom did not farm. Ties of kinship became important, class distinctions arose, and leaders achieved power through religious, military, and/or political means. This structure was maintained by taxes, force, and the construction of monuments. Craftsmen emerged as an important class. These artisans, together with writing and the hints of science and art, led to a society with central authority and enough resources to carry out work through some rational structure. The resultant development of public buildings and monuments gave specific impetus to the creation and application of knowledge.

In the early birth of civilization we see the seedbed of organizations. Although the world moved slowly—and was simple and quiet compared with our world of today—management, roles and relationships, specified objectives, specialization, and class structures formed the brew within the crucible from which man created the modern world. The egg of the butterfly that was to move the world 6000 years later was fertilized in the rich land of the Euphrates Valley.

THE CATERPILLAR IS BORN

In the mid 1920s, the Czech Egyptologist Jaroslav Cerny began the excavations that would span his entire career, in Deir el-Medina on the west bank of Luxor. This was the site of a village which housed a community of workmen, artisans, and artists that built and furnished the tombs in the Valley of the Kings and the Valley of the Queens during the eighteenth to twentieth dynasties (1550–1069 B.C.). Each craftsman had a house in the village, a hut in the Valley, and a tomb, as well as some livestock, and even slaves. Each craftsman also had a plot of land, which he was free to build upon—and if he built upon it during his free time, it was truly his, and could be sold and passed on to his family (Strouhal, 1992).

Craftsmen were free to wander throughout the village, but could not depart to other duties without permission of their superiors. "For the most part they were tied to their place of work" (Strouhal, 1992, p. 187). Until the nineteenth dynasty there was social equality, but as creativity began to be more valued, work requiring less creativity (plasters, blacksmiths, guards, etc.) was relegated to the semedet people (including the young, unmarried, and unskilled). The semedet people, a lower order who assisted the craftsmen, were not counted as members of the community and lived in simple huts scattered outside the village. They were considered outsiders, and used primarily for menial support jobs such as removing rubble.

The craftsmen who built the tombs were called "The Ship's Crew," and were organized, very much as Egyptian oarsmen, into "left" and "right" teams. Each team had a foreman, and each foreman had a deputy. Though many foremen and deputies were following in their father's footsteps, a large number were also elected (by the artisans) into these roles. Foremen assigned tasks and assured task completion. The deputies acted as representatives and spokesmen for the community as well as standing in for the foremen in their absence (Strouhal, 1992).

One man, the Overseer of All the King's Works, directed the massive labor force required to build a pyramid. "His position required him to be a man of science, an architect and a figure of commanding authority and outstanding leadership abilities" (Silverman, 1997, p. 174). The ruling official was a scribe. "His palette and papyrus scroll were symbols of the authority of knowledge, and bureaucratic lists and registers were the tools of political and economic power. Cultural knowledge, which was also conveyed through writing, brought a different sort of power" (Silverman, 1997, p. 90). Literature was prized because of its influence over others, and brought fame to the scribe. In short, knowledge, demonstrated by writing, was considered an authority, whether it took the form of literature, a medical recipe, or a list.

Education was offered to the ruling class (1–2 percent of the population) to prepare children to enter the "pharaonic bureaucracy." Only the son of a scribe could expect to be educated. Temples, the palace, and departments of state were centers of learning, with temples containing extensive libraries where learned men copied manuscripts. The close link between religion and bureaucracy, which will be examined later in this appendix, was already in play.

THE CATERPILLAR AS BUREAUCRACY IN GOVERNMENT

Leapfrogging 3000 years of history and landing in China, the beginnings of a bureaucracy became visible alongside the supposed feudal order. Bureaucratic elements were introduced under the Qin dynasty (221–206 B.C.), and a system of bureaucratic government was formalized in 202 B.C. under Emperor Gaozu. Many of the features of this structure were to last "initially for two centuries and subsequently for two millennia" (Roberts, 1999, p. 27). Gaozu, a man of peasant origins and outstanding virtue, demonstrated the potential for the common man. In his ruling structure, Gaozu was assisted by three senior officials, and under these "Three Excellencies" were nine ministers, each with a defined area of responsibility. These ministers, often assigned in pairs, were controlled through dependent, overlapping terms.

Though Gaozu held contempt for scholars, he embraced the ethical standards for the new dynasty written by a Confucian scholar named Lu Jia in a writing focused on the shortcomings of the Qin dynasty. These ethical standards "marked the beginning of Confucian values as the basis for imperial government" (Roberts, 1999, p. 28).

The bureaucratic structure waned and rose over the next centuries. As an example, let's take a look at the reign of Taizong (626–649 A.D.), which is considered the golden age in Chinese imperial history. The central government was composed of the secretariat (which drafted edicts), the chancellery (which reviewed them), and the department of state affairs (which put them into effect). There was also a body called the censorate (which investigated abuses) and a supreme court (which reviewed sentences for crimes). The country itself, divided into prefectures and districts, was, respectively, administered by prefects and district magistrates. Taizong's "equal field" land system called for the registration of households and the periodic redistribution of landholdings.

Taizong worked to firmly establish his imperial family line as superior to that of leading Chinese families. "His actions relating to education and scholarship suggest a motive" (Roberts, 1999, p. 54). Taizong instituted a system of state schools and colleges, one of which was reserved for children of the imperial family and those of the highest imperial officials. Following the advent of regular examinations, many of the highest positions in the government tended to go to those who passed these literary exams. Thus, the value of learning and knowledge was recognized and used to expand the imperial family's influence throughout the bureaucracy.

The success of this monarchical bureaucratic government was a direct result of Taizong's strong leadership and management approaches built on a solid cultural and military base and his careful avoidance of alienation with the Buddhist Community until he was firmly ensconced as emperor. His thinking is captured in a text written by him in 648 A.D., "Emperor Taizong on Effective

Government" (Ebrey, 1993). This text appears to represent what we would consider his guiding principles or, from a different perspective, the key success factors in his reign as emperor. Here are some primary points from that writing:

- *Establishing Relatives.* Since the responsibility of evenly governing a huge country is too great for one man, the emperor should grant land in equal amounts to any relatives and spread them throughout the empire. If family members are granted too much power they are a threat; not enough and they cannot protect the throne. This process of evening power and investing relatives is called "enfeoff."
- *Evaluating Officials.* The ranks and duties of officials must be differentiated, choosing the right person for the right job. If this occurs, the empire is governed with ease.
- *Welcoming Advice.* Since the emperor lives in a palace and is blocked from direct access to information, he must set up ways to elicit information, then listen attentively. He must determine what is right and wrong regardless of who delivers the information.
- *Discouraging Slander.* Beware sweet flattery that leads to destruction, and accept criticisms that benefit the country.
- *Avoiding Extravagance.* Character is cultivated through frugality and peacefulness. The ruler must restrain himself so as not to tire or disturb his people.
- Confucius said, "Not teaching people how to fight is the same as discarding them." Military might benefits the realm.
- *Esteeming Culture.* Play music when a victory is achieved; establish ritual when the country is at peace. Literature spreads manners and guides customs; schooling propagates regulations and educates people. The way of the realm spreads through culture; learning leads to fame. You must visit a deep ravine to understand how deep the earth is; you must learn the arts to realize the source of wisdom. The country needs both military and culture; which to emphasize depends on circumstances (Ebrey, 1993).

As his flexibility tightened, and the separation between his imperial bloodline and other Chinese families increased, the effectiveness of Taizong's bureaucracy began to decline. By the time of his death in 649 A.D., his foreign wars and extravagant building had drawn him into difficulties in court. As a memorial, his mentor, Wei Zheng, said of him: "In the early years of his reign the emperor had always made righteousness and virtue his central concern [...]; [but now he] had become increasingly arrogant, wasteful and self-satisfied" (Roberts, 1999, p. 55). Apparently the keys to success were lost in the exuberance of authority and power. Is this not often the history of modern organizations? We now jump ahead in time and from China to Rome in space.

THE CATERPILLAR AS BUREAUCRACY IN RELIGION

The papacy is the central governing institution of the Roman Catholic church under the leadership of the pope. The origin of power of the Bishop of Rome comes from the teaching that Jesus Christ directly bestowed ruling and teaching authority on the apostle Peter. This supreme power was then passed on to his successors, the Bishops of Rome. Recognizing the importance of environmental forces, in 313 A.D. the church granted toleration of all religions and allowed Christians to worship freely. This early part of the Middle Ages underwent a backward shift from towns to rural villages and hence became a more agrarian society, as violence and political turmoil increased with the influx of Germanic tribes. Cities and towns were continuously attacked. For example, Gothic warriors ravaged the unfortunate peninsula of Italy for decades and in 410 A.D. captured and sacked the city of Rome. The attack sent shockwaves throughout the west and led Augustine to write his great work, *The City of God* (Dwyer, 1998). Cities and towns were continuously attacked until, by the eighth century, towns and the use of money both had virtually disappeared.

The papacy was as unable to lead the peasants, as were the emperors. Both vied for authority with no clear winner. During the period from the sixth to the fifteenth century, the papacy varied in their power from being subservient to the power of emperors to negotiating peace treaties and alliances with nations and kingdoms. The church reached its height of power circa 1200 A.D. during the Pontificate of Innocent III when the papacy experienced almost universal power and supervised the religious, social, and political life in the west. The papacy governed through a centralized administration that ensured its power over the bishops and by tapping the church's financial resources. Thus the key success factors were money and power, with religious beliefs and rituals serving as the framework and justification for authority. For example, Innocent III (1199 A.D.) directed all bishops to pay a fortieth of their revenue to Rome. A tax was levied on all monasteries, convents, and churches that came directly under papal protection. One half of the first year's revenue of a newly elected bishop was required by the pope as a fee for confirming his appointment (Durant, 1950). Thus the papal "bureaucracy" exercised and expanded its power by influence, pressure, and taxation. It also took the lead in codifying Canon Law and became "an effective supranational monarchy" (LeGoff, 1990, p. 101). In addition, it established the concept of a world theocracy that later formed the justification for the Crusades (*Encyclopedia of Religion*, 1987).

Popes were originally elected only by cardinal bishops. Around 1180 A.D. this was expanded to include all cardinals, although they were required to stay in a locked room until their election of a new pope was completed. During the following centuries the papacy declined because of corruption within its bureaucracy and because of the failure to see the effect of nationalism on church–state relationships. As the organization became more centralized and administratively complex, the cardinals assumed increasing power and began restricting papal authority. Between 1414 and 1418 A.D. the General Council of Constance dealt with a scandal of three would-be popes and set about reforming the leadership and its members.

For the next 300 years the pope's authority was severely challenged due to internal decay and the loss of vision. The heavy taxation, extravagant building projects in Rome, and the overall religious, social, and economic problems throughout Europe led eventually to the Protestant Reformation. With the rise of skepticism, rationalism, and secularism during the Enlightenment came strong opposition to the bureaucracy and rigidity of the papacy. This culminated in the French Revolution in 1789 A.D. and its new political order in Europe. Note the similarity with the collapse of the Taizong dynasty.

For centuries the church treated its external environment as a necessary obstacle to overcome and its internal members as people to rule. A major change occurred when Pope John XXIII (in 1963 A.D.) created a new set of success factors and began promoting ecumenism and world peace. He pressed for a reformation that would bring new vitality into the church. He instituted a collegial style of leadership and built upon the idea of authority for service as distinct from monarchical authority. This was another example of a strong organization, heavily run by ritual, caste, and bureaucracy that yielded to forces external to its formal boundaries. Although frequently its knowledge of the true state of its internal constituency and external detractors was blinded by narcissism and self-aggrandizement, as with most organizations, as the external forces increase in intensity, adaptation or extinction becomes the only alternative.

SPINNING THE COCOON

Implementation of the bureaucratic model reached its full height with the advent of the Industrial Age, whose seeds were sown in the dominance of the scientific view over the religious.

Around 1800 A.D. English industrial organizations could not rely on dogma and rigid disciplines as the church and military organizations could, and industrial managers thus had to find new methods for handling labor problems. Increasing competition had led to larger factories to gain economies of scale, which in turn led to increased problems in training and inducing the employees to work harder. One response was to deskill jobs (increased specialization) (Wren, 1972).

The archeologist R. J. Braidwood suggested there have been two principal economic revolutions in human history since the earliest times when men and women first began using tools. The first revolution came around 6000 B.C., when there was a shift from hunting and gathering food to producing it by planting and cultivating. The second revolution occurred with the invention of the steam engine, around 1770, and ultimately brought about factories, mass production, and consumer-oriented economies (McKelvey, 1982).

This second revolution transformed societies in almost every possible aspect: economic, political, technological, sociological, and managerial. Since our interest is organizational, we shall focus on the transformation that created the ultimate form of bureaucracy and through evolution, led to the information/knowledge revolution, both of which are precursors to the knowledge-networked future and the age of complexity. Daft and Steers note that: "Prior to 1850, organizations were family owned and did not need more than the most elementary administrative structures. Railroads were one of the first industries to require organization. In the United States, railroads were increasing in size and there was a need to manage these larger organizations. The wisdom of the day was that long railroads were not efficient. The preferred size was a small railroad of about 50 miles in length. [...]; Gradually, managers did learn to develop systems and structures for managing organizations of large size"(Daft and Steers, 1986, p. 223).

With the rise of the tycoons of oil, railroads, steel, and automobiles, came the great test of bureaucratic theory. While economically successful, it took a large toll on human freedom. Specialization, limited learning and initiative, and assembly lines turned workers into robots. As new technology was developed, it was frequently misunderstood or misapplied and ended up restricting employees rather than liberating their potential.

Max Weber (1864–1920 A.D.) developed the formal theory recognized today as the bureaucratic model. Weber, a lawyer familiar with power politics, economics, and religion, migrated to sociology through his attempt to understand how capitalism came into existence. His thoughts and words spread across a remarkably wide range of topics in the social sciences. While he did not believe in holistic concepts or universal laws of history, Weber's world of ideas was multidimensional. He recognized the importance of considering a wide variety of influences and perspectives and, in particular, conflict. For conflict is not merely just one more factor among others, it is an expression of the very multidimensionality of things, the plurality of different groups, interests, and perspectives that make up the world. Ultimately, the world does not hold together as one great social or metaphysical unity. Though there is consensus and solidarity inside some components of society, the whole thing is a mixture of contending parts (Collins, 1994).

The bureaucratic framework cited by Weber called for a hierarchical structure, clear division of labor, rule and process orientation, impersonal administration, rewards based on merit, decisions and rules in writing, and management separated from ownership (Cummings and Huse, 1989). Conflict is a theme throughout this model, postulating that forces exist in organizations that perpetuate conflict and class separation. Weber dealt primarily with the conflict between capitalist and worker, the owner of the means of production versus the producer of labor, differentiating these "classes." He also believed that the ever-increasing importance of expert and specialized knowledge created a conflict between the "specialist type of man" and the older type of "cultivated man" [management]. Weber states, "This fight intrudes into all intimate cultural questions," then continues, "During its advance, bureaucratic organization has had to overcome those essentially negative obstacles that have stood in the way of the leveling process necessary for bureaucracy" (Gerth and Mills, 1946, p. 243).

Yet the bureaucratic model was built on management power over workers in what Weber called "imperative control," with legitimacy as the common ground for maintaining imperative control. "Although domination or authority may be based," Weber says, "on custom, interest, affectual or 'value-rational' motives, a secure order is usually characterized by a belief in its legitimacy" (Outhwaite and Bottomore, 1993, p. 328). In his eclectic writings, Weber goes on to distinguish between three types of legitimate authority: legal, traditional, and charismatic.

Legal authority is legitimized through a belief in the legality of enacted rules, and the right of those who have authority under those rules to issue commands. Traditional authority is based on culture and tradition and a belief in the legitimacy of people exercising authority in a traditional, culturally accepted manner. Traditional authority also entails rules, but these rules are seen as customs and traditions. Charismatic authority is best explained through the example of Jesus. This authority is demonstrated through the devotion of followers to "the exceptional sanctity, heroism or exemplary character of an individual person, and of the normative patterns or order revealed or ordained by him" (Outhwaite and Bottomore, 1993, p. 38).

Using Weber's model, the legitimate authority of managers is based on tradition, with that authority derived from the legal legitimacy of owners. The charismatic element of legitimacy would be totally individual-dependent. From this we see that the key success factors of Weber's bureaucracy rest on authority and its acceptance by workers, and on the design and management of processes and rigid rules and procedures.

Although Weber did not see knowledge as a form of legitimacy, he did link knowledge with power. He believed that "Every bureaucracy seeks to increase the superiority of the professionally informed by keeping their knowledge and intentions secret" (Gerth and Mills, 1946, p. 233). Weber felt that since the pure interest of the bureaucracy is power, secrecy would increase with the increase of bureaucracy. We still live with the legacy of this insight.

REFERENCES AND RELATED READING

Collins, R. *Four Sociological Traditions*. New York: Oxford University Press, 1994.

Cummings, T. G. and E. F. Huse. *Organization Development and Change* (4th ed.). New York: West Publishing Company, 1989.

Daft, R. L. and R. M. Steers. *Organizations: A Micro/Macro Approach*. New York: HarperCollins Publishers, 1986.

Durant, W. *The Age of Faith (The Story of Civilization)*. New York: MJF Books, 1950.

Dwyer, J. C. *Church History*. New York: Paulist Press, 1998.

Ebrey, P. B. (ed.). *Chinese Civilization: A Sourcebook*. New York: The Free Press, 1993.

Encyclopedia of Religion. New York: Simon & Schuster Macmillan, 1987.

Gerth, H. H. and C. W. Mills (eds and trans.). *Max Weber: Essays in Sociology*. New York: Oxford University Press, 1946.

Haywood, J. *Historical Atlas of the Ancient World*. New York: Barnes & Noble, 1998.

LeGoff, J. *Medieval Civilization*. Cambridge: Blackwell Publishers, 1990.

McKelvey, B. *Organizational Systematics*. Berkeley, CA: University of California Press, 1982.

Outhwaite, W. and T. Bottomore (eds). *The Blackwell Dictionary of Twentieth-Century Social Thought*. Malden, MA: Blackwell Publishers, 1993.

Roaf, M. *Cultural Atlas of Mesopotamia and the Ancient Near East*. Oxford: Andromeda, 1999.

Roberts, J. A. G. *A Concise History of China*. Cambridge, MA: Harvard University Press, 1999.

Siliotti, A. *Guide to the Valley of the Kings*. New York: Barnes & Noble, 1997.

Silverman, D. P. (ed.). *Ancient Egypt*. New York: Oxford University Press, 1997.

Strouhal, E. *Life of the Ancient Egyptians*. Norman, OH: University of Oklahoma Press, 1992.

Tarnas, R. *The Passion of the Western Mind*. New York: Ballantine Books, 1991.

Wren, D. A. *The Evolution of Management Thought*. New York: Ronald, 1972.

BIBLIOGRAPHY

Ackoff, R. L. *The Art of Problem Solving: Accompanied by Ackoff's Fables.* New York: John Wiley and Sons, 1978.

Adams, J. *The Care and Feeding of Ideas, A Guidebook to Encouraging Creativity.* Reading, MA: Addison-Wesley Publishing Co., 1986.

Argyris, C. *Overcoming Organizational Defenses: Facilitating Organizational Learning.* Needham, MA: Allyn Bacon, 1990.

Argyris, C. and D. A. Schön. *Organizational Learning: A Theory of Action Perspective.* Philippines: Addison-Wesley Publishing Co., 1978.

Argyris, C., R. Putnam, and D. McLain Smith. *Action Science.* San Francisco: Jossey-Bass, 1985.

Arms, K. and P. Camp. *Biology,* 3rd ed. New York: Saunders College Publishing, 1987.

Ashby, W. R. *An Introduction to Cybernetics.* London: Methuen, 1964.

Ashkenas, R., D. Ulrich, T. Jick, and S. Kerr. *The Boundaryless Organization: Breaking the Chains of Organizational Structure.* San Francisco: Jossey-Bass, 2002.

Auyang, S. Y. *Foundations of Complex-System Theories in Economics, Evolutionary Biology, and Statistical Physics.* Cambridge, England: Cambridge University Press, 1998.

Axelrod, R. *The Complexity of Cooperation: Agent-Based Models of Competition and Collaboration.* Princeton, NJ: Princeton University Press, 1997.

Axelrod, R. and M. D. Cohen. *Harnessing Complexity: Organizational Implications of a Scientific Frontier.* New York: The Free Press, 1999.

Bar-Yam, Y. *Unifying Themes in Complex Systems.* Cambridge, England: Perseus Books, 2000.

Battram, A. *Navigating Complexity: The Essential Guide to Complexity Theory in Business and Management.* Sterling, VA: Stylus Publishing, 1996.

Bendaly, L. *Organization 2005: Four Steps Organizations Must Take to Succeed in the New Economy.* Indianapolis: Park Avenue Productions, 1999.

Bennet, A. "The Virtual Town Hall: Vehicle for Change," *CHIPS Magazine,* Fall, 1999, 6–7.

Bennet, A. *Knowing: the Art of War 2000.* Washington, DC: Department of the Navy, 2000.

Bennet, A. and D. Bennet. "Characterizing the Next Generation Knowledge Organization," *Knowledge and Innovation: Journal of the KMCI,* 1, No. 1, 2000, 8–42.

Bennet, A. and D. Bennet. "Designing the Knowledge Organization of the Future: The Intelligent Complex Adaptive System," in C. W. Holsapple (ed.), *Handbook on Knowledge Management 1: Knowledge Matters.* New York: Springer-Verlag, 2003.

Bennet, A. and D. Bennet. "The Partnership between Organizational Learning and Knowledge Management," in C. W. Holsapple (ed.), *Handbook on Knowledge Management 1: Knowledge Matters.* New York: Springer-Verlag, 2003.

Bennet, A. and R. Neilsen. "The Leaders of Knowledge Initiatives: Qualifications, Roles, and Responsibilities," in C. W. Holsapple (ed.), *Handbook on Knowledge Management 1: Knowledge Matters.* New York: Springer-Verlag, 2003.

Bennet, D. *IPT Learning Campus: Gaining Acquisition Results Through IPTs.* Alexandria, VA: Bellwether Learning Center, 1997.

Bennet, D. *Assessing the Risks of Management.* Mountain Quest Institute Website: www.Mountain QuestInstitute.com 1998.

Bennet, D. "AAV RAM/REBUILD: Management Review Integrated Product Team Report," Marine Corps Report, 2000.

Bennet, D. and A. Bennet. "Exploring Key Relationships in the Next Generation Knowledge Organization," *Knowledge and Innovation: Journal of the KMCI*, 1–2, 2001, 91–108.

Bennet, D. and A. Bennet. "Rise of the Knowledge Organization," in R. C. Barquin, A. Bennet, and S. G. Remez (eds), *Knowledge Management: the Catalyst for Electronic Government*. Vienna, VA: Management Concepts, 2001. Reprinted in C. W. Holsapple (ed.), *Handbook on Knowledge Management 1: Knowledge Matters*. New York: Springer-Verlag, 2003.

Bennis, W., G. Spreitzer, and T. Cummings (eds). *The Future of Leadership: Today's Top Leadership Thinkers Speak to Tomorrow's Leaders*. San Francisco: Jossey-Bass, 2001.

Birchall, D. and L. Lyons. *Creating Tomorrow's Organization: Unlocking the Benefits of Future Work*. Washington, DC: Pitman Publishing, 1995.

Boar, B. H. *The Art of Strategic Planning for Information Technology: Crafting Strategy for the 90's*. New York: John Wiley and Sons, 1993.

Boden, M. *The Creative Mind, Myths & Mechanisms*. London: Basic Books, 1991.

Bohm, D. *Thought as a System*. New York: Routledge, 1992.

Bolland, E. and C. Hofer. *Future Firms: How America's High Technology Companies Work*. New York: Oxford University Press, 1998.

Briggs, J. and D. Peat. *Seven Life Lessons of Chaos: Timeless Wisdom from the Science of Change*. New York: HarperCollins, 1999.

Brown, J. S. "Conversation," *Knowledge Directions: The Journal of the Institute for Knowledge Management*, 1, Spring, 1999.

Brown, J. S. and P. Duguid. *The Social Life of Information*. Boston: Harvard Business School Press, 2000.

Burgoon, J. K. "Spatial Relationships in Small Groups," in R. Cathcart and L. Samovar (eds), *Small Group Communication*. Dubuque, IA: Wm. C. Brown, 1988.

Cairncross, F. *The Company of the Future: How the Communication Revolution Is Changing Management*. Boston, MA: Harvard Business School Press, 2002.

Calaprice, A. *The Expanded Quotable Einstein*. Princeton, NJ: Princeton University Press, 2000.

Capra, F. *The Hidden Connections: Integrating the Biological, Cognitive, and Social Dimensions of Life into a Science of Sustainability*. New York: Doubleday, 2002.

Carlzon, J. *Moments of Truth*. Cambridge: Ballinger Publishing Co., 1987.

Chowdhury, S. *Organization 21C: Someday All Organizations Will Lead This Way*. New York: FT Prentice-Hall, 2003.

Clavell, J. (ed.) *The Art of War: Sun Tzu*. New York: Dell Publishing, 1983.

Coleman, D. *Groupware: Collaborative Strategies for Corporate LANs and Intranets*. New Jersey: Prentice-Hall, 1997.

Collins, J. C. and J. I. Porras. *Built to Last*. New York: Harper Business, 1997.

Collins, R. *Four Sociological Traditions*. New York: Oxford University Press, 1994.

Conner, D. R. *Leading at the Edge of Chaos: How to Create the Nimble Organization*. New York: John Wiley & Sons, 1998.

Couger, J. *Creative Problem Solving and Opportunity Finding*. Danvers, MA: Boyd and Fraser Publishing Company, 1995.

Coulson-Thomas, C. *The Future of the Organisation: Achieving Excellence Through Business Transformation*. London: Kogan Page, 1997.

Coveney, P. and R. Highfield. *Frontiers of Complexity: The Search for Order in a Chaotic World*. New York: Fawcett Columbine, 1995.

Cross, R. and L. Prusak. "The People That Make Organizations Stop—or Go," *Harvard Business Review*, 80, No. 6, 2002, 104–112.

Cross, R., S. Borgatti, and A. Parker. "Making Invisible Work Visible: Using Social Network Analysis to Support Human Networks," *California Management Review*, 44, No. 2, 2002, 25–46.

Cross, R., N. Nohria, and A. Parker. "Six Myths About Informal Networks—and How to Overcome Them," *Sloan Management Review*, 43, No. 3, 2002, 67–76.

Csikszentmihalyi, M. *Flow: The Psychology of Optimal Experience*. New York: Harper Perennial, 1990.

Cummings, T. G. and E. F. Huse. *Organization Development and Change*, 4th ed. New York: West Publishing Company, 1989.

Cunningham, I. *The Wisdom of Strategic Learning*. New York: McGraw-Hill Book Company, 1994.

Daft, R. L. and R. M. Steers. *Organizations: A Micro/Macro Approach.* New York: HarperCollins, 1986.

Davenport, T. H. and L. Prusak. *Working Knowledge: How Organizations Manage What They Know.* Boston, MA: Harvard Business School Press, 1998.

Davis, S. *Lessons from the Future: Making Sense of a Blurred World.* Oxford: Capstone Publishing, 2001.

Deal, T. and A. Kennedy. *Corporate Cultures: The Rites and Rituals of Corporate Life.* New York: Addison-Wesley Publishing Company, 1990.

De Furia, G. *Interpersonal Trust Surveys.* San Francisco: Jossey-Bass, 1997.

de Geus, A. *The Living Company: Habits for Survival in a Turbulent Business Environment.* Boston, MA: Harvard Business School Press, 1997.

Denning, S. *The Springboard: How Storytelling Ignites Action in Knowledge-Era Organizations.* Boston, MA: Butterworth-Heinemann, 2001.

Department of the Navy. *Information Literacy Toolkit for a Knowledge World.* Washington, DC: DON, 2000.

Dimancescu, D., P. Hines, and N. Rich. *The Lean Enterprise: Designing and Managing Strategic Processes for Customer-Winning Performance.* New York: AMACOM/American Management Association, 1997.

Dotlich, D. and P. Cairo. *Unnatural Leadership: Going Against Intuition and Experience to Develop Ten New Leadership Instincts.* San Francisco: Jossey-Bass, 2002.

Drucker, P. "The Effective Decision," *Harvard Business Review,* January–February, 1967.

Drucker, P. *Innovation and Entrepreneurship: Practice and Principles* (Special Edition for the President's Association). New York: Harper & Row, 1985.

Drucker, P. F. *The New Realities: In Government and Politics/In Economics and Business/In Society and World View.* New York: Harper & Row, 1989.

Druckman, D. and R. A. Bjork (eds). *Learning, Remembering, Believing: Enhancing Human Performance.* Washington, DC: National Academy Press, 1994.

Durant, W. *The Age of Faith (The Story of Civilization).* New York: MJF Books, 1950.

Dwyer, J. C. *Church History.* New York: Paulist Press, 1998.

Ebrey, P. B. (ed.). *Chinese Civilization: A Sourcebook.* New York: The Free Press, 1993.

Edelman, G. M. *The Remembered Present: A Biological Theory of Consciousness.* New York: Basic Books, 1989.

Edelman G. and G. Tononi. *A Universe of Consciousness: How Matter Becomes Imagination.* New York: Basic Books, 2000.

Ellinor, L. and G. Gerard. *Creating and Sustaining Collaborative Partnerships at Work. Dialogue: Rediscover the Transforming Power of Conversation.* New York: John Wiley & Sons, 1998.

Emig, J. *The Web of Meaning: Essays on Writing, Teaching, Learning and Thinking.* New Jersey: Boynton/Cook, 1983.

Erlbaum, L. *Writing: The Nature, Development and Teaching of Written Communication,* Vol. II. Lawrence Erlbaum Associates, 1982.

Ernst & Young. *Embracing Complexity: Exploring the Application of Complex Adaptive Systems to Business.* Ernst & Young Center for Business Innovation, 1996.

Espejo, R., W. Schuhmann, M. Schwaninger, and U. Bilello. *Organizational Transformation and Learning: A Cybernetic Approach to Management.* New York: John Wiley & Sons, 1996.

Firestone, J. M. and M. W. McElroy. *Key Issue in the New Knowledge Management.* Burlington, MA: KMCI Press/Butterworth-Heinemann, 2003.

Forrester, J. W. *Principles of Systems.* Portland, OR: Productivity Press, 1971.

Fulmer, W. *Shaping the Adaptive Organization: Landscapes, Learning, and Leadership in Volatile Times.* New York: AMACOM, 2000.

Gardner, H. *Frames of Mind: The Theory of Multiple Intelligences,* 10th Anniversary Edition. New York: Basic Books, 1993.

Gerow, J. *Psychology: an Introduction.* New York: HarperCollins, 1992.

Gerth, H. H. and C. W. Mills (eds and trans.). *Max Weber: Essays in Sociology.* New York: Oxford University Press, 1946.

Gladwell, M. "Six Degrees of Lois Weisberg," *The New Yorker,* 11 January 1999.

Gold, M. and E. Douvan. *A New Outline of Social Psychology.* Washington, DC: American Psychological Association, 1997.

Goleman, D. *Emotional Intelligence: Why It Can Matter More than IQ.* New York: Bantam Books, 1995.

Gorman, M. *Simulating Science: Heuristics, Mental Models, and Technoscientific Thinking*. Bloomingdale: Indiana University Press, 1992.

Greenfield, S. *Journey to the Centers of the Mind: Toward a Science of Consciousness*. New York: W. H. Freeman and Company, 1995.

Guns, B. *The Faster Learning Organization: Gain and Sustain the Competitive Edge*. San Francisco: Jossey-Bass, 1995.

Haeckel, S. H. *Adaptive Enterprise: Creating and Leading Sense-and-Respond Organizations*. Boston, MA: Harvard Business School Press, 1999.

Hammer, M. and J. Champy. *Reengineering the Corporation*. New York: HarperCollins, 1993.

Handy, C. *Understanding Organizations: How Understanding the Ways Organizations Actually Work Can Be Used to Manage Them Better*. New York: Oxford University Press, 1993.

Harmon, F. *Business 2010: Five Forces that Will Reshape Business—and How to Make Them Work for You*. Washington, DC: The Kiplinger Washington Editors, 2001.

Havens, C. and D. Haas. "How Collaboration Fuels Knowledge," in J. W. Cortada and J. A. Woods (eds), *The Knowledge Management Yearbook 2000–2001*. Boston, MA: Butterworth-Heinemann.

Haywood, J. *Historical Atlas of the Ancient World*. New York: Barnes & Noble, 1998.

Heller, R. *Charles Handy: The Pathfinder and Prophet of Change in the Workplace*. New York: Dorling Kindersley, 2001.

Hesselbein, F. and P. Cohen (eds). *Leader to Leader: Enduring Insights on Leadership from the Drucker Foundation's Award-Winning Journal*. San Francisco: Jossey-Bass, 1999.

Hesselbein, F., M. Goldsmith, and R. Beckhard. *The Leader of the Future: New Visions, Strategies, and Practices for the Next Era*. San Francisco: Jossey-Bass, 1996.

Hesselbein, F., M. Goldsmith, and R. Beckhard. *The Organization of the Future*. San Francisco: Jossey-Bass, 1997.

Hilgard, E. R. and G. H. Bower. *Theories of Learning*. New York: Appleton-Century-Crofts, 1966.

Holland, J. H. *Hidden Order: How Adaptation Builds Complexity*. New York: Addison-Wesley Publishing Company, 1995.

Holland, J. H. *Emergence from Chaos to Order*. Reading, MA: Helix Books, 1998.

Holsapple, C. W. (ed.). *Handbook on Knowledge Management 1: Knowledge Matters*. New York: Springer-Verlag, 2003.

Holsapple, C. W. (ed.). *Handbook on Knowledge Management 2: Knowledge Directions*. New York: Springer-Verlag, 2003.

Ingber, D. E. "Biological Design Principles that Guide Self-Organization, Emergence, and Hierarchical Assembly: From Complexity to Tensegrity," in Y. Bar-Yam (ed.), *Unifying Themes in Complex Systems*. Cambridge, England: Perseus Books, 2000.

Janis, I. L. *Groupthink: Psychological Studies of Policy Decisions and Fiascoes*, 2nd ed. Boston: Houghton Mifflin Company, 1982.

Jensen, B. *Simplicity: The New Competitive Advantage in a World of More, Better, Faster*. Cambridge, MA: Perseus Publishing, 2000.

Kahneman, D., P. Slovic, and A. Tversky. *Judgment Under Uncertainty: Heuristics and Biases*. New York: Cambridge University Press, 1982.

Kaku, M. *Visions: How Science Will Revolutionize the 21st Century*. New York: Anchor Books/Doubleday, 1997.

Katzenbach, J. R. and D. K. Smith. *The Wisdom of Teams: Creating the High-Performance Organization*. New York: HarperCollins, 1993.

Kauffman, S. A. *The Origins of Order: Self-Organization and Selection in Evolution*. New York: Oxford, 1993.

Kauffman, S. A. *At Home in the Universe: The Search for the Laws of Self-Organization and Complexity*. New York: Oxford University Press, 1995.

Kayser, T. A. *Building Team Power: How to Unleash the Collaborative Genius of Work Teams*. Burr Ridge, IL: Irwin Professional Publishing, 1994.

Kelly, R. and J. Caplan. "How Bell Labs Creates Star Performers," *Harvard Business Review*, 71, July–August 1993, 128–139.

Knowles, M. S. *Journal of Continuing Education and Training* May, 1972. Printed by permission in M. S. Knowles, *The Adult Learner: A Neglected Species*. Houston: Gulf Publishing Company, 1990.

Knowles, M. *The Adult Learner*. Houston, TX: Gulf Publishing Company, 1998.

Koenig, M. and K. Srikantaiah (eds). *Knowledge Management Lessons Learned: What Works and What Doesn't.* Oxford, NJ: Plexus Books, 2003.

Koestler, A. *The Act of Creation.* New York: Dell Publishing Co., 1975.

Kolb, D. A. *Experiential Learning: Experience as The Source of Learning and Development.* Englewood Cliffs, NJ: Prentice-Hall, 1984.

Langer, E. J. *Mindfulness.* Reading, MA: Perseus Books, 1989.

Langer, E. J. *The Power of Mindful Learning.* Reading, MA: Perseus Books, 1997.

LeGoff, J. *Medieval Civilization.* Cambridge: Blackwell, 1990.

Leonard-Barton, D. *Wellsprings of Knowledge: Building and Sustaining the Sources of Innovation.* Boston, MA: Harvard Business School Press, 1995.

Lesser, E. L. *Knowledge and Social Capital: Foundations and Applications.* Boston: Butterworth-Heinemann, 2000.

Lesser, E. L., M. A. Fontaine, and J. A. Slusher. *Knowledge and Communities.* Boston: Butterworth-Heinemann, 2000.

Macmillan. *Encyclopedia of Religion.* New York: Simon & Schuster Macmillan, 1987.

Malafsky, G. P. "Technology for Acquiring and Sharing Knowledge Assets," in C. W. Holsapple (ed.), *Handbook on Knowledge Management 1: Knowledge Matters.* Lexington, KY: Springer-Verlag, 2003.

Marquardt, M. J. *Action Learning in Action.* Palo Alto, CA: Davis-Black Publishing, 1999.

Maturana, H. R. and F. J. Varela. *The Tree of Knowledge: The Biological Roots of Human Understanding.* Boston: Shambhala, 1987.

McDermott, L. C., N. Brawley, and W. W. Waite. *World Class Teams: Working Across Borders.* New York: John Wiley & Sons, 1998.

McKelvey. B. *Organizational Systematics.* Berkeley: University of California Press, 1982.

McMaster, M.D. *The Intelligence Advantage: Organizing for Complexity.* Boston: Butterworth-Heinemann, 1996.

Merriam, S. B. and R. S. Caffarella. *Learning in Adulthood: A Comprehensive Guide.* San Francisco: Jossey-Bass, 1999.

Merry, U. *Coping With Uncertainty: Insights from the New Sciences of Chaos, Self-Organization, and Complexity.* London: Praeger, 1995.

Modis, T. *Conquering Uncertainty: Understanding Corporate Cycles and Positioning Your Company to Survive the Changing Environment.* New York: McGraw-Hill, 1998.

Mohrman, S. A., J. A. Galbraith, E. E. Lawler, III, and Associates. *Tomorrow's Organization: Crafting Winning Capabilities in a Dynamic World.* San Francisco: Jossey-Bass, 1997.

Morecroft, J. D. W. and J. D. Sterman (eds). *Modeling for Learning Organizations.* Portland, OR: Productivity Press, 1994.

Morgan, G. *Images of Organization: The Executive Edition.* San Francisco: Berrett-Koehler, 1998.

Morowitz, H. J. and J. L. Singer (eds). *The Mind, The Brain, and Complex Adaptive Systems.* Reading, MA: Addison-Wesley Publishing Company, 1995.

Nisbett, R. and L. Ross. *Human Inference: Strategies and Shortcomings of Social Judgment.* New Jersey: Prentice-Hall, 1980.

Nonaka, I. "A Dynamic Theory of Organizational Knowledge Creation," *Organization Science,* 5, No. 1, 1994, 14–37.

Nonaka, I. "The Dynamics of Knowledge Creation," in R. Ruggles and D. Holtshouse (eds), *The Knowledge Advantage.* Oxford, England: Ernst & Young, 1999.

Nonaka, I. and H. Takeuchi. *The Knowledge-Creating Company: How Japanese Companies Create the Dynamics of Innovation.* New York: Oxford University Press, 1995.

Olson, E. and G. Eoyang. *Facilitating Organization Change: Lessons from Complexity Science.* San Francisco: Jossey-Bass/Pfeiffer, 2001.

Outhwaite, W. and T. Bottomore (eds). *The Blackwell Dictionary of Twentieth-Century Social Thought.* Malden, MA: Blackwell, 1993.

Pasternack, B. and A. Viscio. *The Centerless Corporation: A New Model for Transforming Your Organization for Growth and Prosperity.* New York: Simon & Schuster, 1998.

Pinchot, G. and E. Pinchot. *The End of Bureaucracy and the Rise of the Intelligent Organization.* San Francisco, CA: Berrett-Koehler, 1993.

Poincaré, H. *The Foundations of Science: Science and Hypothesis, The Value of Science, Science and Method.* New York: Modern Library, 2001.

Polyani, M. *Personal Knowledge: Towards a Post-Critical Philosophy.* Chicago: The University of Chicago Press, 1958.

Porter, D. and A. Bennet. "The Force of Knowledge: A Case Study of KM Implementation in the Department of Navy," in Holsapple, C. W. (ed.), *Handbook on Knowledge Management 2: Knowledge Directions.* New York: Springer-Verlag, 2003.

Porter, D., A. Bennet, R. Turner, and D. Wennergren. *The Power of Team: The Making of a CIO.* Alexandria, VA: Department of the Navy, 2003.

Prigogine, I. *The End of Certainty: Time, Chaos and the New Laws of Nature.* New York: The Free Press, 1997.

Ray, M. and R. Myers. *Creativity in Business.* New York: Doubleday, 1989.

Reid, T. *Essays on the Intellectual Powers of Man* (ed. D. Stewart). Charlestown: Samuel Etheridge, 1785, 1813.

Roaf, M. *Cultural Atlas of Mesopotamia and the Ancient Near East.* Oxford: Andromeda, 1999.

Roberts, J. A. G. *A Concise History of China.* Cambridge, MA: Harvard University Press, 1999.

Robinson, A. and J. Stern. *Corporate Creativity: How Innovation and Improvement Actually Happen.* San Francisco: Berrett-Koehler, 1997.

Rose, C. and M. J. Nicholl. *Accelerated Learning for the 21st Century.* New York: Delacorte Press, 1997.

Rosenberg, M. J. *e-Learning: Strategies for Delivering Knowledge in the Digital Age.* New York: McGraw-Hill, 2001.

Sadler, P. *The Seamless Organization: Building the Company of Tomorrow,* 4th ed. Dover, NH: Kogan Page US, 2001.

Schank, R. C. *Designing World-Class E-Learning: How IBM, GE, Harvard Business School, & Columbia University Are Succeeding at e Learning.* New York: McGraw-Hill, 2002.

Senge, P. M. *The Fifth Discipline: The Art and Practice of the Learning Organization.* New York: Doubleday, 1990.

Shelton, K. (ed.). *A New Paradigm of Leadership: Visions of Excellence for 21st Century Organizations.* Provo, UT: Executive Excellence Publishing, 1997.

Shingo, S. *A Study of the Toyota Production System.* Cambridge: Productivity Press, 1989.

Siliotti, A. *Guide to the Valley of the Kings.* New York: Barnes & Noble, 1997.

Silverman, D. P. (ed.). *Ancient Egypt.* New York: Oxford University Press, 1997.

Simon, H. A. *The Sciences of the Artificial.* Cambridge, MA: The MIT Press, 1984.

Skyrme, D. J. *Knowledge Networking: Creating the Collaborative Enterprise.* Boston: Butterworth-Heinemann, 1999.

Smith, H. A. and J. D. McKeen. "Creating and Facilitating Communities of Practice," in C. W. Holsapple (ed.). *Handbook on Knowledge Management 1: Knowledge Matters.* New York: Springer-Verlag, 2003.

Snowden, D. "The Paradox of Story: Simplicity and Complexity in Strategy," *Journal of Strategy and Scenario Planning,* November 1999.

Snowden, D. "Liberating Knowledge," in *Liberating Knowledge.* London: Caspian Publishing, 1999.

Spears, L. C. (ed.). *Insights on Leadership: Service, Stewardship, Spirit, and Servant-Leadership.* New York: John Wiley & Sons, 1998.

Stacey, R. D. *Complexity and Creativity in Organizations.* San Francisco, CA: Berrett-Koehler, 1996.

Stacey, R., D. Griffin, and P. Shaw. *Complexity and Management: Fad or Radical Challenge to Systems Thinking.* New York: Routledge, 2000.

Strouhal, E. *Life of the Ancient Egyptians.* Norman, OK: University of Oklahoma Press, 1992.

Sveiby, K. *The New Organizational Wealth: Managing & Measuring Knowledge-Based Assets.* San Francisco: Berrett-Koehler, 1997.

Swanson, R. C. *The Quality Improvement Handbook: Team Guide to Tools and Techniques.* Del Ray Beach, FL: St. Lucia Press, 1995.

Swap, W., D. Leonard, M. Shields, and L. Abrams. "Transferring Tacit Knowledge Assets: Mentoring and Storytelling in the Workplace," *Journal of Management and Information systems,* Vol.18, 95–114, Summer 2001.

Tapscott, D. *Blueprint to the Digital Economy: Creating Wealth in the Era of e-Business.* San Francisco, CA: McGraw-Hill, 1998.

Tarnas, R. *The Passion of the Western Mind.* New York: Ballantine Books, 1991.

Tiwana, A. *The Knowledge Management Toolkit: Practical Techniques for Building a Knowledge Management System.* Upper Saddle River, NJ: Prentice-Hall, 2000.

"21st Century Corporation," *Business Week,* August 2000, 153.

United States Marine Corps. *Warfighting: The U.S. Marine Corps Book of Strategy.* New York: Doubleday, 1994.

van der Heijden, K. *Scenarios: The Art of Strategic Conversation.* New York: John Wiley & Sons, 1996.

Vennix, J. A. M. *Group Model Building: Facilitating Team Learning Using System Dynamics.* New York: John Wiley & Sons, 1996.

von Bertalanffy, L. *General Systems Theory: Foundations, Development, Applications.* New York: George Braziller, 1968.

von Krogh, G., K. Ichijo, and I. Nonaka. *Enabling Knowledge Creation: How to Unlock the Mystery of Tacit Knowledge and Release the Power of Innovation.* New York: Oxford University Press, 2000.

Webster's Encyclopedic Unabridged Dictionary of the English Language. New York: Portland House, 1996.

Weick, K. E. *Sensemaking in Organizations.* Thousand Oaks: Sage Publications, 1995.

Wenger, E. *Communities of Practice: Learning, Meaning, and Identity.* Cambridge: Cambridge University Press, 1998.

Wheatley, M. J. *Leadership and the New Science: Learning about Organization from an Orderly Universe.* San Francisco, CA: Berrett-Koehler, 1994.

Whyte, W. H., Jr. *The Organization Man.* New York: Simon and Schuster, 1956.

Wiig, K. *Knowledge Management Foundations—Thinking about Thinking—How People and Organizations Create, Represent, and Use Knowledge.* Arlington, TX: Schema Press, 1993.

Wiig, K. *Knowledge Management Methods—Practical Approaches to Managing Knowledge.* Arlington, TX: Schema Press, 1993.

Wiig, K. *Knowledge Management: The Central Management Focus for Intelligent-Acting Organizations.* Arlington, TX: Schema Press, 1994.

Womack, J. P., D. T. Jones, and D. Roos. *Machine That Changed The World.* New York: McMillan Publishing Co., 1990.

Wren, D. A. *The Evolution of Management Thought.* New York: Ronald, 1972.

Zuboff, S. *In the Age of the Smart Machine: The Future of Work and Power.* New York: Basic Books, 1984.

INDEX

Note: Page numbers followed by *f* and *t* indicate figures and tables respectively; those followed by *def* indicate where a term is defined.

Alex and David Bennet are co-founders of the Mountain Quest Institute. Previously Alex was the Co-Chair of the Federal Knowledge Management Working Group while serving as Chief Knowledge Officer and Deputy Chief Information Officer for Enterprise Integration for the Department of the Navy. Extensive experience as a change agent and a passion for learning propelled her on the ICAS journey. Previously David was co-founder, CEO and Chairman of the Board for a professional services firm in Northern Virginia. He combines industry, government, and military experience to explore the future of organizations.